DEFINING RELIGION

DEFINING RELIGION
Essays in Philosophy of Religion

ROBERT CUMMINGS NEVILLE

Cover design of the cosmos by Beth Neville

Published by State University of New York Press, Albany

© 2018 State University of New York

All rights reserved

No part of this book may be used or reproduced in any manner whatsoever without written permission. No part of this book may be stored in a retrieval system or transmitted in any form or by any means including electronic, electrostatic, magnetic tape, mechanical, photocopying, recording, or otherwise without the prior permission in writing of the publisher.

For information, contact State University of New York Press,
Albany, NY
www.sunypress.edu

Production, Diane Ganeles
Marketing, Michael Campochiaro

Library of Congress Cataloging-in-Publication Data

Names: Neville, Robert C., author.
Title: Defining religion : essays in philosophy of religion / Robert
   Cummings Neville.
Description: Albany, NY : State University of New York, 2018. |
   Includes bibliographical references and index.
Identifiers: LCCN 2017027471 (print) | LCCN 2017046558 (ebook) |
   ISBN 9781438469591 (e-book) | ISBN 9781438469577 (hardcover
) | ISBN 9781438469584 (paperback   )
Subjects: LCSH: Religion--Philosophy.
Classification: LCC BL51 (ebook) | LCC BL51 .N435 2018 (print) |
   DDC 200.1--dc23
LC record available at https://lccn.loc.gov/2017027471
Further information is available at the Library of Congress.

10 9 8 7 6 5 4 3 2 1

*Dedicated to the memory of Nancy Ellegate,
extraordinary SUNY Press editor*

CONTENTS

LIST OF TABLES ⚜ ix

PREFACE ⚜ xi

Part One: Heuristics
PRELIMINARY REMARKS ⚜ 1

CHAPTER ONE ⚜ 3
Problems of Definition

CHAPTER TWO ⚜ 19
A Heuristic Definition of Religion

CHAPTER THREE ⚜ 37
Theory of Religion in a Pragmatic Philosophical Theology

CHAPTER FOUR ⚜ 55
Modeling Ultimate Reality: God, Consciousness, and Emergence

Part Two: Pragmatics
PRELIMINARY REMARKS ⚜ 73

CHAPTER FIVE ⚜ 75
A Pragmatic Approach to Religious Experience

CHAPTER SIX ⚜ 95
Semiotics versus Phenomenology: Existential and Hermeneutic Dimensions

CHAPTER SEVEN ⚜ 117
Hermeneutic and Validity Dimensions of Religious Experience

CHAPTER EIGHT ⚜ 133
Self-Reliance and the Portability of Pragmatism

Part Three: Religious Studies

PRELIMINARY REMARKS ♣ 145

CHAPTER NINE ♣ 147
Why All Theology Should Be Comparative

CHAPTER TEN ♣ 163
Does the Study of Religion Need Philosophy?

CHAPTER ELEVEN ♣ 177
Some Recommendations for the Future of Liberal Theology

CHAPTER TWELVE ♣ 193
Naturalism: So Easily Wrong

Part Four: Philosophical Theology

PRELIMINARY REMARKS ♣ 211

CHAPTER THIRTEEN ♣ 213
A Respectful Alternative to Process Theology:
A Letter of Grateful and Affectionate Response to David Ray Griffin's *Whitehead's Radically Different Postmodern Philosophy: An Argument for Its Contemporary Relevance*

CHAPTER FOURTEEN ♣ 243
The Triune God and Creation *ex Nihilo*, or
"The One and the Many" Strikes Again

CHAPTER FIFTEEN ♣ 255
Perpetual Apophasis and the Existential Implosion of Worldviews

CHAPTER SIXTEEN ♣ 273
Ultimate Realities for the Sciences and Humanities

Part Five: Players

PRELIMINARY REMARKS ♣ 291

CHAPTER SEVENTEEN ♣ 293
John E. Smith: Doing Something with American Philosophy

CHAPTER EIGHTEEN ♣ 303
Richard Rorty: Pragmatism, Metaphysics, Comparison, and Realism

CHAPTER NINETEEN ♣ 319
William Desmond's Philosophical Theology

CHAPTER TWENTY ♣ 337
Nancy Frankenberry: Philosopher of Religion, Radical Empiricist, Herald of Contingency

INDEX ♣ 355

TABLES

TABLE 6.1 ⚜ 98
Dimensions of Religious Experience

TABLE 6.2 ⚜ 100
Existential Dimensions of Religious Experience

TABLE 6.3 ⚜ 112
Hermeneutic Dimensions of Religious Experience 1

TABLE 7.1 ⚜ 125
Hermeneutic Dimensions of Religious Experience 2

TABLE 7.2 ⚜ 129
Validity Dimensions of Religious Experience

TABLE 7.3 ⚜ 131
Summary Dimensions of Religious Experience

PREFACE

For some philosophers, scholars, religious thinkers, and intellectually curious people, defining religion is a gripping topic. For others, it is of little or no interest. In the latter group fall both people who have no interest in religion whatsoever and people whose interest in religion is so great that they are concerned only to become better at being religious, thus finding questions of definition a distraction.[1] This book is directed at the first group, those with an interest in defining religion. Among the authors who have made recent important contributions are Terry F. Godlove, Timothy D. Knepper, Jeffrey J. Kripal, Thomas A. Lewis, Kevin Schilbrack, and Wesley J. Wildman.[2] Of course, if those with no interest in religion suddenly realized that religion *properly defined* includes something that does interest them, this book might be of significant help. People who dismiss religion but respect spiritual depth might be among these. And perhaps those sharply focused on becoming better at being religious might find that this book reorients them in profitable ways, especially as it might point out hitherto neglected dimensions of religion.

The controversies about defining religion come from several sources, as will be explored in the first two chapters. One source is that in public discussions everyone knows what religion is at the same time that there is huge disagreement about what it is. Another source is the common postmodern view that "religion" is a Western category and that its use in understanding other cultures is colonialist. A third source is the practice of the various university disciplines studying religion to define it in terms of their own discipline, reductively leaving out other perspectives.

Yet religion in any of the many ways it is defined seems to be a very potent social and personal force these days for many people and thus worth studying. The essays in this book collectively work at defining religion on many levels and from many angles. Recently, I have completed a very large *Philosophical Theology* in three volumes (with small print). This is a systematic presentation of a theory of religion with detailed defenses of its main contentions.[3] But for many people, system is hard to take. Sometimes, brief essays that come at the topic from different angles and in different genres of conversation are much more effective. Except for the first, all the essays here were written during the years I was working on the *Philosophical Theology* trilogy. Some of the essays were invited presentations, some conference presentations, some for Festschrifts, and one a long letter. Some have been previously published and some not. Some are formal, whereas others are relaxed and joshing with friends. I have not tried to smooth out these differences.

Nevertheless, I have rewritten most of the essays somewhat to relate them to one another. I have updated many notes, and in some instances, have changed my mind about what I had said earlier. Where possible, I have eliminated repetition, although the coherence of an essay sometimes requires treating topics treated in other essays, hopefully with a new contextualization. I have also inserted some references to *Philosophical Theology* where that might be helpful.

The essays are grouped into five thematic parts for the sake of focus and continuity. To be sure, the essays relate in many different ways and there could be other ways of grouping them, though this one makes the most sense. The first part, entitled "Heuristics," contains four essays on the definition of religion itself, both about the nature of definition and the proposal of a definition that will be defended in various ways in the other parts. The definition proposed is not intended to be primarily descriptive, phenomenological, scientifically reductive, or discipline oriented. I propose it heuristically as a helpful way to delimit and characterize religion so as to get at religion in its multifarious dimensions while allowing religion to be distinguished from other domains of human experience such as the political, artistic, psychological, and economic. All of these dimensions relate to but are not the same as religion. The second part, entitled "Pragmatics," contains four essays that develop a specifically pragmatic approach to religious experience and the study of religion. This twenty-first-century approach to the definition of religion builds on American pragmatism (not neo-pragmatism) but also incorporates Confucian sensibilities. European resistance to pragmatism is also discussed. The third part, "Religious Studies," contains four essays that approach the nature of religious studies regarding comparison, the role of philosophy in the study of religion, the role of nonconfessional theology in religion, and the limits of religious naturalism. The fourth part,

"Philosophical Theology," contains essays dealing with four first-order issues in philosophical theology, understood in accord with the definition of religion given throughout the book, namely, conceptions of God, creation, the breakdown of all religious worldviews, and how ultimate realities can be studied in the sciences and humanities, defending, of course, a specific theory of ultimate realities. The fifth part, "Players," contains essays about the work of four philosophical theologians with whom I have engaged for a long time, John E. Smith, Richard Rorty, William Desmond, and Nancy Frankenberry. (Rorty probably would duck the label of philosophical theology, although his work has important theological implications and he is the grandson of Walter Rauschenbusch, one of America's most important philosophical theologians.) By "players" I mean to signify that they are personal friends who have played with me the academic rituals of inquiry into matters of our common interest. David Griffin (chapter 13, in part 4) and Joseph Bracken (chapter 14, in part 4) are also friends with whom I have grown for decades, but those chapters are more about specific problems and less about my responses to their overall work.

Chapter 1 has been written for this volume. Chapter 2 began as an invited lecture at the Goethe University in Frankfurt, Germany, March 8, 2016, and has not been published before. Chapter 3 began as a presentation entitled "Pragmatism and the Theory of Religion" at a conference of the same title at the Max Weber Center, University of Erfurt, Germany, February 16; it was published under the title "Theory of Religion in a Pragmatic Philosophical Theology" in *The Varieties of Transcendence: Pragmatism and the Theory of Religion*, edited by Hermann Deuser, Hans Joas, Matthias Jung, and Magnus Schlette (New York: Fordham University Press, 2016), and reprinted here in a modified version by permission. Chapter 4 began as a presentation at the 2010 Annual Meeting of the American Academy of Religion that was part of a multiyear project on modeling God directed mainly by Jeanine Diller; it was published in *Models of God and Alternative Ultimate Realities*, edited by Jeanine Diller and Asa Kasher (Dordrecht: Springer, 2013), and is reprinted here in modified version by permission. Chapters 5, 6, and 7 began as my fairly large contribution to a project on religious experience funded by the Metanexus Foundation and run under my direction at the Danielsen Institute at Boston University when I was its executive director. They were published in greatly altered form as one long chapter in *Experience, Interpretation, and Community: Themes in John E. Smith's Reconstruction of Philosophy*, edited by Vincent M. Colapietro (Newcastle upon Tyne: Cambridge Scholars, 2011), 43–78, of which

I hold the copyright; the current chapters are very different from the originals. Chapter 8 began as a presentation entitled "Self-Reliance and the Portability of Pragmatism Back to Its European Roots" and delivered at the annual meeting of the Institute for American Religious and Philosophic Thought in Pamplona, Spain, in July 2013; it was published in modified form in *American Journal of Theology and Philosophy* 35/2 (May 2014), 94–107, and is reprinted here with more revisions by permission. Chapter 9 began as a lecture called "Comparative Theology and a Theory of Religion" at the Harvard University Center for the Study of World Religions, January 27, 2012, and is published here for the first time. Chapter 10 was delivered at Dartmouth College, at the invitation of Nancy Frankenberry and the Religion Department, in 2010 and is published here for the first time.

Chapter 11 began as a presentation to the Institute for American Religious and Philosophical Thought at the November 2008 meeting of the American Academy of Religion and was published as "Some Recommendations for the Future of Liberal Theology," in *American Journal of Theology and Philosophy* 30/1 (January 2009), 101–116, reprinted here with modifications by permission. Chapter 12 began as a presentation to the annual meeting of the Institute for American Religious and Philosophical Thought in June 2012 and was published in *American Journal of Theology and Philosophy* 34/3 (September 2013), 199–213, reprinted here with modifications by permission. Chapter 13 is a letter I wrote to my friend David Griffin in response to a chapter he wrote about my work in one of his books; he arranged for my letter to be published as "A Letter of Grateful and Affectionate Response to David Ray Griffin's *Whitehead's Radically Different Postmodern Philosophy: An Argument for Its Contemporary Relevance*," in *Process Studies* 37/1 (Spring/Summer 2008), 7–38. David and I have been writing about one another's work for decades. Chapter 14 was commissioned for a Festschrift for Joseph Bracken and was published as "The Triune God & Creation Ex Nihilo, or, 'The One & the Many' Strikes Again," in *Seeking Common Ground: Evaluation & Critique of Joseph Bracken's Comprehensive Worldview*, edited by Marc A. Pugliese and Gloria L. Schaab, SSJ (Milwaukee: Marquette University Press, 2012), 53–65, and is reprinted here in modified form by permission; copyright 2012, Marquette University Press, all rights reserved. Chapter 15 was a presentation at the Society for the Study of Process Philosophies session at the 2010 annual meeting of the Metaphysical Society of America and is published here for the first time. Chapter 16 was published as "Research Projects for Comparative Study and Appreciation of Ultimate Realities through the Sciences and Humanities," in *Journal of East-West Thought* 1/1 (December 2011), 123–136, and is reprinted here with many modifications. Chapter 17 was first presented as part of a memorial service for John E. Smith at the 2010 annual meeting of the Society for the Advancement of American Philosophy and was published as "John E. Smith: Doing Something with American Philosophy," in *The Pluralist* 6/3 (Fall 2011), 117–126. Chapter 18 was commissioned by Randall Auxier for the Library of Living Philosophers volume *The Philosophy of Richard Rorty*, edited by Randall E. Auxier and Lewis Edwin Hahn (Chicago and LaSalle: Open Court, 2010), 139–154, and published with the title "Pragmatism, Metaphysics, Comparison, and Realism," reprinted here with modifications by permission. Chapter 19 was published in *Louvain Studies* 36/2–3 (Summer–Fall 2013), 239–255, as "William Desmond's Philosophical Theology" and is reprinted here with permission. Chapter 20 was originally presented at a philosophical forum at Dartmouth College on the occasion of the retirement of Nancy Frankenberry in May 2015 and was published as "Nancy Frankenberry: Philosopher of Religion, Radical Empiricist, Herald of Contingency," in *American Journal of Theology and Philosophy* 37/1 (January 2016), 5–20, reprinted here with modifications by permission.

My debts to people supporting the development of these essays are too numerous to mention. I thank all the inviters, editors, and critics in my community of scholars. Let me mention special thanks here only to those whose work I dialogue with in single essays in this volume: Joseph Bracken, S.J., William Desmond, Nancy Frankenberry, David Ray Griffin, Richard Rorty, and John Edwin Smith.

All quotations from the Hebrew and Christian bibles, unless otherwise noted, are from the New Revised Standard Version, copyrighted in 1989 by the Division of Christian Education of the National Council of the Churches of Christ in the United States of America.

The cover art on this book is by Beth Neville, my wife. This is the twentieth SUNY Press book of mine for which she has designed the cover or created cover art. This one is a freehand, asymmetrical drawing executed with colored pens on Bristol paper. It depicts ontological creativity issuing in four ultimate conditions of the cosmos, all of which is explained in the text. If you buy the book for the cover and do not read it, that is just fine too because art is beauty aimed to be enjoyed for its own sake. I am grateful for decades of collaboration with her and hope for a few more covers to come.

I am grateful also to my new editor at SUNY Press, Christopher Ahn. This book is dedicated to my previous editor at SUNY Press, Nancy Ellegate, whose untimely death saddened a great many SUNY Press authors and staff members. To work with her on many projects over the years has been a high point of my career, and I'm sure others feel the same way.

NOTES

1. My friend Hans-Guenter Heimbrach, Professor of Practical Theology at Frankfurt's Goethe University, had the latter reaction upon hearing an early version of chapter 2 in this book. I hope this book whets his interest in definition.

2. See Godlove's *Kant and the Meaning of Religion* (New York: Columbia University Press, 2014), Knepper's *The Ends of Philosophy of Religion* (Basingstoke: Palgrave Macmillan, 2013), Kripal's *The Serpent's Gift: Gnostic Reflections on the Study of Religion* (Chicago: University of Chicago Press, 2007) and *Comparing Religions* (Malden: Wiley Blackwell, 2014), Lewis's *Why Philosophy Matters for the Study of Religion and Vice Versa* (Oxford: Oxford University Press, 2015), Schilbrack's *Philosophy and the Study of Religions* (Malden: Wiley Blackwell, 2014), and Wildman's *Religious Philosophy as Multidisciplinary Comparative Inquiry* (Albany: State University of New York Press, 2010).

3. *Ultimates: Philosophical Theology Volume One* (Albany: State University of New York Press, 2013), *Existence: Philosophical Theology Volume Two* (Albany: State University of New York Press, 2014), and *Religion: Philosophical Theology Volume Three* (Albany: State University of New York Press, 2015).

Part I

HEURISTICS

PRELIMINARY REMARKS

What is religion? Does this question call for a definition of religion that allows us to identify it and provide ways for distinguishing religion from what is not religion? Many people would say no. Given that there are so many kinds of religion, perspectives on religion, disciplines studying religion, public voices reporting on religion, and feelings of religious people, would it not be better simply to not raise the question? We can say that there are family resemblances among many things that are called religious and leave it at that. There is no reason to define religion, as if it had an essence distinct from and related to other things, so long as we can keep moving and talking about religious matters as the conversations unfold. This is a heuristic argument, claiming that inquiry would be better served by not raising the question of how to define religion.

The claim in these essays, however, is that the heuristic case is just the opposite: inquiry proceeds more fruitfully by defining religion a certain way. The nature of definition, however, is a complicated problem in itself. Everyone knows what religion is, and yet there are huge disagreements. Furthermore, religion is not like an Aristotelian substance that can be defined in a genus/species classification system. Rather it is a harmony of many different aspects of reality. The definition to be put forward is that religion is the human engagement of ultimacy, which requires harmonizing semiotic cultural systems, aesthetic achievements, social institutions with their own dynamics, and psychological structures, along with intentional relations with what is ultimate. All these things can be present, but not harmonized so that something ultimate is engaged. Chapter 1 explores some of the problems of definition.

How can a definition of religion be understood? This requires an explication of basic notions, for instance, ultimacy, ontological creativity, universal traits of existence, their human bearings, and so forth. Chapter 2 provides a formulaic definition of religion and begins the explication of its basic notions.

How can we understand what is involved in religion, defined in accordance with the hypothesis proposed here? That requires a theory of religion, expanding on the definition. The initial presentation of such a theory is the topic of chapter 3. Chapter 4 continues that presentation, deepening the introductory discussions.

All the arguments in the chapters of this part are intended to be hypotheses about religion that are presented as heuristically good ways forward. The hypotheses are not deductive, but are speculative nets that need to prove their worth by how neatly they allow religious phenomena to be identified and connected, and how they allow religion to be distinguished from things that are not religious.

Part of religion as the engagement of ultimacy is religious experience. But religious experience is only a part, not the whole of religion. Religious experience is the main topic of part 2 of this volume.

Chapter 1

PROBLEMS OF DEFINITION

CONFUSIONS OF DEFINITION

For some people, religion means a spiritual path. For some people, religion means a community of practice and belief within which members live out a spiritual path. For some people, religion means a set of beliefs about ultimate things, whatever ultimacy is construed to be. For some people, religion means belief in supernatural beings, whether or not they are ultimate. For some people, religion means a tradition of beliefs and practices with a special vocabulary and a history of development and definition over against other traditions. For some people, religion means a rich evolving culture whose images and institutions prompt great literature, music, dance, architecture, and art.

For some people, religions mean ingroups, often ethnically based, with markers of behavior, institutions, beliefs, and gut feelings of propriety and impropriety, distinguishing themselves from outgroups. For some people, religions mean cultural and institutional systems within a larger society that identify themselves in religious terms. For some people, religions mean political forces representing the beliefs, attitudes, and moral programs of such religiously identified social systems. For some people, religion means moral leadership for change in a larger society. For some people, religion means leadership in opposing change that would weaken a prized cultural and institutional system. For some people, especially in the media, religions mean denominationally named social groups that have political agendas and organized activities.

For some people, religion means an interior, individual, search for meaning and fulfillment. Religion means an affair of the heart, whether this involves approaching God, realizing identity with Brahman, entering into harmony with the Dao, or some other orientation to what is of ultimate concern. For some people, religion means extraordinary experience, transformative, wild, or mind-blowing experience, something sharply contrasting with quotidian experience. For some people, religious experience merges with the erotic and excessive. From these perspectives, membership in religious groups, participation in religious movements, and cultural conditions and contributions are of secondary importance. Sometimes the ecstatic experiences are communal, however.

For some people, religion is one of the great engines of civilization. The Axial Age religions in their various ways developed conceptions of the cosmos as a whole, of the fundamental sources of things being one or few and hence of the interrelatedness of the world, of the greater importance in certain circumstances of one's humanity than of one's tribal or kinship membership, of the recognition of all people as among one's extended kin, of the need to be just and compassionate to all, not only those within one's ingroup, and of the greater virtue of achieving peace than victory. The world's civilizations are still trying to live in to these high religious ideals that have been laid down on fractious ingroups of ethnic, tribal, and cultural factions.

For some people, religion is one of the most mischievous forces in a world struggling to survive with peace and prosperity because religion means loyalty to one's ingroup. Religion fuels denominational wars among factions in Islam today as it did among Christian denominations in centuries past. The struggles about the effects of European colonialism are fashioned in religious terms pitting Muslims, Christians, Jews, Buddhists, Hindus, and African tribal religions against one another. Religious groups that feel threatened become fundamentalistic, exaggerating ingroup-outgroup boundary conflicts. Religions sometimes reject reason, scientific inquiry, and good counsel in favor of some inappropriate authority. Despite the veneer of universal compassion, many self-proclaimed religious people are bigoted, nasty, and profoundly disrespectful of people outside of their ingroup, and this is what religion means to some people.

For some people, religion is to be identified with popular folk expressions in festivals and local celebrations, in popular scientific views about supernatural beings, magical causal principles, and superstitious interpretations of the circumstances of life. For some people, all those popular folk practices really are manifestations of much deeper and more sophisticated religious engagements. For some people, religion is to be identified with the most sophisticated teachings of the great founders such as Confucius, the Buddha, Mohammed, Moses, and St. Paul, as interpreted in the great commentarial and theological traditions; for many of these people, the folk expressions of religion are the compromises made when the great religious traditions are embodied in local folk cultures.

"Some people" in the preceding examples of what religion means usually refers to particular perspectives on some aspect or role of religion, and a given individual can occupy many or perhaps all of the perspectives at some time or other. Religion means many more things than are mentioned, of course, but all of these mentioned are recognizable meanings in common public and scholarly discourse. Even if we personally reject some of those meanings as illegitimate, mistaken, or reductive, we know what people are talking about when they use the word "religion" in any of these ways. But it is confusing when religion has so many meanings, often contradictory to one another.

It might be tempting to follow the lead of some postmodernists and reject the whole idea of "religion" as a colonialist imposition of a Western conception on a global array of cultures whose social organization might be very different from the West's. "Religion," for these postmodernists, has validity only when referring to Western religious denominations, especially Protestant ones, and its wider application distorts other cultures.

Our first response to the postmodern criticism of the idea of "religion," of course, should be to amend our understanding of religion so that it does not distort other cultures. Most of us know, for instance, that it is a mistake to define religion exclusively as worship of a supreme personal deity, however common that assumption has been in the recent past in America. When monotheistic European colonialists encountered cultures with swarms of gods, sometimes with none of them regarded as supreme, the first reaction was often to regard these cultures as deficient because not monotheistic. The second response was to hunt for some deep analogue to a supreme deity, as Matteo Ricci did in China with his focus on Shangdi, even when the analogue was not particularly important. The third response has been to reconsider the whole nature of the object of worship as involving different metaphorical systems. The West Asian religions (including Europe as West Asian) developed personifying metaphors, elaborating the notion of the person as ultimate. The South Asian religions, including the many kinds of Buddhism and Hinduism, developed the root metaphor of consciousness for the various conceptions of ultimacy and regarded personified deities as subject to karma. The East Asian religions developed the metaphors of spontaneous emergence and harmony for the ultimate realities. As we come to have more comprehensive and less biased views of these theological constructions, we can observe their interactions over the millennia but also their important differences with only local priorities of one over the others. Paul Tillich taught us to speak of "ultimate reality" instead of God and to have an extremely capacious view of what might count as ultimate; he himself, though a Christian theologian, was dead set against thinking of God or ultimate reality as "a being" of any sort, much less a personal being.

Tillich also recognized that "worship" should not be confined to liturgical practices. Like the ancient "prophets" who thundered against hollow, hypocritical, inauthentic participation in religious rituals, he regarded institutional religious life as suspect and looked to other areas of life for what he called the "depth dimension." Instead of worship, he suggested we think of "ultimate concern," however that is worked out existentially. At the same time, we have come to regard at least some instances of religious rituals as much more than vehicles of worship or the expression of ultimate concern. Rather, as in Purva Mimamsa and Levitical Judaism, they are ontological practices that are taken to constitute the world in some sense and bring it to right order. Regarding rituals mainly as vehicles for worship or expressing ultimate concern is a locally Protestant perspective.

In these and many other ways, our understanding of religion has been correcting its biases for the last three centuries and continues to do so. The basic languages for religious expressions have been studied for their underlying commitments. Translations have been made of an increasing array of religious texts and historical representations of religion. A comparative base for religion and theology is now often presupposed even by postmodern scholars who disapprove of such large theories. And the scholarly world now includes representatives of all the world's cultures, not just the European and American. Although the scholarly study of religion and the broader intellectual understanding of it may never be free from bias, self-consciousness about bias and the concern for self-correction of bias have made our reflections on religion generally vulnerable to correction. This is our proper first response to the postmodern suggestion that we abandon the category of religion.

The second is to look at the history of the category itself. "Religion" derives from the Latin *religio*. Cicero thought the word came from *re-lego*, where *lego* meant considering and *relego* meant considering over again. Lactantius, a third-century Christian writer, followed by Augustine, thought it came from *re-ligo*, where *ligo* meant binding together. Its main meaning in the ancient Roman world was the scrupulous, conscientious, strict observance of the services owed to the gods or to God. It meant taking the cults and their observance seriously, or as we might say "religiously." Thus, the study of religion as the Romans might have practiced it would be the study of the nature of cults worshipping or serving the gods, and how people are or should be deeply invested in that.

For Thomas Aquinas, *religio* was the duty owed to God. All people, he thought, originally had a natural knowledge of God and an impulse to worship and love God. But this natural inclination to *religio* was distorted by original sin and, hence, needs to be supplemented by revealed faith, which only Christians have, according to him. Whereas religion is natural and generally universal, for Thomas, revealed religion is reparative. Thus, he could debate the natural aspects of religion with Jews, Muslims, and, in his case, the Cathars. One of the most intriguing ways to understand the history of the concept of religion is to see it working with regard to a deep problem, the problem of religious violence. Roger A. Johnson's outstanding study, *Peacemaking and Religious Violence: From Thomas Aquinas to Thomas Jefferson*, gives a careful account of the definition and redefinition of religion in the works of Aquinas, Ramon Lull, Nicholas of Cusa, Herbert of Cherbury, and Thomas Jefferson. The point to notice is that "religion" as a term comes from the classical Latin period and has been historically reworked in the West ever since. The nineteenth century did see it redefined to apply beyond the Jewish, Christian, and Muslim discussions to the texts being translated into European languages from South and East Asia. Of course, the translators, led by Max Muller and James Legge, used European words such as the cognates of "religion" to make translations. Of course, there are European biases that might distort the non-European religious cultures. Of course, this applies to translating any foreign culture into the languages of Europe. Of course, these biases all need to be corrected one by one. European and American scholars have spent over a century and a half working explicitly on the biases of European conceptions with a history. Of course, this book of essays is another attempt to define religion in ways that do not distort other cultures and that do pick up on some common threads that are important for noting differences and similarities.

DEFINING RELIGION AS A HARMONY

The customary concept of definition assumed in Western thought reflects Aristotle's theory of formal causes in which he describes a hierarchy of genus-species relations, with differentia distinguishing the various species within a genus. In defining things, we usually want first to say what they are, their essence or genus, and then to say how they differ from other things under the same genus. Definitions are more or less rich depending on the depth of layers of genus-species relations. In most contemporary thinking, especially in the sciences, a given level in a genus-species hierarchy can be explicated by an entire theory. Many variations exist on this conception of definition by classification and then distinction from other things in the same class. But they all suppose something like the Aristotelian view that things are substances that bear properties and that the properties can be explicated by classification systems. On this approach to definition, everything that can be defined at all can be treated as a substance bearing its properties. The properties exhibited in a definition inhere in the substance, just as predicates are predicated of a subject.

Let us suppose, however, that things are not unitary substances but rather are harmonies. Some form or pattern unifies the various components of a harmony. Some of the components are essential for unifying the harmony, but others are conditions arising from other things and thus have a reality in part that is external to the harmony in question. Without the latter, which I call "conditional components," the thing would not be determinate with respect to other things because it would contain no components that connect with the other things. Without the former, which I call "essential components," the thing would have no being of its own aside from the potential influences of other things that would condition it, but those other things would have nothing to condition and therefore could in fact have no real potential to condition. This analysis of harmony is developed in a number of the chapters to follow.

The characterization of things as harmonies is so abstract as to be a characterization of determinateness itself. To define a thing, anything, from a biological entity to a landscape, to a form, theory, quark, a quantum of energy, or dark matter, to a thought, a perception, or an emotion, or to a society, an economy, the climate, or religion, is to define it as a harmony with a form unifying components that relate the thing to other things through its components, thus intrinsically referring to a field of mutually conditioning things in which the defined thing has an existential location. Any harmony also has the achieved identity or value of unifying its components with its particular form in its place relative to other things in the existential field. Because everything is a harmony, every component of every harmony is a harmony, and so on.

One of the pragmatically significant things about saying that things are harmonies rather than substances is that they cannot be defined by themselves. Rather, the harmonies are defined in part and necessarily by the things in the existential fields in which they lie or in which they interact with other harmonies that condition them and that they condition. The conditional components of a harmony are just as necessary as its essential ones, and those conditional components might not be contained wholly within the harmony they condition. The definition of a harmony includes its environment as well as those essential components that give it a real position in the environment, and the form by which it unifies the conditional and essential environment. Thus, a harmony, strictly speaking, does not "bear" the properties that define it, as a substance might be said to bear properties, but rather harmonizes components in a certain way in an existential field relative to other things. The things in the environment themselves might be changing according to dynamics partly external to the harmony within the environment. By convention we might choose to ignore the external variables in the environment and treat the thing as having definite boundaries because of the properties it bears in abstraction from the environment. So Aristotle could define a duck without making reference to its metabolic systems in the environment, its need for a kind of atmosphere, a temperature range, and gravity; he could assume that those things are a steady environment for duck definition. The languages that emphasize subject-predicate structures reinforce the conventions of thinking of things as being externally related to things in their environment. But even in biology we now realize that things are defined in significant part by internal and sometimes dynamically shifting relations to things in their environment. We are coming to think of things as focal points discriminated within a background, not as things that can be defined or even articulated without a background of conditioning connections. The Chinese language is much friendlier to seeing things as harmonies, defined internally by the other things with respect to which they are determinate.

Now suppose we define religion as *human engagement of ultimacy expressed in cognitive articulations, existential responses to ultimacy that give ultimate definition to the individual, and patterns of life and ritual in the face of ultimacy.* This is the definition that will be developed in the essays in this book. In a preliminary way, we can say what some of its components are. I will mention them here and develop them systematically later, especially in chapter 2. There are five main kinds of components.

First are the components having to do with the worship of whatever is taken to be ultimate. Huge differences exist among ways of understanding and symbolizing ultimacy, and these will be discussed in subsequent essays in this volume. Huge differences also exist among ways of worship, ranging from hot theistic worship of the ultimate as something like an adored or hated person to the cool worship of the ultimate as a ground of being or source of existence.

Second are the components that concern the aesthetic grasp of things as having beauty or the special integrity of a harmony. All religions have art, music, usually dance, architecture, and aesthetically tinged rituals. Lying behind this is the aesthetic grasp of harmonies as the very being of harmonies as determinate: to be a thing is to be a harmony with a particular value. Within religion, there are components that have to do with the appreciation of, response to, and the impulse to enhance the beauties of determinate things. This point will be developed in subsequent essays, but it is the old point expressed in Western theologies as the goodness of all things, in their places.

Third are the components that concern the self, its integration of disparate elements, its overcoming of brokenness with wholeness, with practices of spiritual development, with psychological states. These psychological or spiritual components are often those that function as essential components to integrate the larger aspect of a person's or groups' religious harmony.

Fourth are the components that concern the social and environmental contexts within which religion takes place. All dimensions of human life take place with some social arrangement or others, perhaps of a group defined politically, perhaps with different social roles for people with different kinds of engagements of ultimacy, perhaps with very dense interpersonal relations as within a monastery, or perhaps with thin interpersonal relations as in the case of isolated hermits. The social arrangements within which human engagement of ultimacy can take place vary tremendously, and different arrangements condition those engagements differently.

Fifth are the components that concern the cultures, traditions, and historical trajectories that supply the terms within which religious interpretations take place. Religion as the engagement of ultimacy cannot take place without symbolic signs for imagination and interpretation, whether or not a religious person embraces or attempts to transcend, reject, or revolutionize the semiotic systems at hand.

As a preliminary hypothesis, let me suggest that there are these five kinds of components of religion, to give them handy names: worshipful, aesthetic, psychological, social/environmental, and semiotic. Much more will be said about each of these. Moreover, excepting the first, each is a dimension of experience that can be understood and studied on its own, irrespective of the roles it plays in a larger harmony of religion. Each is a kind of harmony of its own, with its own components.

Religion is when these and countless other components are harmonized so that ultimacy is engaged. When ultimacy is not engaged, those and other potential components can be present but are not harmonized to constitute religion. This is so even when the components are labeled as religious, for instance, churches and worshipful experiences described as mystical. If religion is defined as a harmony, and its components in a situation do not harmonize, then the thing at hand is not religion. Of course, the customary association of a component with engaging ultimacy can give it a family resemblance label as religious. For instance, ancient Greek temples were components of religion in large part because basic rituals took place within them, and the rituals at least sometimes presumably were engagements of the gods. But the temples in Hellenistic times were also the city butcher shops because animals were ritually slaughtered and their meat sold there. In those times, butchering thus had a religious dimension that it lacks in most places today, kosher butchering being an exception. But major architectural features of Greek temples are commonly used today in American for banks and other financial institutions; perhaps banks fail to be religious through family resemblance.

ECOLOGIES OF HARMONIES

Return for the moment to the matter of definition. If things are defined as harmonies of components rather than as substances classifiable by their properties, then harmonies are defined and characterized by their relations with one another. One kind of relation is for one harmony to be in another harmony as a component. Another kind of relation is for the form of a harmony to have the character it does by virtue of accommodating another harmony as a component. A third kind of relation is for a harmony to be in a field constituted by other harmonies conditioning one another, embracing some of the harmonies in the field as among its own conditions but embracing the structure of the field itself as constituted by all the harmonies in it. The field itself, of course, can be a harmony.

Given the lingering influence of Aristotle, at least in the West, it is tempting to think of these kinds of relations in a hierarchical way. That is, a harmony is a component in a larger harmony that is itself a component in a larger harmony, and so on up. Or, a harmony accommodates itself to a component that itself accommodates to its components, and so on down. A harmony has existential location in a field that itself has existential location in a larger field, and so on out. But this model is too rigid because it does not reflect the multifarious ways by which harmonies harmonize components and are themselves involved in other harmonies.

A better metaphor for the relations among harmonies is that they are ecological systems relating to one another. Consider a pond that has a particular ecological balance, where, for the moment, all things are supported by the conditions they need to exist. One of the kinds of component harmonies in the pond ecology is a number of fish of a certain kind. Those fish need the right plants and other nutrients to flourish and multiply to fill their niche in the pond, the niche being the existential field relevant to those fish. The plants in turn are defined as ecologies that have their nutrients as components, including perhaps the by-products of the fishes' metabolism, including their decomposing dead. For the fish to decompose, they need bacteria and other microbes. And the microbes in turn need many, though perhaps not all, of the other component harmonies in the pond ecology. Each of these things—the pond, the fish, the plants, the microbes, and all else within the pond—is an ecological system of its sort.

The harmonies as ecologies were represented in the previous paragraph as if they were static or stable, and we know ponds are not like that. New elements enter the pond, say, a chemical from a new runoff that alters what plants can grow, which alters how the fish can flourish and what microbes are present. Ecologies are constantly evolving and changing as the components required for a certain harmony are altered so that the harmony has to accommodate itself anew or disappear. So, the definition of that pond's harmony must be open to a very complex history of changes over time. The definition on one level can be very vague and denotative, such as "Turner's Pond in Milton, Massachusetts, USA, during the twentieth and twenty-first centuries CE." This gives it an Aristotelian genus-species location without many descriptive properties. But to specifically define the pond as the harmony it is, is to accommodate all the things that came to exist in it and how they interacted and altered over time. To define the pond in a non-Aristotelian way that acknowledges that it is a harmony requires indicating its components in some way, showing how the pond as a harmony has to harmonize specific components, and components of components, and so forth.

The difference between a definition and an understanding or explanation seems to be slipping away here. Inquirers need to define their subject matter and then proceed to investigate how to understand or explain it. Even when the definition of the subject changes as it becomes better understood, there needs to be some intentionality in the inquiry that comes from at least a preliminary definition of the harmony to be understood. So, definition as defining a harmony needs to be open to all the things that necessarily or accidentally function as components relating to the harmony.

For instance, religion is defined in this book as *human engagement of ultimacy expressed in cognitive articulations, existential responses to ultimacy that give ultimate definition to the individual, and patterns of life and ritual in the face of ultimacy.* The harmony that is religion, in this definition, is the actual engagement of ultimacy. But the definition supposes that there are kinds of components that are required for this engagement to take place. The previous section identified five kinds of components that pretty much have to be involved in engaging ultimate realities: worshipful, aesthetic, psychological, social/environmental, and semiotic. Consider the ecological dimensions to these.

Worshipful components of religion need to have focused engagements of what is real, especially what is ultimately real, some kinds of psychological states, some kinds of social contexts in a natural environment, and some semiotic system or network to allow for the discriminations involved in all this. To refer to ultimate realities as components in an engagement may seem to beg some questions, but subsequent essays in this volume will address this point at length. For the moment, we can say that worshipful components of religion need to engage what worshippers believe is ultimate. Perhaps those people are right who think that there is no real reference to anything ultimate because there is nothing ultimate. Solipsists believe there is no real society with the result that the social aspects of religion are illusions. Mechanists believe there is no self (or at least say they believe that and defend it with all their soul), with the result that there are no psychological components of religion. We will come back to this point.

The aesthetic components of religion are the graspings of things as having determinateness, importance, and value insofar as these are involved in engaging ultimacy. Art and music are often involved in rituals of worship. But the arts have natures of their own, definitions that orient attention to them, and these need not be focused on the religious use of the arts, or of aesthetic imagination. All that can be studied on its own. Art history can indicate how art has played roles within religion, and it can indicate how religious institutions and people have shaped and sponsored art. All the components of religion can be components within aesthetic engagement. But the aesthetic elements themselves can be present without engagement of ultimacy taking place; they sometimes do not contribute to any religious harmony of ultimate engagement.

The psychological or spiritual components too are necessary for religion, although there are many different psychological conditions that can fit the bill. Moreover, religious aesthetic, social/environmental, and semiotic conditions can be components of a person's psychological makeup, as well as experiences of worship.

It is obvious that semiotic traditions go into engaging ultimacy and also that religion as engaging ultimacy conditions the semiotic harmonies of culture and history. And the history and contemporary structure of a semiotic culture can be studied without paying much attention to how it is a component of religious engagement. As prophets have often cried, the semiotic elements of a culture can lose the capacity to facilitate genuine engagement of ultimacy.

The upshot of this section is that definitions as harmonies define things as interdefined. Inquiry into the nature of what is defined involves investigating just how they are interdefined. In the case of religion as human engagements of ultimacy, this means inquiry into how worshipful, aesthetic, psychological, social/environmental, and semiotic components are involved in religion, when religion is actual. Each of those kinds of components, however, has been called "religion" when no actual engagement takes place. Worship rituals, religious art, spiritual practices, religious organizations, and the semiotics of religious traditions have all been called religion itself, even when they fail to come together in a harmony such that ultimacy is engaged. This leads to reductionism and destructive bias, as well as to illusions about what religion really is.

TUNNELS OF DEFINITION

Different perspectives on religion, such as those listed early in this chapter, are often like tunnels, isolated from one another, working with their own assumptions and procedures, and sometimes crossing one another. Sometimes those tunnels come out at one or another of the important components of religion, oblivious to the others. Because religion is a harmony of so many different kinds of components, each of which is an ecology of components in larger ecologies, it is easy for these perspectives not to be coordinated. But the lack of coordination is as much a function of the different assumptions and procedures of the perspectives as it is a function of the diverse parts of religion. This section shall examine several different kinds of perspectives, beginning with the scientific.

The social and natural sciences that deal with religion differ in their structural patterns and evolved historically in different ways. Each has its own process of socialization with specialized journals, graduate programs, post-doctoral positions, and a cumulative ethos that defines expertise. Judgment of good work is made within systems of "peer review" in which the peers are others who have been socialized into the scientific specialty. Of course, the scientific disciplines are always changing, developing new ways, and are required to redefine themselves as old theories are found wanting and new roads of inquiry open. But, generally, the sciences are conservative in the sense that they respect the authority of their systems of cumulative peer review and are very careful to accept findings that require rejecting what was previously thought to be known only with extremely persuasive evidence. This is true even with so-called "revolutionary science" that involves the overturning of basic paradigms, because the community of that science needs to understand the reasons for the revolution.

The social and natural sciences are often contrasted with one another, and for many good reasons. But they share the common trait of understanding a subject such as religion by "explaining" it. Explanation in this context means the redescription of the subject matter into some language or theoretical model that is supposed to be understood and accepted on its own. Some people think that human affairs should be explained by being reduced to the models of psychological interaction, as in Plato's *Republic*. Psychology in turn should be able to be redescribed in the terms of biology, which itself is explained in terms of the functions of chemistry, which then are translated into the terms of physics, which ideally can be expressed purely mathematically. Plato's hope was that mathematics could be the ultimate model or language in terms of which everything could be explained because he had the intuition that all harmonic relations could be expressed mathematically. His mathematics was not up to the task, and Aristotle's program for explaining by location in a genus-species classification system was more attractive for two millennia. Most scientists today, I suspect, lean in the Platonic direction.

But most scientists today are not so interested in the chain of reductions down to mathematical physics except for the mathematical physicists. They rather are interested in the topics of their own science, inquiring how to explain them in terms of their own theories, methodologies, instrumentations, and the like, building consensus in the journals and books of their science.

In studying religion, a discipline such as sociology naturally will see religion as something to be explained by sociological paradigms. Durkheim took his paradigms from political and cultural aspects of religious social structures, defining religion in terms of sacred legitimations of authority. Structuralists such as Lévi-Strauss and, in different ways, functionalists such as Talcott Parsons analyze social structures in terms of dynamic systems. Marxists define the social aspects of religion in terms of a large historical story. Pressed to be more empirical in the sense of collecting data, many sociologists focus on what can be learned through the methodologies of polling and interviewing. Not much in any of these sociological approaches has the capacity to recognize and explain worship of ultimate realities except in terms of institutions of ritual, or to deal with the psychological aspects except to see how psychological states in religion affect and are affected by institutions, or to deal with the aesthetic dimensions of religion. This situation is not bad so long as the various social sciences know what their assumptions are, know what the alternative assumptions might be, and know what aspects of religion are opened to them by those assumptions and what aspects are closed.

Proper scientific reductionism, in the tradition of Kant, says that it is not studying the thing in itself, religion, but rather only what can be represented of the thing in itself when reconstructed through the theories, methodologies, instrumentations, and socialized communities of judgment of the scientific discipline at hand. But how can any science know what aspect of religion it is studying if it does not have a definition of religion that indicates the other aspects? The very integrity of the tunneled discipline that gives it its standards of objectivity makes any robust definition of religion highly unlikely to be grasped in any but an amateurish way. Remember that the scientific meaning of "objectivity," deriving however indirectly from Kant, means not religion as a real thing but rather a picture of religion as represented through the constructs of a discipline. For all the good empirical data that can be found through proper scientific reduction, the isolation of the scientific tunnels, controlled by both the tools and assumptions of the particular science and the aspect of religion focused on, contributes to the confusion as to what religion is.

The ecological approach to definition as delineation of harmonies would help resolve some of the confusions by insisting on drawing out the lines of ecological dependence. For instance, when evolutionary biologists and anthropologists "explain" religion by showing how it does or does not contribute to making primitive social groups stronger and thus more adaptive competitively, it is showing how religion is a component of political order and solidarity. What really is being explained is politics and social authority structures. The same is true for Durkheim's kind of analysis. But when sociologists show how social dynamics determine changes in religious institutions such as church denominations, they show how the overall harmony of religion as engaging ultimacy is affected by the social dynamics.

The humanities also can be discipline tunnels when it comes to understanding religion. This is especially true in philosophy where analytic and Continental philosophers still do not talk with one another with much respect. Postmodernists have their own "discourses" and think systematic philosophers are slightly immoral because they commit the sins of logocentrism. But all have interesting things to say about religion. So do the art historians of all kinds of religious art. Art and literary criticism are helpful regarding understanding religion. Intellectual historians as well as social historians deal with religion. "History of religions" deals with the great religious traditions, and each tradition has its own mode of study, with its own journals and habits of good judgment. Sometimes history of religions finds its home in religious studies departments, sometimes in history departments, and sometimes in area studies. Many of the nuances of these distinctions among the different disciplines' approaches to religion will be discussed in chapters to follow.

Academic disciplines are not the only approaches to religion to characterize it variously. Religion plays many roles in public life in which politics, economics, social dynamics, the arts, and popular entertainment interact. These interactions are represented in journalism and popular media in newsworthy ways. Religious people represent themselves in public life in many different ways. Various continua between popular culture and sophisticated high-brow culture manifest many forms of popular religion and sophisticated theology. Each presents representations of religion and religious life that are usually partial.

The moral to be drawn from all this is not to disparage the many perspectives on religion, each of which seems to have its valid point in some context or other. Rather the moral is to call for a robust definition of religion in terms of which those who are interested can explore how the many perspectives relate. This interest in understanding religion in its wholeness is itself another perspective. Its particular virtue is being able to orient discussions of partiality. The following chapter presents such a definition and sets up a line of inquiry to be pursued throughout the essays in this volume.

NOTES

1. My remarks here defending the concept of religion parallel in many particulars the arguments of Kevin Schilbrack in his *Philosophy and the Study of Religions: A Manifesto* (Malden: Wiley Blackwell, 2014), chapter 4.

2. Roger A. Johnson, *Peacemaking and Religious Violence: From Thomas Aquinas to Thomas Jefferson* (Eugene: Pickwick/Wipf & Stock, 2009).

3. I have defended this supposition at length in *Ultimates: Philosophical Theology Volume One* (Albany: State University of New York Press, 2013), chapter 10 and passim.

4. This is the formulaic definition given throughout my three-volume *Philosophical Theology*: *Ultimates: Philosophical Theology Volume One* (Albany: State University of New York Press, 2013), *Existence: Philosophical Theology Volume Two* (Albany: State University of New York Press, 2014), and *Religion: Philosophical Theology Volume Three* (Albany: State University of New York Press, 2015). The first occurrence of the definition is in *Ultimates*, 4. The three volumes flesh out and defend the definition in great detail.

Chapter 2

A HEURISTIC DEFINITION OF RELIGION

ON DEFINITION

The controversies about defining religion come from so many angles, as in the informal list in the first section of the previous chapter, that, no matter where one starts, someone will say that you should have started somewhere else. So as not to seem as if I am endlessly postponing giving a definition, I shall repeat my hypothesis (from the previous chapter) for such a definition. *Religion is human engagement of ultimacy expressed in cognitive articulations, existential responses to ultimacy that give ultimate definition to the individual, and patterns of life and ritual in the face of ultimacy.* The short form of this is: *religion is human engagement with ultimacy.*

My hypothesis is that religion is best defined heuristically. A heuristic definition is one that is taken up to guide inquiry (from the Greek *heuriskein*, to discover). Its virtue is that it gives definiteness to what counts and does not count in the inquiry. According to the previous chapter, the definition should guide inquiry around the connections among the components of religion, and the components of components, and how they harmonize in cases of engagement of ultimacy. The justification of a heuristic definition is that inquiry is fruitful when it operates on that definition. A heuristic definition is proposed for use in inquiry, as I propose the preceding hypothesis that religion should be regarded as human engagement with ultimacy.

For some people, a "heuristic" approach is associated with a denial of realism in inquiry, a denial that inquiry can engage real things. For them, an inquiry is heuristic in the sense of being engaged with its own discourse but not with reality. Postmodernism in many forms takes "heuristic" definitions to be this: concern with correcting a trajectory of a discourse. My approach is pragmatic rather than postmodern. Inquiry in pragmatism is interaction, transaction, or engagement (to use my favorite word for being in the world) with things as guided by interpretations that employ signs. The signs and interpretations, of course, are vulnerable to correction as their objects give feedback. The employment of a heuristic definition of religion is to be justified by showing how it cuts reality at its real joints.[1]

We can understand the force of the heuristic character of a good definition of religion by contrasting it with three other definitional strategies: definition from historical beginnings, definition through phenomenology, and definition from reductive angles so that religious people would not recognize themselves in the definition, once it had been explained thoroughly.

In the Western social science traditions, there has been a strong propensity to define religion in terms of what are taken to be its early or "primitive" forms. Durkheim worried about the early establishment of political legitimacy and solidarity.[2] E. B. Tyler, Gerardus van der Leeuw, and Mircea Eliade worried about religious forms in primitive cultures.[3] Freud was concerned with religion in the formation of the primitive psyche.[4] We need not worry about the obvious problems of identifying "primitive" cultures. Evolutionary biologists and cognitive scientists push the locus of religion back even further into the past of human development.[5]

The first problem with defining religion with its "beginnings" is that those "beginnings" are also the "beginnings" of political order and educational organization. They are the beginnings of science; after all, belief in various kinds of supernatural beings is cognitive commitment to the kinds of things there are, what they do, and how they work. If Durkheim has a good point, the beginnings he calls religious are components of social organization having to do with legitimation. They are also components of economic organization, and a whole host of disciplines, practices, or dimensions of life that we now distinguish. There would be no point in seeking a definition of religion if there were no interest in seeing how it differs from but relates to science, politics, the arts, and the other dimensions of life, dimensions that have come to be through historical developments of many sorts. The "beginnings of religion" are the beginnings of all those other things, too, and so reference to the beginnings is not a good heuristic way of defining religion.

The second problem with defining religion in terms of its "beginnings" is that the whole category of "religion" has come under attack as a Western construction, reflecting Christian or at least monotheistic models. It often is associated with colonialism and is criticized by post-colonialist thinkers.[6] The category of "religion" surely does have a history, though that history goes back to the days of Cicero or earlier and was not a nineteenth-century invention. The category evolved through history and that history is fascinating, especially as the term went through translations into non-European languages. The fact that the category is historically conditioned and evolved makes it anachronistic to apply to prehistorical phenomena. A better heuristic definition of religion starts by investigating what religion is today, treating the development of the linguistic category of religion and its cognates as a matter of historical evolution. Far from delegitimating the category of religion, as anti-colonialist thinkers often assert, the fact that it has a history means that we can look to see what it has come to mean. Under criticism from anti-colonialists, scholars can now define religion in a much broader, more nearly unbiased, comparative way.

In point of fact, there is no such thing as religion that lies nakedly before us as a phenomenon to be described. It has no natural boundary identities, and phenomenology of religion, as well as various explanatory approaches, always presupposes some heuristic definition to guide the identification of the phenomenon.[7] Many social and natural scientists heuristically define religion as relating to beliefs in supernatural beings, gods, or a supremely transcendent supernatural monotheistic God. This works fine with dominant religions in Western theistic cultures and seems to be reinforced in studies conducted on people who live in the terms of these cultures. But, in point of fact, beliefs in supernatural beings are cognitive matters, that is, matters of science. As science has gotten more sophisticated and dropped most references to supernatural beings, they fall out of sophisticated religion. Buddhisms, Hinduisms, and Daoism arose in cultures that believed in a great many supernatural deities and devils. The folk religion forms of those traditions today still involve those beliefs and practices relating to them. But sophisticated Buddhists, Hindus, and Daoists today who have been educated into modern science, dropping the folk science of supernaturalism, usually drop literal belief in supernatural beings in their religious lives. The *metaphors* of supernatural personhood are more deeply entrenched in the monotheistic traditions. But even in these religions today, more natural philosophies of what is ultimate often replace any but metaphorical approaches to supernatural divinity.

The point is that there is no obvious phenomenological description of religion that is not itself a function of heuristic commitments such as defining religion through reference to supernaturalism, which is just a theistic bias against nontheistic religions. How should we go about getting a good heuristic definition of religion?

First, we should look at how religion relates to what we have called dimensions of human experience, such as politics, social order, the passing on of tradition, education more generally, the economy, psychological considerations including developmental stages, various kinds of consciousness, the arts, and the interactions of different cultures or "civilizations," as Samuel Huntington called them.[8] For instance, we have come now to think of politics as the symbolization and exercise of power and authority in social life, especially as this is institutionalized in governments of groups. In European and North American societies, politics has become quite distinct from religion when the latter means acting in reference to and on behalf of God or some other ultimate condition. For well-known reasons arising in the European wars of religion in the sixteenth and seventeenth centuries, religion came to be regarded as private relative to the public character of politics. This distinction aimed to keep the peace between warring religious factions, even though religious organizations such as churches are public, and hence political, in their ways. This is a complex story.

But it is quite different from the relation between politics and religion in Islam, which from the beginning has sought to identify political and religious leadership in constantly changing historical forms. The religious political wars between the Sunnis and Shia continue today. But the so-called "Arab Spring" has seen attempts to bring a sharp separation of Islamic religion from economic practices that would allow contemporary people to interact in a global, technologized economy. The separation of Islamic religion from government is much more confused because of the confused, and frequently plainly incompetent, forms of government in many Islamic lands. Islamic governments in the Middle East run from the Caliphate model of early Islam to attempts at imposing democracy in forms whose conditions arose from centuries of history of separating politics as public authority from religion as private practice in Europe and North America. If we define religion heuristically, as different from our heuristic definition of politics (and other dimensions of human experience), we can investigate how they have interacted throughout history, sometimes closely and sometimes distantly. Politics has been a component of religion in different ways throughout history, and religion has been a component of politics in many different ways also.

Another kind of consideration in forming a contemporary heuristic definition of religion is to pay attention to the state of the intellectual disciplines for studying the various aspects of religion. In the Western academic tradition, these include the social sciences, the humanities and literary critical disciplines, and more recently evolutionary biology, neuroscience, and cognitive science. All have been evolving, many at a fast rate. Postmodern critical approaches to religion are barely half a century old, however much they had their roots in nineteenth-century Marxism. The biological approaches to religion were advocated by William James and others in the last third of the nineteenth century but did not become flourishing research projects until the last thirty years or so; now they are changing every year with new directions and standards for research projects. Meanwhile, the internal self-understanding of religion, religious people, and what they take to be ultimate, that is, "theology," to use the old word, has taken on multifarious new forms, especially in reference to increasing contact among different religious traditions and symbol systems and in reference to the sciences. Each of these disciplines has its own set of heuristic definitions of religion that themselves have evolved historically and are now still changing. A good definition of religion should be heuristically helpful in picking up on what is interesting in the understanding of religion in each of these disciplines. It should also provide intellectual space within which attempts at integrating the various disciplines can flourish.

To say that *religion is human engagement of ultimacy expressed in cognitive articulations, existential responses to ultimacy that give ultimate definition to the individual, and patterns of life and ritual in the face of ultimacy* allows for asking how any of the dimensions of human experience are involved as components in ultimate engagements. It also allows for any disciplined inquiry that involves treating components in ultimate engagements as an inquiry into religion insofar as it does so. Two stumbling blocks to this heuristic definition of religion are obvious. One is that most of the disciplines that claim to be studying religion do not acknowledge or have any internal way of dealing with ultimacy. The exceptions would be metaphysical forms of philosophy and religious philosophies and theologies themselves. The other stumbling block is that just about any dimension of experience, including politics, tradition, and the flow of consciousness, might or might not involve engaging ultimacy. So, obviously, a defense of my heuristic definition of religion requires a treatment of ultimacy that could make sense to the disciplines involved and to the historical realities of the various dimensions of experience, the topic of the next section.

But first, a further word needs to be said about a good heuristic definition of religion. While it is tempting to allow heuristic definitions to arise out of the disciplines studying religion, those disciplines might access only certain components of religion and not how the components hang together, as noted in the previous chapter. Just what is the harmony of the components? To answer this, it is worth recalling the old saw that religious people ought to be able to recognize themselves in what is called religion. Most people who consider themselves religious understand themselves to be engaging whatever they take to be ultimate (although they are not likely to put it in that philosophical way). The reality of their religion is the reality of that engagement. Of course, there are many understandings of ultimacy, several classes of which will be discussed in chapter 4. But religion for religious people is when the engagement happens, episodically or regularly (see chapters 6 and 7). The great religious traditions have highly developed and complex ways of testing the authenticity of engagement. So a good heuristic definition of religion cannot exclude the problematic of real, authentic engagement, even when it articulates "religious" definitions of components such as institutions and psychological states that might or might not be involved in actual engagement of ultimacy.

The preceding point is controversial for at least two reasons. First, many people studying religion understand their methodologies to be disengaged from engagements with ultimate realities. But for them a heuristic definition that includes what is most important to religious people should be all the more important so they can see how the tunnel of their own approach relates to others. Second, many people who study religion believe that there are no ultimate realities. What if there are no ultimate realities, not even one? If this were the case, then Freud would be right that religion is an illusion. But then this would be an important thing to know about religion. How would we know whether religion is an illusion? Only by studying ultimacy! That many scholars have abandoned supernatural or other beliefs about ultimacy does not solve the problem of whether there are ultimate realities. That must be studied on its own.

To say as, my heuristic definition does, that *religion is human engagement of ultimacy expressed in cognitive articulations, existential responses to ultimacy that give ultimate definition to the individual, and patterns of life and ritual in the face of ultimacy* demands that the inquiry be taken very seriously into what, if anything, is ultimate, and how people variously understand ultimacy. To this we now turn.

ULTIMACY AND ENGAGEMENT IN RELIGION

This section spells out in brief fashion a complex hypothesis about ultimacy that will be developed from many angles in the chapters that follow.

One of the most pervasive and basic philosophical questions is that of the one and the many or, put differently, how different things can be sufficiently unified so as to relate as determinately different from one another, and at the same time be external enough from one another so as to be different in the first place. Heidegger framed this as the ontological question: what is being such that beings have it in being related to one another and yet different? Plato considered many hypotheses about the one and many in his dialogue *Parmenides*. But the problem occurs in one form or another in just about every philosophical or theological tradition around the globe. Because the explicit answers, or implicit assumptions, about unity in diversity affect nearly every other philosophical topic, the problem of the one and the many is about as fundamental as a philosophical question can be. A thinker in any field can avoid addressing this philosophical problem, as most scientists do. But then such thinkers are vulnerable to unexamined assumptions about the one and many, or unity in diversity. When philosophers do get around to examining those assumptions and developing theories of the one and many, their arguments count, and scientists and other thinkers about religion can either accept the philosophical conclusions blindly or take responsibility for relating themselves to the philosophical discussion.

My own approach to the one and many is to analyze it in terms of determinateness as such.[9] No matter what the world might consist of, it is determinate. If something is determinate, it has to be determinate with respect to something else. Therefore, there must be a plurality of determinate things, determinate relative to one another in some respects or other. These determinate things must be other than one another to be determinate with respect to one another. On the other hand, they must condition one another relationally to connect as mutually determining. This means that each determinate thing is a harmony of two kinds of components. First, each must have conditioning components stemming from the other things with which it is determinate; otherwise, they would not be connected in their very determinateness. Second, each must have essential components that integrate all the components so that the thing has its own being; otherwise, they would reduce to the ways they are conditioned without being anything to be conditioned in the first place. Determinateness requires harmonizing both kinds of components, and both kinds of components need to be harmonized with one another to make up a determinate thing.

The mutual conditionings of a plurality of determinate harmonies constitute a kind of relational togetherness, which I call "cosmological togetherness." But the togetherness of the determinate harmonies themselves includes their respective essential components, which are precisely what is beyond their mutual conditioning components and yet are necessary for the things to be external enough from one another to be other than one another. I call this the "ontological context of mutual relevance" because it is the context in which determinate things have being relative to one another, both internally related as mutually relevant and externally related as different. What can this ontological context of mutual relevance be?

Perhaps the most popular philosophical answers to this question are monistic ones, claims that the one contains the many in some sense or other of "contains." The problem with these answers is revealed in the further question: is the one as container itself determinate over and above the determinate things contained? If the answer is yes, then the many things contained and the container constitute a larger many and a yet larger determinate container is required, which is a bad infinite regress. If the answer is no, the question is how an indeterminate container can be said to contain anything. Perhaps the contained things just fit together, but then we would not have explained how their diverse essential features can be together. Some other singular indeterminate thing is needed to be an ontological context of mutual relevance.

Yet another possible answer to the question of what the ontological context might be is a radically pluralistic one, namely, that each determinate thing is a unity for the other things with respect to which it is determinate. According to this answer, there is no one for the many, but many ones in each of the many. Paul Weiss has developed this philosophical strategy most thoroughly, though it lies in William James and in most forms of the Buddhist emphasis on suchness.[10] The difficulty with this answer is that each determinate thing unifies only the conditional components of the other things and is in principle incapable of grasping the essential components of those other things. The result is that each thing is a world unto itself with no real internal relations with other external things, and therefore nothing could be determinate.

The only answer I can imagine to the question of what the ontological context of mutual relevance can be is that it is an ontological creative act that in itself is indeterminate but that simply and singularly creates all the determinate things as ontologically together. Everything in the nature of the ontological act, including its very occurrence, is the result of the act, part of the complex, plural, determinate product. One can liken this to a monotheistic creator God, but only in a metaphorical sense that needs to be shriven of any sense of divine potential, intention, agency, or will.

Everything that is determinate, such as a divine character, must be the result of the ontological creative act, not an antecedent condition. The act is a sheer making, creating both time and place for determinate makings. This ontological creative act is the ultimate condition for there being anything determinate at all. I call it the "ontological ultimate."

Nevertheless, there could be no ontological creative act without creating something, and whatever things are created are determinate. Therefore, the conditions of determinateness as such are also ultimate. They would obtain in any cosmos, and so I call them "cosmological ultimates." The ontological ultimate and cosmological ultimates are equally ultimate; there cannot be one without the other.

There are at least four cosmological ultimates: form, components formed, existential location, and harmonic identity. Any determinate harmony has a form or pattern according to which its components are integrated; otherwise, they would not be harmonized. Any determinate harmony has components with a nature of their own, often extending beyond the harmony to other harmonies; otherwise, there would be nothing determinately distinct to be components, conditional and essential, within the harmony. Any determinate harmony has an existential location relative to the other things with respect to which it is determinate, constituted by the mutual interplay of conditional components; the components connecting with other things constitute an existential field, perhaps several such fields; without such existential fields, things could not be determinate with respect to one another. Any determinate harmony has the value or harmonic identity of getting its components together with its form in its existential location relative to other things; although more needs to be said about value than I shall say here, each determinate thing has a determinate, contextualized identity in its conditioning environment. These four cosmological ultimates—form, components formed, existential location, and harmonic identity—are ultimate conditions for any determinate world whatsoever. So is the ontological ultimate.

FIVE PROBLEMATICS OF RELIGION

Let us move from the absolute metaphysical generality of determinateness as such to how these ultimate conditions show up in the scale of things relevant for human life. For human beings, these five ultimates set five problematics for religion as the engagement of ultimacy, a point to be elaborated in greater detail in chapter 3 and subsequent chapters.

The ontological ultimacy of the ontological creative act shows up in human life as the problematic of responding to radical contingency. This problematic has many forms, such as affirmation or denial of existence, blissful appreciation, profound gratitude, and sometimes disciplined attempts at mystical comprehension of, even close union with, the ontological creative act, symbolized one way or another.

Form is ultimate for human life insofar as it is future possibilities among which people sometimes have to choose. Future possibilities sometime have alternatives among which choice must be made, and the different alternatives have different values. Therefore, there is the problematic of righteousness, or living under obligation, that is an ultimate condition for every individual, singly and collectively. The problematic is complex, with different kinds of possibilities, issues of discerning the values in the future, perfecting abilities to choose, coping with mistakes and guilt. Religions handle the problematic of righteousness in diverse ways. But all religions with any depth have to develop the problematic of righteousness because form is an ultimate condition of human life as facing possibilities. It can no more be ignored than the weather.

"Components to be integrated" is an ultimate condition insofar as each person has to integrate a wide variety of kinds of components that often do not easily go together. This constitutes the religious problematic of the quest for wholeness. When wholeness is missing, there is suffering, of diverse kinds. Models of human wholeness differ radically from one another, but any religion has to have models or ideals or practices for questing wholeness. All religious engagements with the need for human wholeness are bound by this as an ultimate condition of human life.

The ultimacy of existential location shows up on the human scale as the need to engage others as relative to oneself but also as having identity and value on their own, with their own otherness in the environment, their own essential components. Religions have long recognized the issues of engaging other people with devices such as the Golden Rule that allow persons to imagine themselves in the places of others. Now we are becoming sensitive to treating the natural environment as something to be respected on its own, not just relative to human interests. The problematic of engagement of others as others is an ultimate condition of human life.

The ultimacy of achieved harmonic identity or value shows up on the human scale as the quest for meaning in the world, or as the search for salvation in the cosmic context, however understood. All religions deal with this problematic of meaning, with a wide range of answers, from living forever in a place with ultimate value to seeking oblivion or enlightened extinction. Although not everyone attends to this problematic, it is an ultimate condition for human life that the question can be asked.

My basic claim here, expressed only in the most hurried way (but detailed elsewhere in this volume), is that there are five ultimate conditions of existence that can be understood somewhat by philosophy that anyone can read or understand if they work at it enough. Each of these ultimate conditions needs to be engaged by human beings. Religious traditions, social groups, and psychological structures, among other things, have provided complex problematics for doing so. The problematics themselves are human constructions and can be studied in part as merely human constructions. But they are ways of engaging ultimate realities that are there, really there, however well they are engaged, and thus can be understood with pragmatic realism. Of course, people can ignore the problematics, and the negative feedback punishing such inattention is much slower to come in than corrective feedback from ignoring the weather. But because the five ultimate realities are real, the problematics of radical contingency, righteousness, selfhood, interactions with others, and the meaning of life are fully embedded in human life.

COMPONENTS OF AUTHENTIC RELIGION

Given these problematics, what are some of the main components of human engagement with ultimacy that allow them to be addressed? Let us set aside temporarily the background components that are important functions for any human endeavors, such as habitable climates, economies that furnish nourishment, shelter, and education. But let us not set them too far aside, because they are all fragile and might suddenly become religious concerns. Moreover, these and many other conditions are necessary components of those components that are specifically important for religion as the engagement of ultimacy, ecosystems within ecosystems. I shall focus on some of the conditions specifically involved in human engagement with ultimacy.

The components are involved in the direct, albeit symbolically mediated, engagement with the five ultimates. For shorthand, I call the components involved in religion *worship*. Worship is a good term for direct engagement of ultimate realities because it suggests the contingency of the four cosmological ultimates and of the *nature* of the ontological creative act on the ontological act itself.

Although there are five ultimate objects of worship, perhaps most people would identify worshipful engagement of the ontological creative act on which all things determinate depend to be the first thing they think of as worship. There are semiotic components providing the symbols for worship, social/environmental components such as liturgies and liturgical calendars, aesthetic components, and psychological components. The harmonizing of these components through the intentionalities of taking self-involving signs to engage the ontological creative act is the worshipful engagement. Chapter 4 will say more about the personhood, consciousness, and spontaneous emergence kinds of signs worship or mystical engagement.

In addition to the worshipful engagement of the ontological creative act are worshipful engagements of what I have called the cosmological ultimates.

So, the second set of religion's components are those involved in worship of the radically contingent fact that there is form in the world, as a trait of any determinate world, and that form is the appearance of contingent existence: without form, there would be nothing. Moreover, form is the bearer of beauty, the intrinsic value native to form. An elementary kind of worship is toward the ultimate beauty of formed existence. All the arts—visual, musical, architectural, and those of movement—can function as components of this kind of worship. There is an intrinsic beauty in liturgical and other spiritual practices that in other respects are functional for other things. There is a beauty in persons and a different kind of beauty in nature. Kant spoke of the sublime beauty of the starry heavens above and the moral law within. According to the metaphysics I am suggesting, any harmony whatsoever has some beauty in its form, however harmful that might be to other things. Therefore, the worship of the ultimacy of beauty in form can be a dimension of everything. But in religious practice, the beauties mentioned are important components. Worship of the ultimacy of radically contingent beauty of course requires the appreciation of beauty in various contexts, and cultivation of this appreciation is a component of religious worship. So too are the disciplines for the creating of the arts, liturgical practices, and the rest. The social and natural sciences have not paid much attention to the components of the worshipful appreciation of the ultimacy of beauty in all form.

The third component of religion as engagement of ultimacy is the psychological. By "the psychological" I mean the range of things studied by William James in his *Varieties of Religious Experience*, and the things Kierkegaard, Freud, empirical psychologists, and more recently cognitive sciences have studied. The psychological component of religion is as various as are the worshipful, social, and semiotic components. It most often functions in my definition of religion, as a harmony that constitutes human engagement of ultimacy, as supplying essential components. Conditional components connect a harmony with somewhat external things, whereas essential components are internal and function to integrate themselves and the conditional components into a coherent form. The psychological components of religion have to do with existential choice, spiritual quests, unifying bliss, and the dark night of the soul. Everyone has rich and complex, sometimes mutually conflicting, psychological states, and some of these states with some people are components of engagements with ultimacy. When they are, those psychological states are components of religion and are appropriately studied by psychology of religion. But just about any psychological state can also be present without being involved with engaging ultimacy. In that case, it is not part of religion, even if it is expressed with religious symbols, such as perceptions of spirits or voices that claim to be God. Psychological elements are what make thinkers such as William James and Alfred North Whitehead say that religion is essentially solitary, not a group phenomenon.[11] Of course, solitary states are affected by hosts of external conditions, but they are not to be reduced to the external conditions. And the components of life are not harmonized into engagements with ultimacy without them. As with religious traditions and social groups with religious components, psychological elements are not only components of engaging ultimacy; engagements with ultimacy in turn can be components in one's psychological states. These psychological elements are components of religion in the ways and degrees to which they engage the ultimacy of truth of the diversely related self. The wholeness of the self has an intrinsically dyadic element, being true to the components of the self and those external elements to which the self is conditionally related, while attempting to be true to its own unity. In classical theological terms, this is a version of the ultimacy of truth. It is a kind of worship of the contingency of being a self.

The fourth kind of component of religion as symbolic engagement of ultimacy is social and natural environmental context. Everyone has a social context and that affects how an individual engages ultimacy. Every society is set in a natural environment, or moves through several. The variation in social contexts as components of religion is astonishing, however. In some, the religious culture is virtually congruent with the society's organization and the entire society is a venue for engaging ultimacy; in others, the society contains many religious traditions; in yet others, religious people might hide out in caves or be forest dwellers with little social intercourse. A religious person needs some social setting or other in order to engage ultimacy. But not all religious people take membership in a religious culture in a social setting to be the venue for engaging ultimacy, even though that is what sociologists might measure. For some authentically religious people, church attendance is a crucial social venue for engaging ultimacy; others can attend church without ever engaging ultimacy; yet others find church attendance or religious traditional affiliation to be counterproductive or irrelevant for engaging ultimacy.

I have spoken of social context as a component in religion as engaging ultimacy. As with religious cultures, however, religion as engaging ultimacy might also be an important component in the formation of social groups. A society is an ecologically shaped harmony within which religions is often, although perhaps not always, a component. As mentioned, Durkheim and others think they are "explaining" religion by showing it to be a helpful component in the formation of legitimated social structures. Some evolutionary biologists think they are explaining religion when they show how it strengthens primitive group solidarity. In fact, it would be better to say that they are explaining social structures by showing how religion is a component. Neither the social nor scientific modes of inquiry tend to be curious or even open about understanding religion as engaging ultimacy.

The components of religion that involve social and natural contexts reflect the fact that persons are part of a larger togetherness, a larger unity. Each person is together in some specific or vague sense with everything else that is determinate; all are creatures. There is no overarching unity to the whole of creation. But the fact that the ontological creative act creates all things as determinate with reference to one another, more or less, gives it a singularity that the classic Western tradition has called divine unity. All the social and natural connections of human life can function as components of religion as engaging ultimacy, in this instance, the unity or singularity of the ontological creative act.

The fifth kind of component of religion is the need for cultures that supply the symbolic systems for identifying ultimacy and how to engage it. These are the semiotic components of religion. Countless cultures have existed with such symbolic systems, from the time human groups developed sufficiently complex semiotic systems that they could conceive of ultimate conditions, conditions that themselves are not conditioned. We are accustomed to thinking of these cultures of symbols for ultimacy as religious traditions. Sometimes we think of the history of these cultures as history of religions, and those histories are histories of changes. Sometimes religious traditions are important for religious identity. But sometimes changing or breaking with a tradition is also important for identity. On the one hand, religious traditions can be understood as components of religion as symbolic engagement of ultimacy and, on the other, symbolic engagements of ultimacy can function as components within the ongoing changes of a religious tradition or culture. A religious tradition itself is a developing harmony that can be understood on its own. Religion as the engagement of ultimacy can be part of such a tradition, but then again the tradition might have its own dynamic that can carry on, at least for a while, without any authentic engagement of ultimacy. Prophets complain about the latter condition quite a lot. Existential theologians such as Paul Tillich worked hard to transform their religious tradition so that it had symbols that facilitate rather than blunt authentic engagement with ultimacy. Many scholars who study the history of religious traditions and cultures do not bother to consider whether authentic symbolic engagement of ultimacy is taking place within them. But these semiotic cultures are necessary for the engagement of ultimate questions of the meaning of life or of the existence of the cosmos. The various semiotic components are religious insofar as they help articulate how the world achieves an actual identity that has the value of actualizing the possibilities it does with the components it has in diverse harmonies, in the places where those harmonies are located with respect to one another. This is a cumulative appreciation and assessment of what good the world has, and insofar as the ontological creative act derives its nature from what it creates, it is the goodness of that act that is worshipped through the semiotic components.

Obviously, the engagements of the five ultimates are not separate. The components of one kind of engagement are also components of the other kinds. I have tried here to address the question of how the components can be harmonized to effect real religious engagement, while also having their own nature that does not necessarily effect real engagements. The classic Western monotheistic traditions have transcended personification symbols by calling God the creator, beauty, truth, unity or singularity, and good. These notions also appear in many other traditions in their articulations of symbols of the radical contingency of things, as we shall see in subsequent chapters.

In addition to the cultural, social, and psychological kinds of components I have mentioned here, there are hosts of historical, familial, and biological conditions that can function in religion as engagement with ultimacy. I've given a terribly simplified view. But the discussion is sufficient to grasp the point that these kinds of things can be components of *religion* only when they are involved in engaging ultimacy. When they do not come together so as to constitute that special harmony that is *human engagement of ultimacy expressed in cognitive articulations, existential responses to ultimacy that give ultimate definition to the individual, and patterns of life and ritual in the face of ultimacy*, they are not religion or components of religion. They are only cultural traditions with religious names, social organizations with religious names, or psychological states and historical conditions that are religiously named for their association with religion, but are not in this case religion.

Of course, we cannot make much of this point about authentic religion if we cannot make sense of ultimacy, as I have begun to do in the second section of this chapter and will supplement in subsequent chapters. History and anthropology of religions, sociology of religion, psychology of religion, and the new combinations of scientific inquiries into religion usually define themselves as sciences in part by the fact that they do not and cannot deal vulnerably with ultimacy. But this means that they are tone deaf to the distinction between authentic religion and religion that fails to engage ultimacy and is reduced to the dynamics of its historical cultures, social organization, and psychological states. They do not hear the prophets' cry against dead symbols and liturgical forms, against social structures that are only power plays, and against supposedly divine madness that is only pathological madness. They cannot take at face value the disciplines in so many religions focused on spiritual discernment and on the vetting of allegedly religious engagements with ultimacy as to whether they are the real thing.

Now I admit that inquiry into ultimacy is philosophy on a profound and fundamental scale. Even most philosophers do not want to do this these days, claiming that such metaphysical inquiries are impossible. Far less are most scientists willing to learn from philosophy because they confine "learning," as scientists, to what takes place within the disciplines of their science. But I shall march ahead as a philosopher to marshal arguments for the knowledge of ultimacy needed to work in interdisciplinary ways with my definition of religion as engagement of ultimacy.

In this chapter I have tried to defend the thesis that religion should be defined as a harmony of integrating various components so that people can engage ultimacy. First, I have argued that definition of something like religion ought to treat it as a harmony of components, some of which can be understood on their own and as not necessarily religious. They are religious only to the extent that they are harmonized so as to produce engagement of ultimacy. They can be understood as components of religion defined as engaging ultimacy, and religion defined that way can be understood as a component of those other dimensions such as the awesomeness of the ontological creative act, the aesthetic, the personally integrative, matters of social and natural environment, and the semiotic. The definition of religion as the engagement of ultimacy needs to have a theory of ultimacy, which I have provided with the discussion of determinacy and the problem of the one and the many. There are five ultimates, I have argued: the ontological creative act, which is what the radically contingent world consists of; form; components formed; existential location; and achieved identity, all ultimate conditions in any cosmos that is determinate. Not everyone has to believe in these ultimates. But when the problem of the one and the many is considered, these ultimates should be accepted, or some better theory needs to be proposed. I have then sketched briefly how these ultimate conditions are addressed on the scale of human life with the basic religious problematics of righteousness, the quest for wholeness, the engagement of others, the quest for meaning or value in the cosmic context, and ways of addressing ontological contingency or the ontological creative act. When I say that religion is *human engagement of ultimacy expressed in cognitive articulations, existential responses to ultimacy that give ultimate definition to the individual, and patterns of life and ritual in the face of ultimacy*, the content of religion is engagement of ultimacy through at least these five problematics that have found articulations in all the world's religions. The components of such religious engagements are themselves religious when they harmonize to effect the engagements, and I have classified these as those involved in engaging the ontological creative act, aesthetic ones, personally integrative ones, engagements of others in social and natural contexts, and semiotic elements in culture and tradition. Subsequent chapters will spell these distinctions out more.

NOTES

1. In *Philosophy and the Study of Religions: A Manifesto* (Malden: Wiley Blackwell, 2014), chapter 5, Kevin Schilbrack defends a "heuristic" definition of religion with a realistic metaphysical or reference base; he sometimes calls his definition "strategic." His definition is not the same as mine, depending too much on reference to superempirical realities, to my way of thinking.

2. Emile Durkheim, *The Elementary Forms of the Religious Life*, translated from the French by Joseph Ward Swain (New York: The Free Press, 1965; original edition, London: George Allen & Unwin, 1915).

3. Edward Burnett Tyler, *Primitive Culture: Researches into the Development of Mythology, Philosophy, Religion, Language, Art, and Culture*, fourth edition, revised, in two volumes (London: John Murray, 1903; original edition, 1871). Gerardus van der Leeuw, *Religion in Essence and Manifestation*, two volumes, edited by Hans H. Penner, translated by J. E. Turner (New York: Harper, 1963). Mircea Eliade, *Patterns in Comparative Religion*, translated by Rosemary Sheed (New York: Meridian Books, 1963; original French edition, 1949).

4. Sigmund Freud, *The Future of an Illusion*, translated by W. D. Robson-Scott, revised and newly edited by James Strachey (Garden City: Doubleday Anchor, 1964) and *Totem and Taboo* (London: W. W. Norton, 1989).

5. See Wesley J. Wildman's review of the evolutionary biology approach to religion in his *Science and Religious Anthropology: A Spiritually Evocative Naturalism Interpretation of Human Life* (Farnham: Ashgate, 2009), chapter 3.

6. See, for instance, Tomoko Masuzawa, *The Invention of World Religions: Or, How European Universalism Was Preserved in the Language of Pluralism* (Chicago: University of Chicago Press, 2005).

7. See my defense of this in *Religion: Philosophical Theology Volume Three* (Albany: State University of New York Press, 2015), chapter 1.

8. See Samuel P. Huntington, *The Clash of Civilizations and the Remaking of World Order* (New York: Simon & Schuster, 1996).

9. See the extensive argument in my *Ultimates: Philosophical Theology Volume One* (Albany: State University of New York Press, 2013), part 3.

10. See Paul Weiss, *Modes of Being* (Carbondale: Southern Illinois University Press, 1958).

11. See my discussion of James and Whitehead on "solitariness" in *Existence: Philosophical Theology Volume Two* (Albany: State University of New York Press, 2014), introduction.

Chapter 3

THEORY OF RELIGION IN A PRAGMATIC PHILOSOPHICAL THEOLOGY

I write here not as a scholar of pragmatism but as a pragmatic philosophical theologian with a theory of religion. The first step in the pragmatic theory is to propose a definition of religion intended as an hypothesis for organizing the inquiry. The hypothesis is that *religion is human engagement of ultimacy expressed in cognitive articulations, existential responses to ultimacy that give ultimate definition to the individual, and patterns of life and ritual in the face of ultimacy.*[1] Obvious topics of the inquiry into religion will have to include (1) ultimacy or ultimate reality in the several senses included in the definition, (2) the cognitive articulations of ultimacy, (3) ways by which individuals are defined existentially through their responses to ultimacy, and (4) the issues of everyday living in the face of ultimacy. Equally important is the theory of symbolic engagement presupposed, which is dealt with in the fourth section of the following chapter and all of part 2 of this volume.[2]

ULTIMATE REALITIES

For the purpose of sketching a pragmatic theory of religion, I shall briefly state but not defend here an hypothesis about ultimate realities. The hypothesis is that *there are five ultimate realities: an ontological creative act that creates everything that is determinate and four transcendental traits of anything whatsoever that is determinate: namely, form, components integrated in the form, existential location relative to other determinate things, and achieved value-identity.* The philosophical argument for saying that there is an ontological creative act of everything determinate comes from an analysis of determinateness as such, as sketched in the previous chapter. That analysis also yields the transcendental traits of determinateness. Thus, the five ontological realities are interlocked and the hypothesis about them is indifferent as to just what determinate things might be found to be created. I shall not rehearse the philosophical arguments for this theory of ultimate realities.[3]

The interest of a theory of religions in ultimate realities is less for what they might be in themselves than for their bearing on human life. The ontological creative act is the source of all determinate existence, including all the things making up the human world.[4] How do we comport ourselves toward the fact that there is this world rather than nothing at all? The appreciation, affirmation, or denial of existence is a pervasive theme in all religions, albeit symbolized in different ways. The act itself cannot be symbolized in an iconic way: iconic reference asserts some kind of isomorphic modeling of the object, and the act has no shape to model except in its termini, namely, the things of the world. In a sense readily understandable to pragmatic semioticians, any real reference to the act must be through a kind of indexical pointing, perhaps of the sort supplied by a dialectical argument.[5]

To engage it, however, people still do need to find intimate ways to symbolize the ontological creative act because it is an ultimate reality resident in every determinate thing. The religious cultures of the world have developed three main symbolic systems to express this, each with many variants and many crossovers from one to another, as the next chapter shall spell out. One of these is the symbol of the person, elaborated variously in different kinds of theism. Another is the symbol of consciousness as an underlying reality, the objects of which are the determinate things of the world; the metaphors of underlying consciousness are prominent in Buddhism and various forms of Hinduism. A third symbolic system, more prominent in Daoism, Confucianism, and Chinese Buddhism, is based around metaphors of spontaneous emergence, the Dao that cannot be named giving rise to the Dao of process that can be named. As the great civilized theological systems have elaborated their symbols, all have recognized that their symbols are broken and cannot refer iconically even at their most abstract. The monotheistic God is beyond personhood in any determinate sense, however much personal metaphors find some application. The Brahman without qualities that is somehow identical with atman is still beyond any finite determinations of consciousness. The Ultimate of Non-being that spontaneously blossoms into the Great Ultimate is beyond even the quality of fruitfulness. The ultimate ontological creative act simply cannot be modeled, and can be grasped only through the indexical reference that connects with an act of sheer making.

Now let us examine briefly the four cosmological ultimates. The cosmological ultimates of form, components formed together, existential location, and value-identity are conditions for the possibility of any world because they are traits of determinateness as such. Any world whatsoever must have determinate things in it insofar as it is something rather than nothing and thus must exhibit the transcendental traits.

Form as an ultimate condition for human life is most prominent as the structure of possibilities for the future. The future contains the possibilities that might get actualized, and sometimes what gets actualized is affected by human choices. A fundamental aesthetic sense is involved in grasping form's inner structure as bearing value. Sometimes the possibilities in the future are structured to be alternatives for choice and often, when this is so, the alternatives differ in value. Sometimes the difference is in measurable degrees, as one choice being better than another, and sometimes the difference is in kind. In either case the choices a person makes have two related deep effects. On the one hand, they determine what gets actualized, to the degree the person influences this, and so contribute to the value of the world for better or worse and for the kinds of values that get actualized. On the other hand, the choices determine the kind of moral character the chooser acquires insofar as this is a function of this or that choice, and of choices cumulatively. The objectivity of the value-structure of possibilities and the moral self-definition of choosing define any person with a choice as lying under obligation. To be in a position of having to choose among alternative possibilities with different values is to lie under obligation. All religions develop problematics of lying under obligation.

Having components, from the human standpoint, means that people have to integrate these components with the dynamic forms they actualize in their lives. Important components include family, social, cultural, and ethnic conditions; physical traits related to genes, health, age, and living conditions; the traits of a person's neighborhood, ecological habitat, and historical conditions; and a host of particular elements such as friendships and enmities, career and other aspirations, and the accidents of life. Each of the components has a formal structure of its own, hence a value, and hence a moral bearing. But in addition to facing the ultimate reality of lying under obligation is the human need to balance a proper deference to each of the important components of life with the requirements that they be integrated together in a life with some wholeness. So there is an ultimate condition for human life, deriving from the need to integrate components, which consists in healing brokenness and suffering and striving for wholeness or integration. All religions have problematics of suffering and wholeness.

In reference to the ultimate reality of existential location is the fact that people are in existential fields with other things and people to whom they are related but that are external to them in significant ways. We are accustomed to thinking of people as others and recently have become more conscious of various aspects of the natural environment as others. Institutions and cultures are others as well. In some ways, others such as family, friends, and environmental factors are components of a person's life and function as issues for personal wholeness. But in addition, others also have their own integrity that might be quite irrelevant to their roles in that person's life, and there is an ultimate obligation of the person to respond to the others as "others." The ultimate reality of having existential location in a field that includes others constitutes an ultimate condition of relating to others for better or worse. Religions all have problematics of relating to others with such practical dispositions as respect and appreciation, kindness and compassion, forgiveness, mercy, reconciliation, and repair, or perhaps as rejection of others as members of the outgroup.

The bearing on human life of the ultimate condition of any determinate thing having a value-identity pertains to the meaning or value of a person's life in ultimate perspective. Individuals differ in how much they conceive the meaning of their lives in this sense of value-identity in personal or in social terms. Religions problematize value-identity in enormously diverse ways as the problem of salvation, or meaning, or justification. Sometimes the nature of value-identity is framed in terms of a cosmic or grand historical narrative; other times, it is framed in terms of more local relations to the ontological creative act.

The shape of this pragmatic theory of religion is now coming into view. Every religion with depth and reflective subtlety must cope with each of the ultimate realities, with problems of obligation, wholeness, otherness, meaning, and contingency on the ontological creative act. Every religion develops the complex problematic of obligation, with concerns for righteousness in choice, for knowing what righteousness is, for success and failures at righteousness, moral training and heroism, guilt, punishment, forgiveness, and the like. Every religion develops the problematic of wholeness, with health, healing, exercise, coping with suffering, spiritual integration and maturation, reconciliation in many senses, fragmentation, activity and passivity. Every religion develops the problematic of relating to others, and the Axial Age religions agree vaguely that everyone, even those outside the ingroup, should be treated with compassion, love, care, and justice. Every religion develops ways of dealing with the question of the meaning of life, especially in circumstances of deep and widespread suffering, loss of identity through the destruction of one's ingroup or loss of home territory, or deep shame and guilt. Every religion develops the problematic of responding to the gratuitousness, arbitrariness, undeservingness, and surprisingness of the creation, articulating ways of affirming or denying this reality, enjoying or hating, bliss or nihilism. Religions think all of these things through metaphoric systems of personhood, or consciousness, or spontaneous emergence for the ontological act of creation on which all dimensions of determinateness are contingent.

To think that there is just one thing religion pursues, "salvation," as it is put in the terms of Western religions, is a mistake. To think that each religion has its own particular kind of salvation to pursue is also a mistake.[6] Rather, it is in the nature of the reality that all religions engage for the ultimate conditions of existence to determine that five ultimate realities must be articulated in some way or another and engaged, each determining a complex religious problematic. Of course, the religions have radically different approaches to these ultimate realities according to their different cultural sets of symbols, to which we now turn.

COGNITIVE ARTICULATIONS

The cognitive articulations of the five ultimate realities can be called "theology" in the most comprehensive sense. Included within theology are the engagements of the various ultimate realities with the symbols involved in the interpretive aspects of the engagements. These are the symbols that would be included within what Peter Berger might call a sacred canopy.[7] In a settled, unchallenged religious culture, the symbols of a sacred canopy would be shared by those in the group whose culture it is. But few if any religious cultures are settled, unchallenged, and so each individual can have a sacred canopy of first-order religious symbols that is only more or less shared with others. Theology inquires into the symbols of ultimacy in sacred canopies that differ widely from culture to culture. This is more complex than might be apparent.

Included within the engagements of the ultimate realities with the symbols of a sacred canopy are all the questions of the personal and cultural interpretations of the problematics of how the ultimate realities bear upon life. This is to say, a theology needs to include some critical understanding of the complicated problematics of obligation, wholeness, existential engagement, achieved value-identity, and response to the ontological contingency of determinate existence, hermeneutically enriching the intimacy of such symbols with philosophy and its symbolic surrogates. This understanding of the problematics of the ultimate reality constitutes the backstory of how the symbols of ultimacy refer, the conditions for their making sense, and is a necessary part of theology.

The theological articulations of symbolic engagements in addition need to be critical, that is, to ask whether in fact the ultimate realities are engaged truly in the actual or potential engagements at hand. So, built into the theology of the symbols of the sacred canopy and the various interpretations of the problems of human life they address in ultimate ways are various disciplines crucial for criticism. These include all the disciplines that interpret the symbols and their functions in actual engagement, including semiotics, philosophy, sociology, anthropology, psychology, empirical studies of the origins and development of religion, practical disciplines such as ethics, jurisprudence, politics, and the arts, insofar as they register something ultimate. To make the cognitive articulations of symbolic engagements of ultimacy vulnerable to correction, as they should be, all these disciplines become proper parts of theology.

The scene of cognitive religious articulations is even more complicated, however. A sacred canopy is only a small portion of the worldview that gives orientation to a person's or community's life. The concept of worldview is a central construct in this theory of religion. Life has many different domains—home life, personal career, neighborhood activities, political involvements, the workplace, geographical location, social positions, national and cultural identities, historical roles, and the like; a sacred canopy, or set of symbols for engaging ultimacy, is one such domain found in many but not all worldviews. People orient themselves within each of these domains differently, with more or less coherence. The domains too are oriented toward one another, more or less. A worldview is a set of symbols that provides orientation within and among domains. Some worldviews orient the sacred canopy domain to other domains of life, and when this happens to a great degree the worldview can be called a "sacred worldview." When a worldview connects symbols from the sacred canopy to another domain, as when it places eating in a religious context by praying before meals, then that domain can be said to have an ultimate or religious "dimension" even though its principal structures concern proximate, not ultimate things.

Therefore, the cognitive articulations of ultimate realities include also their bearings on other domains of life where those bearings exist.

Another distinction needs to be made concerning the symbolic engagements. On the one hand, the interpretations involved should aim at the ultimate realities in their transcendent ultimacy as fundamental conditions for existence and human life. On the other hand, the interpretations need to be intimate to life in order to connect with life's practical domains. This means symbolic interpretations that might be far from the ultimate conditions, as when interpretations of the ontological act are highly anthropomorphic and involve worship as due a king, as when lying under obligation is just being like Arjuna in the Bhagavad Gita, when being whole is being like the Buddha, when engaging others is being like Mother Teresa, and when the problem of meaning is being like the Dao.

The transcendent symbols and interpretations of symbols are truer to the ultimate realities and ultimate dimensions of life but also can tend toward irrelevance. The intimate symbols and interpretations seem immediately practical but also founder on problems such as theodicy and ambiguity. Cognitive articulations of ultimacy have an inherent tension between the pulls of transcendence and intimacy. The pragmatic senses of meaning and truth adjudicate these tensions as a proper part of theology.

EXISTENTIAL IDENTIFICATIONS

The pragmatic theory of religion by no means is limited to cognitive articulations of ultimacy, however important that is and however much any engagement has a cognitive element. Another crucial function of symbolic engagement of ultimate realities and ultimate dimensions of various domains of life is the ways by which engaging ultimacy defines who individuals are, and in some extrapolated sense, what communities are.[8] Some people seem to have no ultimate concern whatsoever, moving from one concern to another like Kierkegaard's aesthetic personality. Other people become concerned about ultimate things when crises hit, such as the death of a loved one or the failure of a lifelong project; then they look to ultimate matters to find priorities for their lives. The prioritizing kind of ultimate concern can become stronger and stronger, integrating more and more, until finally the concern for ultimate reality becomes more important than one's own life and its priorities and one gives oneself over wholly to the ultimate as it can be engaged with one's symbols.

People become aware of ultimate issues of self-definition when customary and perhaps taken-for-granted ways of relating to ultimate realities become seriously problematic. Those ways are always human predicaments, built into the nature of human reality in the world. For instance, serious moral failure gives rise to huge problems of guilt; this often leads to initial attempts to deny the obligatoriness of the norms with respect to which one is guilty, but then further to a negative condemnation of oneself. Serious failure to achieve wholeness leads to debilitating senses of suffering, fragmentariness, and internal contradiction; people can attempt to forswear the obligatoriness of self-integration, but then go so far as to despair about their own existence. Unstoppable selfishness and unwillingness to relate to others on their own terms can lead to a retreat to narcissism and then finally to a rejection of oneself as one has rejected others. The ambiguities of value in self-identity can become so great that life despairs of meaning. Life itself is filled with such suffering and always ends in death so that the affirmation of existence as such becomes problematic.

For many people, if not everyone in fact, a primary engagement of the ultimates is with respect to how the individual is defined by them. Perhaps an individual's life is construed as broken relative to obligation, wholeness, engagement with others, value-identity, and comporting oneself to existence as such. This is expressed in different ways according to the vocabularies of different religious and secular cultures, and each individual has particular manifestations of brokenness. Perhaps each individual looks for some remedy to the brokenness. Most look to religion, and the world's religions have developed many responses to human need relative to ultimate things: forgiveness for moral failure, healing for fragmentation, paths of love and reconciliation for estrangement from others, transcendent forms of meaningfulness, and experiences of the beauty of creation in the face of its terrors. One primary form of religion thus is the engagement of ultimate realities and the ultimate dimensions of life's domains as predicaments that define a person as broken and in need of reparative response. William James called this the way of the "sick soul," though I think it is a part of life for many rather than a distinct type of soul.[9]

Another equally primary form, however, is the engagement of the ultimates under what might be called the guise of beauty or beguiling awesomeness. Quite apart from the problematic aspects of the ultimate definitions of the human condition, people have experienced existence as ecstatically good. They have experienced the moral dimension of life as heroic in failure as well as success. They have experienced the wholeness of self as an inspiring ideal and the challenge of otherness as an outpouring of hopeful affection. People have found life to be meaningful no matter how absurd it seems. These are what James would call the "healthy souled" people. It is not that they have any fewer or less serious problems with the ultimate aspects of life. They simply take them in stride because their primary engagement with ultimate realities is to embrace them ecstatically. Such an ecstatic embrace might be the result of long and painful working through of the predicaments of life, especially the brokenness of comporting to the creation itself—such would be the highly successful healing of a sick soul. But for many people the ecstatic embrace is fully compatible with unresolved problems of brokenness with respect to ultimacy. Existential self-definition in ultimate senses is just as possible through ecstatic embrace of the ultimates as it is through the human predicament of failure regarding the ultimates and the accessing of religious remedies.

RELIGIOUS LIFE

To live a religious life is to take orientation from a sacred worldview by means of which the ultimate realities symbolized in the sacred canopy of that worldview bear upon other domains of life given orientation by the worldview. This sense of religious life has many internal complexities and variables. To begin with, not all worldviews contain significant sacred canopies and those that do not are not sacred worldviews. People who live according to nonsacred worldviews are genuinely secular. Another consideration is that sacred worldviews vary in the scope of domains they integrate with sacred implications. Worldviews in general vary with regard to the scope of the domains of life they integrate in some way or another—many worldviews seem to offer little orientation at all to some important domains, with the result that those domains are relatively "meaningless" relative to the other domains or a sense of wholeness of lifeworld. Similarly, sacred worldviews vary with regard to how many and which domains are connected with the sacred canopy in significant ways so as to have ultimate or religious dimensions; some sacred worldviews foster praying around just about every activity, whereas other sacred worldviews limit prayer to a few specific domains, such as attendance at liturgies.

Not only do sacred worldviews vary among themselves, but the ways by which people inhabit them vary. Some people inhabit their sacred worldviews with deep and thorough intensity, whereas at the other extreme are people who hold to the same sacred worldviews but inhabit them lightly: perhaps the integration of the many domains of life with a worldview is simply not very important to them and they can live mostly in the moment. Most people live religiously between these extremes and vary the intensity of the inhabitation of a sacred worldview according to circumstances and their time of life.

Scholars of religion, especially social scientists and ecclesiastically oriented theologians, are accustomed to thinking of worldviews as characteristic of communities, not individuals, and think of individuals as having worldviews because they share the culture of their community. But the nature of communities, cultural and religious, is extremely problematic. The old anthropological model of a relatively isolated homogeneous tribal cultural community has rare application in the contemporary world. Rather, many people in the world today are descended from people who have moved geographically in the last two hundred years, who have absorbed important influences from other cultures, who have changed languages, and who now have means of communication about ultimate matters with people who inhabit broadly different sacred canopies. Furthermore, in developed and developing countries many individuals belong to several different communities with significantly different domains, for instance, the communities of nuclear families (which often themselves are plural when there are mixed ethnic and religious marriages), commodities of the workplace, of the local neighborhood, of geographical connections relating to the local environment, of city, region, and national connections, and so forth. Each of these communities has its own set of domains and thus needs a specialized worldview integrating these domains. So an individual participating in several of these communities needs not only their several worldviews but a kind of meta-worldview that integrates the worldviews. When some or all of the special worldviews are significantly sacred, and when the meta-worldview is also sacred, the complications are all the greater for finding a comprehensive sacred worldview. Given the mobility of modern economic meritocracies determining that many people will have to make a number of significant moves in their lives, those people serially will need a number of somewhat different comprehensive sacred worldviews if they are to lead religious lives. The actual religious situation today, for which we need theological guidance, is one in which communities are multiple, changing, and often very difficult to find such that they can be oriented by a sacred worldview.

Therefore, to approach religious life as if people were already in a religious community with a sacred worldview seems to miss the whole pragmatic meaning of the religious situation. Of course, to think of religious life in terms of historical communities makes it easy for disciplines in the social sciences that are good at studying such communities. And it is helpful for confessional theologians who want to mount apologetic defenses of specific religious communities or to lay down the boundaries of religious identity in communal terms. But these approaches disqualify themselves for looking pragmatically at the real situation. Because of the close interaction of so many groups across the globe, the contemporary religious situation for the world has a great many very different religious positions within it. Some positions might still involve relatively static homogeneous populations with a common sacred worldview. Others might be at the extreme of mobility and multiple cultural and communal connections. Most positions in the contemporary religious situation are in between these extremes, but changing rapidly.

My pragmatic theory of religion thus insists that the analysis of religious life be rooted in the contemporary religious situation and move backward to understand the intertwining of roots from earlier stages.[10] This is a rejection of the common assumption that the Chinese, religiously, are Confucian, Daoist, and Buddhist; that the South Asians are Hindus, Muslims, and perhaps a few remaining Jains and returning Buddhists; and that the West is Jewish, Christian, and Muslim. Whereas that way of thinking might be right by way of preponderance of influence and self-identification, and so helpful to thinkers such as Samuel Huntington who speak of a "clash of civilizations," from the position of people seeking to live a religious life in those parts of the world, that way of thinking is backward. A participant in the current revival of Confucianism in China might be enthusiastic about the title and explicitly Confucian symbols but should know that contemporary Confucianism is sponsored by the Communist government; that its scholars have thoroughly engaged Western philosophy; that it is competing with Christianity now, not so much Buddhism and Daoism; that the heritage from the Neo-Confucian period incorporated many important elements from Daoism and several kinds of Buddhism; that its cultural embodiment now, as much as in the last two and a half millennia, has been in symbiotic relation with shamanism as well as popular Daoism and Buddhism; that business relations will be in community with Western and South Asian cultures as well as East Asian ones; and so on to embrace a vast plurality of communities with different sacred worldviews. To be a serious contemporary Confucian in China thus requires working out a Confucian sacred worldview that embraces domains and communities that earlier

Confucians never could imagine. To be a Confucian in Boston is to have a radically different set of problems, albeit sharing affection and loyalty to a core of texts and traditions.

To understand the religious situation today is to grasp the multiple positions within it with their own sets of problems for working out a sacred worldview that allows for close inhabitation, usually with significant others. Because of the connections among the positions, a global perspective needs to be taken on the religious situation and its historical antecedents and developments. No religious tradition can be understood fruitfully in isolation, but only from a comparative perspective, although of course micro-studies are possible with all their attendant blinkers. Theology needs always to be comparative across cultures. Moreover, historical developments also need to be understood globally and comparatively. For instance, to understand the contemporary religious situation, it is as important to understand the Axial Age revolution that affected the formation of Buddhism, Christianity, Confucianism, Daoism, Hinduism, Islam, and Judaism in similar ways as it is to trace each of these from its founders to the communities and individuals who claim inheritance. Precisely because of the cross-cultural comparative perspective required for this, the important details of the cultural differences will be manifest more clearly than if we maintain a myth of the historical development of each of these individually.

In addition to finding a sacred worldview to inhabit that provides orientation to all the diverse communities in which an individual participates, inhabitation itself is usually fostered by additional senses of community. Two such senses can be mentioned, although they are idealizations of a much richer social matrix.

Most social groups have quasi-public community religious organizations such as congregations, local temples and mosques, and the like. These organizations provide rituals and other services for the teaching of explicit religious traditions and the interpretation of their symbols and have special significance for marking the stages of life, birth and death, coming-of-age, marriage, celebration of children and career goals, care for the sick and needy, and often though not always some professional "pastoral care," as it is called in Christianity. Regular participation in such organizations also offers steady occasions to articulate, express, and perform worship in gratitude for existence, confession of failures in righteousness, exercises for healing, practices of appreciation, care, and generosity toward others, and celebrations of life's ultimate meanings. A congregation or local traditional organization provides balance for the acknowledgment of the diversity of ultimate realities and calls for the engagement of them all with at least traditionally sanctioned symbols.

Organizations such as these can be identified with particular traditions and hence are exclusive of those who are not members, yet they are public and often welcome outsiders for such things as weddings and funerals, and many exhibit general hospitality and cooperation within a larger social unit that has many such religious organizations. These are the organizations that many social scientists identify with religious communities as such. They have core sacred worldviews that can be shared more or less by their members and, in homogeneous societies, this is as far as the problem of finding a sacred worldview goes. But most such organizations have members whose real lives take them into many diverse communities that are not shared by the other members—communities of different occupations, educational classes, cultural interests, age groupings, often ethnic identities. Many domains of life are not shared by all members. Yet the real sacred worldview, the inhabitation of which constitutes robust religious life, needs to orient the real domains of each individual. So some of the most serious sacred worldviews an individual needs to seek out might extend far beyond any congregation that provides a nominal religious identity. Most congregations, even in late-modern and postmodern societies, combine sophisticated theology with folk religion; highly educated people are not likely to find their serious spiritual companions in those congregations but rather in other associations with theologically sophisticated people, perhaps from very different nominal religious traditions.

Why is it necessary for individuals to have religious communities of any sort beyond the symbols carried generally by a given culture? It is not necessary, of course, as evidenced by the highly individualized cultures of many modern societies; no one needs to be religious at all, and connections to ultimate matters can be wholly neglected. Even if individuals do want to be religious, it is possible to be "spiritual but not religious," meaning that explicit religious communities are rejected. But if the religious predicaments of life are hard, then access to religion's remedies requires participation in the religious traditions. Participation can be weak or strong, focused or blurry. But the seriousness of religions' remedies to the human predicament usually requires more rather than less inhabitation of religious communities. This does not necessarily mean participation in an explicit religious organization such as a congregation. But even tradition-rejecting "spiritual seekers" need to go beyond the depth of reading groups and yoga classes to access anything serious in the way of religious engagement of the fundamental predicaments of the human condition. To be seriously religious is to inhabit a sacred worldview relevant to the domains of one's life and through it to engage those domains with ultimate passions and commitments.

The pragmatic theory of religion has now come into view. The theory does not pretend to be neutrally descriptive but rather to analyze the situation so as to achieve ideal ends, as Dewey would say. The theory is first-order theology about how to be religious well. To be religious at all is to inhabit a sacred worldview. The quality of the sacred worldview is a function of how well it orients all the important domains of life with regard to the ways its sacred canopy facilitates engagement with ultimate realities. The qualities of inhabitation are functions of how deeply an individual invests in orienting life in the various domains according to the sacred worldview.

"Inhabitation" is a metaphor halfway between "journey" and "being at home," two other prominent metaphors for the religious life. The limitation of the "journey" metaphor is that any stage can be passed beyond, including the final stage, unless some qualitative change is made to inhabit the end. The limitation of the metaphor of "being at home," or "becoming more at home," is that it falsely assumes that there is such a thing as home: even existence itself is gratuitous, arbitrary, undeserved, and surprising—the identification of home is nearly always idolatrous and bellicose.

The inhabitation of a sacred worldview is how an individual relates to ultimate realities, which defines the individual existentially. The pragmatic theory of religion distinguishes two lines of ultimate existential definition: through coping with existential predicaments and through enjoying ecstatic fulfillment.[11] The existential predicaments characteristic of ultimacy in the human condition arise as problems of comporting life toward the five ultimate realities separately and together. Regarding the ontological ultimate of the creative act of everything determinate, the predicament is the affirmation or denial of existence itself; regarding the ultimate reality of form/possibilities/value/obligation, the predicament is the affirmation or denial of obligation in the face of inevitable failure; regarding the ultimate reality of the integration of wholeness, the predicament is the affirmation or denial of wholeness of self in the face of inevitable fragmentation; regarding the ultimate reality of location in an existential field, the predicament is affirmation or denial of engagement of others with care for their own value; and regarding the ultimate reality of value-identity, the predicament is affirmation or denial of meaning in life when that meaning has no simple location in any one thing, including the self.

Religious traditions offer remedies for coping with the ultimate predicaments, variously interpreted according to culture. Engagement of the five ultimate realities with ecstatic fulfillment similarly takes forms relative to the distinctions among those realities and is a function of finding elements in life that serve as symbolic mediators of the ecstatic feelings of those realities. The significance of the various forms of ecstatic fulfillment and coping with the ultimate existential predicaments is carried throughout life to the extent the person's sacred worldview interpretively mediates the symbolic engagement of ultimacy to life's various domains.

The cognitive forms of symbolic engagement of ultimacy are to be understood in terms of a pragmatic semiotic theory, explored in chapters 5–8. Many kinds of cognitive engagement exist with conventional, iconic, and indexical modes of reference. Theology, among other tasks, has to be the agency of interpretation among the various putative cognitive engagements, ascertaining their contextualized truth as carrying over, or not, what is important in the ultimate realities and the ultimate dimensions of the domains of life into the experience of the engaging individual in matters pertaining to the ultimate predicaments or to ecstatic fulfillment. Given the global scope of the religious situation and the changing contexts of any person's life, theology needs always to have both a comparative public and a facility with any of the disciplines that might bear upon the potential truth of an alleged symbolic engagement of ultimacy. Among these disciplines is philosophy, particularly metaphysics.

Ultimacy in its five forms and indefinitely various dimensions has been symbolized in an astonishingly diverse number ways. The pragmatic theory of religion employs metaphysics to triangulate among them and the ultimate realities it articulates. Metaphysics can provide an appropriate analysis of ultimate reality, on the condition that it deals with the most abstract of topics, the nature of determinateness. The analysis of determinateness supplies a dialectical argument, that is, a proper index, that everything determinate is created by an ontological creative act, the ontological ultimate. It also supplies an articulation of four traits necessarily present in any determinate thing: form, components formed, location in an existential field with other determinate things, and an identity with the value of getting these components together according to this form in this existential location. The metaphysics proves itself pragmatically not only in its fruitfulness in sorting the various symbol systems for ultimacy but in its capacity to stand up in philosophical competition with alternatives.

Thus, the pragmatic theory that *religion is human engagement of ultimacy expressed in cognitive articulations, existential responses to ultimacy that give ultimate definition to the individual, and patterns of life and ritual in the face of ultimacy* has deep ramifications for how to think about symbolic engagement, metaphysics, semiotics, comparative philosophy and theology, the involvement of many disciplines in articulating ultimacy, the nature of existential self-definition, and the social and personal inhabitation of sacred worldviews. This theory also receives practical reinforcement in each of these areas as it enriches them with its understanding of religion. In consonance with pragmatism, the meaning and truth of religion, and the theory about it, lie in the differences they make to how people live, differences that can be seen to be valuable insofar as they carry across into experience what shows itself in the long run to be ultimately important for human life. Chapter 5 will return to this line of argument.

NOTES

1. This hypothesis is the central orienting claim of my three-volume *Philosophical Theology: Ultimates: Philosophical Theology Volume One* (Albany: State University of New York Press, 2013), *Existence: Philosophical Theology Volume Two* (Albany: State University of New York Press, 2014), and *Religion: Philosophical Theology Volume Three* (Albany: State University of New York Press, 2015), and it was introduced in the first two chapters of this volume.

2. On the theory of symbolic engagement, see also my *The Truth of Broken Symbols* (Albany: State University of New York Press, 1996) and *On the Scope and Truth of Theology: Theology as Symbolic Engagement* (New York/London: T&T Clark, 2006). An extended case study of symbolic engagement is my *Symbols of Jesus: A Christology of Symbolic Engagement* (Cambridge: Cambridge University Press, 2001).

3. They were summarized in the previous chapter and are given at length in Neville, *Ultimates*, especially part 3.

4. This analysis of the ontological creative act was given its first and most elaborate defense in my *God the Creator: On the Transcendence and Presence of God* (Chicago: University of Chicago Press, 1968; second edition with a new preface, Albany: State University of New York Press, 1992). A summary statement is in *Symbols of Jesus*, chapter 1, and the long version is in *Ultimates*, part 3.

5. Charles S. Peirce distinguished iconic, indexical, and symbolic or conventional reference. See, for instance, the analysis in Robert S. Corrington, *An Introduction to C. S. Peirce: Philosopher, Semiotician, and Ecstatic Naturalist* (Lanham: Rowman & Littlefield, 1993), or Neville, *The Truth of Broken Symbols*. Chapter 4 of the present volume expands on this point.

6. Thus, this point opposes the position of S. Mark Heim in his *Salvations: Truth and Difference in Religion* (Maryknoll: Orbis Books, 1995) in which he attempts to soften the exclusive claims of different religions by saying that they really are pursuing different salvific goals. The position here is that there are five realities that must be addressed by every religion and so they have something else in common despite their different modes of address.

7. See Peter L. Berger, *The Sacred Canopy: Elements of a Sociological Theory of Religion* (Garden City: Doubleday, 1967). The use of Berger's phrase, sacred canopy, in my theory of religion extends far beyond his restricted sociological use.

8. Paul Tillich is famous for defining the ultimate in one sense as that which defines individuals ultimately, constituting their ultimate concern. He himself reflected out of the heritage of German idealism that took it for granted that the unity or centeredness of the self is an a priori given, and he concluded that each person must therefore have an ultimate concern around which the self is centered. It is much more likely that the unity of the self is an achievement, perhaps fleeting and sometimes eluding some individuals altogether.

9. On the "sick soul" and the "healthy soul," see William James's *The Varieties of Religious Experience: A Study in Human Nature* (New York: Longmans, Green, 1902) chapters 4–7.

10. The notion of "religious situation" was developed by Paul Tillich in his *The Religious Situation*, translated by H. Richard Niebuhr (New York: Henry Holt, 1932). What he meant was the religious situation in Germany in the vicinity of Berlin in the mid-1920s. What is meant in the pragmatic theory of religion is the global religious situation as it obtains at any given date.

11. See my *Existence*.

Chapter 4

MODELING ULTIMATE REALITY
God, Consciousness, and Emergence

INTRODUCTION

Philosophers of religion and religious thinkers in every tradition refer to what they take to be ultimate by means of models.[1] These models range from careful metaphysical constructs to wild symbols and the manners of articulation and justification of the models exhibit astonishing variation. Sometimes the models are referred literally, or nearly literally, and sometimes even the best models are affirmed to be false because the ultimate cannot be modeled. This chapter argues that ultimacy cannot be modeled and that this is the more profound truth than is to be found in any apophatically denied model. The overall question of models of ultimate reality is highly illuminating, however, because it provides a context for deep comparative, critical, and imaginative thinking.

This introduction states in abstract terms the hypothesis to be developed here. The explication of these terms follows in the body of the essay and they have been introduced in previous chapters. The hypothesis is that the primary ultimate reality is an ontological act of creation, the terminus of which is everything determinate, constituting, and unfolding in space-time. This ontological creative act cannot be "modeled" in any sense of *isomorphism* because anything with a form or *morphe* is in the endpoint or terminus of the act, not the act of creation itself. Anything that can be modeled cannot be the ultimate reality of the ontological creative act. Nevertheless, religious engagement of this ultimate reality, which is ancient and multifarious, requires "signs," if not exactly models. At least some of these signs need to be intimate to human life so as to provide orientation to ultimacy, as argued in the previous chapter.

Among the signs that have been used in the history of religion for this ultimate reality are models of persons, as in some personifying monotheisms, models of pure consciousness, as in some Hinduisms and Buddhist schools, and models of process and emergence, as in some Daoist and Confucian schools. These models are not stable, however, being pushed at once in transcendent directions toward the unmodelable ontological act and in intimate directions toward human experience. Reaching for experiential intimacy, for instance, are models of anthropomorphic gods, consciousness of the sort experienced in meditation, or emergence and flow in nature. The philosophical and religious moral of this is that ultimate reality can well be engaged with these models but that the object engaged, the ontological creative act, never should be confused with what is modeled.

Symbolic engagement with the models needs always to be understood as indexical, not iconic in the sense of construing the model to model the object. Rather, the model models an analogue in human experience that is turned into a sign referring indexically to ultimate reality, distinctions that will be explained in the third section here.

The hypothesis also says that there are four cosmological ultimates that derive from the transcendental traits of anything determinate—all created things are determinate to some extent. These are form, components formed, location in an existential field, and achieved value. Relative to human life, these constitute four ultimate conditions: being under obligation, needing wholeness, engaging others with due care, and finding ultimate meaning. These will be explained in more detail in the second section and have been introduced in previous chapters.

So there are three parts of the argument for this hypothesis: (1) a brief analysis of some intimate models of ultimate reality that are or can be legitimate signs of ultimate reality but that model something other than ultimate reality, (2) a defense of the philosophical hypothesis that ultimate reality is the ontological creative act that creates anything determinate, and (3) an explanation of the process of symbolic engagement and its consequences for thinking about ultimate reality.

PERSONHOOD, CONSCIOUSNESS, AND EMERGENCE

As will be argued in detail in the next section, ultimate reality is an ontological act of creation that cannot be modeled, because only determinate things can be modeled. The determinate world and its parts can be modeled, but not the world's status as the terminus of the ontological creative act. The determinate world is the terminus of the creative act and thus part of the act, not a product that might be separated from the act.

Nevertheless, models for ultimate reality have been taken from elements within the world and carefully cultivated within reflective religious traditions to serve as signs for engaging the finite/infinite ultimate realities, ontological and cosmological. In most cases, these models have been subjected to qualifications that, on the one hand, indicate the highly transcendent, abstract, and unmodelable aspects of the ultimate and, on the other hand, function as intimate signs to which human life can be related in ultimate matters.[2] The three models for ultimate reality to be discussed here are those of the person, of pure consciousness, and of emergence. Persons, consciousness, and emergence are all determinate things within the world and can be developed into theological models. They also can be used as signs of ontological ultimate reality. Historically, they obviously have been used as such signs, and the last section in this chapter will explain a bit of how this has worked.

Many kinds of theism build models of human personhood to use as signs of ontological ultimate reality. Gods are not ordinary persons, of course, and perhaps the history of the development of ideas of personified gods should start with the common belief in many early cultures that there are supernatural agents as part of the world, deified ancestors, trees with intentionality, spirits of weather or war. Most models of personhood for ultimate reality have a range of levels of personification. For instance, Vishnu and Shiva are conceived to have very human avatars, such as Krishna, who was Arjuna's charioteer in the Bhagavad Gita and like any other man except for his divine knowledge. Vishnu and Shiva themselves are thought to be able to manifest themselves to human sensibilities, as Vishnu does in the Bhagavad Gita, but also have forms that transcend ordinary or even miraculous human knowing. In the Abrahamic monotheisms, God is conceived to be something like a person with a proper name, such as Yahweh, with intentions, who both creates the world and intervenes within it as an actor in human narratives. Moses speaks with God and sees his backside, and Isaiah sees the hem of his robe in the throne room; Allah speaks or thinks in Arabic. Sometimes the anthropomorphisms are plainly intended to be metaphors, as when the Twenty-Third Psalm likens God to a shepherd (and people to sheep). Other times the signs are taken to refer without much qualification to ultimate reality. And yet in these theistic traditions the personifications are linked within certain systems of thought to understandings of the transcendent indeterminacy of the ultimate, as Vishnu and Shiva are reflectively understood really to be Brahman who is beyond qualities. The author of Colossians says (in chapter 1) that Jesus is the first image of the invisible, that is, beyond determination, God. Christianity, Islam, and Cabbalistic Judaism have been much influenced by the Neo-Platonic idea of the One that is beyond any determinate differentiation. How are these highly transcendent symbols of God as beyond determination linked to the personifying symbols?

Thomas Aquinas had perhaps the most explicit answer. God is the pure Act of To Be, he thought, and as such is simple, without determination, unable to think intentionally about anything outside the pure fullness of Actuality, knowing things in the world only by knowing their causes within the divine actuality, not knowing anything in a way that is different from simply being that thing in infinite fullness, not being a thing in a genus (such as a god, or person), or even a genus itself. Yet Thomas said that this pure Act of To Be is also the personal God of the Bible. He was able to say this because he claimed that finite personhood in ordinary people is a good, positive thing and as such is a finite derivative from the infinite actuality of God. So, God is an infinite person as people are finite persons and personhood can be attributed to God by analogy. There are difficulties with his theory of analogy, because it is problematic to compare the finite and infinite.[3] But he clearly recognized the problem of conceiving of God on a scale from very anthropomorphic personifications to philosophically acceptable transcendent ones. The Neo-Platonic theory of levels of reality addressed a similar concern.

The advantage of the symbols at the personifying end of the spectrum is that people can imagine themselves relating to ultimate reality as a person, praying to it, hoping to be known and loved, conceiving it to be in a narrative in which they also play roles, finding an identity as a subject to a ruler, and loving God like loving a person. Another advantage is that the caprice of the world, the fact its main powers are not scaled to human affairs, and alleged divine promises are not kept, can be imagined in terms of a capricious personal God.[4] Yet another advantage is that the personified signs for ultimacy can articulate religious connections with the four cosmological ultimate realities. Obligations to shape one's life with the right *form* can be understood as divine personal commands. The brokenness of life, manifested in maladjustments to life's *components*, can be understood in terms of divine powers of making whole. Engagements with others in the *existential field* can be understood in terms of divine intentions to love, or fight, or preserve. *Achieved value-identity* can be understood as standing under the judgment of a personal God.

Different religious traditions parse these symbols differently, often with contradictions within a single named religion. But building a model of ultimate reality based on human personhood allows for many ways of intimate connection with ultimacy. At the same time, the reflective thinkers of many of the traditions have known that the personal model does not work iconically. God is not really a person with intentions and agency within the world, but thinking of God that way does pick up on something important about ultimate reality that is metaphysically beyond personification.

A deep motif in South Asian religious thought is that "true reality" is something like consciousness without objects. This motif has had many manifestations in various Hindu, Jain, and Buddhist schools. Roughly put, where there is diversity in experience, especially change, there must be a deeper substratum of experience. The Samkhya tradition distinguishes the self, which is pure consciousness, from nature, which constitutes the objects of consciousness. Most people confuse their true selves with the self in which consciousness has passing objects and need to learn to abstract from those objects to consciousness itself. This tradition was closely allied with the yoga tradition, which has been developed in many schools of Hinduism and Buddhism, but the emphasis on clarifying consciousness of its objects was taken by a variety of traditions to constitute a kind of metaphysical move to deeper reality. Advaita Vedanta, for instance, rejects the reality of diverse nature entirely and identifies consciousness as the true self, which in turn is identical with Brahman, which is imagined as something like consciousness.

The intimacy in the model of consciousness is that everyone can experience it and can practice meditative techniques such as those in Buddhisms and Hinduisms to purify consciousness. Some Buddhist schools, usually associated with Yogacara Buddhisms, say that reality is "consciousness only." Others, associated with Madhyamika Buddhisms, say that even a substratum of consciousness is too ontologically oriented, and the only real things are the risings and ceasings of conscious contents or "dharmas." For most Buddhist schools, "Buddha-mind" is a state of perfected consciousness that does not make mistakes about what is real and what is not, with the result that a person who attains or uncovers Buddha-mind is never attached to anything in a way that causes suffering. For most Buddhist schools also, meditative techniques can bring people into some kind of experience of this Buddha-mind, if not abiding in it fully. In a vague sense, differently specified by different South Asian and some East Asian traditions (such as Chan or Zen Buddhism), consciousness is something that is intimately accessible and yet can be interpreted in highly transcendent, indeterminate ways as the reality that lies behind and is the source of the suchness of the world.

To continue with this highly abstract characterization of models derived from finite determinate reality to be used as signs of the ontological creative act, a deep motif in East Asian thought is the model of emergence, as in the flow of the Dao. Themes of novelty and spontaneity, as well as continuity and inertia, have been developed around emergence. Both Confucianism and Daoism, in different ways, teach living according to the Dao so as to conform to the inertial situations of the past and to act to accomplish things that emerge with novelty. This can be understood in intimate ways. But both also say, as the Daodejing does, that the Dao that can be named, that is, the emergent flow, is not the true Dao, which rather is the source or mother of the flow. In some special sense, the flow emerges from something deeper that cannot be named. For Confucians, the emergent flow is to be understood as the harmonizing of the unruly forces of various processes by the patterns of harmony that come from Heaven or Principle. But underneath that is a deeper emergence that the great Neo-Confucian philosopher Zhou Dunyi describes as follows:

> The Ultimate of Non-being and also the Great Ultimate! The Great Ultimate through movement generates yang. When its activity reaches its limit, it becomes tranquil. Through tranquility the Great Ultimate generates yin. When tranquility reaches its limit, activity begins again. So movement and tranquility alternate and become the root of each other, giving rise to the distinction of yin and yang, and the two modes are thus established. By the transformation of yang and its union with yin, the Five Agents of Water, Fire, Wood, Metal, and Earth arise. When these five material forces are distributed in harmonious order, the four seasons run their course.[5]

So there is a kind of double emergence, the emergence of temporal flow involving the temporal emergence through yin and yang, from something more basic than flow, beginning with the Ultimate of Non-Being, which has no qualities. Thus, in any temporal emerging there is also a nontemporal or eternal emerging of flow from nothing. The relation between the Ultimate of Non-Being and the Great Ultimate is a symbolic way of speaking of the ontological creative act whereby something determinate comes to be.

Personification, consciousness, and emergence are not the only models drawn from modeling finite determinations and used as signs by religious traditions, and they themselves are only broad motifs that have been elaborated in many, often contradictory ways. But they illustrate how reflective religious traditions have responded to the task of developing signs of ultimacy that are usefully intimate on the one hand by virtue of modeling something that is known in the world and that can be pushed or broken into the transcendent kind of reference appropriate for engaging the ultimate reality of the ontological act of creation, which, apart from the creation, is not determinate and that makes the creation gratuitous, arbitrary, undeserving, and surprising. One push in the development of signs for ultimacy is that toward intimacy, for which intimately known and experienced things can be symbolically transformed into models for referring to ontological ultimate reality. A contrary push also is in contention, namely, toward signs that indicate the reality of the ontological creative act that transcends any model.

THE ONTOLOGICAL CREATIVE ACT

To make the point about the push for transcendence in the models of ultimate reality, a metaphysical argument is necessary. This argument stands on its own and is not an induction from a comparative survey of models of ultimacy. But it is reinforced by the intellectual dialectic in so many traditions that moves from the determinacy of personhood, consciousness, and emergence to something that is beyond determinacy, as, for instance, the idea that Brahman with qualities is really a presentation of Brahman without qualities. The metaphysical argument provides the framework for the preceding discussion of models of ultimate reality. The argument begins with an analysis of determinateness, the most universal trait of things.[6]

To be determinate is to be something rather than something else. The "rather than" indicates that determinateness in one thing is always with respect to some other thing. A is determinate with respect to x, y, and z, for instance, but perhaps not determinate with respect to p and q. If a is not determinate with respect to anything at all, it is not determinate at all, not something rather than something else. Therefore, a determinate thing has to have "conditional components" by virtue of which it relates to those things with respect to which it is determinate so as to be different from them, for instance, causal conditions. The things with respect to which a thing is determinate might also, but might not, have conditional components from the thing so that they all are mutually determinate, constituting a field of determinate connections.

But a thing cannot be only conditional components, that is, only the influences from other things. It also needs to have "essential components" by virtue of which it integrates the conditional components into its own being. Without essential components, a thing would be only the conditional influences of other things, but those would be influences on nothing: a thing without essential components could not be a term in any of its conditional relations. Without conditional components, a thing would be only an atom with no internal relations to other things, and thus indeterminate with respect to them. A thing could not have only external relations because it would have no capacity on its own to enter into any relations, internal or external.

A determinate thing is a harmony of essential and conditional components. That it is a harmony means that its components just fit together.[7] If one thing is a determinate harmony, there must be other harmonies with respect to which it is determinate. Therefore, determinateness requires a plurality of determinate things (which may also be indeterminate in some respects, as the present is partly indeterminate with respect to the future).

The plurality of harmonies is such that each exhibits four transcendental traits merely by virtue of being harmonies.[8] One is the trait of form: every harmony has a pattern by virtue of which its features just fit together. Some harmonies are discursive, that is, they play out their parts through time, so that their pattern is an unfolding of temporal development and fit. From the standpoint of a present moment, the future has form under the aspects of possibilities, sometimes with alternative possibilities of differing value. For human beings, facing a future with possibilities of differing value places people under obligation to choose the better rather than the worse insofar as they can act to affect which possibilities are actualized and which excluded. A second transcendental trait of all harmonies is having components or features that are formed in the harmony's pattern. The components themselves must also be harmonies. A third transcendental trait of all harmonies is having existential location with respect to other harmonies. The conditional features that harmonies have from one another and by virtue of which they are determinate with respect to one another constitute an existential field within which the mutually determinate harmonies are located. A fourth transcendental trait of all harmonies is that they achieve the value-identity of getting these components together with this form in this existential location. That harmonies have value, by the very definition of determinateness, is a controversial point that will not be pursued further here, but assumed.[9]

A plurality of harmonies is such that each has both essential and conditional components. The harmonies could not be determinate with respect to one another without their mutual conditional components, which constitute collectively their "cosmological togetherness," their field of relations. But the harmonies also could not be determinate with respect to one another without each having its own essential components, which are required for the harmonies to be terms on their own in relation to one another. Therefore, their cosmological togetherness, accounting for their relations, cannot account for their ontological togetherness that allows them to be together with their own essential components. There must be an ontological context of mutual relevance within which harmonies are together with their essential as well as conditional components. Within the cosmological togetherness alone, one harmony grasps another only in terms of its conditional components. That it does not grasp the other's essential components is what gives the other the status of being other and external, and capable of being determinate on its own. The existence of a plurality of determinate harmonies supposes that they exist within an ontological context of mutual relevance.

What can the ontological context of mutual relevance be? If it is another determinate thing, then for it to be determinate with respect to the other determinate things so as to hold them together, an even deeper ontological context of mutual relevance would be required for the first ontological context to be together with the other determinate things. This would result in an impossible infinite regress of assumptions so that no determinate things would have the possibility of being ontologically together, and hence would be impossible themselves. The ontological context of mutual relevance thus must in itself be indeterminate.

What can in itself be indeterminate and yet constitute the context within which determinate things can be together, each with its own essential as well as conditional components? The answer is an ontological act of creation that simply makes the determinate things together with their essential and conditioning components. The act is indeterminate except in giving itself the nature of being creator of the world of determinate things created. The act is a sheer making, a creating, terminating in determinate things. The determinate things are what they are, with their determinate natures with respect to each other. The kinds of relations and unities they constitute are various; we seem to live in a cosmos with islands of intense connection and order in an ocean, as it were, of minimal connections. What the determinate things are is a matter of empirical determination. The determinate things are also the elements of the terminus of the ontological creative act, which they have in common and which constitutes them as together in the ontological context of mutual relevance. Thus, they are determinate with respect to one another and are determinate together instead of being nothing at all. Each bears its part of the dynamism of the ontological act of creating.

Some people find it difficult to imagine an act creating something new. They cite the old adage that "out of nothing, nothing comes." But this supposes that all the reality in an effect is contained in its cause, an Aristotelian principle. If all the reality in an effect were in the cause, however, how would it be possible for the effect to differ from the cause? It could not, except by the creation of limitations or negations by the cause so as to produce an effect that differs from it by virtue of being less than it. The creation of negations is more obscure than the creation of positive things. Process philosophies of many types have argued that within finite things is some spontaneous capacity to create novel things, often by rearranging old things but also necessarily by the addition of something new that makes a difference to the old things. In the case of the ontological act of creation, there are no old things, only the sheer creation of determinate (and partially indeterminate) harmonies.

The ontological creative act, then, is eternal and immense in the sense of creating things that are temporal and that constitute a spatiotemporal field as they unfold.[10] Eternity is the togetherness of the modes of times and the places of space, a togetherness that modern physics is only beginning to allow us to imagine. The ontological creative act, creating all times, does not take place at a time, not at the Big Bang, if that is how the cosmos started in time, nor now, nor in some consummatory future. It simply creates and the product of creation includes the accoutrements of temporal and spatial things. And the ontological creative act has no nature apart from being the creator of the determinate things. If it did, it would be determinate and therefore could not be the ontological context of mutual relevance.

Given the ontological act of creation, the ontological ultimate reality has a distinguishable tripartite nature. First is the act itself, the making. Second is the world as the terminus of the act, the made. And third is the nothingness that would be the case if there were no ontological act creating the world. In West Asian religions, this has been called creation *ex nihilo*, meaning that the act of creation arises from absolutely nothing. It is not the case that there is absolutely nothing: there is in fact the world as created, and in this sense the ontological act of creation is determinate as the act creating this determinate world. The ontological act is not determinate in any sense apart from the world, however, and so does not need a deeper ontological context of mutual relevance. Creation *ex nihilo* in this sense does not mean that a determinate God creates a world out of no stuff rather than out of a divine stuff, as in Thomas Aquinas's philosophical claim that finite actualities are delimitations of infinite divine actuality (pure Act of To Be). Rather, it means that the ontological creative act is gratuitous, arbitrary, undeserving, and utterly surprising. There is no reason why the world is created—any "reason" would itself have to be created. But the determinate world exists, and it could not exist unless it be created by an otherwise indeterminate ontological creative act. This is my complex hypothesis about primary or *ontological* ultimate reality.

The discussion of the four transcendental traits of harmony, however, exhibits four other ultimate realities that can be called "cosmological" in contrast to the "ontological" ultimate reality. They would not exist unless the ontological ultimate reality created a world of determinate things and thus are secondary to the ontological creative act. Nor could the ontological ultimate reality create a world that did not have determinate, or at least partially determinate, things in it.

But given a determinate world consisting of harmonies, which is what determinate things consist in according to this hypothesis, having form is an ultimate reality. Having components formed within that pattern is an ultimate reality. Having location relative to other harmonies through conditional features is an ultimate reality. And achieving some value-identity by having these components in this location with this pattern is an ultimate reality. So, according to this hypothesis there is one ontological ultimate reality, the ontological act of creation by virtue of which every determinate harmony exists relative to others in an ontological context of mutual relevance. And there are four cosmological ultimate realities, form, components, existential location, and value-identity that are necessary if there is to be anything determinate; these cosmological ultimate realities come to be with the ontological creation of determinate things. Any created world whatsoever, so long as it has some determinacy, exhibits these cosmological ultimate realities.

"Ultimacy," or the "ultimate" in ultimate reality can now be defined more precisely. Of course, it means a final condition beyond which there is nothing more. Relative to human life, it means those final or boundary conditions that define the world. These can now be characterized as finite/infinite contrasts. The finite side of a finite/infinite contrast is some finite thing that defines the world. In the ontological ultimate reality, the act of creation including the determinate world as its terminus is the finite side. The infinite side of a finite/infinite contrast is the counterfactual condition of what would be the case if the finite side were not real. In the case of the ontological ultimate reality, there would be absolutely nothing if it were not for the ontological creative act creating the determinate world. In the case of the ultimate reality of form, form itself is the finite side, and pure unformed chaos would be the infinite side. In the case of the ultimate reality of components, having components to be harmonized is the finite side, and a pure, empty lack of anything to be formed would be the infinite side. In the case of the ultimate reality of existential location, having an existential field of things with respect to which to be determinate is the finite side, having nothing else to be determinate with respect to, with the resulting impossibility of being determinate, would be the infinite side. In the case of the ultimate reality of value-identity, having such an identity is the finite side; having no determinate identity would be the infinite side.

It is possible, of course, to experience the existing world without wondering about how it exists, just as it is possible to experience forms, components, place, and value-identities and think about how they might be different, without wondering about what would be if there were no forms, components, places, and value-identities. This would be experience of only the finite side. But these ultimate realities in fact are the boundary conditions of the world, and sometimes the significance of this is grasped in religious and philosophical thought. Sometimes people have signs that express the finite/infinite contrast. They feel the finite side as well as its radical contingency or what-if-there-were-no-finite-side. These are religious engagements of the ultimate. Precisely because the ultimate conditions are finite/infinite contrasts, religious cultures develop signs for addressing and engaging the radical contingency of the ontological act of creation and the transcendental traits of anything determinate. The concrete feeling of the ultimate realities includes a sense of their mystery as expressed in the felt infinite side. Some experiences of the ontological ultimate in terms of personhood, consciousness, and emergence include also the feel of their counterfactual absence. This raises again the question of experience.

SEMIOTICS OF SYMBOLIC ENGAGEMENT

By what semiotic theory of engaging ultimate reality, understood philosophically as the ontological act of creation, can we understand how these models can be signs of ultimate reality? The theory I propose arises from the pragmatic tradition that concerning this point turns on the problem of reference.¹¹ A model is a conceptual tool whose elements are supposed to be in some kind of isomorphic relation to the object modeled, a mode of reference that Peirce called "iconic."¹² Early modern Western science modeled nature as a machine: knowing how to construct the "machine of nature" meant that nature's own workings were known.¹³ Mathematical physics models certain natural processes with the mathematical expressions. Poets model realities with their imagery, so that even when the images are obviously metaphoric, there is a sense in which reality is like what the images project.

Only determinate things can be in iconic or isomorphic relation to a model. Ultimate reality is not only determinate things—it is also a making of the Dao itself. Therefore, any model of ultimate reality must be false insofar as it is understood to refer iconically. The ultimate reality of the ontological creative act cannot really be in iconic relation to the model of a person, or of human consciousness, or of the emergent flow within time. So if those models are taken to be signs for the engagement of ultimate reality, they are necessarily false in their iconic reference.

Another form of reference, however, is indexical, by which is meant the establishment of some kind of real connection between the object engaged and the signs of engagement so that something true is picked up in the engagement. Pointing with the index finger causes the interpreter to look and see something that otherwise would be missed. All interpretations that engage real things have some indexical characters in their references. So the question is whether models of ultimacy such as personhood, consciousness, and emergence might point to ultimate reality, establish some kind of real connection with it, and allow for what is important in ultimate reality to be carried across in the symbolic engagement. They might do this even though, iconically, the ultimate reality of the ontological creative act cannot be personal, conscious, or emergent.

How can we tell whether such models indexically refer to ultimate reality in true ways? To answer this question, several observations need to be made about symbolic engagement. First, the signs in an interpretation are neither true nor false unless the interpretation actually engages its object. An interpretation takes the signs to stand for the object in a certain respect. The engagement intends the object by means of the sign. And the interpretation itself is a third thing that relates the object and sign intentionally; it is part of the experience of the interpreter. Second, interpretive engagements are always particular and contextual, depending on actual people making them. Signs that are used to interpret truly in one context might be false in another, true for one person but false for another. Therefore, third, some external way needs to be found to discern whether for this person in this context this sign of ultimacy as a personal being, pure consciousness, emergence, or some other, carries over what is important about the ontological act of creation.[14] The great religions have profound traditions of spiritual discernment and direction, aimed to determine just what difference the engagement of ultimacy with this sign or other makes to a person's experience.

Such individualism in the discernment process is unwieldy for the cultural processes of religion, however. So, religious traditions have evolved to focus on the symbols that engage truly for the most part, for most people, in most contexts that then are taken by the culture to be the normative contexts for engaging ultimate reality, usually ritualized contexts. This remark vastly oversimplifies the complex character of the cultural embodiment of religion, but it can serve its purpose in the present argument. Pragmatically effective markers for habitual engagements of ultimacy with certain signs are developed in religious cultures. St. Paul, for instance, talked about "living in the Spirit," by which he meant, at least partly, living in a community of people who think of themselves as "belonging to Christ Jesus" and who interpret ultimate reality in terms of Jesus and his teachings about the God of the Hebrew Bible. The fruit of living with these signs in their particular lives, he said, "is love, joy, peace, patience, kindness, generosity, faithfulness, gentleness, and self-control."[15] In the case of individuals who live in this community but who are conspicuously lacking in these fruits of the Spirit, the signs are not engaging them with ultimate reality truly. What is true for many of the others is not true for them.

Paul's point can be generalized in terms of the metaphysics of ultimacy. The ontological creative act whose terminus is the determinate world unfolding through space-time was described previously as gratuitous, arbitrary, undeserved, and surprising. The act is gratuitous because there can be no reason in any reality prior to the act for the act to happen. The act is arbitrary because there can be no reason prior to the act for it to be one way rather than another. The act is undeserved from the human perspective because whatever good is found in the determinate world does not justify or fulfill some prior need. The act is surprising from the human perspective because everything in the world just is what it is, contrary to expectations.

Now, the fruits of getting these points, these values, in the ontological act of creation are something like the following. You can tell if people have grasped the point about the gratuity of the ontological creative act if they have a deep acceptance of being, of the field of existence, of their own lives; most people are ambivalent about this. Whether the symbols for ultimacy are personifying ones, matters of pure consciousness, or emergence, they are true if engaging the ultimate with them produces what Jonathan Edwards called "consent to being in general."[16] With respect to arbitrariness, you can tell that their symbols are indexically true if they result in acknowledgment and acceptance of the singularity of the world, especially people's own singular position, rich or poor, educated or not, belonging to a powerful group or not, and so forth. With respect to the undeservedness of the ontological creative act, you can tell that people's symbols are indexically true if they produce a kind of ontological humility, a profound feeling of not deserving to be what one is. With respect to the surprisingness of the world created, you can tell that people's symbols are indexically true if they spark self-transcending awe and astonishment. Acceptance of being, and of singularity, ontological humility, and self-transcending astonishment and awe are all modes of gratitude toward the ontological creative act.

These last remarks have focused on signs for engaging the ontological ultimate reality. There are also the four cosmological ultimates mentioned earlier, of form, components, existential location, and value-identity, all engaged as finite/infinite contrasts. The same signs, or systems of signs, that engage the ontological creative act also engage the transcendental traits of anything determinate. From the human perspective, engaging form is a matter of choosing among alternative possibilities of different values, in respect to which people live under obligation. If people's signs of ultimacy give them discernment of justice and mercy with regard to human failings, they are indexically true to the ultimate reality of form. If people's signs of ultimacy give them increasing wholeness and personal integrity, they are indexically true to the ultimate reality of having components in their life with respect to which they should comport themselves appropriately. If people's signs of ultimacy lead them to engage others with care and respect, including nature and institutions as well as other people among the others, then they are indexically true with respect to the ultimate reality of having existential location in a field with others. If people's signs of ultimacy lead them to achieve the best value-identity they can and to accept that achievement as what they really are, those signs are indexically true to the ultimate reality of having value-identity.

A thousand qualifications need to be added to what has just been said. Every time the signs are said to be indexically true, the statement should be amended to say they are true to a certain extent, in some respects but not others, and so forth. Those limitations should be tied to the particulars of the ways the signs are used and the intentionality behind them.

But enough has been said to indicate how it is possible to use models of ultimate reality, such as personhood, consciousness, and emergence, to engage the ultimate reality of the ontological act of creating the world in ways that might be indexically true. By implication, enough has been said to indicate when those very same symbols are false in their engagements of ultimacy, namely, when they reinforce injustice, an arrogant sense of self, bigotry toward others, despair, and ontological ingratitude.

The philosophical theology that advocates judging the truth of signs in symbolic engagements of ultimacy by their fruits needs to stay in close touch with the metaphysics that shows that ultimate reality is the ontological creative act and that this cannot be modeled because it is not wholly determinate. In practice this means constant vigilance against any serious claim that the models such as personhood, consciousness, and emergence might be iconically or literally true. First naiveté in cultural religion is dangerous and second naiveté is difficult to attain. The skepticism that rejects the first without attempting the second is simply a withdrawal from attempts to engage the ultimate matters of life. The other kind of skepticism that negotiates between first and second naiveté is where most reflective people are on ultimate matters. In this day, when so many people are not simply located within any one rich religious tradition but instead are moving through several with ambivalence for all, the simple pragmatic tests previously mentioned might be too vague to be helpful. In the short run, at least, most reflective people are more like individuals seeking personal spiritual discernment than like congregants finding meaning in common rituals. This is all the more reason to pay attention to the metaphysical arguments about ultimate reality, arguments that build in the denial that ultimate reality can be modeled with anything determinate, such as a person, consciousness, or emergence.

This chapter has taken three very different approaches to the question of modeling ultimate reality. The first section has examined three very common models, that of the person, resulting in some form or other of theism, that of consciousness, resulting in some ontology of mind and its purification, and emergence, resulting in an ontology of change with both continuity and novelty. These models provide experientially intimate ways of referring to ultimate reality. And yet ultimate reality cannot be captured by a model that supposes that its object is isomorphic with the model. So the traditions associated with personification, consciousness, and emergence also include transcending impulses that say that the ultimate is "beyond" anything registered in the respective models.

The second section has directly argued for the claim that ultimate reality is an ontological creative act and therefore cannot be modeled. This argument is highly metaphysical (and therefore unpopular in the current intellectual climate), but it shows how ultimacy can be defined in terms of the most abstract of all notions, determinateness. That definition of ultimacy is ontological, in accounting for the possibility of determinateness, and cosmological, in accounting for the ultimate conditions of all determinate things. However unpopular such metaphysical arguments are, they must be dealt with by anyone who would like to say that ultimate reality can be modeled in isomorphic ways.

The third section shifted gears to reflect on the semiotic theory according to which models and other signs might refer to ultimacy. It claims that people engage ultimate realities by means of interpretations with signs, which can refer iconically and indexically, among other ways. Models aim to refer iconically, but they cannot in the case of ultimate reality because of the arguments in the second section. Yet they can refer indexically if there are means for determining whether they carry over what is important in ultimate reality into the experience of the interpreters. Some religiously common and powerful tests for carryover were discussed, albeit briefly, and will be revisited in the chapters to come.

NOTES

1. See Jeanine Diller and Asa Kasher, editors, *Models of God and Alternative Ultimate Realities* (Dordrecht: Springer, 2013). An early version of the current chapter appeared in this volume.

2. The problem of the tension in religious symbolism between needs for transcendence and needs for intimacy is very complicated and is the subject of chapters 6 and 7 of my *Ultimates: Philosophical Theology Volume One* (Albany: State University of New York Press, 2013).

3. See the detailed argument in Neville, *God the Creator: On the Transcendence and Presence of God* (Chicago: University of Chicago Press, 1968; revised edition, Albany: State University of New York Press, 1992), chapter 1.

4. See the elaborate discussion in Jonathan Goldstein's *Peoples of an Almighty God: Competing Religions in the Ancient World* (New York: Doubleday, 2002), chapter 1, of the devices used by the authors of the Hebrew Bible to explain how God is both predicted and unpredictable, especially in times of apparent abandonment of His people by the One who promises protection.

5. Zhou Dunyi, "An Explanation of the Diagram of the Great Ultimate," translated by Wing-tsit Chan in his *Source Book in Chinese Philosophy* (Princeton: Princeton University Press, 1963), 463.

6. The argument to come in the next few paragraphs restates in slightly different and more expansive terms the argument for the ontological creative act given in chapters 2 and 3; if readers are persuaded by the earlier discussions, they can skip to the next section, but if they are not yet persuaded, they should work through the discussion here.

7. Whitehead called this "just fit" a "contrast." See *Process and Reality*, corrected edition, edited by David Ray Griffin and Donald W. Sherburne (New York: The Free Press, 1978), 22.

8. This point summarizes an elaborate theory of harmonies in my *Recovery of the Measure* (Albany: State University of New York Press, 1989). The point is made in several of the chapters of this volume.

9. But see the argument in *Recovery of the Measure*.

10. See my *Eternity and Time's Flow* (Albany: State University of New York Press, 1993).

11. This argument summarizes the more elaborate analysis in my *On the Scope and Truth of Theology* (New York: T&T Clark, 2006).

12. For a closer analysis of Peirce's terminology in semiotics, see Robert S. Corrington's *An Introduction to C. S. Peirce: Philosopher, Semiotician, and Ecstatic Naturalist* (Lanham: Rowman & Littlefield, 1993); see also his *A Semiotic Theory of Theology and Philosophy* (Cambridge: Cambridge University Press, 2000). My treatment of Peirce's semiotics is in *Realism in Religion: A Pragmatist's Perspective* (Albany: State University of New York Press, 2009), chapters 6–7.

13. For a sophisticated defense of this sense of modeling nature, see C. R. Gallistel's *The Organization of Action: A New Synthesis* (Hillsdale: Lawrence Erlbaum Associates, 1980).

14. An elaborate defense of the claim that truth is the carryover of value or importance from the object into the experience of the interpreter in the respects in which the signs stand for the object is to be found in *Recovery of the Measure*, part 1.

15. Galatians 5:22–23, NRSV translation.

16. See Edwards's *The Nature of True Virtue*, in *Jonathan Edwards: Ethical Writings*, edited by Paul Ramsey, volume 8 in *The Works of Jonathan Edwards* (New Haven: Yale University Press, 1989).

Part II

PRAGMATICS

PRELIMINARY REMARKS

The chapters of part 1 have considered basic issues regarding the definition of religion, and the argument was put forward that religion is human engagement of ultimacy in cognitive, existential, and practical ways. The chapters of part 2 investigate basic issues regarding religious experience. Religion is more than human experience, although perhaps there are dimensions of experience in all engagements of ultimacy. Religious institutions, art, authority, rituals, sacred places, and the like are components of the engagement of ultimacy, but not necessarily to be understood as experiencing or engaging ultimacy interpretively.

Experience is a topic to be investigated on its own and it is the hallmark of American pragmatism. Chapters 5 and 8 will focus on the pragmatic theory of experience and show how it relates to alternatives, dealing with the topic of religious experience. One of the chief questions on that topic is how to understand what is religious in religious experience, and how to distinguish religious experiences from others that can be mistaken for them. The heart of the American theory of experience is Charles S. Peirce's semiotic theory. Chapters 6 and 7 will develop a scheme inspired by Peirce that examines many dimensions of experience and says how these dimensions might relate to ultimacy and, hence, be religious. Chapters 5, 6, and 7 were originally parts of a much larger and more unwieldy paper and have been separated here with much revision. Chapter 8 was an independent essay contrasting the pragmatic and European approaches to experience.

Chapter 5

A PRAGMATIC APPROACH TO RELIGIOUS EXPERIENCE

RELIGIOUS EXPERIENCE

The suspicion that central Jewish and Christian religious symbols do not refer as they seem to reached a crisis in the nineteenth century, and the crisis came for Islam in the twentieth. There were problems with scriptural symbolism earlier, of course, when the determinism of early modern science threatened to make belief in miracles impossible and when early modern astronomy displaced the Earth from the center of the universe. The crisis came, however, when the popular European and American imagination was so formed by modern science as to be overwhelmingly out of scale with the scriptural imagination. The cosmos that science measures is so much bigger and older than the cosmos imagined in the Bible (and the Qur'an) that they seem like different worlds. They cannot be imagined together. The same holds for the imaginative worlds of the scriptures of South and East Asia when they are confronted with the world of science, but the conflict was first addressed in the West.

The conflict of the two imaginations is the crisis. One can remain within the biblical world and still try to reconcile apparent miracles with scientific principles. One can form one's life by biblical symbols and stories and still appreciate that many are metaphorical and never were meant literally: who, after all, ever thought that geology is the proper discipline for studying the Rock of our Salvation? Thinkers such as Origen and Augustine in the ancient world, and Anselm, Bonaventura, Bernard of Clairvaux, Maimonides, the Kabbalists, Al-Ghazali, Ibn al-ʿArabi, and Ibn Rushd in the European Middle Ages had worked through interpretative issues of symbolism and allegory. But when the fundamental imaginative frame by which we live—the ways we take ourselves to be in space and time, the elementary kinds of things we understand to inhabit our cosmos—cannot be registered within the biblical imagination of those things, and vice versa, religion hits a crisis. The crisis is that the biblical symbols cannot make a religious difference to the imagination with which we live in fact. They do not connect sufficiently to do so.

One way to handle the incommensurability of fundamental imaginative worlds is to segregate and alternate them: Accept the imagination of late modernity for six days a week and switch to the biblical world for the Sabbath. Unfortunately, this solution is impossible in any literal sense. We cannot simply turn off the way we apprehend the world for one day a week and adopt another way. What happens instead is that we pretend to adopt the imaginative world of the Bible all the while assuming after divine services we can watch television, which is not a talking piece of wood like Moses's burning bush but a device that sorts and displays electrons created in the Big Bang thirteen billion years ago. Pretense is not always a bad thing. But in matters religious it is disastrous. Religious practice shaped by the central symbols of the faith is assumed to have a transformative power for individuals and communities. In every religion, not only the theistic ones, symbolically shaped religious practice is taken to transform souls so that they better apprehend and conform to the Ultimate that is symbolized. The segregation of the religious biblical imagination from the real imagination of late-modern life makes religion impotent at the most important level.[1]

That problem is even worse with the other common ploy for dealing with the incommensurability of the biblical and late-modern imaginations. Some people segregate not just their time but their very lives, inhabiting the biblical world for part of their lives and the late-modern for other parts, counting on the former being religious and the latter secular. Think of the fundamentalist engineer who builds space shuttles but who also believes that Jesus Christ will return from the sky in clouds of glory. The problem with this strategy is that it is simply impossible to divide life cleanly according to different fundamental imaginations. The result is that the infinite religious passion rightly roused and focused by the religious symbols easily gets attached to finite projects such as patriotism and particular forms of culture with devastatingly demonic distortions of the religion's intent.

Charles S. Peirce's pragmatic philosophy of religious symbols allows a way forward from this crisis of imaginations. It allows us to believe, employ, and shape our lives by central biblical symbols within the reality of our late-modern imagination. It does so with tools that allow us also to criticize biblical symbols from the perspective of what we have learned so that we can appreciate the biblical world and its ways of presenting God to us without having to buy into its approval of slavery, the subordination of women, or rejection of homosexuals, to name only a few issues. Peirce's theory equally allows us to criticize the imaginative frame of late modernity so that the prophetic edge of the Bible is not lost: though the twentieth century knew vastly more about the cosmos than the first, it has also been vastly more wicked according to many measures. Peirce's theory does not by itself suggest just how we should live with religious symbols, nor pick which ones. It does not itself engage in criticism of biblical symbols, nor does it provide a criticism of our own culture from a biblical standpoint. But it does allow for those activities, which other conceptions of symbolic religious imagination do not do.

In the following I shall defend this judgment about Peirce by discussing the following topics:

- That interpretation is engagement with the reality interpreted, which in biblical matters means engagement with the divine, with divine manifestations, and with the ways human life is impacted by its relations with the divine.
- That interpretations, including religious ones, are true or false, and that this means either carry over what is important or valuable from the reality interpreted to the interpreters, in the respects in which the symbols represent the realities, or they do not.
- That the *carryover* in allegedly true symbols means two things: on the one hand, the reality interpreted needs to be carried over into the real imagination of the interpreters, and on the other hand, the carryover affects, indeed transforms, the interpreters and their imaginations.
- Although not all religious interpretations operate at such a level as to employ basic imaginative structures differentially, most do. In the occasions when the religious symbols are biblical, the imaginative structure of the Bible is connected to that of late-modern interpreters insofar as the question of truth is pursued and tested. Thus, the imaginations are made commensurate, with the possibility of determining whether the interpretations are valid—the truth in the symbols—and with the possibility of determining whether the imaginative frame that receives them can accommodate them without change, which is to judge late-modern imagination.

ENGAGEMENT AND REFERENCE

The principal distinguishing characteristic of Peirce's semiotics or theory of interpretation is its claim that interpretation is the way by which people engage the world.[2] The more usual approach to semiotics is to say that it is the way by which people engage texts. This has been the claim from Spinoza and Schleiermacher through Saussure and Derrida. The connection of semiotics, hermeneutics, or interpretation theory with religion has usually come from the fact that the main text to be interpreted is the Bible. Peirce's paradigm case of interpretation, by contrast, is experimental science, epitomized in the laboratory but generalized to mean an engagement with nature (Americans, the frontier, and all that) and indeed the long natural-historical engagement of the evolutionary process.

Roughly put, for Peirce the form of an interpretation is an hypothesis about what the real is relative to the interest of the interpreter that is disconfirmed, reinforced, or corrected somewhat when the interpretation is put into play. Or to put the point from the opposite point of view, all human interactions with nature that involve any kind of human response are shaped by interpretations, from the most passive perceptions to the most aggressive actions. In his famous early papers on "The Fixation of Belief" and "How to Make Our Ideas Clear," Peirce argued that the best if not the only way to improve our ideas about things is to put them in the way of being corrected if they are wrong, as a scientist does.[3]

Peirce was a speculative metaphysician of very great originality and power, and he extended his semiotics beyond the usual scale of interpretation theory. For instance, he argued that the human self is not an entity that uses signs or makes interpretations but is itself a living sign whose reality consists in interpreting.[4] Moreover, he argued that all physical and other causal processes can be analyzed according to the developmental structure of interpretation. Material causation he regarded as "frozen mind" and the line between that and "psychical" or "mental" causation is not sharp.[5] He generalized the main categories of his theory of interpretation into phenomenological categories with which he constructed an entire evolutionary cosmology. These are his famous categories of firstness, secondness, and thirdness, related so as to give rise to synechism (continuity), tychism (chance), and agapism (evolutionary love or development).[6] These fascinating parts of Peirce's philosophy are not to our direct interest here except to note that they go a long way to making good on his claim that interpretation is engagement with the world; bodily processes metabolizing the world are as much interpretations as flights of fantasy and directed intellectual inquiries. Peirce's general claim that interpretation is engagement was taken up in many diverse and fruitful ways by Dewey, who called it "transaction" in his early writing and "interaction" in the later.[7]

The most pertinent point of Peirce's semiotics for the claim about engagement is his theory of reference. Peirce argued that semiotics has three main topics: meanings and meaning systems (which he called signs), reference or how the signs stand for their objects in interpretation, and the interpretation itself in which signs are actually taken to stand for objects in the concrete context of the interpreters.[8] Engagement has first to do with how the interpreters' signs relate to their real objects.

Reference has three main kinds, according to Peirce. The simplest reference is iconicity in which a sign or set of signs is taken as an icon of the world.[9] Or rather, in an interpretation, the world is taken to be like the iconic sign. In an icon, there is some kind of mirroring or iconic mapping of the object. This was the only kind of reference admitted by Wittgenstein in the *Tractatus*, and everything else that he believed to be real was mystical and should be treated with nonreference (silence).[10] In religious symbols, an icon might be a crucifix referring to Jesus's crucifixion, Peirce's example. But his idea has much greater generalizability. A religious mythic world is taken to be iconic of reality. In mythopoeic times, no distinction between the myth and the reality is recognized. In Axial Age religions, however, such a distinction is recognized and problematized. This is not the place to dissect the many levels of myth in human culture. But at deep levels it structures elementary imagination about the size, shape, age, and contents of the cosmos, as well as basic causal patterns. The distinction between biblical and late-modern imaginations made earlier can now be called a distinction between basic myths, and the religious conflict between those two imaginations can be recognized to be a clash of mythologies. It does not matter that we late-modern sophisticates know our scientific worldview is a myth: we have no other myth congruent with the rest of our knowledge with which to image or mirror the world. Though we know our scientific myth is fallible, indeed doubtless inadequate in ways to be proved sooner rather than later, we have no practical choice save to take the world to be like the late-modern myth says, at least in certain crucial respects.

The positivist conception of science took scientific theories to be iconic of their objects. So too do positivist theologies that believe the function of theology is to describe religious realities. This is plainly true of conservative theologians who defend propositions about religious realities. But it is also true of many theologians who talk in narratives, metaphors, and paradoxes. In a sense, the entire modern era as defined by Descartes has supposed that mental representations are supposed to be iconic of extramental realities, and the problem from the beginning has been how to compare them.

The second kind of reference Peirce called indexical.[11] An index is a sign that refers by some kind of causal connection with its object. A pointing finger (Peirce's example) employs the perceived physical geometry of the scene to indicate its object. More generally, indexically referring signs connect the interpreter causally with the realities interpreted. Indexical reference, if valid, should align the interpreters with the causal processes of their reality insofar as the referring signs interpret those realities in respect to those processes. For religions, indexical reference is very important indeed, because it is crucial for any kind of attunement to ultimate realities that might be attained. When religions speak of people realizing religious truth, that is not so much having true icons of religious states of affairs but rather the people becoming true to those realities. To become a saint, to be more holy, to actualize religious truth, is to interpret reality with those indices that align people to what is objectively and causally real in their objects. Indexical reference is necessary for engagements with reality that allow interpreters to learn from their experience. Many religious themes put soteriological interests ahead of theological ones, claiming that interpretations that are a bit silly when interpreted as having iconic reference are true and valuable when interpreted as having indexical reference. A person indexically related to Jesus such that love of God and neighbor animate the person's life has a true reference, even though the person might be hopelessly naive and false in matters of ascertaining who the historical Jesus really was and whether he really gave the Great Commandment.

The third kind of reference Peirce called "symbolic," and I call it "conventional."[12] Conventional signs refer by virtue of the structure of a semiotic system. The semantics and syntax of a language system is a good example of the complexities of conventional reference. The semiotic system is structured so as to spell out the meanings of signs in codes, to indicate possible versus impossible references to other signs within the systems, and to shape possible interpretations where an interpretation is a complex sign taking another sign to stand for yet a third sign.

Any sign we can think about and mention must be in the semiotic system of some language or gestural matrix. Therefore, the iconic and indexical references previously mentioned really are abstractions from a richer kind of reference that includes the conventions by which we speak of crucifixes, myths, fingers, and religious practice. In point of fact, any religious reference we might discuss is at least conventional and is likely also to involve indexical and iconic elements. What the conventional reference adds is the connections of simple mirroring or brute causal interaction with other signs, other meaning systems, other mirrorings, and other interactions. Thus, religions have very complex symbols. The crucifix is an icon of Jesus's crucifixion, but the meaning of that is connected with his life and teaching, the culture of the Messiah, the significance for disciples and others, and nearly the whole of Christian thought and practice. Moreover, the conventionality of religious symbols is what allows religion to be connected with the rest of life, with morality and politics, with art, and with domestic living. Conventional reference is what can imbed religion in larger practice.

Peirce's point that interpretation is engagement with the realities interpreted requires all three kinds of reference. Conventional reference is required because all interpretations take place within the ongoing contexts of living, with a physical and social situatedness, with inherited practices and habits, with expectations and purposes. Conventional systems of meaning make the integration of these possible. Moreover, conventions are publicly learned. Whether or not Wittgenstein was right in saying there is no such thing as private language, there certainly is not a lot of private language. The evolution of human society depends on communication through shared semiotic systems.

Our interpretations are not solely functions of internal mentalistic fantasy, however. Because of indexical reference those conventional signs can be oriented to connect interpreters causally with the reality around them. Indeed, the elaborate conventional systems of civilized life evolved precisely because the signs that can refer conventionally within the system can be used indexically to engage reality. If the conventions did not have some crucial indexical reference, they would be pragmatically and evolutionarily useless. Not all religious interpretations need to be iconic in explicit ways, though a great many are. Nevertheless, religious interpretation supposes that its fundamental system of images, its basic imagination, picks up on what is important in reality and mirrors it. For practical purposes, it assumes that what its imagination can register as what is important to register really. Actually, what I just said is false. Nearly every religion, especially the biblical ones, have an element of apophatic theology. They say that no image or idea is adequate to some religious realities. But at a higher level of reflection they are saying that the inapplicability of any finite images or ideas is just the way the religious things are, meta-iconicity if you will.

If iconicity is the paradigmatic reference for positivists and indexicality of thinkers of praxis, religious and otherwise, conventionality is the paradigm for postmodern deconstructionists. Peirce himself worried about the view that reduces iconicity and indexicality to convention. He called this "degenerate" firstness and secondness and suspected Hegel of the fault.[13] In our time deconstructionists have argued that, because any iconic and indexical reference can itself be represented within a conventional semiotic system, and because any speaking about iconic and indexical reference is done within the signs of a semiotic system, there is no reality outside the system of signs. Everything is a text and nothing is signified except more signifiers. If everything is internal to the semiotic system, then there is no reality to engage, and human life is only discourse, conversation.

But both indexical and iconic references involve a dualism of the interpreting sign system and the objective reality to which the signs refer; this is so even when the objective reality is something in the semiotic system itself. Peirce's theory of reference shows how semiotic systems themselves arise through human evolution as they provide ever more sophisticated ways of interacting with the environment so as to survive, multiply, and flourish. It also explains why semiotic systems have structures that appear to refer to real things outside the systems. Peirce's theory not only saves the appearance but provides a ground for engaging reality with more deliberation and the desire to make our interpretations vulnerable to correction.

A deep problem has lurked beneath the surface of this discussion of reference in engagement, showing itself so far only in the brief allusion to apophatic theology. Most of the traditions of biblical religion have a point at which they say that God is not an object or thing and transcends all that. Moreover, all the finite manifestations of God in burning bushes, leadership of Israel, still small voices, or even in Jesus, are not religiously interesting in their finitude alone. The finite elements can be referred to without difficulty, or with only the difficulty of historical and other kinds of inquiry. What makes them religiously interesting is their connection to a divine ground that in some sense is not finite, that is infinite, otherwise indeterminate. Reference to the finite elements has to be made an analogy to refer to the infinite elements. I have argued elsewhere that any serious religious object is what can be called a finite/infinite contrast.[14]

Theological traditions affirm the apophatic character of the religious object in different ways, depending on their affinities for reference. The Aristotelian tradition that fed Aquinas assumed that something like the syntax of language is iconic of reality, so that reality is made up of substances with properties whose icons are propositions with predicates. So Thomas Aquinas affirmed the apophatic character of the religious object by saying that God is not a substance, nor in a genus of substances, nor even a genus itself. Theologians with an affinity for indexical reference begin with stories about God's participation in their story, usually put the other way around, but they end the dialectic of avoiding idolatry by embracing mysticism, the practical plunge of the soul into the Abyss drawn by the index of love. Theologians with an affinity for conventions, such as in the rabbinic tradition, talk as if the talk defined God but move to the margins if not the center of the Kabbala, a language that so intensifies finite reference as to become incommensurate with finite things of life.

If the religious object, God, the Ultimate, the Ground of Being, is beyond any kind of reference to finite things, is God beyond reference? If the answer is yes, then God cannot be engaged, and Peirce's theory of interpretation is of no help here. If the answer is no, then we must speak to the issue of nonfinite reference. Peirce's semiotics suggests two responses.

First, there is a distinction between a logical object and the kind of reality that object might have. A logical object is simply something that is or can be referred to. What that object is, for instance finite, infinite, or a finite/infinite contrast, makes a difference only to the signs that are used to interpret it. If the sign is complex enough, as is the case with a fancy apophatic theology, it can refer to a logical object that is not a finite thing, or at least is more than a finite thing. The question then becomes one of meaning, of getting the right signs and theories.

Second, Peirce severely criticized nominalism, which he called the great error of all modern philosophy (where it is in error).[15] Only a nominalist would expect that the objects of reference be objects in the sense of finite things, especially particular finite things. On the contrary, said Peirce, most of the important things in life are quite general. Why is there a universe? In what does the ideal of the good life consist? What is the spirit of an age? On a more prosaic level, we can enter a room full of people and pick up its mood, its tensions, frustrations, or glee. None of these "objects" are finite particulars, yet we refer to them in discussion and assume them in life. The reference to them is very complex, because we identify them through a great many integrated details. Most of us could not even say what particular things we notice when we pick up on tension in a group. The signs by which we refer to such things are extraordinarily complex, referring in mediating ways to a great many other things but integrating all those other references by means of what Peirce would call an hypothesis or theory. On the intellectual side of religion, it takes a whole theology to refer to God; that's why theologians are so verbose—the fragment of a theology fails of its ultimate reference. On the practical side of religion, it takes a vast nest of symbolic networks, supplementing and balancing one another.

With these two observations about why reference to a transcendent God might not be impossible, we move from reference to meaning or the symbol systems themselves.

WHAT MAKES RELIGIOUS SYMBOLS RELIGIOUS?

Signs, including religious symbols, have content, and the question of truth is whether that content applies to the reality referred to in the respect in which the symbol is taken to represent the reality. Peirce had an extraordinarily original and creative theory of signs, dividing them into trichotomies of trichotomies and into ten different classes. His theory of the internal structure of sign systems is not to the particular point here, however.[16] More important is to develop Peirce's theory to characterize the structure of systems of religious signs or symbols.[17]

The fundamental intent of this and the following two chapters is to provide a semiotic framework to distinguish religious from other kinds of experiences. This framework will include a categorial scheme of various dimensions of religious experience so that, when inquiring into a religious experience, or a kind of religious experience, the scheme presents something like a checklist of questions to be explored. Cumulatively, the checklist facilitates saying how a given experience is religious in some respects but not others. Few if any experiences are exclusively religious and it is likely that many experiences ordinarily not considered religious have religious dimensions.

The preliminary statement of the hypothesis for distinguishing religious experiences is that a religious experience is the experiencing of something religious, whereas nonreligious experiences do not experience anything religious. This is a semiotic approach to defining religious experience because it is based on the relation of signs to their objects and to their interpretations. Experiences, of course, can be partly religious, or religious in some respects but not others: to the extent an experience *is* religious, however, that is because it is the experiencing of something religious. "Something religious" I define, following Paul Tillich and a rather broad tradition of philosophy of religion, in terms of ultimacy—ultimate objects, ultimate human projects, ultimate dimensions of various aspects of life, and the personal and institutional behavior of religious and spiritual people insofar as that relates to ultimacy.[18] The previous four chapters discussed this at length.

For religious people the most general representation of ultimacy is in what sociologist Peter Berger calls their society's "sacred canopy."[19] This is the more or less coherent set of symbolic interpretations that defines the boundaries of the "world" of a cultural group. Berger points out that religions' sacred canopies are artifacts of the religious tradition, internalized so that individuals in the group see their world as bounded in their particular canopy's ways. They act upon these internalized representations, and sometimes reality gives feedback that reinforces or problematizes the sacred canopies. In the latter case, either the canopies are repaired or there is a religious crisis. Most sacred canopies are in constant states of revision in small if not large ways. People take their sacred canopies to be signs of the ultimate or ultimacy, signs by which the ultimate is to be engaged. If people are asked, however, to define their ultimates, and so identify which of their experiences are religious, they would usually name elements articulated in their sacred canopy. Social scientists studying what people believe to be religious experiences would thus relate the experiences to the culture's sacred canopy, prescinding from the question whether the canopy in fact can function as a complex sign of ultimacy as well as from whether it actually does in an alleged experience under investigation. The semiotic theory of interpretive engagement defended here, however, would insist that whether the experience in question is a religious experience depends on determining whether in fact it engages the experiencer with what is really ultimate through the mediation of a train of signs that might include a sacred canopy. "Really ultimate" here, of course, needs a properly theological explication, which is given in other chapters of this volume; its functional meaning in the present context is that the ultimate, or aspects or elements of ultimacy, provide the boundary conditions for the human world, as expressed in sacred canopies but not limited to the culture-wide venue of sacred canopies. Not all signs mediating religious experiences need to be connected with a sacred canopy but might be novel, circumstantial, poetic, or idiosyncratic. The elements in a sacred canopy might mediate religious experiences very well and still be false in how they do so. In modern times, traditional sacred canopies are often thought to be filled with misleading symbols (if not downright falsehoods). For people skeptical of a traditional sacred canopy, that canopy might be unable to effect engagement with anything ultimate and thus could not be involved in religious experience. For people gulled by a false sacred canopy, it still might mediate genuine, though false, engagement.

I argued in the chapters of the first part of this volume that there are five ultimate realities that are addressed in one way or another and with varying contextual validity by the symbol systems of the world's religious cultures, particularly the Axial Age religious cultures.[20] One is the radical contingency of the determinate world on something that makes it exist. This can be called "ontological ultimacy," and it has been modeled with three basic forms taken from familiar experience: personhood (giving rise to personalistic theisms), consciousness relative to its contents (the fundamental ontological motifs in both Buddhism and most forms of Hinduism), and emergence (as in notions of Dao, the arising of yang and yin, and other ontological themes of Chinese religion).[21] The character of determinateness itself involves four more ultimate realities that define the human world, which can be called cosmological because they are transcendental traits of the existing world. Any determinate thing has form, components formed in its harmony, existential location relative to other things, and achieved value. Relative to human beings, form means primarily possibilities with alternative values, giving rise to obligation; not particular obligations but obligatoriness itself is an ultimate boundary condition of life. Having components constitutes an ultimate boundary condition of achieving wholeness. Having existential location constitutes an ultimate boundary condition of engaging others, both human beings and nature in a larger sense. Having the achieved value of getting components together with the form at hand in existential relation to others constitutes the human boundary condition of the meaningfulness of life. All developed religions employ symbols for engaging these five "ultimate realities" in some way or another, often in ways that connect them. This metaphysical discursus on ultimate realities is not germane in particular to the semiotic theory of religious experience: other things might turn out to be ultimate on further analysis. The point is only to show that some things that can enter engaged experience can be ultimate in the sense of being boundary conditions for human existence and experience.

In addition to ultimacy in the sense of ontological and cosmological ultimate realities, ultimacy as relevant to religious experience can also mean *anthropologically* ultimate things, such as the Buddhist quest for release from suffering, or the search for enlightenment, harmony, righteousness.[22] The cosmological ultimates orient ultimate quests for righteousness, wholeness, proper engagement with others, and with meaningfulness. In most religions, there is a connection between ontological ultimates and ultimate aspects of human life. But this should not suggest that religious experiences of ultimate aspects of life, such as one's blissful state, or one's horrible guilt, are not in the genre of religious experience. Just how those aspects are ultimate is a matter for theology, broadly considered, to understand.[23]

An underlying supposition in this semiotic theory about religious experience is that the most fundamental element for defining a class of experiences is what the experiences are about, rather than the cognitive apparatus in the experiences that might be shifted contextually the better to address what the experience is about. Religious experiences are about something religious, which is to say, something ultimate. Religious experiences can be very much like nonreligious experiences, for instance, in their subjective feelings, the symbols and signs they use, their occasions for occurrence, their evolution as social and personal possibilities, and the like. But those nonreligious experiences are nonreligious because they do not experience something religious, however much they are like religious experiences in various respects.

A great many different kinds of experience, sometimes apparently unrelated, have been called "religious," and they can be examined from many different points of view and with different methods. For example, some religious experiences have extraordinary immediate qualities or subjective feels, such as that of radical oneness with the universe. Some students of mysticism concentrate on the quality itself and ask how the brain functions when that quality is brought to consciousness. The quality, however, might also occur in experiences that are not religious at all. Some mystical experiences are very like the experiences of certain people with temporal lobe epilepsy when a seizure is about to take place. The trancelike states of whirling dervishes are very like the experiences of small children who spin for the sake of delicious dizziness; only the former would be rightly called religious experiences. The subjective quality of religious experience is only one aspect of those experiences and might not be unique at all to religious experiences.

Collaborative, multidisciplinary, and cross-disciplinary studies of religious experience often are confused by this peculiar complexity: nonreligious dimensions or elements of religious experience can be abstracted from the experience of something religious and studied on their own. The study of these dimensions can thus neglect or explicitly bracket precisely what makes the concrete experience religious. Such scientific reductionism is commendable if it is explicit about bracketing out the issues concerning the experiencing of something religious. It might focus on the social function of the experience, or its subjective feel, or some other element. If that study, however, goes on to identify its abstracted dimension with religious experience itself, it reduces what makes the experience religious to something else, often to what is common with other kinds of experience. The reductionism is vicious if it neglects to be explicit about its bracketing and claims, or allows the claim, both that it is still analyzing religious experience and that religious experience is "nothing but" the abstracted element studied.

REDUCTIONISM

The purpose of this and the next two chapters thus has negative and positive sides. The negative side is to ward off vicious reductionisms. The positive side is to produce a framework within which scientific, historical, philosophical, and theological reductionisms can be integrated as valid approaches and contributions to the study of religious experience, which is the experience of something religious. The next two chapters shall develop the positive side. The remaining discussion in this section shall sketch some of the issues of vicious reductionism.

The first critical move against vicious reductionism is a preemptive defense against those scholars who themselves believe that there is nothing ultimate the experience of which might be defined as religious. They identify "religious experiences" as experiences that someone has identified as religious in the sense of engaging something ultimate but that are, in fact, according to these scholars, fictions, illusions, delusions, projections, evolutionary expediency, or whatever. They go on to say or suggest that the "alleged" religious experiences are "nothing but" those validity-scrambling "projections" (to use Feuerbach's term), thus discrediting religious experience in its primary intentionality of experiencing something religious. This kind of argument is classically associated with the intellectual heritages of Feuerbach, Marx, and Freud, and more recently with biological materialists such as Richard Dawkins and Daniel Dennett.[24]

Now surely religious experiences employ culturally constructed signs and, hence, are made of "fictions." Sometimes religious experiences really do mean something other than what they seem to mean and, hence, involve illusion. Sometimes they serve to hide unpleasant truths and, hence, can be delusory. Sometimes they have or once had evolutionary, social, or personal adaptive value and, hence, are prized for something other than what appears on their face. Discernment of the validity of religious experiences and their further interpretation is an important dimension of the spiritual strains of most religions, recognizing these common distortions. But vicious, hostile, genuinely unscientific reductionism results if scholars go on to assert that religious experiences are "nothing but" these negative elements.

The point of contention here is subtle and difficult to express. Religious experiences are those, I argue, that have an *intentionality* that engages something religious, something having to do with ultimacy; intentionality shall be analyzed later.[25] That these experiences have this intentional engagement does not mean, however, that the experiences interpret their religious objects well or correctly. The signs involved in the experiences are often inadequate or misleading; the point of apophatic theology is that even the best of signs fail in the end. Religious experiences with intentionality toward something religious often involve layers of interpretation with inconsistencies and misleading connections to semiotic systems that betray the basic intentionality. Religious experiences can be vaguely true but hastily overinterpreted so as to be specifically false. Religious experiences can be set within contexts that distort their fundamental intentionality. Alas, for people who look to religious experiences as experiential evidence for religious doctrine, it is difficult indeed, if not impossible, to get crisp epistemological verifications; religious experience has many functions other than verifying theological claims.[26]

None of these failings, however, disqualify experiences *as religious* if their intentionality engages something of ultimacy. They only complicate the task of the philosopher of religion or philosophical theologian who needs to assess the respects in which religious experiences do engage ultimacy.[27] They never justify a scholarly perspective that says that all alleged religious experiences are "nothing but" some aspect of the experience that does not acknowledge the religious intentionality engaging something ultimate.

So much for warnings about vicious reductionism. How can the many different vital disciplinary approaches to the study of religious experience be understood as coordinated to explicate the various dimensions of religious experience, when that is recognized to be the experience of something religious? The next element of the hypothesis about religious experience is a definition of religious experience based on a semiotic theory of experience. The definition will allow us to set boundaries for recognizing, at least in principle if not always in practice, what counts as a religious experience, and how the dimensions of religious experience under study fit in. This will help us understand our context when analyzing some dimensions of the experience that might also function in nonreligious experiences, such as subjective feels, religious symbol systems, adaptive advantages, and so forth. It will also help us be open to religious experiences that might be different from our preferred examples, where that preference comes from the particularities of our own culture or from appreciating what shows up best in our particular mode of analysis.

NOTES

1. The crisis of imagination has been worst for Christian Protestantism. Like liberal and conservative, if not Orthodox, Jews, Protestants have embraced the culture of European modernity, including its scientific imaginative formation. But unlike any of the other religious movements, Protestantism defined itself from the beginning by the doctrine of *sola scriptura*, the view that the Bible alone is sufficient for faith and the repository of the only important symbols. Both the Eastern Orthodox and the Western Roman Catholic traditions had grown since biblical times, introducing Trinitarian theology, metaphysical systems that imagined a far vaster cosmos than the biblical one and shaping Christian life by liturgies that pointed to mysteries far beyond biblical Christianity. All these might have been helpful in mediating a scientific understanding. But instead Protestant theology had to retreat to a biblical vocabulary foreign to the Christian traditions since the second century. Orthodoxy and Catholicism retreated from acknowledging the scientific imagination until recently. And European Christian theology, paralleled within Judaism, developed a dual track: one was the biblical theology of Protestant confessionalism and the other was the philosophical tradition of reconceiving God in light of scientific and other developments, the tradition of Descartes, Leibniz, Kant, Hegel, and Whitehead. Those philosophers all sought to provide reconstructions of religious symbols so as to bring together the modern and late-modern imaginations with the imaginative frame of the Bible. But is so doing, they relativized the exclusive authority of the Bible. The divergence of these two traditions important for Protestant theology—the confessional with an insistence on biblical language for theology, and the philosophical with an insistence on reimagining the biblical symbols before believing them—is one of the major fault lines between conservatives and liberals in America.

2. References to Peirce are given in the *Collected Papers of Charles Sanders Peirce*, volumes 1–6 edited by Charles Hartshorne and Paul Weiss, volumes 7–8 edited by Arthur W. Burks (Cambridge: Harvard University Press, vol. 1 1931, vol. 2 1932, vol. 3 1933, vol. 4 1933, vol. 5 1934, vol. 6 1935,

vol. 7 1958, vol. 8 1958), hereafter, CP; references are given by volume and paragraph number, for example, 2.274 for the beginning of the discussion of reference in volume 2, paragraph 274. Although discussions of semiotics are spread throughout Peirce's works, the concentrated discussions are in volume 2 in the section the editors call "speculative grammar." A good general introduction to Peirce that focuses upon his semiotics is Robert S. Corrington's *An Introduction to C. S. Peirce: Philosopher, Semiotician, and Ecstatic Naturalist* (Lanham, MD: Rowman & Littlefield, 1993).

3. CP 5.358–410.

4. See, for instance, CP 6.238–271, "Man's Glassy Essence." For an excellent study, see Vincent M. Colapietro's *Peirce's Approach to the Self: A Semiotic Perspective on Human Subjectivity* (Albany: State University of New York Press, 1989).

5. CP 6.66–87, 102–163.

6. CP 1 entire!; CP 6.7–87. For good discussions of Peirce's system as arising from semiotics, see Douglas R. Anderson's *Creativity and the Philosophy of C. S. Peirce* (Boston: Nijhoff, 1987) and *Strands of System: The Philosophy of Charles Peirce* (West Lafayette: Purdue University Press, 1995).

7. For Dewey on this point, see John E. Smith's discussion in "John Dewey: Experience, Experiment, and the Method of Intelligence," in his *The Spirit of American Philosophy*, revised edition (Albany: State University of New York Press, 1983). For an excellent comparison of Dewey with Peirce on the points made in the text here, see Smith's *Purpose and Thought: The Meaning of Pragmatism* (New Haven: Yale University Press, 1978), chapter 4.

8. In terms of his categories, signs are "firsts," which can be understood in terms of their own systems; reference is "secondness," which relates signs to their objects; interpretation is "thirdness," which connects the signs to objects by making an interpretation or giving rise to what he called an "interpretant."

9. CP 2.274–282.

10. Ludwig Wittgenstein, *Tractatus Logico-Philosophicus* (London: Routledge and Kegan Paul, 1922), propositions 6.41–7.00.

11. CP 2.283–291.

12. CP 2.292–308. I prefer "conventional" because in religion, nearly all signs are called symbols, and it should be said that there are three kinds of symbolic reference: iconic, indexical, and conventional.

13. CP 1.521–544.

14. See my *The Truth of Broken Symbols* (Albany: State University of New York Press, 1996), chapter 1.

15. CP 1.15–42; 6.619–624. This point was so important to Peirce that his editors, Hartshorne and Weiss, put his strong statements in the first and last paragraphs of their six-volume edition.

16. See Anderson's two books referred to earlier for an exposition of the theory of signs.

17. On Peirce's approach to religion as such, see Michael L. Raposa's *Peirce's Philosophy of Religion* (Bloomington: Indiana University Press, 1989) and Hermann Deuser's *Gott: Geist und Natur: Theologische Konsequenzen aus Charles S. Peirce's Religionsphilosophie* (Berlin: Walter de Gruyter, 1993). Peirce's writings on religion have not been collected in English, except for those in the Hartshorne-Weiss-Burks *Collected Papers*, which contain only a small fragment of Peirce's writings. They have, however, been collected by Deuser in *Charles Sanders Peirce: Religionsphilosophische Schriften*, Übersetzt unter Mitarbeit con Helmut Maassen, eingeleitet, kommentiert und herausgegeben von Hermann Deuser (Hamburg: Felix Meiner Verlag, 1995).

18. Paul Tillich discusses ultimacy at many places in his work, but most especially in his *Systematic Theology*, volume 1 (Chicago: University of Chicago Press, 1952) and in *Dynamics of Faith* (New York: Harper, 1957). The discussions treat both the metaphysics of ultimacy and the various ways it is symbolized. See *Ultimate Realities*, edited by R. C. Neville (Albany: State University of New York Press, 2001), a collaborative study by the Cross-Cultural Comparative Religious Ideas Project that focused on ultimate objects, ultimate projects or concerns, and the ways different traditions treat ultimacy. I have treated ultimacy in many dimensions in various writings, including *God the Creator* (Chicago: University of Chicago Press, 1968; second edition, Albany: State University of New York Press, 1992), *Eternity and Time's Flow* (Albany: State University of New York Press, 1993), *The Truth of Broken Symbols, On the Scope and Truth of Theology* (New York: T&T Clark, 2006), and *Ultimates: Philosophical Theology Volume One* (Albany: State University of New York Press).

19. Peter Berger, *The Sacred Canopy: Elements of a Sociological Theory of Religion* (Garden City: Doubleday, 1967).

20. See chapter 4.

21. Although personhood, consciousness, and emergence might be most associated with West, South, and East Asian cultures, respectively, in fact all three models play roles in nearly all the religious cultures.

22. This distinction is the result of long discussions in the Comparative Religious Ideas Project, reported in its volume *Ultimate Realities*. The point was hammered home by Malcolm David Eckel, a senior participant in that

project, who insisted that some kinds of Madhyamika Buddhism claim that anthropological ultimacy (the overcoming of suffering) requires the rejection of any kind of ontological ultimacy.

23. Theology should not be construed only as the intellectual work of members of a religious community for other members, although that kind of theology is common: Christian theology, Jewish theology, Buddhist theology, among others. For a detailed study of the publics for which theology is undertaken, see my *On the Scope and Truth of Theology*. That study indicates some of the ways in which theology necessarily includes the sciences.

24. The works of Feuerbach, Marx, and Freud are well known. For Richard Dawkins, see *The God Delusion* (Boston and New York: Houghton Mifflin/Mariner, 2008), and for Daniel C. Dennett, see *Breaking the Spell: Religion as a Natural Phenomenon* (New York: Viking/Penguin, 2006).

25. For the naturalistic sense of intentionality involved in the present theory, see Robert Cummings Neville, *Recovery of the Measure* (Albany: State University of New York Press, 1989), part 4.

26. For a critique of the attempt to use religious experience as evidence for religious doctrines, see Wayne Proudfoot's *Religious Experience* (Berkeley: University of California Press, 1985). The account of religious experience given in the present essay is both more restrictive to experiences of ultimacy) than Proudfoot allows and more capacious in allowing various means of engagement of ultimacy.

27. My *On the Scope and Truth of Theology* lays out a number of these complications.

Chapter 6

SEMIOTICS VERSUS PHENOMENOLOGY
Existential and Hermeneutic Dimensions

DEFINING RELIGIOUS EXPERIENCE: PHENOMENOLOGY AND SEMIOTICS

The definition of religious experience comes from the theory of experience understood as interpretive engagement discussed in the previous chapter. By spelling out the elements of that theory, it is possible to articulate dimensions of religious experience based on the logic of interpretive engagement. The dimensions are aspects of every interpretive engagement, and when the engagement is religious, of every religious experience. Every religious experience can be analyzed in terms of any and all of the dimensions. In most instances, not all of the dimensions are interesting, only some. But we know immediately that an analysis is reductive if it is not set within an array of analyses of the other dimensions, and that it is reductive in a vicious sense if it prevents or inhibits the analyses of those other dimensions.[1]

A religious experience is an interpretive engagement of ultimacy or some aspect of ultimacy, structured by some hermeneutical intentionality, by means of signs referring to the ultimate object in some respect and context; the religious experience might be true or false.

This is a semiotic definition of religious experience, not a phenomenological definition, although phenomenological elements are embedded within it. The remaining sections of this chapter will explain what makes the definition semiotic and introduce the relevant semiotic theory. Because most current approaches to religious experience are phenomenological, however, a word should be said about this distinction.

Phenomenology is the study of experiences as they appear and sometimes, as in Hegel, as they unfold internally. The strength of the phenomenological approach is that its drive to meticulous description aims at completeness and guards against reductionism. It exposes and surmounts the biases of scientific approaches that, perhaps unwittingly, limit what counts as religious experience to only that which is amenable to study by the particular scientific method and conceptuality at hand.[2] Phenomenology also criticizes approaches that give a theological or metaphysical interpretation of the authenticity or truth of the experiences. Phenomenology explicitly brackets concerns about whether experiences are true or valid, or have any real referent that is engaged.[3] Thus it is proof against scientific and other debunkers of religious experience as well as against theologians who read their theology into the experience, by claiming that the proper study of experience (religious or otherwise) eliminates questions of referential engagement or validity.

While phenomenology is valuable for the reasons mentioned, it is inadequate for a fully oriented study of religious experience precisely because it does bracket the questions of whether something really ultimate is engaged and, if engaged, engaged truly. Built into a religious experience (and most other experiences) is the intention that it is referring to what it seems to be referring to and does so truly. No religious person would think his or her experience is fully explicated unless the explication includes an assessment of the genuineness of its engagement. An experience that does not engage a religious "object" is not a religious experience, however much it might be like a religious experience in its subjective feel, proximate neural causes, or place in a pattern of religious behavior: nothing religiously significant is experienced.

One must be careful to observe the distinction between engagement and truth. Engagement concerns connecting with the ultimate object; truth concerns what the experience asserts or enjoys about the object. Some mystical experiences are thought to be so profound that they do not assert anything: they only enjoy the engagement. While these experiences are neither true nor false and in fact are praised because they transcend that distinction, the question that needs to be asked is whether their reference is engaging: is it something ultimate that is enjoyed?

Precisely because it brackets questions of real reference and validity and sticks instead to description, phenomenology is viciously reductive right at the most interesting points from the perspective of people with putative religious experiences. Therefore, the better analytical frame for studying religious experience is the semiotic one that builds into the interpretive elements of the experience the connection of the subjectively describable experience as a sign with the realities referred to, along with definitions and criteria of truth. This is the justification for using the theory of interpretive engagement to derive a scheme for the dimensions of religious experience.

The theory of "interpretive engagement" is an extension of the American pragmatic tradition of Charles Peirce and John Dewey.[4] The distinctive focus of the theory is that experience is an interaction or "transaction," to use Dewey's word, between an experiencer and the environment containing the object experienced.[5] This is to say experience is of real things, not just ideas of real things, although ideas themselves can be experienced because they are a kind of real thing. "Engagement" connotes that the real thing is attended to, taken up for response, related to the experiencer's purposes and life context, and discriminated in ways that bear upon attention, response, purpose, and context; engagement connotes interest in the object.

That experiential engagement is interpretive means that it is shaped by signs. Engagement takes the object engaged to be as the sign says in the respect in which the sign refers to the object. This means, among other things, that the experiencer always brings to engagement a semiotic set of signs that mediates the relation between the experiencer and the object. Because engagement is dynamic, a kind of transaction, signs sometimes are modified in the engagement, old signs found wanting, new signs invented by analogy or wit. But there is no unmediated experience. Signs are always involved because we only engage the world in certain respects, relative to our contexts and purposes, and as enabled by the signs we have at our disposal.

This claim to the mediated quality of all experience, including religious experience, seems to stand in contradiction to the claims of some mystics in various religious traditions that some religious experience is unmediated, immediate, or intuitive. True, many mystical experiences have the subjective quality of immediacy, with no sense that they refer to something else. Moreover, they often have such intensity that all aspects of the experience except for the subjective quality of the signs are obscured. But if the main point of the theory of interpretive engagement is true, it would be misleading to say that there is no mediation of the religious object in such immediate experiences. The experiences would be forgotten immediately if they contained no signs networked with other signs in a semiotic system. The better way to understand them is to say that the signs involved refer to the object as being no different from the powerful signs themselves. In the technical language introduced in the previous chapter, those experiences approach referring with perfect "iconicity," saying that the sign approximates the object in all possible respects. This explains the quality of immediacy of engagement while acknowledging that the mediation of signs is involved.

In its theory of interpretive engagement of real things in the world, the American pragmatic tradition stands in some contrast with a tendency in European semiotics to say that interpretation is always of other interpretations, usually of texts. For the Americans, the paradigm for interpretation is the interpretation of nature; for the Europeans, the paradigm is the hermeneutics of texts. So the emphasis on engagement of real things is important. Of course, when we talk about the objects engaged, we use interpretations to refer to the objects. It is possible, then, to treat all aspects of an interpretation as being within one large semiotic system. In technical language, this is to treat the extension of interpretation. The theory of interpretive engagement, however, emphasizes the intention of interpretation, in which the signs and the entire semiotic system containing their extension are employed as mediators to shape the interactive engagement with the object. Engagement is interpretation construed intentionally, which means that interpretations are always concrete and contextual. Religious experience is the intentional engagement of ultimacy as the religious object. "Intention" here does not always mean purposive or directed, although it sometimes does. The basic meaning of intention is the framing of experience so that it is "of" something, or "about" something.

The explication of the semiotic theory of religious experience will elaborate six kinds of basic dimensions, all of which relate to ultimacy, although they also characterize many kinds of experiences that do not involve ultimacy. There are existential dimensions, four kinds of hermeneutic dimensions, and validity dimensions. This chapter will explore the existential dimensions and the hermeneutical dimensions of intentionality and signs. The hermeneutical dimensions of reference and context as well as the validity dimensions will be treated in chapter 7. Table 6.1 shows the three basic kinds of dimensions of religious experience.

TABLE 6.1 Dimensions of Religious Experience

Existential Dimensions
Hermeneutical Dimensions
Validity Dimensions

EXISTENTIAL DIMENSIONS OF RELIGIOUS EXPERIENCE

It is possible to identify four *existential dimensions* of religious experience, all having to do with whether the experience is a genuine engagement of ultimacy in some respect. They can be labeled roughly: the intentionality dimension, the objective reality dimension, the formal reality dimension, and the causal connection dimension. These can be called "existential dimensions" because they existentially relate the interpreter to ultimate realities through engagement. That experiences have these existential dimensions does not mean that they necessarily involve engaging ultimacy truly: the validity dimensions deal with the question of truth and will be treated in the next chapter.

Intentionality. The first thing to determine regarding whether an experience is a genuine engagement with some aspect of ultimacy is whether the ultimacy is *intended* in the experience. Presumably, ultimate realities, whatever they are, are constantly present and modify or condition every experience. But an experience is not *of* them unless its intentionality includes them. As mentioned, an experiencer intends a real thing by means of engaging it with signs in their semiotic system. The dimension of intentionality will be analyzed in greater detail later because it also falls within the class of hermeneutic dimensions.[6]

Objective reality. Another thing to determine regarding genuine engagement in a religious experience is how the ultimacy appears to the experiencer, how it is "objectified" in the experience. The objective reality of ultimacy is what people think is ultimate. "Objective reality" was distinguished from "formal reality" by the medievals as the reality a thing has for a knower versus the reality it has in itself.[7] For people in cultures deeply shaped by religious traditions, the sacred canopy of their culture supplies the main parts of their objective "take" on ultimacy. Or, the sacred canopy in conjunction with understanding its existential relation to their particular lives does so. For people with little connection to more or less coherent sacred canopies, other symbols supply their objective ultimate realities. Objective realities for ultimacy depend on the signs and semiotic systems at hand for engaging ultimacy.

Formal reality. The formal reality dimension of actual engagement of ultimacy pertains to whether the experience engages what is really ultimate as intended and objectified in its signs. This dimension cannot be explored fully through the analysis of religious experiences alone, because a determination must be made regarding what is really ultimate. This is a theological or philosophical problem that shall not be addressed here.[8] The formal reality dimension of religious experience, however, has to do with whether the really ultimate is what is engaged by an experience whose objective ultimate is shaped by the signs at hand. This requires coming at the experience from an external as well as internal point of view.

Causality. The causal dimension of engagement has to do with whether there is an actual, albeit complex and indirect, causal link between the formal reality of the intended ultimacy and the experiencer so that some character of the ultimacy is carried over into the experience through the medium of the interpreting signs. It is one thing merely to think about some kind of ultimacy, and another to experience it. *Thinking about* ultimacy might be merely extensional, limited to thinking about ideas and judgments within a semiotic system. The *experience* of ultimacy itself depends upon a causal relation such that, in the relevant senses for the hermeneutics of the experience, the formal reality of the intended ultimate causes the experience. The formal reality of the ultimate is not the only cause, of course, because individual purposes, semiotic systems, peculiarities of reference, and various contexts are also contributing causes to any religious experience. Nevertheless, through whatever indirect means the causality works, the causal process by which ultimacy is engaged in some properly hermeneutical way reverses the intentionality in the experience. Religious experience is something like a perception. The more we emphasize the experiencer's causal contributions to the experience, the more the causal contributions of the ultimate intended are like feedback, reaffirming or denying the objective intent. But sometimes, religious experience just blows away the experiencer, and the experiencer grasps desperately for hermeneutical contributions in order to be

TABLE 6.2 Existential Dimensions of Religious Experience

| *Intentionality* |
| *Objective Reality* |
| *Formal Reality* |
| *Causality* |

able to grasp and hold the ultimate. Unless the experience can be framed in a sign, it will be forgotten.

These four existential dimensions of religious experience all pertain to whether the experience is a genuine engagement. The engagement is also interpretive, however, and so it is a related but separate question as to whether what the experiencer gets out of the experience is true. Paul Tillich liked to say that genuine but false religious experience is demonic! We will return to the question of truth in chapter 7. Table 6.2 shows the four existential dimensions of religious experience.

HERMENEUTIC DIMENSIONS: INTENTIONALITY

An interpretation takes a sign to refer to its object in some respect that is selected by the interpretive purpose at hand. Peirce's language is worth citing here:

> A sign, or *representamen*, is something which stands to somebody for something in some respect or capacity. It addresses somebody, that is, creates in the mind of that person an equivalent sign, or perhaps a more developed sign. That sign which it creates I call the *interpretant* of the first sign. The sign stands for something, its *object*. It stands for that object, not in all respects, but in reference to a sort of idea, which I have sometimes called the ground of the representamen.[9]

The semiotic theory of interpretive engagement gives rise to an array of dimensions in terms of which the meaning of a religious experience can be understood, summarized in table 7.3.[10] An object can be interpreted in any number of respects. Another way of thinking about the "respect" of interpretation is to see it as a category for interpretation. To interpret a terrain with respect to the category of roads, use a road map; with respect to topography, use a topographical map; with respect to weather, a weather map; and so forth. The selection of the respect in which to interpret the object is a function of the purpose at hand. The purpose might be conscious and explicit, or only implicit. It can be borne by the culture in which the experiencer lives without ever being more than a cultural habit in the individuals.

Purposes can be of innumerable sorts, and many purposes can be involved in shaping a given experiential engagement. Nevertheless, there are at least four underlying hermeneutical intentionalities within which purposes fall. The intention of an interpretive engagement, it will be remembered, is how the interpreter engages the object by means of signs in their semiotic system. The four underlying *intentionalities* are modes or ways of engagement. They are: imagination, assertion, synthesis, and practice.

Imagination. Imaginative intentionalities guide interpretations that attempt to produce or discover images by means of which the object can be engaged. "Images" by themselves are neither true nor false but only are to be judged according to whether they enable engagement. Imagination runs very deep in human experience, from the development of very basic spatiotemporal orientation to discriminating focal points from backgrounds, to identifying objects in an environment, to linguistic expressions for articulating experience, to special concepts, narratives, theories, and so on. Once imagined, an image can be used in assertion, in synthesizing experience, and in guiding practical life by means of patterns of images. Without images, the logical object cannot be engaged with any discrimination.

Religious experience depends on having, or if lacking, developing or discovering, images of ultimacy. "Images of ultimacy" are not limited to the transcendent images of the sophisticated literati of the religions of high civilization; sacred trees, ghostly spirits, and things that go bump in the night are also images of ultimacy for people for whom they define boundary conditions for the world. Many religious experiences encounter ultimate matters as so mysterious that the experience itself is of attempting to come up with signs as images that allow the experience to have some interpretable shape. The authors of scripture had imaginative experiences in which they composed stories or sacred cosmologies so as to bring to voice what they were attempting to experience. Religious "founders" such as Confucius, Laozi, Buddha, Moses, Jesus, and Mohammed all experienced the ultimate in imaginative ways. Poets in our own day experience ultimate matters through the process of image-making.

These verbal images are not the only kind of signs involved in religious experience, however. Brute, sensuous subjective images of the sort involved in some kinds of mysticism such as the feelings of Samadhi, of one oneness with the universe, or of falling into the abyss of God are signs that allow for engagement with ultimate matters. The subjective feeling of unity in the experience of the whirling dervish is a sign that perhaps was taken from the experience of the spinning child and used as an image of unity. The same for the subjective feeling of expansiveness surrounding a grand mal seizure. The extreme dissociative feelings of a peyote or LSD trip can be taken as images of the numinous transgressive qualities of some ultimate realities. This is not to say that in these religious experiences there first is an experience of mystery that is then interpreted with signs brought in from elsewhere. Rather, it is to say that those subjective feelings, when they arise (say, from dancing, or ingesting LSD), are taken as signs of the ultimate if the experience is in the intentional mode of imaginative engagement of ultimacy. Not everyone who trips on LSD has a religious experience; but when Walter Pahnke did his famous experiment in 1962 with Andover Newton seminary students in the basement of Marsh Chapel at Boston University during a Good Friday service, the intentional mode of imagining ultimacy with the resulting subjective feelings was not surprising.[11]

Imagination is productive in two senses. In one, there is the creative moment when an image is first constructed and placed in a semiotic network. This is the work of the religious geniuses. In another, each individual has to acquire the image in his or her personal life, like a little child learning Bible stories, or spinning until dizzy, or remembering what it was like to be in the womb (Freud's explanation for the source of the "oceanic feeling" of certain mystics).

Imaginative intentionality shapes a religious experience so that its ultimate object is engaged by means of an imagined sign that might interpret it in a certain respect. By itself, the imaginative intentionality of a religious experience does not assert that the sign interprets the ultimate object, only that the sign is a sign for interpreting the ultimate object. Perhaps very few religious experiences are of a purely imaginative intentionality. The great religious founders most likely thought their imaginative constructions were also true of the object and asserted them.

Assertion. Assertive intentionalities attempt to say what or how the logical object is or should be. They aim to say that the object is truly referred to by the sign at hand in the respect in which the interpretation is being made. Propositions are the most obvious linguistic form of assertive purposes in experience, but by no means the only ones. An automobile driver in heavy traffic makes zillions of assertive interpretations at once that pick up on road conditions, speed, other vehicles, and so forth. These are all under the intention of asserting what the situation is and what to do to get to one's destination. While some assertive purposes are explicit and conscious, others, like the driver's, are habits of orientation to the environment, and yet others are given by the culture's determination of what is important to attend to.

Whereas religious experiences must first have some imaginative structure if they are to engage some aspect of ultimacy, they also usually involve some assertion as to what's what and should be. Under most circumstances, religious experiences whose signs come from a traditional sacred canopy take the signs to be true of the ultimate references. Mystical experiences of unity, or depth, or indifferent detachment, or comprehensive attachment, or universal compassion take the universe to be ultimately unified, or deep, or inhumanely factual, or available to empathy, or loveworthy. Religious experiences of command, such as to leave home, change one's life, undertake a special work, are taken to be assertively normative. Religious experiences of oneself as living in illusion, or deeply guilty, are taken to be true characterizations. Religious experiences of a people's founding identity, as in a mythic story or a sacred geography, are taken to be true.

The question of what is true in an assertion is complicated by the fact that so many experiential signs in religion are metaphoric and are not meant literally; this will be explored in the discussion of iconic and indexical modes of reference to come. Moreover, there is an assertoric complication in the fact that in a group, some people can take their founding myth, for instance, to be naively true in a literal sense, learn that literally it is false, and then return to a second naiveté that asserts a true experiential point in the myth while accepting its literal falsity. The explication of intentionally assertoric religious experiences is often in the form of doctrines or claims about some aspect of ultimacy.

Synthesis. Synthesizing intentionalities guide interpretive engagements to take a unified view of things, to be systematic, to come at things from many angles, to articulate how the various respects of interpretation themselves hang together. The most obvious examples of this are theoretical interpretations. But this intentionality also sometimes functions when interpretations are embedded in symbolically expressed worldviews.

In religion, theology is an intellectual means of synthesizing interpretive engagement. For some people, theological ideas, with all their attendant arguments, can become signs for engaging "the whole." This is to say, the contemplative process of moving about in a systematic theology might be used in a genuine engagement with ultimacy in some synthesizing sense. Some theologians can pray using a complicated theology as a unified if complex "name of God." But people like this are rare. Most people take more concrete signs to symbolize wholeness. The Axial Age revolution in religion was remarkable for its development of synthesizing signs. It invented notions of how the cosmos is One instead of a congregation of local environments beyond which was ignorance. It invented notions of unitary fundamental ontological realities undergirding the one cosmos, such as monotheistic Gods, interaction principles like the Chinese Heaven and Earth, and cosmos-controlling pantheons as in Hinduism, all replacements for tribal gods who were in competition with the gods of other tribes. It invented notions of universal commonality of human beings, transcending cultural and tribal differences, all of whom should be treated justly and cared for compassionately. Confucianism, Daoism, Buddhism, Hinduism, Judaism, classical paganism, Christianity, and Islam all, in their many denominations, assert these traits as characteristics of what is experienced ultimately.[12] The different religions have very different semiotic systems for symbolizing these traits, and it would be a mistake to assume too much parallelism without examination. Nevertheless, in all the Axial Age religions, fundamental religious experience for at least some of the people is shaped by the signs that are the result of synthesis. To be sure, that experience has imaginative and assertive intentionalities. But it also has a synthesizing intentionality. Signs that are helpful for these synthesizing intentionalities include many that short-circuit the heavy-duty theological symbols. For instance, the unity of the cosmos might be experienced in terms of the Chinese qi (material force), easily taught to be recognized in the play of taijiquan, or it might be experienced through the symbols of a vast network of ecosystems as in contemporary religious Deep Ecology. Experience of underlying ontological conditions can be mediated by signs of God as creator, the balance of process and pattern in harmony, or in the consciousness that underlies all consciousness of objects. Experience of the commonality and unity of human kind can be mediated in stories of particular interactions, such as Jesus's parable of the Good Samaritan. By no means are all religious experiences shaped by a synthesizing intentionality, but many are.

Practice. Although all intentionalities are practical in some sense, some interpretive engagements of the ultimate are set within the *practical intentional* frame of guiding a larger domain of life. The importance of this point is seen in the fact that many people, who would never claim to have "a" religious experience, nevertheless pattern their lives in religious ways and in this sense interpretively engage ultimacy. Their patterns shape the ways they handle birth and death, sickness and triumph, meaningfulness and gratitude for existence. Perhaps no single experience is "of" the ultimate. But the way by which they live through the patterns of religious experience is "of" the ultimate. An "experienced" religious person might be far closer to God or the Dao, in the sense of having a life that itself is a sign engaging the ultimate, than individuals with unique, deep, or outrageously transforming experiences. Of course, an individual can have specific religious experiences that are included within a life of patterned religious experience. The experience at hand is set in the context of patterning or guiding practices beyond the experience itself.

In terms of practice, religion consists of ways of living in the light of what the religion takes to be ultimate, and this includes all sorts of patterns of worship, spiritual development, thinking and communicating about what is ultimate, and so forth. In many respects, the cognitive aspects of experience are devoted to guiding life in its practical aspects.[13]

Moreover, the long-run tests of whether interpretive engagements are true or false pertain to the feedback that comes from living with them as guides for how to discriminate what is real and valuable in the ultimate environment. More on the truth question later. Now we look at the dimension of signs.

HERMENEUTIC DIMENSIONS: SIGNS

Signs function in an interpretation so as to mediate the reality interpreted to the interpreter in a semiotic way. A sign has network meaning as defined within a semiotic system or code; the semiotic system has syntactic (grammatical) structures as well as semantic (meaning) structures. Thus, when a sign mediates an object to an interpreter, it brings along the network of meanings within its semiotic system; this is not to say that the whole semiotic system is brought to consciousness, only that it functions in defining the sign and its mediating work.[14]

Interpretive engagement is a natural causal process.[15] In other natural causal processes, the "effect" might synthesize its "causes" with mechanical or chemical or other "nonexperiential" forms of synthesis. In experiential natural causal processes, however, the forms of synthesis include the semiotic organization of the signs. The semiotic systems of many animals might not be very sophisticated. The contractions of an empty stomach might signal (sign) a move toward getting something to eat. Human beings have semiotic systems with vast arrays of signs for mapping the world; hunger pangs might trigger the contemplation of choices among Italian, Chinese, Abyssinian, or French restaurants, with pros and cons for each, none of which are in the immediate environment. Semiotic systems that include religious symbols, for instance, those dealing with elements of a sacred canopy, are very complex indeed and include comporting the interpreter toward ultimate realities far distant from things touched or seen. Or perhaps they symbolically locate ultimacy in the ordinary things touched or seen. Religious experiences, however, are still natural causal processes involving semiotic systems that interpret ultimacy in the environment with which the interpreter engages.

A sign in an interpretive engagement has four elements to be acknowledged, separately and in combination. In a shorthand way, the first three can be called, respectively, "quality," "decisiveness," and "connection." They correspond roughly to what Peirce called "firstness," "secondness," and "thirdness." Firstness, for Peirce, is what a thing is just in itself; secondness is what a thing is strictly in opposition or difference from something else; thirdness is what a thing is as mediating between two other things (if a thing differs from another thing in a certain respect, the "respect" is a mediating third). Although Peirce thought he could do without a category of fourthness, it would be the immediate harmony of firstness, secondness, and thirdness.[16] Peirce (and I) use these categories analogically to exhibit relations among elements. Quality has to do with immediate in-itselfness (firstness); decisiveness with opposition (secondness), and connection with mediation (thirdness). The fourth element is the semiotic embeddedness of the sign, which would illustrate fourthness. All four are crucial for the dimensions of religious experience to be explored in this chapter.

Quality. Quality is the immediate subjective feel of the sign as it functions in an interpretive engagement. Some religious experiences have very intense immediate qualities, so that all other aspects of the interpretation are suppressed. The qualities of signs need not be homogeneous but might be internally complex and unfolding through time, such as the quality of listening to a symphony. Sometimes the quality of a sign in an interpretive engagement is at the center of consciousness, and other times the quality might not be noticed except in retrospect. The Buddhist admonition to attend to the "suchness" of things points to the project of attending to quality.

The qualities of certain religious experiences are extraordinarily intense, vivid, and exotic, and some thinkers would limit the category of "religious experience" to those dominated by such subjective qualities, although this essay argues that any interpretive engagement of ultimacy is a religious experience, regardless of the vivacity of its subjective quality. One line of reflection on religious experience argues that the intensity, vividness, and uncanny exoticness of such experiences, like Rudolf Otto's *numinous mysterium tremendum et fascinans*, must be caused by an ontologically real ultimate. This view can be called a "naive realism" by analogy with that philosophical position that says that perceptions are caused by objects as the perceptions refer to them. The causal line is difficult to establish, however, because, like the child spinning, the subjective feel of the experience might be caused by something else entirely. Naive realism is not helpful, even though it is common in popular religion. Another line of reflection is taken by cognitive scientists and neuroscientists who are interested in discovering how those experiences are functions of brain activities. Results of such research greatly enrich our understanding of those experiences. Opposite to the naive realists, some thinkers would argue that demonstrating a neural cause for an experience proves that it is *not* caused by the ultimate object to which it refers and that the belief that it is so is merely a projection. The assumption in this reductionist argument is that for the experience to be asserted as true, it must be alleged to be planted in the mind by a miraculous intervention that does not employ the usual forms of physical embodiment of experience, an assumption made by some naive realists. Nevertheless, the success of neural explanations of the exotic qualities of certain religious experiences only deals with the proximate neural elements in what are much larger causal networks. Links to ultimate realities might or might not be found in those larger causal networks, a question for empirical inquiry. Perhaps there is indeed a causal connection, however indirect this is when understood through the complications of the hermeneutical conditions. By analogy, that we understand how the optic nerve works does not mean that there is nothing real and distant that we see by means of the nervous activity in a larger causal network; on the other hand, sometimes we have visual illusions.

The point of these causal considerations is that the qualities of exotic religious experiences are simply immediate qualities of the experiences. Those qualities have their causes, which include neural and larger environmental causal networks. But the question whether the causes link in some way to real religious objects cannot be addressed without attending to the relevant factors of meaning, reference, purpose, context, and the integration of these in alleged interpretive engagements. This is to say, the immediate quality of an exotic religious experience (or of an ordinary one) is not by itself a religious experience. It is not a religious experience except insofar as it is implicated in an interpretive engagement with something ultimate. So the proximate neural causes of the subjective quality itself do not discriminate between religious and nonreligious experiences that share the same qualities.

Whereas all religious experiences have signs whose immediate qualities can be studied, not all have signs that are especially intense, vivid, or exotic; not all religious experiences need to be *numinous* with *mysterium tremendum et fascinans*. Augustine's much analyzed conversion experience contained only ordinary qualities, for instance, personal agitation, sharing a dilemma with a friend, the voices of children singing beyond the wall, and reading and interpreting a scripture chosen by chance. In certain meditative experiences the subjective qualities might seem unusual to non-adepts, but would seem ordinary to adepts.

Decisiveness. Decisiveness is that aspect of a sign by virtue of which it is this sign and not some other sign. Because of the decisiveness of signs, they can be true or false within interpretations. Sometimes the decisiveness is shocking, running contrary to what was expected. Other times, the decisiveness is almost unnoticed because the sacred canopy is taken for granted.

In religious signs, decisiveness can give rise to an intensity different from the intensity of quality. Decisiveness in religious signs can be intense because they can give rise to the singularity, the particularity, the oddness, of the experience, and hence of the experiencer. Moreover, because the signs are in interpretive engagements of the ultimate, in some sense they are ultimately important for the experiencer. If a sign is decisive so as to make a serious difference to the experiencer, a difference that would be denied or neglected by some other sign in the interpreting experience, then it has a dyadic, either/or, or better, this/not that character. Signs distinguishing hope from despair, a personal from an impersonal ultimate, a benevolent from malevolent deity, a humanly framed versus indifferent cosmos, guilt from innocence—all are decisive. In understanding religious experiences, the investigation of the decisiveness of the signs is extremely important, both for understanding the experience itself and understanding its consequences for the experiencer that might be indicated in secondary self-reference.

Connection. Connection in signs consists in the way by which the interpreter engages the reality in the respect in which the sign in its semiotic system stands for the reality in the experience of the interpreter. The sign is what it is as a connector because it brings the object into the experience of the interpreter in the respect signified by the sign. Connection can be understood either extensionally or intentionally, as distinguished earlier. Extensionally, a sign performs its mediating function within a semiotic system. Intentionally, a sign performs its mediating function between a real logical object and a real interpreter, orienting the interpreter toward the object in the ways the sign signifies.

The world is a vastly complicated environment for human life. But we can discriminate its elements only insofar as we have signs that allow us to do that. At a basic level, we need signs to pick up on the things that are necessary for survival. Most of us Bostonians would not see the things necessary for survival in an Amazon jungle; and the inhabitants of the jungle would never make it across Commonwealth Avenue if they had not been taught the signs of modern civilization. The conditions for the ultimate characters of life and existence cannot be noticed without signs for them. And then, the signs pick up on what is real only in the respects in which the signs can stand for the ultimacy objects. Pre–Axial Age religions have signs for local gods and ultimate discriminators of ingroup membership, history, and place, and these among others form their worldviews. Axial Age religions developed signs for the universe as a whole, for underlying principles or super-intenders of the whole, for universal commonality in human nature, and the rest; Axial Age religions might lose facility with the ingroup signs orienting local communities. Imagination gives rise to signs that *might* pick up on what is important and real concerning an ultimate matter. But, whether the signs can *actually* do that depends on their being used in interpretive engagements with assertive, synthetic, or practical intentionalities.

Because it is the actual connection that makes a sign a sign, the issue of literal versus metaphoric connection is not a great problem. Whatever signs actually work to make the connection in the respect in which the interpretation takes the signs to stand for their ultimate objects are the functionally important ones. Of course, much work is to be done to understand the roles of literal and metaphoric signs. In religion, it might be the case that all signs are metaphorical and none literal. Paul Tillich said once that only the sign of Being-itself could be construed as a literal sign of the ultimate; he said on other occasions that no signs are strictly literal.[17]

All signs have quality, decisiveness, and connection, and so can be analyzed in terms of all three elements. Peirce pointed out, however, that these aspects can be overlaid. Thus, there can be a quality of decisiveness—the subjective feel of singularity or difference. There can be a quality of connection—the subjective feel of the interaction itself. There can be a decisiveness of quality—the singularity of the subjective feel, and a decisiveness of connection—the singularity of the connection. There can be a connection within quality, as the structure of a symphony is complex beneath its subjective feel, and a connection within decisiveness, as when one group's distinctiveness is a function of its mythic story.

Semiotic embeddedness. Any sign employed in religious experience is embedded in a semiotic system of other signs. Sometimes these systems are the complicated networks of symbols in a traditional religion. But other times these might not be traditionally religious at all but come from a semiotic system idiosyncratic to a life. For instance, a secular, religiously uneducated person might have a life-shattering experience, such as the death of a friend, that suddenly points to ultimacy in life's meaning and leading to the transformation of the person's life. Understanding a sign, including a religious sign, involves noting its quality, decisiveness, connection, and semiotic embeddedness.

Because of their highly metaphorical quality, religious signs are often involved in any number of symbolic networks, some of which fit together and others do not, even when they resonate with one another. For instance, one of the most ancient, typical, and powerful religious experiences among Christians is that of feeling redeemed from heinous sin by the sacrifice of Jesus Christ, with the result that one is reconciled to God, at one with God; the word for this experience, atonement, means literally at-one-ment. This is an odd sign for us late moderns, because we do not participate in the rich culture of sacrifice that permeated the first-century Mediterranean world. Moreover, the specific Christian senses of Jesus's "sacrifice" come from two very different symbolic networks. On the one hand, Jesus is called the Paschal Lamb, referring to the Passover sacrifice by which painting one's doorframe with the blood of a lamb or goat warded off God's agent to kill all the firstborn in Egypt. As Paschal Lamb, Jesus wards off death. On the other hand, he is said to be "the Lamb of God who takes away the sins of the world," a reference to the atonement rite of ancient Israel in which the sins of the people and High Priest are put on a goat who is sent into the wilderness to be taken by an evil demon. That is a purification ritual that allows people to come close to the presence of God, not a warding off of the murderous God ritual like Passover. To complicate things further, the Judaism of Jesus's time had been influenced by Persian Hellenism so as to believe that God is in a mortal combat with Satan, the Prince of Evil. Because humankind had been wicked, their souls were owed to Satan, but Jesus's sacrifice redeemed them, ransomed them. All of these symbol systems resonate together in the writings of St. Paul, for instance, and other early Christians. To understand the experience of "redemption," which is so powerful for many people even today, requires sorting out how these different networks of signs work together. It is easy for skeptical scholars to derogate the claims to experiences of redemption through Jesus's death on the cross by noting inconsistencies in the networks of signs in play, and it is hard for theologians to sort them out so as to make sense of them. Whether the alleged religious experience makes actual connection in interpretive engagement depends in part on the efficacy of the signs' networking within semiotic systems that allow for intentional engagement. That an actual connection is made in the appropriate respect does not mean that the interpretation mediated by the sign is true. It might be an actual but false interpretive engagement. More on truth in the next chapter. Table 6.3 shows the hermeneutic dimensions of religious experience discussed so far, those of intentionality and signs; the dimensions of reference and context will be discussed in chapter 7.

TABLE 6.3 Hermeneutic Dimensions of Religious Experience

DIMENSIONS OF INTENTIONALITY	DIMENSIONS OF SIGNS
Imagination	*Quality*
Assertion	*Decisiveness*
Synthesis	*Connection*
Practice	*Semiotic Embeddedness*

NOTES

1. The array of dimensions of religious experience deriving from the theory of interpretive engagement, of course, is not the only way to classify elements of religious experience. In a loose sense of the term "phenomenology," there are many phenomenologies of religious experience, beginning

with Hegel's, which will be discussed later; the classification here is not a phenomenology. In the long run, the helpfulness of the array of dimensions developed here will depend on how it is reinforced by and in turn throws new light on the other approaches to religious experience, although that is not the topic of this chapter.

2. The life and work of William James is a *locus classicus* for the tension between phenomenological exactness and the reductive interests of scientific approaches. See Robert D. Richardson's deeply philosophical biography of James, *William James: In the Maelstrom of American Modernism: A Biography* (Boston: Houghton Mifflin, 2006).

3. Edmund Husserl was the classical phenomenologist. In his *Ideas: General Introduction to Pure Phenomenology*, translated by W. R. Boyce Gibson (New York: Macmillan, 1931; Collier edition 1962; German original, 1913), Husserl made the point about bracketing any concerns for reference to a real world or for the existence of the objects of experience by saying that those concerns come from what he called a "natural" standpoint. Proper phenomenology takes what he called a "transcendental standpoint," using the language of Kant. He thus attempted to explain the a priori structure of experience in terms of the conditions for the possibility of experience as such, limiting discussions of experience to the sheer description of them. By cutting experience off from the realities to which the experience might refer and from the questions of truth, Husserl made experience into a kind of thing-in-itself accessible to consciousness. In terms of the pragmatic theory of interpretation employed in this chapter, experiences in the phenomenological sense are limited to being subjective signs that might have reference and truth. Pragmatists, however, have rejected that understanding of experience in favor of what Husserl condemned as experience from the natural standpoint. For Peirce, Dewey, and my theory of interpretive engagement, experience includes the realities experienced as well as the signs by which they are experienced, and experiencing always makes the elementary truth claim that, insofar as the signs refer, they might do so truly. From the natural standpoint of pragmatism, Husserlian phenomenology is a reductive limitation to the subjective signs involved in experience. Many kinds of phenomenology exist, of course, not only Husserl's pure kind. Hegel's phenomenology of religion in *The Phenomenology of Spirit*, translated by A. V. Miller (Oxford: Oxford University Press, 1977) and in his *Lectures on the Philosophy of Religion*, translated by E. B. Speirs and J. Burdon Sanderson in three volumes (New York: Humanities Press, 1962), unfolded religious experience as a cultural phenomenon in narrative form.

E. B. Tyler, J. G. Frazer, Rudolf Otto, G. van der Leeuw, and Mircea Eliade, have produced compendious phenomenologies of religion, including religious experience as such. All, like Hegel, have been accused of reading in their own religious philosophies and categories, and all are subject to the critique Husserl made of failing to bracket out all reference to reality and concern for truth in experience. Charles Peirce called part of his work "phenomenology," but he did not mean description; he meant, rather, the classification of things, not necessarily experiences, into his three basic categories derived from his relational logic, firstness, secondness, and thirdness, which shall be explained briefly later in the chapter.

4. For an interpretation of recent philosophy that justifies the move to a theory of interpretive engagement, see Warren G. Frisina's *The Unity of Knowledge and Action: Toward a Nonrepresentational Theory of Knowledge* (Albany: State University of New York Press, 2002). The theory will be sketched only briefly here, to the point sufficient to derive a taxonomy of dimensions of religious experience. For a formal statement of the theory, see my *The Truth of Broken Symbols* (Albany: State University of New York Press, 1996). For an extended application of the theory, see my *Symbols of Jesus* (Cambridge: Cambridge University Press, 2001). That the theory guides an entire approach to theology, see my *On the Scope and Truth of Theology* (New York and London: T&T Clark, 2006).

5. Dewey's classic and most comprehensive text on this is *Experience and Nature* (LaSalle: Open Court, 1925); it is volume 1 of *John Dewey: The Later Works*, edited by Jo Ann Boydston (Carbondale: Southern Illinois University Press, 1981). But he wrote on this topic for nearly seventy years, and just about any of his books will give a version of his theory of experience as interaction or transaction.

6. A detailed exposition and defense of the theory of intentionality used in this chapter is found in my *Recovery of the Measure: Interpretation and Nature* (Albany: State University of New York Press, 1989), especially chapter 15.

7. This language has become complicated in philosophy since Kant because he used the medieval meaning of objective reality to say that this is the only reality we know; things in themselves, formal realities, were utterly irrelevant for Kant with regard to knowledge. In contrast to Kant, we can ask whether our objective realities are proper measures of their formal realities.

8. But see the discussions in part 1 of this volume.

9. *Collected Papers of Charles Sanders Peirce*, edited by Charles Hartshorne and Paul Weiss, volume 2, paragraph 228 (cited as CP 2.228) (Cambridge: Harvard University Press, 1932), italics in the original. Although I do not

follow Peirce's language exactly in this essay, the passage cited contains the main items in his semiotic analysis.

10. The generation of the tables of dimensions of religious experience comes not only from Peirce's semiotic theory, as modified by me, but also from his metaphysics within which it is embedded. Within that metaphysics, Peirce distinguishes between firstness, secondness, and thirdness, which are explained in more detail in the section on signs. Roughly, firstness refers to things as they are in themselves, secondness to things as in opposition to others, and thirdness to things that mediate between other things in certain respects. Using these categories analogically, the first element in a dimension is a First, the second is a Second, the third is a Third, and the Fourth represents what Peirce should have recognized as fourthness, the togetherness of the first three categories. So, there is more system in these tables of dimensions of religious experience than is apparent on the surface.

11. Pahnke was a Harvard graduate student and the experiment was part of his dissertation, directed by Timothy Leary and Richard Alpert; Huston Smith, then of MIT, took part in the experiment.

12. Buddhism is a tricky case here, because its Madhyamika forms especially do not make ontological reality assertions. But they do assert universal ultimate conditions of the cosmos—all is suffering, the universality of attachment, and so on.

13. This is the argument of my *On the Scope and Truth of Theology*.

14. For further analyses of network meaning for religious signs, see my *The Tao and the Daimon* (Albany: State University of New York Press, 1982), chapter 11, *Recovery of the Measure*, chapters 13–14, and *The Truth of Broken Symbols*, chapter 3.

15. For a detailed defense of the causal theory of interpretation, see my *Reconstruction of Thinking* (Albany: State University of New York Press, 1981), chapters 5–8.

16. I argue for supplementing Peirce's three categories with fourthness in "Intuition," *International Philosophical Quarterly* 7 (December 1967), 556–590, reprinted in my *Realism in Religion* (Albany: State University of New York Press, 2009) as chapter 8.

17. Paul Tillich, *Systematic Theology* (Chicago: University of Chicago Press, 1951), part 2.

Chapter 7

HERMENEUTIC AND VALIDITY DIMENSIONS OF RELIGIOUS EXPERIENCE

HERMENEUTIC DIMENSIONS: REFERENCE

Reference is the mode in which signs are taken within an interpretation to stand for their objects. The mode of reference is determined in part by the kind of signs involved, by the context of interpretation, by the intentionality underlying the interpretation, and by the kind of logical object engaged. Reference can be of three kinds, according to Peirce: iconic, indexical, and conventional (Peirce called the last "symbolic"). To Peirce's three we need to add a fourth kind of reference, secondary self-reference. A given interpretation can have one, two, three, or all four modes of reference, although often one is of greatest importance.

Iconic reference. Iconic reference takes the object to be *like* the sign. The most obvious iconic reference is when the sign stands in a one-to-one mapping relation to the object in some respect. A road map is an icon of a territory with respect to roads; a topographical map is an icon of the territory with respect to topographical features. One understanding of scientific explanation is that the mathematically expressed scientific theory is taken to be iconic of its subject matter; if the theory is understood to be iconic only in a certain respect, it is reductive (to that respect) but not viciously so; the scientific theory is viciously reductive if it assumes that it is iconic in all respects (for instance, assuming that, because value does not show up in mathematical relations, the object of the theory is value free).

Descriptions of any sort are iconic, even when they use metaphors. Narratives are among the most important religious signs, and their reference is perhaps iconic but always metaphorical. This is to say, a narrative selects certain elements in an indefinitely complex series of events to create a story line that has a narrative unity. All the other things going on in the events are left out. Those other things perhaps play roles in other narratives. But then again, perhaps no narrative could give them their rightful place regarding what is important. For instance, narratives generally lie when they tell the story from the standpoint of the protagonists, being very reductive and dismissive of the antagonists. But even a story told from both standpoints leaves out the issue, mainly of suffering, that ordinary people go through in a narrative of conflict. How many biblical narratives pick up on the effects of human affairs on the environment? Almost none. But the narratives become partially free-standing metaphors for defining the people who make those stories their stories. The story of the Exodus aims on the one hand to be iconic about the development of a special relation between God and Israel. But it has become a metaphor for Jews ever since for what it means to be a Jew standing before God. Metaphysics attempts to be as literally iconic as possible, and it is often not satisfying to an ingroup approach to religion because it insists on being indifferently related to all that might fall under it.

Indexical reference. Indexical reference modifies or establishes a causal connection between the object and the interpreter so that the object can be engaged in some respect. Literally, a pointing finger (index finger) causes the interpreter to turn to look at something otherwise not noticed. Often descriptions point out things otherwise not noticed, so that in each interpretation both iconic and indexical modes of reference are involved. It is also often the case that reference is indexical without much or any iconic reference, as in pointing, surprises, double entendre, and so forth. This latter is especially common with regard to religious symbols that, though highly descriptive, sometimes in phantasmagorical ways, are not really iconic at all but are intended to cause the interpreter to change so as to be able to pick up on something ultimate. The Hindu image of Kali, the heavyweight goddess wielding swords and wearing a belt of skulls, is not intended to *describe* a real deity but rather to be an object of meditation the purpose of which is to scare away our clinging. Peirce's example of *iconic* reference was that of a cross in a church referring to the cross on which Jesus was executed; there is an iconic similarity of shape. Religiously, however, the important mode of reference in the cross is not to an instrument of execution but rather, indexically, to transforming the Christian into someone who understands suffering, guilt, mercy, atonement, and love, which might come about through a long period of meditation on the cross.

In traditional religions there are many signs or symbols that require long years of meditation to understand, signs that are repeatedly used in rituals because they need to transform the experiencer so as to be able to ascertain what the symbols are about.

Religious experience, in contrast to many other domains of experience, is rarely about merely getting new information. Rather it concerns finding ways of positioning people in appropriate fashion with regard to what is ultimate. That means usually that people need to be developed, transformed, so as to be able to defer to ultimate matters correctly. So the indexical character of reference in religious experience is often if not nearly always more important than the iconic elements of reference.

Because interpretive engagement is a causal relation between the object engaged and the experiencer, indexical reference must be involved somewhere in the engagement, either directly in the interpretation at hand or indirectly through connections between this interpretation and others that are directly indexical. Naive realism is not a good way to understand the causal relation between the ultimacy in religiously experienced objects and the experience. Tracing out the complications of the indexical reference system, through all the turns of the hermeneutic dimensions, is the better way.

Conventional reference. Conventional reference is between a sign in a semiotic system and another sign in that system that functions as the logical object of an interpretation that is itself yet a third sign (or complex set of signs—Peirce's interpretant) within that system. By itself, conventional reference is strictly extensional. Of course, conventional reference is hardly ever "by itself." Most experiences, perhaps especially religious ones, refer in conventional, indexical, and iconic ways at once. Any reference we can talk about is at least conventional. Peirce (as quoted earlier) labeled the signs involved within a semiotic system in conventional reference (which he called symbolic reference) as the "object," "sign," and "interpretant." The interpretant is a sign taking the "sign" to stand for the "object" (another sign) in a certain respect.

Through conventional reference, we can connect iconic and indexical interpretive references in present circumstances with other such references far distant. An experiencer with a conventional road map can figure out, on the basis of the conventional references, how to get from a present location to a distant destination. An experiencer with a conventional understanding of a network of religious symbols would know that engaging God as the "rock of salvation" does not entail the study of geology. Precisely because religions have worldviews, most abstractly expressed in their sacred canopy, it is possible for religious experience to move from one part of the "religious world" to another. Moving within the conventions of the extensional semiotic system is not by itself religious experience. But a genuine religious experience can interpretively engage a range of ultimate matters because of the connections within the conventions of the semiotic system. Most of the religious experiences in the synthetic intentional dimension involve making connections through the conventions of the system.

All language involves conventional reference. Hence, any interpretive engagement we can talk about at the very least has conventional reference. Also, we can talk, with conventional reference, about many things that do not involve engagement, as when interpretations are all merely extensional, not intentional. But conventional reference can also be involved in complex religious experiences that shape the conventions into an iconic map and lay down diverse indexical connections with the real objects intentionally engaged. Because of conventional reference, "a" religious experience need not be of an ultimate matter directly confronted but might be of diverse ultimate matters in different temporal, spatial, and spiritual locations.

Secondary self-reference. Secondary self-reference is when the character of the interpreter, irrespective of the purpose and context at hand, affects the readiness of the sign to interpret the object in a certain respect. For instance, stage of life makes a difference with regard to religious experience; a child might not be able to have the experience an adult can. The "state of the soul" might also make a difference; people who have been sexually abused by their father when they were children might never be able to experience God as a father, even though they know how their tradition uses that term and can distinguish the sense in which God is a father from the sense that their male parent is a father.

More dramatically, secondary self-reference might affect religious experience when the experience reveals something about the experiencer when referring in its primary ways to something ultimate: "O my God! I'm guilty!" "I've been blind all these years!"

All interpretive engagements change the experiencer because the experiencer takes in what is carried over from the object. In secondary self-reference, however, the way the engagement refers to the ultimate object involves, as well, a reference to the experiencer. The experiencer is not merely the interpreter but also part of the object of interpretation along with the elements of ultimacy. Perhaps no thinker has been more acute than Søren Kierkegaard to point out that every reference to the ultimate is also a reference to the referrer. Sometimes this is not important:

experiencing the Creator in a beautiful sunset can be merely a calming, settling, integrative experience of ultimate contingency in beauty. Other times, it is ferociously important: the sudden experience of the immensity of God immediately implicates the depravity of human beings (to paraphrase the beginning of Calvin's *Institutes*).

HERMENEUTIC DIMENSIONS: CONTEXT

All interpretive engagements are in some *context* or other. No interpretive engagement is a free-floating proposition. Every experience is contextual. Without understanding the context of interpretation, it is impossible to tell whether an interpretive engagement is true. The context in part determines what purposes and intentional stances are relevant to the engagement at hand. Contexts, like purposes, are innumerable. Moreover, one experience might take place in many significant contexts at once, for instance, a biological context, a cultural one, a context of power relations, a context of a particular historical moment. Yet there are four having to do with the character and significance of the *occurrence* of the experience that are especially important for a semiotic approach to religious experience: episodic, discursive, repetitive, and identity-formative contexts.

Episodic. An episodic context is bounded by a particular situation and a relatively short duration of time. Most of the time, what we mean by "a" religious experience is that its context is an episode, a happening. It might be an episode in a long career that gets some of its meaning from the rest of the story. St. Paul's Damascus Road experience was an episode in his larger story, but it was an isolated religious experience, different from the ones where he claimed to have been caught up in the heavens. The same was true concerning Moses's encounter with God in the burning bush. Some episodic contexts for religious experiences might have only loose connections with the rest of a person's life, being unexpected, and having few consequences save being remembered. Most religious experiences in episodic contexts, however, do have decisive consequences for the person's later life. Sometimes episodic religious experiences have intense, relatively homogeneous qualities; often they have the qualitative form of a brief narrative.

Repetitive. Repetitive contexts are those patterned by religious practice, such as liturgies and regular worship, prayer, the articulation of the year by a religious calendar, and the repetition of life stages in generations of people.

Part of the meaning of the experience comes precisely that its context is that of repetition. Repetition helps define its mode of reference. It also helps define the relevant semiotic systems within which the signs of the experience have meaning; this is to say, immature systems might be in play early in one's life, but mature ones come into play later. The repetition means that the religious experience at hand is also an experience of the growth of the religious experience. That the contexts are repetitive does not mean that the content of the religious experiences in them is repetitive. Hopefully, in fact, people grow and find new meaning through the repetition. Repetitive contexts are particularly important for the work of indexical religious symbols that require the transformation of soul in order to connect the experiencer with the religious object.

Discursive. A discursive context is of somewhat long duration and involves an internal development of interpretation, like the context of listening to a symphony. But the discursive context might be much longer than that. Consider the religious experience of sophomore year: throw off parental religion, become an existentialist, then a skeptic, and finally a know-it-all (perhaps this experience is autobiographical and not universal). Although there are thousands of experiences during sophomore year, and perhaps a great many religious ones of various sorts, the year as a whole has a unifying developmental quality, something of a narrative, that itself can be a sign for engaging something ultimate. In the long run, of course, a person's whole life is a sign by which that person engages the ultimate: in Christian terms, that is the meaning of standing in ultimate judgment. Or consider the more limited religious experience of growing up in a church, raising one's family in the church, growing old, surviving one's spouse as a single person in church, and finally dying and being put to rest in the churchyard. There is a unity to religious experience (the interpretive engagement of ultimacy) in this sense that needs to be recognized. Such discursive contexts for religious experience are often lost sight of when the paradigms of religious experience are limited to the episodic or repetitive experiential contexts.

Identity formative. Identity-formative contexts are those in which the experience is significant for forming an individual's or group's identity. Not all episodic, discursive, or repetitive experiences are significant for identity formation, although all important religious experience might have consequences for personal or group identity. But many do. Identity-formative contexts are transformative, perhaps even contexts for conversions. Experiencing God one more time in a beautiful sunset (think of Kant's "sublime") might add to or solidify one's identity. But it is not in an identity-formative context unless it evokes a significant change in the person's identity. This might happen, of course. A person in deep despair about life, caught in a vortex of narcissistic self-absorption, might be blown loose from this by the experience of God in a beautiful sunset, becoming a humbler, more grateful, and happy person because of it.

Contexts for experiences can be nested so that an episodic experience can also be an item in a larger discursive experience, which can also be repeated, all of which contribute to identity formation. There need not be any single context within which an interpretive engagement takes place. But all of the contexts that obtain help determine purposes, which help determine the respects in which the object is interpreted and the modes of reference with which the interpretation is made. When applied to religious experience, this nesting of contexts illustrates just how complex a religious experience can be, and how complex our analysis needs to be if we are to understand it as an interpretive engagement of some aspect of ultimacy.

The complex discussion of the hermeneutic dimensions of religious experience can be illustrated by Paul's (Saul's) famous (in Christianity) experience of the Risen Christ on the road to Damascus. As described in Acts 9, it goes:

> Now as he was going along and approaching Damascus, suddenly a light from heaven flashed around him. He fell to the ground and heard a voice saying to him, "Saul, Saul, why do you persecute me?" He asked, "Who are you, Lord?" The reply came, "I am Jesus, whom you are persecuting. But get up and enter the city, and you will be told what you are to do." The men who were traveling with him stood speechless because they heard the voice but saw no one. Saul got up from the ground, and though his eyes were open, he could see nothing; so they led him by the hand and brought him into Damascus. For three days he was without sight, and neither ate nor drank. (Acts 9:3–9)

Previously, Saul had been a kind of prosecuting attorney attacking Christians; after the experience, he sought out Christians for instruction and became a great Christian preacher and thinker. In the next chapter of Acts, the disciple Barnabas told others that in Paul's meeting with the risen Jesus on the road, he had seen (as well as heard) him.

With regard to the hermeneutical dimensions of intentionality, Paul had to have in his imaginative repertoire signs of heavenly voices and visions with which to interpret the experience of God; most of us twenty-first-century people can imagine heavenly encounters but do not have them within the intentional frame for interpreting God. The experience was assertive in that Jesus confronted Paul and Paul took that confrontation to be veridical. The experience was not synthetic in itself in a formal theological sense, although Paul took the next several years to work out its systematic theological significance. But it was synthetic in that it brought the whole of Paul's life into a new relation with the Christian movement. The intentional purpose obviously determined Paul's responses, causing him to shift from persecuting to defending the way of Jesus.

With regard to the dimensions of signs, the qualities in the experience seem to be a kind of sensory overload: a light that blinds, a voice that even his companions could hear but only Paul could understand. The quality also was decisive: a confrontation of two life plans posed by a supposedly dead man. If Paul had heard or seen Jesus before the crucifixion, he might have added the quality of recognition to the experience. The experiential signs connected Paul to God in a kind of literal way, if you understand Jesus to be divine in some sense, and it was this engagement with Jesus's ultimacy that transformed what before might have been only Paul's interest in defending his own style of Judaism against Jesus's. Paul's understanding of Jesus, and the Lordship of the confrontational voice, came from the semiotic systems involved in that style of Judaism; Paul was a well-educated Hellenistic Jew, and he came quickly to interpret the significance of Jesus in terms of Greek philosophy as well as traditional Judaism.

With respect to the dimensions of reference, the voice and perhaps the visage of Jesus were iconic of Jesus, in Paul's experience. The dramatic occurrence of the experience was definitely indexical for Paul, reorienting him from his personal religious project of purifying Judaism to being able to take in something about God (in Christ) to which he was blind before. The experience involved many conventional connections that affected the way Paul related to his previous Judaism and suddenly to his new acknowledgment of Jesus as Lord. And there was a powerful secondary self-reference in the fact that Paul encountered not only Jesus but also himself as a persecutor of God, when he had thought he had been God's agent.

With regard to the dimensions of context, Paul's experience was episodic and not repetitive. That particular experience was an episode in the much larger discursive experience of Paul's relation to God, first as an unwitting persecutor and then as a devoted follower. The experience occurred also in an identity-formative context, symbolized by the change of name from Saul to Paul.

If we ask, in what sense was Paul's experience a religious experience, all these dimensions need to be discussed in answer. A religious experience is an actual interpretive engagement with some aspect of ultimacy. The dimensions analyzed here can be found in experiences that are not religious. Nevertheless, the dimensions together constitute the hermeneutic of religious experience, and when coupled with connections to ultimacy and analyses of the consequences of the experiences in the lives of the experiencers, allow us to raise questions of the validity of religious experiences. Table 7.1 shows the hermeneutic dimensions of religious experience of reference and context; compare this table with table 6.3.

TABLE 7.1 Hermeneutic Dimensions of Religious Experience

DIMENSIONS OF REFERENCE	DIMENSIONS OF CONTEXT
Iconic	*Episodic*
Indexical	*Repetitive*
Conventional	*Discursive*
Secondary Self-reference	*Identity Formation*

VALIDITY DIMENSIONS

Truth is a very complicated question, and the previous discussion has issued many promissory notes about the topic. In general, truth, on the causal theory of experience as interpretive engagement, consists in the character of the object being carried over into the experiencer in the ways mediated by the interpretation.[1] Philosophers have long debated about the "character" that is carried over. Aristotle thought it was the form of the object that is carried over by various kinds of "touch" into the mind. A good case can be made, however, that it is the value or importance of the object that is carried over into the experience of the interpreter. That value might have one form in the object and a very different form in the interpreter's experience. Roughly speaking, interpretive engagement, when it is true, picks up on what is important in the object relative to the purpose of the interpreter, in context, as expressible by signs in the interpreter's semiotic system.

An interpretive judgment says that the sign adequately refers to the object in the respect in which the sign stands for the object in the actual engagement. "My car is red" says that, with respect to color, red adequately represents my car. That is either true or false, a dyadic dichotomy. If my car indeed is red, and someone tells me "your car is silver," that interpretation is false. Truth versus falsity is not always clear-cut, however. The signs are dichotomous only to the extent that the semiotic system allows. Moreover, many signs are vague, meaning that they can be made more specific by contraries. For instance, crimson and scarlet are two specifications of red. If my car is crimson, it is not scarlet. To call it red is true if by red crimson is meant, and false if by red scarlet is meant.

Determining whether an interpretive engagement is true requires "triangulating" on the object and the experience to see whether the character of the object is carried across into the experience in the respect in which the interpreting sign refers to the object. To do this requires further interpretive engagement. Part of that further inquiry involves getting straight about the details of the semiotic system, the modes of reference involved, the kinds of purposes or intentionalities driving the selection of the respect or category of interpretation, and the nests of contexts; this analysis is hermeneutics. Another part involves independent access to the object and to the experience of the interpreter. Sometimes all of this is unproblematic. To test the judgment about my car's color, it is usually sufficient to look again, or ask an independent person to go to the parking lot and look. Often enough, however, testing interpretations in human experience is more complicated, involving deep hermeneutics about symbols, reference, intentionality, and context, as well as independent interpretive engagements by people who might not communicated with hermeneutical transparency. In religious matters, the truth question is complicated indeed because the hermeneutics of understanding the truth claim involves vast layers of religious symbolism, the idiosyncrasies of purpose and context, and self-referential aspects of reference that are hard to access. Moreover, the feedback from ultimate matters is rarely just a matter of looking again, or working with others to confirm experience; it might take a lifetime, or a community of spiritual adepts working for generations. The Christian tradition says that the long-range tests of the truth of religious interpretive engagements have to do with whether living according to the consequences of those engagements leads to peace, joy, love, and other virtues, but then, there might be many different causes that can lead to those virtues. Inquiry about the truth of interpretive engagements is what Peirce rightly called a "triadic" matter of more interpretations, making those interpretations vulnerable to correction, even when truth itself is a "dyadic" relation.

Truth is important in matters of religious experience. Suppose, for the sake of argument, that a religious tradition's semiotics have adequate ways of distinguishing signs of God as being loving and merciful, on the one hand, and wrathful and punitive, on the other, and that these are contraries. Some people experience God as loving and merciful, and others as wrathful and punitive (or the same person experiences God first one way and then the other). Suppose, for the sake of argument, that a hermeneutical analysis of the experiences shows that the disagreement about God is not a matter of confusing respects of interpretation; that is, the situation is not that God is loving and merciful in some respects and wrathful and punitive in others. Suppose also that there is no confusion over purposes and contexts, or modes of reference. Suppose that the experiences are real, that is, genuine engagements; some people really do experience God one way, and others the contrary way. Then, one or both sets of experiencers are mistaken. Yet enormous practical consequences for how to relate to ultimate things flow from experiences such as this, and relating to ultimate things affects how people relate to everything else.

From what has been said here about truth, it is apparent that there are *four dimensions of validity* regarding religious experiences: truth as such, vulnerability to correction, spiritual discernment, and proof in practice.

Truth and falsity. Insofar as a religious experience does in fact engage ultimacy and asserts something about what is experienced, it is either *true or false*. What it asserts is right or wrong. Of course, it can be too vague to be decisive, in which case the truth question cannot really be raised; the semiotic systems involved might not be able to give sufficient meaning to the signs employed. Perhaps it is the case that all experiences of ultimacy at a certain basic level are too vague to be decisive. Some mystics claim this. Nothing definite is asserted in this case, and the experience is "beyond" the question of truth. The ultimate as engaged is simply enjoyed, and that enjoyment might be so vast as to trivialize any truth question. The question of whether the experience genuinely engages something ultimate is a different question from that of whether the experience asserts something that can be true or false.

To understand what is involved in being true or false, when that is the issue, the experience has to be understood in terms of all the hermeneutical dimensions. This is what clarification requires. The assertive elements of the religious experience are true or false irrespective of whether we can determine whether they are true or false. Here lies one of the great ironies of religious experience. Because religious experience is so very consequential for both individuals and communities, their truth or falsity are extremely important. But because religious experience is so hermeneutically complex, and because getting feedback to support or modify the interpretive elements in the experience is so long term and often indirect, it is extremely difficult to judge the validity of religious experience. Religious people themselves, even the most devout, experience the ambiguities of their own experiences. The more sophisticated they are, the more practiced they are at the hermeneutics of suspicion.

Vulnerability to correction. The second dimension of validity regarding religious experiences is their vulnerability to correction. Experiences of color are easily vulnerable to correction because you can look again, or ask someone else. Religious experiences are so complicated that they often seem private and internal. In many religious experiences, a mere hermeneutical analysis sometimes can make the experience vulnerable to correction because there are often complications of inference and interpretation internal to the experience that can be straightened out. In cases like St. Paul's, the validity of his experience in some respects is vulnerable to correction by the transformation in his life and its subsequent effects. For most individuals, the validity of any one religious experience is made vulnerable in part by the accumulated force of the religious life. To understand whether a religious experience is "true" in its assertive interpretive elements, it is necessary to discover where it is vulnerable to correction. Those experiences that are most vulnerable to correction are likely to be truer, because they and their interpretations can be refined through corrective processes.

Spiritual discernment. For any given individual, however, spiritual discernment is required to test the places where the experience is vulnerable to correction. Spiritual discernment is something that most thinking people practice automatically, although they might not think of it in those terms. Spiritual discernment connects backward looking with forward looking. Spiritual discernment needs to understand how a religious experience is the result of a person's life, however novel it might seem, and life changing. Spiritual discernment needs to understand what might follow for one's life if a religious experience is truly what it seems. And then spiritual discernment needs to ask whether the experience and its surrounding interpretation cheats on giving perspective to the past and hope for the future. This is to say, spiritual discernment finds ways to ask whether the things experienced as ultimate really are so in the life of the experiencer. We all do this when we tell ourselves to "get real" with how we experience ultimate matters. Within traditional and new organized religions, people can go to spiritual directors for help with spiritual discernment, despite the fact the spiritual directors might be self-deceived or just incompetent.

Moreover, it helps to live in touch with a religious community of fellow spiritual discerners, people who from their own experience can help interpret the blind spots, blockages, and cheats of their fellows, despite the fact that religious communities can be ideological distorters of humble discernment.

As spiritual discernment advances, it makes more and more sense of accumulating religious experience. "Making sense" might mean coming to terms with experiences that disrupt one's entire view of ultimacy, rending the sacred canopy. "Making sense" might also mean coming to terms with experiences that just do not make sense in ordinary human ways. Some religious people say that God is wild, and that is beyond human understanding; this makes sense.

Practice. The long-range kind of making sense is whether *practiced* living according to the consequences of religious experiences makes sense of life in regard to ultimate matters. There are at least two aspects of this. On the one hand, is living with one's experiential view of ultimacy comprehensible? Even when one's experience is that the ultimate is mysterious and beyond fathoming, this gives rise to an appropriate humility in life before the ultimate, and a hardiness for living with ambiguities when sacred canopies flash in and out of intelligibility. On the other hand, does one's treatment of other people, oneself, one's society and culture, and the natural environment follow from one's experiences of ultimacy in such a way as to lead to appropriate recognition and deference? This is to ask, does one's cumulative religious experience concerning ultimacy lead in practice to realistic engagement with the rest of the world. Does it lead to respect where it is due, to love, justice, mercy, and the virtues that all the great religions advocate? If so, it makes sense of the non-ultimate in light of the ultimate. To experience oneself as engaging the non-ultimate in light of one's engagements of the ultimate is itself a religious experience. Table 7.2 shows the validity dimensions of experience.

TABLE 7.2 Validity Dimensions of Religious Experience

Truth or Falsity
Vulnerability to Correction
Spiritual Discernment
Practice

SUMMARY DIMENSIONS OF RELIGIOUS EXPERIENCE IN SEMIOTIC ANALYSIS

This and the previous chapter have sketched a classificatory scheme of dimensions of experience that apply to religious as well as other experiences. Religion experiences are always oriented intentionally to ultimacy, according to the theory here, and with this theory it is possible to say in various experiences just what is religious about them and what not. The classificatory scheme provides a checklist of dimensions of an alleged religious experience that can be analyzed. The various disciplines inquiring into religious experience can be understood as focused on some but not others of those dimensions, and the connections between the dimensions indicate some important parameters of collaborative investigation. Much further work is necessary to spell out these elements of collaboration, and of course it is never wise to say what some line of inquiry might be able to do. The classificatory scheme is summarized in table 7.3.

This and the previous two chapters have attempted to answer the question, what makes an experience a religious experience?

NOTES

1. I have defended this at great length in *Recovery of the Measure: Interpretation and Nature* (Albany: State University of New York Press, 1989).

TABLE 7.3 Summary Dimensions of Religious Experience

DIMENSIONS OF RELIGIOUS EXPERIENCE
Existential Dimensions
Hermeneutical Dimensions
Validity Dimensions

EXISTENTIAL DIMENSIONS OF RELIGIOUS EXPERIENCE
Intentionality
Objective Reality
Formal Reality
Causality

HERMENEUTIC DIMENSIONS OF RELIGIOUS EXPERIENCE			
DIMENSIONS OF INTENTIONALITY	DIMENSIONS OF SIGNS	DIMENSIONS OF REFERENCE	DIMENSIONS OF CONTEXT
Imagination	*Quality*	*Iconic*	*Episodic*
Assertion	*Decisiveness*	*Indexical*	*Repetitive*
Synthesis	*Connection*	*Conventional*	*Discursive*
Practice	*Semiotic Embeddedness*	*Secondary Self-reference*	*Identity Formation*

VALIDITY DIMENSIONS OF RELIGIOUS EXPERIENCE
Truth and Falsity
Vulnerability to Correction
Spiritual Discernment
Practice

Chapter 8

SELF-RELIANCE AND THE PORTABILITY OF PRAGMATISM

AMERICAN PHILOSOPHICAL EXCEPTIONALISM

Flush with the juices of adolescence, American philosophy declared independence from its European parentage in the work of Ralph Waldo Emerson and his generation. In 1837, Emerson addressed the Harvard Phi Beta Kappa on the occasion of its inaugural meeting for the year, which he called a "holiday." Emerson began:

> I greet you on the recommencement of our literary year. Our anniversary is one of hope, and, perhaps, not enough of labor. We do not meet for games of strength or skill, for the recitation of histories, tragedies, and odes, like the ancient Greeks; for parliaments of love and poesy, like the Troubadours; nor for the advancement of science, like our contemporaries in the British and European capitals. Thus far, our holiday has been simply a friendly sign of the survival of the love of letters amongst a people too busy to give letters any more. Perhaps the time is already come when it ought to be, and will be something else; when the sluggard intellect of this continent will look from under its iron lids and fill the postponed expectations of the world with something better than the expectations of mechanical skill. Our day of dependence, our long apprenticeship to the learning of other lands, draws to a close. The millions that around us are rushing into life, cannot always be fed on the sere remains of foreign harvests. Events, actions arise, that must be sung, that will sing themselves.[1]

Many will remember that Emerson proceeded to argue that for the arising of American genius, the "first in time and the first in importance of the influences upon the mind is that of nature."² After nature come the influences of the minds of the past, which is to say nature encountered through the experiences of others rather than directly. Emerson insisted on the danger of the influences of the minds of others, keeping them a distant second. In fact, he argued in many places that one cannot understand the minds of others in matters of encountering nature unless one first has a direct and original relation to the universe. Among the many implications he drew from this is the importance of distancing American philosophy from that of Europe until the Americans know their own mind. The third important and necessary influence, after the direct encounter with nature and the proper appropriation of the minds of the past, is learning from action. By action he meant the enormous energy of American business and agriculture in his time. He knew that Europeans believed such "action" to be the primary image Europeans had of America, all push and shove, no serious philosophy. He himself complained about the predominance of action in American culture, giving the American Scholar a "*love* of letters" when Americans were too "busy" to give letters more than love. Yet he knew that learning from action was a key influence needed for the flourishing of American philosophy. For all its adolescent rebellion and enthusiasm, Emerson's clarion call to self-reliance announced the themes that would mature in American philosophy to which I shall return shortly: nature, relating to the mind of the past from the present, and learning from action.

Before that, however, I want to point out that American philosophy also had a promising childhood. Jonathan Edwards, a century before Emerson, was surely a child of Europe who thought of himself as contributing to the European conversation quite directly, however far west in the colonies. From Edwards's many original contributions to that conversation let me signal three. First was his emphasis on relating to the world through what he called "dispositions," which later would be developed as the concept of habit. The importance of dispositions in Edwards was that it gave him a significant protection from the nominalism that was so rampant among those, such as John Locke, from whom he learned so much. Charles Peirce much later would claim, with only some exaggeration, that all of philosophy's major errors derived from nominalism and the basis of that criticism was Peirce's robust theory of habit.

Edwards's second main contribution was his theory that interpretations of religious matters, which he called "religious affections," can be assessed only by judging their consequences, a point later identified with the heart of pragmatism. Edwards said that the immediate feelings of religious judgments all could be counterfeited by the Devil and therefore could not be trusted. Those immediate feelings later would be analyzed by Peirce and others as the "material qualities" of signs, which are only one part of the reality of signs as triadic mediators between objects in nature, including God, and the interpreting subject. Today we find Edwards's respect for the projective epistemological powers of Satan to be quaint. But we have great respect for the powers of psychoactive drugs, neurological diseases and traumas, disorienting activities such as whirling in place or singing hypnotic music, and other interventions to cause intense feelings with religious content. We can understand Edwards's point to be that the immediate qualities of experience, no matter how vivid or persuasive, have no truth value unless they interpretively connect the person with the religious object in ways that can be checked up on by assessing transformed behavior. If a person's behavior is indeed transformed through powerful feelings to be more loving and godlike, then it does not matter where the signs in their material quality come from. Edwards's Calvinism was quick to insist that Satan unwittingly works for God. What matters is whether the signs in immediate experience genuinely carry across or mediate the divine realities so that the interpreter, through a host of dispositions, is disposed more correctly toward the divine.

Edwards's third major contribution to American philosophy was his emphasis on the aesthetic dimensions of experience as the development of dispositions. The aesthetic theme was as old as Plato and flourished in an interesting if diminished way in Calvin's theology. But Edwards provided an original analysis of beauty as involved with ontological dispositions to consent and harmony. For Edwards, things, including God, are themselves dispositions to other things, and those dispositions aim to delight in the harmonic beauty of those other things. Beauty is not just an immediate feeling but a way of acting. To appreciate the beauty of something is to appreciate its dispositions as harmonized, God being the paradigm. The theistic orientation of Edwards's philosophy of beauty lessened in discussions after his time, but the aesthetic theme was taken up by Emerson, and then by Peirce, James, and Dewey in the maturity of American philosophy.

Indeed, it was Peirce, James, and Dewey, in the generation after Emerson and continuing two centuries beyond Edwards, who brought American philosophy to its creative maturity. They were the ones who turned an emphasis on the first importance of the encounter with nature into a deep and complex naturalistic philosophy. They engaged the minds of the past European traditions in a massive critical and revolutionary transformation. And they lay the foundation, and perhaps even the first two or three floors, for the hall within which a global philosophical conversation might take place. The many varied ways in which pragmatism developed a naturalistic philosophy have been much discussed, especially by and among members of this society. I want to focus on the other two themes, how pragmatism appropriated and revolutionized the European tradition of philosophy, which might be of interest to our European colleagues, and how this in turn transformed the American interest in action and aesthetics into a language for engaging a global philosophy, particularly with East Asian thought.

TRANSCENDENTAL PHILOSOPHY

Despite its extraordinary diversity of positions and traditions, many of which do not communicate well with one another, European philosophy looks astonishingly monolithic from the standpoint of American philosophy. I include within European philosophy British empiricism as well as German idealism and its multitude of descendants in phenomenologies, existentialism, hermeneutical philosophies, and postmodernisms. The general name I would give to this monolithic look is "transcendental philosophy," a term that comes from Kant. His paradigmatic statement of the foundation and program of transcendental philosophy was in the preface to the second edition of the *Critique of Pure Reason*, which I quote at length to give a sense of its aggressive character:

> When Galileo caused balls, the weights of which he had himself previously determined, to roll down an inclined plane; when Torricelli made the air carry a weight which he had calculated beforehand to be equal to that of a definite volume of water; or in recent times, when Stahl changed metals into oxides, and oxides back into metal, by withdrawing something and then restoring it, a light broke upon all students of nature. They learned that reason has insight only into that which it produces after a plan of its own, and that it must not allow itself to be kept, as it were, in nature's leading-strings, but must itself show the way with principles of judgment based upon fixed laws, constraining nature to give answer to questions of reason's own determining. Accidental observations, made in obedience to no previously thought-out plan, can never be made to yield a necessary law, which alone reason is concerned to discover. Reason, holding

in one hand its principles, according to which alone concordant appearances can be admitted as equivalent to laws, and in the other hand the experiment which it has devised in conformity with these principles, must approach nature to be taught by it. It must not, however, do so in the character of a pupil who listens to everything that a teacher chooses to say, but of an appointed judge who compels the witnesses to answer questions which he has himself formulated.[3]

(I hope you note the humorous irony in Kant's third example of the triumph of experimental physics, namely Stahl's proof of the existence of phlogiston.) Kant's overall point is that nature is to be understood insofar as it conforms to the transcendental conditions of human subjectivity. This, of course, is his brilliant solution to the problem bequeathed by Descartes and his generation, including Locke, who distinguished nature described as body from mind and said we have immediate intuitive access only to mind. The problem was how to infer from mind intuitively known to nature outside of mind.

Kant's immediate target was David Hume who had argued that we cannot make that inference. For Hume, the immediately intuitive elements of mind are impressions and ideas. For his more recent successors in analytic philosophy, the immediately intuitive mental elements are language formal and informal, logic, and theories of possible worlds based on logical formalisms. For most analytic philosophy in the Humean tradition, philosophical argument consists in getting clear about things that can be understood intuitively, often by means of counterexamples, rarely if ever by interacting with the subject matter so as to learn to perceive and handle it with more discrimination. Although most descendants of Hume would not call themselves transcendental philosophers, a term Kant invented to oppose Hume, in fact they are attempting to study the mind in its intuitive "show" in order to find out about nature and usually think, as Kant did, that nature is known only through science, not philosophy. Philosophy of science, in that tradition, is about the nature and procedures of the scientific enterprise, not about philosophical cosmology.

Kant's own philosophy elaborated a complex structure of the transcendental conditions for the possibility of experience within which science can be practiced properly. Successor idealists such as Fichte and Schleiermacher developed aspects of this structure in various directions. Hegel rightly argued that to do the critique, Kant had to be beyond the transcendental conditions himself. But when Hegel developed his own theory of how the subjectivity of experience is transcended, the starting point is still the subject and the ending point is an objectified and resubjectified, or *Geistliche*, subject. In both continental and analytic philosophy, the subject matter is consciousness; experience is the inner experience of consciousness and its contents. Edmund Husserl defined the world as that which can be known through human experience and then distinguished between the natural standpoint of experiencing the world, which is how it appears to us and the transcendental standpoint by which philosophy analyzes consciousness without any commitment to the realities of things appearing in the world of experience. The hold of the transcendental suppositions about the primacy and ultimacy of human consciousness was so great that it never occurred to Husserl that the real world might have all sorts of things and dimensions to which human experience is simply inadequate now and about which we need to change experiential capabilities in order to learn. Continental hermeneutics, in many different ways, has taken its venue to be the interpretation of texts, or of subjectively appreciated cultures, so that hermeneutical progress is made by the fusion of horizons of differently structured consciousnesses. The pragmatic alternative is that hermeneutics has nature as its object about which it learns through experimental engagement, or experience in the American sense as distinguished from experience in British empiricism. Existentialism in its many forms, from Kierkegaard and Nietzsche to Heidegger and Sartre, remains within the transcendental subjective frame and supplements consciousness with subjective will, in some version or other, not with natural things about which we might achieve some consciousness. Marxism, of course, is a form of materialism in direct opposition to the subjectivity of consciousness Marx found in Hegel, but it is an inversion of Hegelian idealism that interprets the history of material culture as if it moved like a dialectic of concepts with assertion and opposition. Its materialism cannot be understood without its opposition to false consciousness. Its moral force comes from assuming the conscious or preconscious standpoint of the oppressed. Postmodernism pushes that point to the legitimation of the meaning structures of any group's consciousness as such without requiring, in fact by banning, the examination of the validity of those meaning structures.

Much modern science, as opposed to modern European philosophy, aims to be thoroughly materialistic as opposed to the materialism that has the form of the dialectic of concepts. In doing so, however, it cuts itself off from accounting for the obvious features of mind, such as intentionality, consciousness, purpose, and most importantly the critical judgments required to do science well. Only in the recent work of a few scientists such as Terrence Deacon, a Peircean pragmatist, is an effort being made to elaborate scientific materialism into an account that is fair to mind and to science's own suppositions.

I apologize, though halfheartedly, for the sweeping generalizations I have made about modern European philosophy. It is truly more complicated than represented in my account here, and it contains many movements in addition to those I have cited. In particular, the tradition of Scottish commonsense philosophy is not a transcendental philosophy in any real sense. But, to be fair, that is the only form of modern philosophy that Charles Peirce, the pragmatist, could cite as his own, in addition to his peculiar appropriation of Kant as nontranscendental. My remarks have been intended to show how European philosophy appears to American pragmatism, not how it really is in a sophisticated historical sense.

PUTTING NATURE FIRST

Now let me say why I think pragmatism sees European philosophy the way it does. The parts to this story are well known but perhaps not told the way I shall. Pragmatism, beginning with Peirce, took Emerson's advice and put nature first in the way of learning. But how could it do this, given the European heritage? Much has been written about the role of the frontier, the actual encounter of sophisticated, book-learned people with a natural environment that was relatively unworked by their own educated hands, though of course the Native Americans did modify their environments. In some sense, American nature did shock the European immigrants to a new awakening. But how could the American philosophers get there, starting with the European transcendental frame from which they came? Their European contemporaries have remained locked within the transcendental frame to this day, by and large.

The answer lies in the first works of brilliance of Charles Peirce, his 1868 essays, "Questions Concerning Certain Faculties Claimed for Man" and "Some Consequences of Four Incapacities." The arguments of those essays are well known and I shall not rehearse them more than I have. They conclude that there is no such thing as an "intuition" that is in "immediate relation to its object," which is how Kant had defined intuition. Every cognition is in a mediated relation to its object. Much of Peirce's life work was to show how this mediation is in the form of an interpretation, with signs being taken to stand for objects in a certain respect. Peirce's arguments against intuition were many and mostly dialectical, coming at the topic from different angles. But the conclusion was extraordinarily radical. Descartes had held that we have intuitive, that is immediate, knowledge of the mind and that true judgments can be drawn about this by the intuitive capacities of the light of reason or the light of nature. Descartes's own arguments had to show how intuition can be trusted even under the circumstance that we might be deceived by an evil genius when our reason is absolutely clear and distinct. The show of consciousness by itself is immediately given, and Husserl rang the final changes on the project of bracketing out all sources of erroneous inference so that the givenness of the intuitions stands true in their immediacy, and that project failed. There are no intuitions in immediate relation to their objects, or immediately being themselves. British empiricists such as Locke and Hume had argued that what the latter called impressions, and the ideas too, are immediately given, even if, in Hume's case, nothing can be inferred about what they are supposed to represent beyond them. No, showed Peirce; not even impressions and ideas are immediate intuitions. They are inferences.

Kant was far subtler than Descartes and Hume, arguing that appearances in experience are constructs of both immediate sensible intuitions and constructive imagination; perhaps this was the point that inspired Peirce's admiration for Kant, even though he rejected the entire transcendental status of Kant's view of experience. But for Kant, all the constructed appearances are functions of subjective representations. The representations within appearances are mediated to one another by the transcendental structure of mind. But they are not mediated to the real world. As Kant put it, the world as constructed subjective experience is empirically real but transcendentally ideal. That is, empirical reality in the sense known by science, is an ordering of subjective representations by objective rules learned through experiments answering to the strictures of the transcendental categories of mind, as Kant argued in the Second Analogy. Its empirical objectivity consists precisely in not referring to transcendent things in themselves, about which we can have only ideas and no knowledge. Transcendental ideality is cognition that cannot determine real things. In this sense, for Kant the entire realm of experience is immediate in its subjectivity relative to things in themselves, that is, cut off from any relation to them. To exist, for Kant, is to occupy a moment in inner sense and perhaps a place in outer sense. The sensibility, that is, inner and outer sense, is Kant's version of consciousness, mediated by the imagination with the use of categories in the complex ways he described. Peirce's argument proved there can be no such thing as an inner and outer sense of Kant's sort. That is a devastating conclusion.

Put another way, Peirce demonstrated that there is no such thing as consciousness in the sense of mental immediacy. Rather, consciousness itself is a consequences of inferences that come from interacting with the things supposedly represented in consciousness, that is, interactions with nature. This seemed almost impossible to comprehend from within the prejudices, in the Heideggerian sense of prejudice, of the European transcendental frame. What could be more obvious than the immediacy of consciousness, say, the visual field? The most powerful of Peirce's arguments in those early papers was his experiment with the coins. Put two coins, he said, on a sheet of white paper, close your left eye, stare at one coin with the right eye and slowly move the other coin up and to the right. The right coin will suddenly disappear when it gets to the visual point where the optic nerve enters the eye and there are no rods and cones to pick it up. That "blind spot" is present in all of our visual experiences, except that we automatically infer what would fill in that spot. Most of us never are aware of those inferences. We evolved with an automatic Photoshop airbrush function, and it is a shock to realize that our visual field is not an immediate determinate whole but a tissue of inferences. The same is true of all dimensions of consciousness. Nothing is immediately given. Everything is mediately taken up. Thus, the entire European philosophical suppositions about experience being contained within consciousness is mistaken, and this is why the pragmatists see all those different strategies for coping with the given and attempting to leap beyond consciousness to the world, or to define the world as what fits with actual or potential consciousness, as simply a dead end. It is hard for American pragmatists to get interested in phenomenology of the European sort, or hermeneutics, or postmodern studies of meaning, or most forms of analytic philosophy, when they blindly cannot get beyond the prison house of conscious immediacy.

THE PRAGMATIC MODEL

If the human situation is not to be bound by transcendental consciousness, what is the philosophical alternative? Here is where the positive contribution of pragmatism must arise. If experience is not based on the immediacy of consciousness but is instead a tissue of inferences, what does this involve? The pragmatists in their diverse ways argued that experience is the interaction of human beings with their environment. That interaction is the direct and primary engagement of nature. In fact, human beings are parts of nature, parts that have evolved to have the inferential capacities that give rise to what we experience. Consciousness is part of experience, but it waxes and wanes and in the long run is not very important for the pragmatists. Here pragmatism has a fundamentally new model, that of organism in the environment, to use Dewey's phrase, that stands alongside as an alternative to the European model of the transcendental frame. That model is so deeply and subtly different that it cannot be comprehended by those in the thrall of the transcendental model based on the immediacy of consciousness, just as the European model is hard now for the pragmatists and their heirs to take seriously.

The pragmatic account of its model is complex and diverse in the ways it has been elaborated. For Peirce, who thought of himself as a logician, the model required an account of inferences that took the form of a causal interpretive interaction with real things, that is, with nature. The object of an interpretation is not a representation of a real thing but is the thing itself. Of course, any real thing to be interpreted is also a mediated reality, determinate because it has a nature connecting it with other things. Peirce's own cosmology construed natural causation to have the form of an effect being the interpretation of a cause by means of a general law functioning as a sign. With regard to the human interpretation of the world, Peirce's early conclusion, worked out over his lifetime, was that it is all fallible. This is to say, all interpretations are hypotheses. The hypotheses might be so steady and reinforced over time that we take them for granted, as we generally trust our visual experience. But something might come up that causes us to question the hypotheses; even Descartes noticed that a straight stick looks bent when half submerged in water and developed an optical theory to explain this, that is, a more general hypothesis that the commonsense one. In philosophy, Peirce said, we deliberately look for ways to question our basic hypotheses. Metaphysics, for him, was the development of the most general hypotheses for the most basic structures and values of existence. All of these hypotheses are fallible. Peirce's enthusiastic nineteenth-century hope was that the community of investigators in the infinite long run would test all the possible ways in which the hypotheses might be mistaken, and the truth would be the last hypotheses that remain standing.

Kant argued against the metaphysical use of hypothesis in the Dialectic of Pure Reason at the end of the first *Critique*. He said that you could never say what counts as evidence for or against the truth of an hypothesis unless you already had a transcendental account of what the world is. Peirce answered, No, you only need a good hypothesis about what the world is relative to a given hypothesis. Whereas European philosophy manifesting the transcendental stance now assumes that metaphysics is impossible because it cannot be carried out within that stance with the certainty that comes with foundational work, American philosophy assumes that metaphysics is not only possible but thriving as the development of hypotheses of the most general range, with a by now long conversation about the pros and cons of various hypotheses. Whitehead's process philosophy is at the center of this discussion, although the pragmatists had their own alternatives. When postmodern philosophers dismiss metaphysics as logocentric and colonialist and attempt to delegitimate those who engage in metaphysical philosophy, this seems simply ignorant as well as arrogant to the pragmatic tradition.

One more element of the pragmatic engagement of nature through hypotheses needs to be mentioned at this point, namely, the role of purpose. For Peirce, all interpretive interactions with things are guided by human purposes, some evolved into our instinctual bones and others tending toward conscious awareness. Purpose is needed to select the respects in which things are to be interpreted.

William James was different from Peirce in many ways, not only in temperament. In his radical empiricism, with Peirce he stoutly rejected the transcendental stance for consciousness. Rather, the stuff of experience is just there and requires the intervention of purpose to sort it into the experiential career of an individual, the person's personal or subjective experience. It also can be sorted, according to other purposes, into the enduring or changing things of the world rather than any personal form for an experiencer. In fact, the neutral stuff of the experience can be sorted in many different ways, but it is important to see what it is first. Do not assume, James said, that experience must be privileged with the forms of personal subjectivity. Nor should we assume that experience has to be privileged with the theories of scientific materialism. Look for the real connections that are there. James was especially important for his observation that certain things cannot be experienced without taking on strong purposive stances, for instance, toward the reality of God or the worthwhileness of life. It is not that those things are not real; it is that they cannot be engaged without certain vigorous, willful, and fallible approaches to life.

John Dewey learned from both Peirce and James and thematically rejected all the dualisms he saw inherent in the European history of modern philosophy in what I have called its transcendental stance. Most dualisms attacked by Dewey, and he attacked as many as he could find, express the mind-body dualism that pushed philosophy into the mind alone and left science with material bodies and mindless self-accountability. Dewey's masterwork, *Experience and Nature*, was titled to reflect his basic hypothesis that experience could be interpreted either in terms of the natural world or in terms of human intentionality toward the natural, and social, world. Experience for Dewey is neither nature without intentionality nor intentionality without nature, but both.

A crucial lesson for all the early pragmatists and their heirs has been that when we assume the naturalistic stance of organisms engaging their environments, we discover that those engagements always have valuational aspects. Some of the valuational aspects are functions of the purposes that the interpreters bring. But others are the values in things that accommodate or afford being engaged with those purposes. In the long run, it is the values in things that are crucial even for the evolution of interpreters with purposes. For Peirce, the most important question is what purposes are worth having, and that question is to be answered by studying the world. The exception to this is the kind of interpretation that goes on in modern science that so strictly, methodologically, and metaphysically separates facts, which are knowable, from values, which are merely projections that can be avoided in careful objective science. All the pragmatists were enthusiastic about science but highly critical of its separation of fact from value. Philosophical inquiry, as opposed to strictly scientific inquiry, needs to be open to recognizing and giving accounts for the value elements experienced in the world. For Dewey, experience is an art. We learn to experience by learning to perceive better and better the valuational elements in the world. Dewey sometimes called his philosophy of science "instrumentalism," not because science is merely for the sake of accomplishing human technical purposes, but because it is the revelation of what is valuable in reality.

With regard to religious experience, the transcendental traditions cannot comprehend easily the pragmatic claim that ultimate realities can be engaged. The previous chapters in this part have spelled out how ultimacy can in fact be engaged, sometimes truthfully. But it is difficult to make this persuasive to the dominant forms of European philosophy of religion.

NOTES

1. "The American Scholar," in *Selected Writings of Emerson*, edited by Brooks Atkinson (New York: The Modern Library, 1940), 45.
2. Ibid., 47.
3. Immanuel Kant, *Critique of Pure Reason*, translated by Norman Kemp Smith (London: Macmillan, 1956), 20, B xii–xiii.

Part III

RELIGIOUS STUDIES

PRELIMINARY REMARKS

The chapters in the first two parts of this volume have been oriented to developing my own definition of religion and the theory of religion that goes with it, including a theory of religious experience. Those chapters have been extensively rewritten from the essays or addresses with which they began. The chapters in this part, as well as the next two parts, are more lightly rewritten. They read much more like independent essays.

The topics addressed in this part concern ways to study religion. Chapter 9 is a defense of comparative theology. Chapter 10 defends my reliance on philosophy in the study of religion and reviews some of the philosophical aspects of the theory of religion developed in this volume. Chapter 11 is a philosopher's analysis of what liberal theology ought to do in the current situation; more than other chapters in this volume, it addresses primarily Christian theology. Chapter 12 is a playful but very serious discussion of the contours of religious naturalism, a "liberal theology" not restricted to Christian theology. It defends my own religious naturalism as hospitable to the truth of religious symbolism that, if taken non-symbolically, can be supernaturalistic.

Chapter 9

WHY ALL THEOLOGY SHOULD BE COMPARATIVE

All serious theology should take place in and arise out of a solid grounding in the comparison of religious ideas. This is my hypothesis. Too many people believe that theology should be the reflection of religious ideas from the standpoint of a religious tradition by itself, exclusively in its own terms. For instance, many Christian theologians, influenced by Karl Barth, think that theology is a reading of the Christian word of God on its own terms without any serious mention of Jewish, Buddhist, Daoist, or Muslim theology. Sometimes this kind of theology is called "confessional" because it takes its rise from some theological starting point to which it confesses allegiance and then derives what follows from that. While confessional theology can be helpful for the fulsome expression of the implications of the theological starting point, it runs the grave danger of abandoning theology for intellectual sociology. "This is what Christians believe" is a sociological statement. It differs from a related theological statement, "this is what Christians believe and for good reason." Christian theology ought to say, "this is what is true, and therefore Christians should believe it."

The nature of theological truth is an enormously complicated topic, and here I am going to address only a small part of it. Theological truths are not to be understood merely as propositions offered for religious belief. They arise out of long traditions of experience, traditions that have debated formulations and used beliefs to guide religious life, giving rise to new experiences. The traditions reflect back on symbols having to do with their founding, and they look forward to offering guidance to new situations of religious life. The symbols in theology are on many different levels, some more abstract, others more concrete; these levels are hard to sort. My thesis is that theological reflection should take place within a public in which different religious traditions, with their symbols, their histories, their experiences, and their practices, compete for attention. Indeed, there are important senses in which the symbols and theological traditions of any one religion cannot be understood without seeing how they are similar to and different from other religions. Max Mueller is famous for saying that to understand only one religion is to understand none.

This general thesis is not helpful without a more precise notion of what comparative theology is. Therefore, the hard work of my remarks is in the spelling out of a logic of comparison. Only then can we see its value in any detail.

My purpose here is to articulate a particular conception of comparative theology as a mode of inquiry. Of course, there are many other modes of theological inquiry, and in fact there are many other very worthy conceptions and methods of comparative theology.[1] Here I mean to articulate one approach and advocate its virtues.

A LOGIC OF COMPARISON

Things can be compared only in some respect or other. Complex comparisons compare things in several respects, perhaps. Even when comparison takes mainly the form of juxtaposition, studying two texts side by side, for instance, comparison supposes that the texts represent their objects in some respect. A preliminary aspect of comparison is to determine what those respects are and whether they are the same for all the texts compared. Only when texts represent their objects in the same respects can it be determined how they agree or disagree in what they say.[2] Comparison fails when there is no respect in which the things compared are connected. For instance, some people have tried to compare the notion of emptiness in Buddhism with that in Paul's letter to the Philippians where he speaks of *kenosis*, usually translated "emptiness." But emptiness in Buddhism has to do with the inappropriateness of things to be objects of ego-driven attachments, whereas emptiness in Paul has to do with Jesus as divine, emptying or humbling himself to the status of a slave. Not only is emptiness an equivocal term in this putative comparison, it does not interpret reality in the same respect—it is about different issues in the two religions.[3]

The respect in which things are compared functions as a comparative category. So, for instance, theologies can be compared with respect to what they say about the human condition, or about ultimate realities, or about the nature of religious truth. The human condition, ultimate realities, and religious truth are the comparative categories in these instances. Each of them can be broken down into subcategories, which in turn might have interesting and relevant subcategories. Aaron Stalnaker has shown how complicated the task is to sort out just what respects of interpretation connect differing interpretations. He calls these "bridge concepts."[4]

1. The first logical step in comparison is to identify a comparative category. A comparative category needs to be logically vague with respect to what might fall under it or specify it. Logical vagueness, a concept first analyzed for comparative purposes by Charles S. Peirce, means that the category can tolerate mutually incompatible instantiations.[5] The law of noncontradiction does not apply to what falls under it. For instance, the comparative category "God" can be instantiated by highly personal and anthropomorphic conceptions, by Thomas Aquinas's pure and simple Act of Esse, as well as by Paul Tillich's conception of the Ground of Being. Each of these contradicts something important in the others and yet they all fall under the category of conceptions of God. The category "God" is properly comparative if it allows each of these, and other theistic theories, to register themselves as proper and nonprejudiced conceptions of God.

Suppose, as we know to be the case, that these three conceptions of God are interesting because they purport to be about what is ultimate. Some religions conceive gods to be merely higher-than-human creatures, themselves subordinate to what is ultimate; popular forms of Buddhism, Daoism, and Confucianism hold this about gods. But those other religions also have conceptions of what they take to be ultimate, for instance, Emptiness or Buddha-mind, the Dao, Heaven and Earth, Principle, and so forth. While it is possible, therefore, to compare just those conceptions of "God" that aim at ultimacy, more to the point is to develop a comparative category of ultimacy that would allow for the vague specification of Buddhism, Daoism, Confucianism, and the rest. A comparative theology project might begin by intending to compare conceptions of God, but then consciously amend its comparative category to something like ultimacy, in order to embrace in a vague and fair way the nontheistic theological conceptions of ultimacy.

But even this comparative category is unstable. Madhyamika Buddhism contends that concern for any ontological ultimate reality is itself a misstep. Concern for ontological realities is the root of attachment, it says, and an important cure for attachment is coming to think of all ontological realities as empty and unreal. What is truly ultimate, says Madhyamika

Buddhism, is the quest for release from suffering. That quest is a kind of anthropological ultimate, to be distinguished from an ontological ultimate. So the comparative category needs to be modified again to be something like "ultimate realities," where that is understood to embrace both ontological and anthropological ultimates.[6]

Now the comparative category is becoming vague and subtle enough to register theologies of the ultimate such as that of Paul Tillich, who uses "ultimate concern," an anthropological ultimate, to identify, sort, and assess dialectically candidates for the ontological ultimate, which he calls the Ground of Being.[7] Probably most personal theists, and Thomas Aquinas, as well as Buddhists, Daoists, Hindus, and Confucians, also would conceive of their ultimates in some dialectical combination of ontological and anthropological reflections. So the amended comparative category, ultimate realities, has become much richer, subtler, and vaguely tolerant of diverse ways in which theologies can specify it.

The moral of this discussion of comparative categories is that they should remain under revision and amendment all through the comparative process. As attempts to specify them reveal biases, or lacunae, the comparative categories need to be revised to be fair and inclusive.

2. The *specification* of the comparative categories is the second step in comparison, bearing in mind that the comparative categories themselves are fluid. Specification means determining what the theologies under comparison each say about the comparative category. How is ultimacy conceived by a notion of a personal God, or the Act of Esse, or the Ground of Being, or the Dao, Brahman, Emptiness, Heaven and Earth, ultimate concern, or the quest for release from suffering? Each notion needs to be specified in terms of what it says about ultimate realities or ultimacy.

Moreover, each theology to be compared with respect to ultimacy needs to be able to register itself without bias or distortion within the comparative category of ultimacy. If the category of ultimacy is framed by a preconscious bias toward monotheism, then Hindu notions of ultimacy, as well as Daoist and Confucian notions, will look like immature or confused conceptions. The comparative category, as I've said, needs to be in constant revision to be fair.

But how do you tell when the category is biased? It would be unempirical to assume that all the theologies are equally right and not confused. Therefore, special care must be taken to let the theologies under comparison speak for themselves when expressed as specifications of the comparative category. I recommend a checklist of five procedures for promoting fairness of specification, which can be called "sites of phenomenological analysis."[8] First, a theology needs to be expressed in its own terms and words as a specification of the category, an intrinsic expression. Second, the theology's own perspective on the world needs to be expressed, including how it sees the other theologies. Third, a conceptual analysis of the theology in theoretical terms, not perhaps its native terms, needs to be given as a specification. Fourth, the practical implications of the theology need to be drawn out to express its identity. Finally, the elements in a theology that are singular and incommensurate with terms that might allow of comparison need to be indicated, expressing the limits of potential comparison. Being scrupulous about these five phenomenological sites of analysis cannot guarantee lack of distortion and bias. Nevertheless, they provide a procedure for making any given specification of the comparative category by a theology vulnerable for correction.

When all the theologies one wants to compare with respect to their conceptions of ultimacy have been articulated as specifications of ultimacy, the vague comparative category has been filled in as containing all the variant theologies. The comparative category is no longer only vague but also specific, containing what might be contradictions. The comparative category thus has two faces: on the one hand, it is vague and empty, ready to tolerate all the theologies to be compared in its respect; on the other hand, it is specific and full, containing all the theologies as specified, with the various specifications being internally complex so as to embody all the sites of phenomenological analysis.

3. The third step in comparison is then to analyze the rich comparative category to see just how the theologies agree, disagree, overlap, lift up different subcategories for comparison, differ in perspectives on the world, imply different practical consequences, and so forth. This is to say, comparisons need to be formulated and tested. Because the language of ultimacy, now very rich, is complex but univocal, it is possible to state just how the different theologies stand with respect to one another on the question of ultimacy. Actual comparisons need to be expressed as hypotheses to be tested by reviewing the enriched category of ultimacy. This is by no means an easy task. Comparisons of complex material are not obvious, although some hypotheses might leap out as obvious. Rather, the comparative judgments need to be tested as hypotheses for describing comparative relations.

The upshot of the logic of comparison, on my view, is that it is an ongoing dynamic process within which three kinds of hypotheses are being tested at once, in relation to each other. The articulation of the comparative category as vaguely tolerant is a process of improving the category as an hypothesis. The articulation of the theologies to be compared as specifications of the category needs to be under constant revision as the sites of phenomenological analysis are explored. And the comparisons themselves need to be under revision. It would seem as if everything is totally fluid: the comparative category does not stay still long enough to be specified, the specifications themselves are under correction, and the comparisons themselves are constantly undermined by changing the category and its specifications. But in practice, if the comparative category, the diverse specifications, and the comparative judgments are made as vulnerable as possible, their expressions will settle down more and more as objections and new evidence come into view and provoke corrective revisions. To be sure, some new discovery, some new point of view, some new insight into the comparison might cause a revision of the whole project. We have seen many such revisions in the last two hundred years. But each makes progress on its predecessors.

THE SOCIAL ORGANIZATION OF THEOLOGICAL COMPARISON

The logic of comparison is one thing. The social organization of comparison in theology is something else, and it is not an innocent matter. Although individual scholars can work in relatively personal isolation, the scholarly ambiance within which they work is a great cloud of witnesses. A responsible scholar will consider the work of antecedent and contemporary thinkers and write for a scholarly venue hopeful for a careful reading and helpful corrections. Nevertheless, the great cloud of witnesses contains so many different languages and approaches that it is hard to reconcile into a consistent pattern of background materials. A "literature review" is almost laughable in setting out a comparative theological project. Moreover, it is extremely difficult, if not impossible, to write for every venue that might have some corrective perspective to offer. Simple wisdom suggests that we should settle for an attitude of quiet resignation to the inevitable partiality of the background we can assemble for a comparative project and to the parochial character of the audience from which we can expect helpful responses. Nevertheless, accompanying this simple wisdom is the pragmatic dictum that, when an obstacle to inquiry, or lacuna of corrective evidence, is discovered, efforts should be made to correct for that bias. At the very least, the fragmentariness of the environment for comparative inquiry can be acknowledged, not in general, but in its particulars insofar as we can identify them.

The social environment for comparative theology does not consist only of the prior efforts of other scholars. Comparison is essentially a collaborative process because comparison needs to be accountable in so many different directions. I have already mentioned three. Comparison needs to be accountable to those who suspect that the comparative categories might be biased in favor of or against some of the ideas compared. It needs to be accountable to the practitioners and experts in each of the ideas, texts, or traditions compared to make sure that the comparison has each of them right. And comparison needs to be accountable to any who might have an interest in the comparative judgments made, testing those judgments as hypotheses. These are the three kinds of accountability that come from the logic of comparison itself. In addition, important issues of temperament affect comparison. Some people have a generalist's flair for creating contexts in which things are seen together. Other people have a specialist's flair for seeing why each tradition, text, or idea complex is unique and singular, not to be compared without distortion. Both temperaments are valuable even when suspicious of and hostile to one another. The comparative process needs to be accountable to the perspectives and criticisms of both.

Ideally, then, a comparative process in theology should be accountable to historical specialists in the theological ideas compared, to practitioners who live by those ideas (if they are living ideas), to theological specialists who work out those ideas' meanings for various dimensions of life, as well as to historical, theological, sociological, psychological, and philosophical generalists. Although it is extremely difficult, not to mention expensive, to set up a particular comparative project involving these diverse kinds of people, it is not so difficult to create a scholarly community of accountability that is this diverse. The comparative theology unit of the American Academy of Religion is in the process of creating just this sort of scholarly community.

The downside of the dense and continuous accountability proper for comparative theology is that it is so much easier to be accountable only to oneself and one's personal projects, or to the few colleagues who are working on the same material, or to blind reviewers in professional journals. Nevertheless, comparative theology is important enough to do well, for various reasons to which I am coming.

MOTIVE FOR THEOLOGICAL COMPARISON

Let me now step back from the discussions of the logic and social dimensions of my program for comparative theology and ask a naive question about the motive for comparative theology. Comparative theology seeks to gain objective knowledge about how theologies compare. We all know the complexities and perplexities of claims to objectivity; we would avoid being foundationalists; we acknowledge our social locations and various other subjective elements of our research perspectives. Nevertheless, as best we can, we want to say how theologies compare in their expressions, claims, theories, and practical consequences. This desire for objectivity is in contrast with a different desire, namely, to adjudicate the theologies normatively, saying which ones are more elegant, precise, important, interesting, and true. I'll say something more about normative elements of comparative theology shortly.

Before that, however, we can note that three approaches to objectivity in comparison are influential in America now. First is comparison by way of classification within a classificatory scheme. The scheme itself, however arrived at with whatever accountability, sets the terms of comparison, the respect in which theologies are compared, or the comparative categories. Theologies (or philosophies) are classified according to the structures of the scheme, without judgment of better and worse. In America, this approach was developed for philosophy by Richard McKeon of the University of Chicago and elaborated by his students, Robert S. Brumbaugh, Walter Watson, and David Dilworth.[9] The drawback to this approach is that the elements of a theology that do not fit the classificatory scheme are relegated to nonimportance, even total neglect; a theology has to be dead to fit into such a pigeonhole.

A second approach to objectivity in comparison is the social science causal approach, to which Peter Berger has contributed so much. Perhaps the most massive comparative study of this sort is Randall Collins's *The Sociology of Philosophies: A Global Theory of Intellectual Change*, in which he traces influences of figures and schools through and among religious and philosophical traditions.[10] Of particular interest is his scrupulously global attention to the Western, East Asian, South Asian, and Islamic traditions, and their mutual interactions. The drawback to this approach is that it focuses only on the influences of figures and schools, not the details of their theories; while the influence of a position might be alive and growing, its living creativity is not recognized.

A third objectivist approach is philosophy of culture, pioneered by F. S. C. Northrop, among others, with his *The Meeting of East and West*.[11] Perhaps the most creative practitioners of philosophy of culture in our time are the late David Hall and his Sinologist philosophical partner, Roger T. Ames.[12] The genius of this approach is to depict in sweeping strokes the assumptions, values, and habits of distinguishing focal elements from backgrounds in the cultures they compare (ancient China and the West). The drawback is that individual figures and schools rarely fit their cultural background exactly and, in fact, can be more in tune with alien cultures. Many creative thinkers transcend their cultural backgrounds to pick up on some of the elements that are registered better in other cultures.

All three of these approaches aim at objectivity in the sense of articulating how their subjects compare, with minimal bias and with an explicit attempt not to evaluate the comparisons or things compared. Moreover, all three approaches can be understood and evaluated according to the philosophical logic of comparison I sketched earlier. The comparative categories for the classifying approach are the structural definitions in the comparative grid; these can be amended as the classification of figures and schools into them proceeds, and the classification itself can be amended as the process continues; comparative judgments consist in commentaries on the relation between the positions defined in the grid. The comparative categories for the social science approach are the articulations of the respects in which figures and schools influence each other; these can be rearticulated as the analysis of influence proceeds, and the comparative judgments consist in summaries of the influences. The comparative categories for the philosophy of culture comparativists are the contrast terms developed to distinguish and relate different cultures, which can be amended through their illustration in specification; comparative judgments consist in summarizing similarities and differences in terms of the contrast terms. All are amenable to the objectivity and minimization of bias that comes from the logic of comparison.

The objectivity sought through the logic of comparison is not value free, however. Its normative element consists, at least, in the implicit argument that the comparative categories are *important* to the theological positions involved. A comparative study might be made of the appropriateness of eating popcorn for a variety of theological positions. This would not be important. Comparisons of dietary prescriptions might very well be important, and popcorn might have a role in this somewhere, but only insofar as that role is understood in terms of the dietary philosophies. Earlier, I illustrated the shifting definition of a comparative category by arguing that comparison of conceptions of God is not as important as comparison of conceptions of ultimacy, because some theologies affirm gods who are not ultimate and thus do not compare with the monotheisms. What makes the monotheisms interesting to compare is the ultimacy in their conceptions, not the fact alone that they ascribe ultimacy to a deity. I argued also that ultimacy resides not only in ontologically ultimate objects but also in anthropologically ultimate projects, and that the ultimacy in objects is connected with the ultimacy in human concerns. What was going on in that rehearsal of the shifting definition of a comparative category was in fact a search for what is important to compare. "Importance" itself is a complex notion that cannot be analyzed here. It includes at least the dimensions highlighted in the phenomenological sites of analysis, namely, intrinsic importance, extrinsic importance in terms of how a position organizes its place in the world, practical importance in terms of consequences, theoretical importance in terms of how the position is understood within larger theories, and the singular importances that cannot be compared. Only a careful elaboration of the dialectic of importance, as illustrated crudely in the discussion of defining ultimacy as a comparative category, can flesh out and defend as a worthy hypothesis the claim that the category does indeed represent something important among the positions compared.

We should not assume that the importance of the comparative category has to be the same for all the positions compared. For instance, in Christianity, Islam, Buddhism, Hinduism, and Chinese religions, their diverse conceptions of human nature are very important. But for Judaism, the universal conception of human nature is strikingly less important than the specific nature of Israel as a particular nation of people in a special relationship with God. For Israel of the Torah, human nature divides into Israel and the Gentiles, and the latter are important mainly for how they impinge on Israel. What is important for Judaism, at least for the pre-prophetic forms, is not so much the human condition but the condition of Israel relative to God. This finding reflects somewhat negatively on the "human condition" as a universal category, a fact that is important to know, and that does not detract from the importance of the category as revealing important things in the theologies compared. One important way of specifying a comparative category is to have no specification of it save to reject alternative ways of specifying it.

That comparative theology is inevitably normative in ascribing importance to the categories of comparison means that it has an obligation to turn its normative ascriptions into hypotheses that can be examined and tested. This moves beyond the logic of comparison to inquiry into what is truly important, which is to say, inquiry into what is true theologically. "Truth" in theology is even more complex than "importance." Inquiry into theological truth at the very least should be grounded in comparative theology, for the pursuit of truth requires consideration not only of antecedent theological resources but also their alternatives. Confessional theology is limited in its claim to truth, because it so easily reduces to sociological observations such as that "as Christians we believe x," or "Madhyamika Buddhists reject ontological belief." Truth in theology also requires analysis of the theological implications of the sciences, literary and plastic arts, and music and dance. Inquiry into theological truth also needs to learn from practical arts such as politics, ethics, and jurisprudence. Of course, theological inquiry needs to work its way through the texts and liturgies of religious practices, through analyses of how these function in religious communities, and through the practical consequences of theological positions for personal, communal, and social life. Inquiry into theological truth is far, far more complicated than the study of theologians, although that is what it has come to mean when theology is defined as an academic profession.[13] The question of what is important in comparison is a normative theological question the truth of which needs to be tested in each case.

NORMATIVENESS IN COMPARATIVE THEOLOGY

Let me close with a double point. The first is that comparative theology cannot separate itself from normative theology in the larger systematic sense. Of course, it can do so preliminarily. Many comparativist historians of theology would be horrified to think that their work still needs to be tested and assessed by normative theologians, because most of them associated normative theology with confessional theology of someone else's religion. But those historical comparativists themselves function as theologians insofar as they assert that the categories according to which they make comparisons highlight important aspects of the religions compared. For comparative theology to be fulfilled and fully assessed in the long run, it needs to imbed itself in, and test itself by, systematic theology in a larger and frankly normative sense. That larger theology would not be Christian, or Buddhist, or Islamic theology, except insofar as it should be able to register what is true and important in each of those religions. It would just be theology, in the sense of collaborative inquiry into theological topics, which in turn are defined in considerable measure by the categories that turn out to be important for comparison. Good comparative categories are those in which the respects in which theologies are compared make an important difference.

The other side of my concluding point is that all theology should operate with sophistication in comparative theology: all theology should operate with a comparative base. Because this point is controversial, permit me to draw it out a bit.

Of course, it is foolish to say what "all theology" should do. Theologians can do whatever they want, and people will pay attention to them if what they do is interesting. Interesting theological projects abound in every religious tradition that remains clueless about how its ideas compare with ideas in other traditions. Who do I think I am, as a philosophical theologian, to tell other theologians what they need to do?

In answer, let me mention for the third time the philosophical point that theological claims based on the fact that some religious group makes those claims reduce quickly to sociology rather than theology. Particular theological positions are part of the religious identity of the people who hold them. The people with that identity of course hold that their theological positions are true, or at least worry about those positions rather than about the theologies of other groups. But if people hold to their theological positions because that is part of their group or personal religious identity, this is a sociological or psychological point. It says nothing about the truth of the theological position in question, except that certain kinds of people believe it to be true. Some theologians hold this to be a good outcome, the reduction of theology from making and justifying truth claims to a kind of sociological study of what truth claims are made within the context of a certain religious identity. The so-called "Yale School" of theology, led by George Lindbeck and Hans Frei, says that theology should examine the deep structure or grammar of a religious group understood as a cultural-linguistic system and then articulate what beliefs and practices are consistent with this deep grammar. Theology is closer to the social sciences in being descriptive of group identity than to philosophy in aiming at truth, they say. Theology of this sort is internal to the group under study and need not refer to the cultural-linguistic systems of other groups. So comparative theology is not interesting, and hardly possible. For this sociological sense of theology as the explication of religious group identity, the terms within a group's theology do not really refer to what they seem to refer to, for instance, ultimate realities or the human religious predicament. The reference really is to consistency with the ways people within a particular religious identity talk about ultimate realities or the predicament.

Nevertheless, giving up any theological quest for truth is an extremely high price for theology to pay. Most religious people, when they think about it, want their theological beliefs and the practices following from them to be true, not just the way their group thinks, although I do not mean to minimize the issues of religious belonging. The vast majority of religious people trust the authority of their group to tell them what is true, and to not engage much in theological inquiry themselves. Yet even for these people, they trust the group's authority to tell them what is true, not merely what the group's identity is to think. If confessional theologians limit themselves to being shepherds of the intellectual consequences of religious identity, then someone else will have to take up inquiry into the truth of theological matters. These are the people I am saying are the theologians who need comparative theology.

How do we inquire into the truth of theological issues? Rarely if ever do we begin a theological inquiry at the beginning. Rather, we have theological beliefs and symbols in hand, with long histories and many levels of nuance. Theological inquiry works to make these beliefs and symbols vulnerable to correction. If they are wrong, we want to find out. If they are biased, we want to find out. If they are true in some contexts but false or even demonic in other contexts, we want to find out. How do we make our theological positions vulnerable to correction? By making them accountable to anyone who might correct them. This means preeminently, by making them accountable to theologians in other traditions who might have reason to disagree with them, or to agree with them in some respects but not others, or to agree with them through alternative sets of symbols that have somewhat different consequences.

Theology, therefore, should take as its public anyone or any discipline or tradition that might contribute to its correction. But how can the theologians of other traditions be in one's theological public if we do not have a common language for assessing how our traditions and various positions compare? Building a proper theological public is extremely difficult. It does not consist only in those who share one's religious identity, for that might be only a sociological public of intellectual consistency. A proper theological public is built through the ongoing, self-correcting work of comparative theology. Comparative theology has a logic of its own, as I have argued here. It also needs a social structure because it is essentially a continuous collaborative theological process. The first and chief purpose of comparative theology is to create and improve a public within which any other kind of theology can make itself vulnerable to correction. Even when other theological projects do not make reference to more than one tradition or position, their vulnerability to correction requires that they be accountable to a public that includes those others. Not to do so would be to make them, to that extent, invulnerable to correction. Invulnerability to correction reduces a theological position to what persons with a particular religious identity happen to hold. Vulnerability to correction gives them a warrant for the truth of holding that position, because if it is mistaken, they might find out about it.

NOTES

1. Among the most distinguished are the studies by Keith Ward. See his *Images of Eternity: Concepts of God in Five Religious Traditions* (Oxford: One World Press, 1987), *Religion and Revelation: A Theology of Revelation in the Word's Religions* (Oxford: Clarendon Press, 1994), *Religion and Creation* (Oxford: Clarendon Press, 1996), and *Religion and Human Nature* (Oxford: Clarendon Press, 1998). See also my several discussions of comparative theology and comparative philosophy in *Ritual and Deference: Extending Chinese Philosophy in a Comparative Context* (Albany: State University of New York Press, 2008). Outside of the Western context, comparative theology is rarely distinguished from comparative philosophy, which opens an even-wider array of approaches. See Robert W. Smid's *Methodologies of Comparative Philosophy: The Pragmatist and Process Traditions* (Albany: State University of New York Press, 2009). On the roles of comparative theology within the broader comparison of religions, see Walter H. Capps's *Religious Studies: The Making of a Discipline* (Minneapolis: Fortress Press, 1995), chapter 6. For a careful comparison of approaches to comparative theology, see Francis X. Clooney, S.J., *Comparative Theology: Deep Learning Across Religious Borders* (Chichester: Wiley-Blackwell, 2010).

2. This sense of comparison by juxtaposition has been elaborated beautifully by Francis X. Clooney, S.J. Among his many books, see especially *Theology After Vedanta: An Experiment in Comparative Theology* (Albany: State University of New York Press, 1993), *Seeing Through Texts* (Albany: State University of New York Press, 1996), and *Hindu God, Christian God: How Reason Helps Break Down the Boundaries between Religions* (New York: Oxford University Press, 2001).

3. See my extended analysis of this example in "Kenosis in Buddhist-Christian Dialogue," chapter 6 in *Behind the Masks of God: An Essay Toward Comparative Theology* (Albany: State University of New York Press, 1991).

4. See Aaron Stalnaker, *Overcoming Our Evil: Human Nature and Spiritual Exercises in Xunzi and Augustine* (Washington, DC: Georgetown University Press, 2006), chapters 1–2.

5. See Peirce's essays, "Issues of Pragmaticism" and "Consequences of Critical Common-Sensism," in *Collected Papers of Charles Sanders Peirce*, edited by Paul Weiss and Charles Hartshorne, volume 5 (Cambridge: Harvard University Press, 1934); the essays are found in several anthologies of Peirce's writings. For a more elaborate discussion of vagueness, see "On Comparing Religious Ideas," by Wesley J. Wildman and myself, in *Ultimate Realities: A Volume in the Comparative Religious Ideas Project* (Albany: State University of New York Press, 2000), chapter 8.

6. This is the move taken by the Cross-Cultural Comparative Religious Ideas Project in its volume *Ultimate Realities*, under the prodding of Malcolm David Eckel. See there, chapter 6, "Cooking the Last Fruits of Nihilism: Buddhist Approaches to Ultimate Reality," by Eckel and John J. Thatamanil.

7. See Paul Tillich, *Systematic Theology*, volume 1 (Chicago: University of Chicago Press, 1951), introduction.

8. These sites of phenomenological analysis are discussed at length in my *Normative Cultures* (Albany: State University of New York Press, 1995), chapter 2, "Importance."

9. See Robert S. Brumbaugh, *Western Philosophic Systems and Their Cyclic Transformations* (Carbondale: Southern Illinois University Press, 1992), Walter Watson's *The Architectonics of Meaning: Foundations of the New Pluralism* (Albany: State University of New York Press, 1985), and David Dilworth's *Philosophy in World Perspective: A Comparative Hermeneutic of Major Theories* (New Haven: Yale University Press, 1989).

10. Randall Collins, *The Sociology of Philosophies: A Global Theory of Intellectual Change* (Cambridge: Harvard University Press, 1998).

11. F. S. C. Northrop, *The Meeting of East and West* (New York: Macmillan, 1946).

12. See Hall and Ames's *Thinking Through Confucius* (Albany: State University of New York Press, 1987), *Anticipating China* (Albany: State University of New York Press, 1995), *Thinking from the Han* (Albany: State University of New York Press, 1998), and *Democracy of the Dead* (LaSalle: Open Court, 1999). They focus on the philosophical elements of the cultures they compare, but these include openly theological themes.

13. I have argued this expansive thesis about the nature of inquiry into theological truth in *On the Scope and Truth of Theology: Theology as Symbolic Engagement* (New York: T&T Clark, 2006).

Chapter 10

DOES THE STUDY OF RELIGION NEED PHILOSOPHY?

Whether the study of religion needs philosophy is an extremely important topic. But there are so many ambiguities about the question that we should begin by clearing away some of that brush.

KINDS OF PHILOSOPHY IN RELIGION

To begin with, religion has been studied fruitfully in many ways, some of which are fairly devoid of philosophy. In fact, since the development of the social sciences in the nineteenth century, many social science scholars of religion have been quite deliberate to keep certain kinds of philosophy out of their study. Thinking primarily of German idealism, they imagine philosophy of religion as a kind of disguised Christian, or Judeo-Christian, theology. There is some truth to that accusation, although this does not settle the question of whether German idealism is good or bad theology. For these social scientists, however, theology itself is bad for the study of religion, for at least two reasons.

First, they cannot conceive of theology as anything other than apologetics for some particular religion, usually Christianity. Confessional theology is ineluctably biased because it begins by presupposing the truth, though not necessarily the meaning, of a particular theological stance.

Second, the antitheological social scientists of religion define their methods in terms of careful reductionism, following the lead of Kant and his followers. They are clear, in effect, that what they discover about religion is only what comes through when religion is examined through their particular methods, instruments, framing theories, and scholarly traditions. This reduces out what does not come through under these conditions and they are careful, usually, not to comment on what does not come through. The nature of the social sciences studying religion has changed in many critical ways over the last several decades, especially regarding the elimination of vicious reductionism. But what is not allowed to come through in any of them is consideration of the truth of first-order claims or suppositions of religions, such as gods, the Dao, Brahman, Buddha-mind, Heavenly Principle, or other candidates for ultimate realities. Whether notions or symbol systems such as these have valid reference is not a question to be asked within social science methodologies, no matter how important it is for many religious people themselves. Theology, some kinds of philosophy of religion, and philosophical theology are disciplines for the study precisely of those first-order questions, among others. So these antitheological social scientists exclude theology and those forms of philosophy that deal with first-order religious questions because they would contaminate the careful reductionism of the sciences in which lies their claim to objectivity.

A second clarifying remark needs to be made about the ambiguities of philosophy as a discipline. Most of the academic world has become aware that philosophy has developed into a number of rather different intellectual approaches that sometimes do not communicate with one another, and that the question of whether philosophy is needed for the study of religion depends on what kind of philosophy you have in mind. Analytic philosophy, for example, the dominant form of professional philosophy in America, has several approaches. One is simply to clarify religious concepts, in the sense of clarification associated with introspective immediacy. Another analyzes the validity of apologetic arguments by which religions sometimes defend their beliefs. David Hume, for instance, gave a very hard time to a number of apologetic arguments, for example, for the existence of God and the probity of miracles. Other analytic philosophers such as D. Z. Phillips have used Wittgensteinian notions of language games in apologetic defenses of religions, particularly Christianity. Yet other philosophers have used the argument styles of analytic philosophy, under the name of philosophical theology, to defend Christian doctrines, in the manner of James F. Ross or, more recently, Eleonore Stump.

I must say that apologetics does not interest me as a use of philosophy for the study of religion because so many more basic philosophical questions need to be asked before justifying an apologetic stance. Nor am I convinced that the conceptual analysis of concepts into meanings that can be introspected immediately is of much help.

Continental philosophies are also various. Some, following Husserl, are as intent as social scientists in bracketing out questions of reference and truth in first-order religious beliefs and suppositions and so are of little help in studying those questions of religion. Nevertheless, phenomenological approaches have had the great virtue of showing that religious experience is far more subtle and complex than many scholars of religion had thought it to be, especially those who treat religious experience, positively or negatively, as bearing upon apologetic issues. Other continental philosophies, following Heidegger, attempt the enormously interesting imaginative job of inventing new symbols and conceptualities for the first-order religious issues. Ostensibly limiting itself to phenomenological analyses of experience, in fact, the Heideggerian tradition has invented imaginative new metaphysical and ontological ideas. Philosophy is far less the analysis of arguments, I believe, than the imaginative or speculative construction of perspectives for thinking things together that otherwise would have to be thought separately. Heideggerian ideas have been useful for thinkers as diverse as the Kyoto School Buddhist philosopher Nishitani and the existentialist Christian Tillich. Yet other continental philosophies identified with postmodernism have taught the important lesson that the meaning of religious beliefs and assumptions depends in large part on their being used in concrete engagements with religious things, and that these engagements are always contextual. The great limitation of most continental philosophy is its general inability to think religion together with science in any detail; naturalistic philosophy is required for that.

So far, I have mentioned only Western philosophical approaches and, in fact, artificially have reduced and demarcated a small selection of them. South Asian, East Asian, and Islamic philosophic traditions have long contributed greatly to the understanding of religion and should be considered for their contemporary usefulness, perhaps even necessity. But I will spare you that tonight and mention that my own preference in matters philosophical is for the American pragmatic tradition and its close cousin, process philosophy. Instead of characterizing those approaches, I shall illustrate them in the rest of my remarks. I shall defend, within the limits of your patience for the remainder of this hour, the following three theses:

1. Philosophy, in the right sense, is necessary for the definition of religion, which in turn leads to tools for controlling for reductionism in other approaches to the study of religion.

2. Philosophy, in the right sense, is necessary for providing a theory for understanding and assessing religious symbolism, which sits within a larger epistemological context of engaging religious matters.

3. Philosophy, in the right sense, is necessary to give a metaphysical account of the ultimate realities religion engages, an account that itself is hypothetical and thus, in the broadest sense, empirical.

PHILOSOPHY IN THE DEFINITION OF RELIGION

Religion needs to be defined because the reductive sciences are incomplete, perhaps even misleading, if it cannot be said what they leave out in their accounts. Note that I am not saying that religion has to be defined in any clear way in order to be studied at all. We could have a bunch of overlapping definitions of religion and still have productive inquiry into religion from many directions. In point of fact, the academic world of religious studies does not have a clear and accepted definition of religion and yet is filled with productive inquiries. My point, rather, is that an important question constantly attends all the scientific and discipline-oriented approaches to religion, namely, what is neglected or obscured when the discipline lifts out of the religious realities those aspects that its methods and categories can recognize? The follow-up question is, how must the results of the reductive study be modified when brought back into context with what had been left out? The discipline per se does not ask that question, although some of its practitioners might by becoming philosophical. The what-is-left-out question is philosophical in the sense that it can never be addressed by an approach that limits itself in principle to what is amenable to its method. In practice, of course, all philosophies are limited by their historical context, social location, style of approach, canon of classics, and all the rest of intellectual particularity. But, in contrast to any science that claims that its objectivity consists in limiting its conclusions to what the subject matter reveals through the constructions of the science's method, philosophy is always in principle committed to leaving nothing out. If someone points out an omission to a philosopher, the philosopher hastens to amend the faulty account where possible.

One cannot know what is left out of an account of religion unless one has a working definition of religion in the first place. Although all philosophers do not have to agree on a definition, each philosopher reflecting on the questions of reductionism needs one for that work. I propose the following definition of religion as the best hypothesis on the matter: *Religion is human engagement of ultimacy expressed in cognitive articulations, communal patterns of life or ritual in the face of ultimacy, and personal and communal existential responses to ultimacy that give ultimate definition to the individual and community*. I shall not defend this definition at length here, although some of its usefulness will come out in the rest of our discussion. You surely will have noted the reference to three kinds of expressions of religion, the cognitive, the social, and the existential. These obviously overlap and interact, and they are themselves broad enough to host the important discussions in religious studies of various kinds of cognition, of structured ritual, social action, and organization, and of existential choices and commitments that define personal and communal identity in various ways. This vague reference to all three is enough in a working definition to serve as warnings about what is left out or pushed into the background in various reductionisms. We are warned that when theologians are concerned about cognitive matters, the first-order questions of truth, they are likely to leave out the social and existential dimensions (though not the *conceptions* of those dimensions). We are warned that scientists are likely to leave out the intellectual truth questions as well as certain kinds of existential issues when focusing on what can be expressed in social structures and linguistic, neurological, and psychological habits. And we are warned that gurus, preachers, and prophets are likely to leave out disciplined concern for the cognitive and social aspects of religion when focusing on the existential issues. Healthy disputes about just what the cognitive, social, and existential issues and boundaries are help vivify this part of the definition for purposes of understanding the costs of reductive analysis.

This definition identifies religion with human *engagement* of ultimacy. Engagement is a term with roots in pragmatism, something like Dewey's terms "interaction" and "transaction," with overlays of habit and intentionality. In fact, it is the key term for my second thesis, to be discussed in a moment, and so will merely be noted now. By identifying religion with engagement expressed in cognitive, social, and existential ways, the definition precisely does *not* identify religion flat out with belief, social practices, and existential issues, which many other definitions do. Religion is engagement of ultimacy as expressed in those three ways, not just the expressions themselves.

The reference to ultimacy is key to this definition of religion, and you can see already why philosophy needs to reach for metaphysics to define ultimacy, a point to be made in my third thesis. "Ultimacy" and its cognates such as "ultimate reality" and the "ultimate dimensions of things" are terms made popular by Paul Tillich, who used them to refer to boundary conditions beyond which one cannot go, the boundary conditions of experience, or of the human world, or determinate reality as such. Religions have various theories of what is ultimate and very many different ways of symbolizing them. The symbols of ultimacy are subject to two kinds of pressure. One is to make sure they are transcendent enough so that there is nothing behind or beyond them. The other is to make them intimate enough to human life that they can be engaged relative to human affairs. For purposes of our definition so far, we need not decide any of these issues, only note that ultimacy means boundary conditions, something like what Peter Berger calls a sacred canopy.

The reference to ultimacy is crucial to the definition because it allows for the discrimination of religious engagements from all sorts of things with which religion is sometimes mistakenly identified. For instance, some scholars, particularly evolutionary biologists these days, identify religion with belief in supernatural agents. They get excited by the observation that all religious traditions have believed in supernatural beings at some time and that nearly every child today goes through a period of believing in invisible persons who can read their minds. Then they identify religion today with belief in supernatural agents, which is true for some people but not others, and conclude that those who do not believe in supernatural agents are not robustly religious. But belief in supernatural agents is not necessarily religious. It is a belief about the kinds of things to be found in the cosmos and thus is budding science. Only belief that supernatural agents are ultimate in some sense would constitute religion; that belief is common in theistic religions. But East Asian religions such as Confucianism, Daoism, and Buddhism have taken some considerable pains to say that the ultimate realities are not supernatural agents, even though they believe, or have believed at some time or other, that the world is filled with angels, gods, and demons. For them, supernatural agents, while plentiful, are not ultimate. Thomas Aquinas's conception of God as the pure, simple Act of To Be is not a supernatural agent either, although through analogy he thought God can be symbolized in supernatural ways.

Similarly, with regard to alleged religious experiences: scholars can study their phenomenological immediacies, neurological underpinnings, and cognitive categories. But whether the experiences are really religious depends on whether they are within engagements of something ultimate. As Jonathan Edwards put the point in his own quaint way, the Devil can counterfeit any experiential feeling whatsoever, and the only way you can distinguish true religious experience from Satanic counterfeits is through judging the engagements and their consequences. This point reflects a particular philosophy of engagement to which I will come in a moment.

One last point about the definition, however. You will have noticed that it is a definition of religion, not religions. Religions are historical and cultural ways of expressing engagements of ultimacy in cognitive, social, and existential forms. This aspect of the definition runs against a long, Kantian, critique of the notion of religion as such. The critique is based on the view that religions are cognitive and social constructions, and that these are different one from the other. To be sure, religion is always expressed in human constructions, in signs, as the pragmatists like to say. But what is expressed is not just the expression but the engagement. To reduce religion to the cultural constructions of religions is to leave out the engagements of ultimacy in all of the religions in favor of their expressions alone. The entry of biological, evolutionary, and cognitive sciences into the study of religion, which deal with matters universal among human beings and not limited to the constructions of any culture (or of all cultures for that matter), has restored religion to the center of the study of religions. An added benefit of this restoration is that we can take a much more empirical look at how cultural constructions work in the actual engagements of life, and how their traditions bob and weave.

PHILOSOPHY AND RELIGIOUS SYMBOLISM

Now let me turn to my second thesis, which is that philosophy, in the right sense, is necessary for providing a theory for understanding and assessing religious symbolism, which sits within a larger epistemological context of engaging religious matters. You know now that I propose that the larger epistemological context be understood as engagement. In this I follow the pragmatist Charles Peirce, who said that we are interpreters of reality by means of signs; we engage reality by interpreting it with signs. This is different from the epistemological stance that says we are conscious of or experience the contents of our own minds and thus worry about how those mental contents mirror the realities to which they refer. It differs from the European semiotic tradition that says that we interpret, not realities, but other signs, by means of signs, as in interpreting texts. Peirce imagined the interpretive situation to be like walking in the wild, trying to figure out what is there and constructing a semiotic system to do so. Dewey imagined the interpretive situation to be like that but with a more problematic character—we recognize suddenly that what we thought was there is not, and it is something else instead. Interpretive engagers, according to my version of pragmatism, are parts of nature interacting with other parts of nature to discriminate aspects of reality by means of signs in intentional, if not always conscious, ways.

Interpretation, said Peirce, is the taking of a sign to refer an object in a certain respect. A given interpretation picks up on only those aspects of the object that can be expressed in its signs. Without the right signs, those aspects are not interpreted. Moreover, any interpretation intends its object only in certain respects, not in all respects. The respects intended depend on many things, including the purposes underlying the interpretation and the semiotic storehouse of signs that can interpret in some respects but not others. The objects of interpretation are taken to be real, and they are real even if the interpretation is wholly mistaken about what their reality is. A thing is real if it is possible to be mistaken about it.

Among the realities of our world are its boundary conditions, the ultimate realities. The various religious cultures have signs for interpreting them in certain respects but not others. Part of the vastly complicated practice of comparative religions is to identify in what respects their interpretations engage ultimate realities, and in what contexts. The same sign, or what seems to be the same sign, might mean radically different things when used to interpret something in different respects, or in different contexts. Even the question of whether the different interpretations are engaging the same thing is an empirical question of analytical semiotics.

Bear in mind now that interpretive engagement is not only cognitive but also social and existential (and probably a lot more besides). This is to say, participation in a structured social form such as a ritual can be a way of engaging something ultimate in which the ritual elements are signs that shape the engagement of ultimacy. Confronting an existential crisis of identity, or loss, or sudden empowerment, can be a way of engaging something ultimate in which the terms of the existential crisis are signs that interpret ultimacy in a certain respect. The signs for interpretive engagement are not only conscious signs as employed in rare and refined kinds of cognitive engagements but also are in the muscles of our social habits and structures, and in the ways we comport ourselves in existential matters.

All this is complicated even more by a peculiarity of reference in interpretation. Developing some of Peirce's ideas, let me say that one dimension of reference in interpretation is conventional, which means that signs interpret other signs in a semiotic system. Insofar as we are interpreting linguistically, say, the syntax and semantics of signs are functions of some language system. A given interpretation can be expressed in something like a sentence, or a theory. This is the "extension" of interpretive signs and is what allowed us humans to develop so far beyond other primates: we can engage the world, not just with a few signs pointing to realities but with whole extensive constructions of signs. We engage the world in particular interpretations with extensions that might be as broad as whole theories. The engagement itself is the "intension" of interpretive signs, the use of the signs to interact interpretively with realities: any given interpretation involves signs that stand for the reality but only as they are embedded in larger semiotic structures.

Now within the intensive engagement of realities there are at least two more dimensions of reference, which Peirce called iconic and indexical. Iconic reference is where the interpretation takes the real object to be like what the sign says, in some sense of "like." The likeness can be mirroring, mapping, describing, theoretical, metaphorical, and a host of other forms. Indexical reference is where the interpretation finds a causal connection between the real object and the interpreter as constituted by the sign. A pointing finger causes the interpreter to look in a new direction. An image of a dancing goddess with a girdle of skulls scares the bejesus out of a laconic worshipper who finds nothing ultimately important. Going to Mass for thirty years finally brings someone around to understand sacrifice and hospitality. Indexical reference changes the interpreter so that the interpreter can pick up on something important in the objects that otherwise would be missed. An indexical reference need not be iconic at all. The worshippers of Kali might not believe that there exists a real dancing goddess with skulls, but the indexical connection refers the worshippers to what is really worship worthy. The Mass is not about the cannibal rite of eating Jesus's flesh and drinking his blood, but about something else that is ultimately important. Many religious symbols have extremely powerful indexical reference, but silly or absurd iconic reference if taken literally. In many instances, the literal interpretation of things with symbols referred iconically needs to be broken.

You will have noticed that the discussion of engagement has slipped into a discussion of truth, as when religious symbols need to be broken. It is one thing to determine whether we have the symbols to engage something ultimate at all. Many people complain that the old symbols of some tradition or another do not engage as they used to in a different context. To determine whether engagement is enabled by the interpretive symbols is an empirical matter. It is another thing to determine whether what the symbol says about the object in the engagement is true or false. If you are looking at a barn in respect to its color and say that it is gray when it is red, you are genuinely engaging the barn, though falsely. In religious matters, Tillich liked to warn that demonic symbols are genuinely engaging with ultimacy, but falsely, and disastrously.

What is the truth of an interpretation? An engagement is true if what is important or valuable in the object is carried over into the interpreter in the respect in which the signs refer to the object. What is carried over is value or importance, not necessarily form, although iconic reference has some carryover of form. But indexical reference might carry over what is relevant and valuable without having the form in the sign be like the form in the object.

The point of this second thesis is that philosophy is necessary to spell out the conditions of engagement and the checking of the truth or error involved. I urge a pragmatic philosophy that understands epistemological issues in terms of engagement. But now more needs to be said about engaging ultimate realities if this is to apply helpfully to understanding religion as the engagement of ultimacy.

PHILOSOPHY AND ULTIMATE REALITY

The third thesis is that philosophy, in the right sense, is necessary to give a metaphysical account of the ultimate realities that religion engages, an account that itself is hypothetical and thus, in the broadest sense, empirical. So let me sketch a brief metaphysical account of ultimate realities. My hypothesis is that ultimate realities, as boundary conditions of the world, should be understood abstractly as finite/infinite contrasts. The concept of a "contrast" comes from Whitehead, who meant by it a thing composed of two or more things that just fit together, holding their differences in a contrast. They do not fit together because of an overarching third term or special relationship: they "just fit," the way things often do in a work of art. A finite/infinite contrast, in my usage, is the "just fit" of something finite and something infinite.

The finite thing is some ultimate condition of the world without which the world would not be what it is in some very basic dimension. Religions symbolize such ultimate conditions in many ways, for instance, as the grounds for possibilities with value, the grounds for personal wholeness, the grounds for interacting with a world of things that are causally connected with us and yet are fundamentally other, the grounds for having or achieving a personal identity that is ultimately important, the grounds for existence itself. The symbols in a rich religious tradition address most or all of these allegedly ultimate conditions. For instance, in Christianity, God is conceived (in various ways) to be the creator of everything, but not only that, to be the judge before whom everyone has an ultimately important identity, to command engagement of others with traits of love that recognize both otherness and intimacy, to offer salvation in terms of wholeness in the face of brokenness, and to present human beings with alternative possibilities for choice that have different values, so that human choosing is under obligation to choose the better, that is, to be moral. Christianity symbolizes the various aspects of these things in many different and sometimes conflicting ways. I would argue on another occasion that Confucianism, Daoism, and Buddhism symbolize a similar array of ultimate conditions, although perhaps without the personifying images of ultimacy typical of Christianity, Judaism, and Islam.

Now as the finite side of a finite/infinite contrast is some such ultimate condition without which the world would not be the world, the infinite side is what would obtain were the finite side absent: no existence, no value-laden possibilities, no complex self to integrate, no relating to other things as other though intimate, or no ultimately important identity (to repeat the brief list given). The ultimate realities are not just the finite things about which claims are made that they are last (or first) in a chain of conditions. As finite/infinite contrasts, they are intended with the ultimacy built into the contrast between the finite condition and the what-if-not infinite side. The infinite side is not some further condition beyond the finite—that would only prove that the finite side is not really an ultimate or last condition. The infinite side is rather the felt negation-affirmation of the ultimacy of the finite side, and this gives ultimate realities the aura of mystery to which religions testify. Symbolizing finite/infinite contrasts in sacred canopies is not merely fundamental philosophical cosmology: it is awesome acknowledgment of the sacred and mysterious givenness of the boundary conditions of the world, without which we would not have the world.

The analysis of the ways by which alleged ultimacies are finite/infinite contrasts offers many new and interesting avenues for understanding the workings of religious symbols. But how do we know what the principal finite/infinite contrasts are? Phenomenologists such as the great Mircea Eliade claimed to do in-depth analyses of a great many religious contexts and, through cumulative comparisons, developed in some inductive way a theory of religion. Yet he was criticized for imposing his own theoretical categories on the material, as of course he could not help but do, despite the discipline of his vast learning.

My argument is the reverse of his. I want to say that philosophy can provide defensible hypotheses about what really is ultimate, and then to claim that all religions with a rich history have to cope with what is ultimately real some way or another, and have done so with varying kinds and degrees of success. Their resources are different but somehow or other they need to symbolize the ultimate realities and their bearings on human life. An historical survey of religious contexts then can serve as a kind of empirical check of reinforcement or inapplicability on the metaphysical hypothesis. The study of religion, in part, can move back and forth between the philosophical hypotheses about ultimacy and the material of religion giving cognitive, social, and existential expression to engagements with what is alleged to be ultimate.

Consider, for instance, the metaphysical hypothesis that to be a determinate thing is to be a harmony. A harmony is a contrast within which many components are fitted together in a pattern or form. As determinate, one harmony is determinately different from another harmony, at least in some respects. In all the respects in which one harmony is determinate, it is determinately different from other harmonies, each of which is determinate in its own ways. Thus, harmonies are in an existential field in which they relate to each other as others with respect to which to be determinate. The ultimate identity of harmonies is the value they have of getting their components together in the form that they have and in the existential location they have relative to others. This is a penultimately abstract characterization of what it is to be a thing: a harmony with form, components to be formed, existential location, and the identity resulting from all these. This account applies to anything determinate whatsoever, whether you believe basic things to be Aristotelian substances, Leibnizian monads, quanta of energy, or ideas in some divine mind. Those traits of harmony—form, components, existential location, and value-identity—are transcendentals found in any determinate thing.

Considering human beings as harmonies, much of life involves the processes of actualizing possibilities that themselves sometimes allow of alternatives with different values. So, the transcendental trait of form shows up in human life as the moral sphere of choice and obligation: being under obligation is an ultimate reality that everyone faces. Similarly, human process requires a constant integration of the components of life into some semblance of wholeness, an integration that involves groundedness in the components as an ultimate condition. Every person faces other things in the world with which they are connected and by which they are intimately defined but which are also genuinely other and should be engaged as such: engaging the other is an ultimate condition. Every person is ultimately conditioned by the need to achieve an identity through life that is ultimately important. These are human versions of four of the five ultimate realities that I listed earlier, now derived from the transcendental traits of harmony.

But why say that to be a determinate thing is to be a harmony? Sure, it is a good organizing hypothesis for pulling together vast themes of human existence. But why believe it? Think again about what it means to be determinate. To be determinate is to be this rather than that. The "rather than" means that "this" must include some components from "that" if they are to be connected enough to be different from one another, and vice versa. These can be called "conditional components" because they constitute how "this" and "that" condition one another. But also "this" has to have some components "that" does not have, and vice versa; otherwise "that" would be merely a component of "this," not something external and determinately different. These are "essential components," each set unique to the different things. Things determinate with respect to one another need both mutually conditioning components and essential components of their own. Thus also, things determinate with respect to one another need to harmonize their own conditioning and essential components, that is, to be harmonies, and we have in hand our abstract theory of what a harmony must be.

Mutually determinate things are together in a cosmological sense by virtue of their networks of conditioning relations, causal nexus, and the like. But through conditioning components alone, the external reality of others is not recognized: only the conditioning components of "that" are included in "this," not the essential components. If the essential components of "that" were included in "this," "that" would not be other, and thus could not be that with respect to which "this" is determinate. So there must be a more basic context of mutual relevance within which the essential components of different things can be together without being completely encompassed within any of the many determinate things. There must be a determinate many if there is to be one determinate thing, and that many cannot be exhausted in any one thing. The very being of determinateness requires a multitude of things that are conditionally connected and essentially other to one another. This is possible only within an ontological context of mutual relevance in which their essential components can be together.

What can that ontological context of mutual relevance be? If it is anything determinate in itself, it is just one more of the many, and a super ontological context would be needed to connect it with the original determinate multitude. Therefore, it cannot be determinate. The only thing that is not determinate but that can be an ontological context of mutual relevance for all determinate things, I would argue, is an ontological creative act that creates all determinate things as together, mutually conditioning but essentially other. That act has no determinateness except being the act that creates this world, whatever that is. The act is not in space or time, does not take place at any time, is not necessary, or motivated, nor does it have possibilities, because all those things are determinate and, as such, creatures. The act as such has no nature but gives itself the nature of being creator of the determinate things. The world of determinate things is the terminus of the ontological creative act and not separate from it. The act and world are absolutely arbitrary, gratuitous, undeserved, and surprising. The array of determinate things, many of which play themselves out in time, is radically contingent, arbitrary, gratuitous, undeserved, and surprising. This is my metaphysical hypothesis about the contingency of existence.

These conceptions are extremely abstract and different from the ways we customarily think about processes in space-time. Finite creators use antecedent resources to make new things, however they add novelty, and the ways religion has found to symbolize the finite/infinite contrast of the ontological act of creation often drag in that finite trait, assuming that the creator has to have some determinate character antecedent to creation. Religion, however, has also found ways to symbolize the breakdown of those finite analogies. The study of religion can be greatly enhanced by analyses of how symbolic resources are developed in various ways to engage the ultimate reality of the ontological creative act.

I apologize for having illustrated the importance of metaphysics in the study of religion by dragging you through the problem of the one and the many. Let me add, however, that your bonus is that you now have a new proof for an ontological creator, just in case you wanted one. Of course, all I have offered are hypotheses, which are fallible and subject to correction. But at the center is the hypothesis about what it is to be determinate, a subject matter so abstract and basic that it holds regardless of debates about what kinds of things there are and how they work. At that very basic level, the result of the hypothesis is a proof for the radically contingent act of creation within which every determinate thing, whatever it might be, is located. This is pretty basic for religious concerns about what is ultimately real and important, concerns expressed in many cultural ways but always engaging the nature of ultimate reality. The study of religion needs philosophy to imagine ultimate reality critically, which it should do, because the ultimate reality of the radically contingent act of creation is the universal condition affecting everything, just as everything has form, components, existential location, and ultimate identity.

Chapter 11

SOME RECOMMENDATIONS FOR THE FUTURE OF LIBERAL THEOLOGY

A NEW FRAMEWORK

The first recommendation is that liberal theology think of itself within a somewhat new framework. This is not to neglect the customary frameworks: Liberal theology develops methods of inquiry that address the plausibility conditions of its contemporary intellectual situation (the "contemporary plausibility conditions" of the eighteenth century differ from those respectively of the nineteenth, twentieth, and twenty-first centuries).[1] Liberal theology is thus science friendly, which means different things as different sciences come to bear upon the study of religion.[2] Liberal theology is also supernaturalism-hostile insofar as religious imagery is treated as science, although it can be supernaturalism-friendly when religious imagery is treated symbolically and demythologized.[3] Liberal theology thus presses hard to develop theories of symbolism such that religious significance is distinguished from scientific claims.[4] Liberal theology takes seriously the moral elements in religion, emphasizing the need for religion to make a difference regarding justice and piety even when central religious symbols might be rejected as literally true.[5] Liberal theology gives greater weight to seeking truth concerning religious topics than to providing theological identity to religious groups.[6] Liberal theology is open to learning from as many religions as might teach something, as well as from the sciences and the secular world.[7] These are some of the important, and often connected, frameworks within which liberal theology has understood itself and has been understood by others. All of them in one way or another found important inspiration in Schleiermacher. In the twentieth century, all of them characterized in one way or another the theology of Paul Tillich, the archetypical liberal Christian systematic theologian, and all of them were anathema to Karl Barth, the archetypical antiliberal. Any discussion of the future of liberal theology needs to track the future developments of these and perhaps other frameworks.

Nevertheless, I propose a new framework within which to integrate these others in characterizing a worthy future for liberal theology. Actually, the framework itself is not new, only its application to understanding liberal theology. The framework is the distinction between Pre–Axial Age and Axial Age religions originally proposed by Karl Jaspers and developed by many thinkers in a variety of disciplines since then.[8] Jaspers observed that in the period of approximately 800 to 200 BCE a global change took place across the Eurasian continent, often without serious communication between its locals, that led to the formation of the great religions as we know them: Confucianism and Daoism, along with other philosophical schools, in China; Hinduism and Buddhism (and Jainism) in South Asia; and Zoroastrianism, Jewish prophetic religion, and Greek philosophical religion in West Asia. All of these religions developed conceptions of universal humanity over against tribal conceptions, of a unified world, of a universal set of ultimate conditions (not necessarily a monotheistic God but a unified pantheon, or interacting first principles—Heaven and Earth, or a Dao). As Jaspers pointed out, it suddenly became possible to think of a universal world history, however differently these religions conceived that history. Individuals came to be understood as related individually to the universal ultimate conditions. Strikingly, all of the religions emphasized some version or other of universal justice and compassion or love.

The revolutionary character of the Axial Age is stark when contrasted with the characters of tribal religions that preceded it. Tribal religions tend to conceive members of the tribe as fully human and others not to be fully human, or if not insufficiently human, the others are in outgroups, not in the ingroup defining the tribe. The geography of tribal religions is limited to the local habitat and its margins. The deities of tribal religions are tribe specific and are often conceived to be in competition with the deities of other tribes. Human beings in tribal cultures are not defined "individualistically" as human in relation to universal defining conditions such as the Dao, God, or Brahman but rather as determined in kinship relations and specific roles within the tribe, related to the graveyard of the ancestors. For tribal religions, the distinction between the ingroup and correlative outgroups is paramount to the sense of religious identity. It is easy to understand, in a commonsense way, how the characteristics of tribal religion build solidarity within the tribe and thus are adaptive for situations in which tribal groups are in competition for scarce resources and safety. The ingroup/outgroup distinction most often marks the difference between friend and foe.

The Axial Age was a time of empire building when diverse tribes were being forced to get along together, to supplement local languages with imperial common languages, sometimes to be moved away from ancestral homelands and graveyards. The tendency to constant tribal warfare with its ingroup/outgroup consciousness was not an adaptive virtue in imperial times but rather a hindrance. Hence there is some adaptive advantage to the Axial Age universalism and individualism in times of empire or large-scale global interactions, such as our own time. Jaspers's hypothesis about the Axial Age is not a strict historical one but rather serves as a framework for looking at large groupings of historical data and interpretations.

Somewhat independent of the Axial Age hypothesis, some social psychologists and evolutionary theorists have developed the hypothesis that primitive human beings, in tribal cultures, evolved five "moral" projects. Jonathan Haidt and his colleagues call these concerns for compassion, fairness, ingroup, authority, and purity.[9] The project relative to compassion concerns developing emotions that react to harm that might befall those within the ingroup, emotions such as love, nurture, sympathy, and care. Fairness pertains to reciprocity, justice, and balanced dealing within the ingroup. "Ingroup" itself as a moral project has to do with developing the signs that distinguish ingroup members from outgroup people, including appearance in dress, hairstyle, tattoos, matters of cuisine, sexual practices, ethnic markers, and so forth; the Holiness Code in Leviticus 17:26 illustrates commandments distinguishing the Israelites as the ingroup from all the neighboring outgroup peoples. Authority involves defining one's place within a hierarchy of elders and dependents, with duties for protecting the authority structure and integrity of the culture; patriotism is a great virtue for defending an authoritative ingroup. Purity is the moral project of developing visceral responses, like cultured instincts, about what is pure and impure; impure things evoke a disgust reaction. Whereas purity concerns might have arisen out of dietary issues of identifying poisons, according to Haidt, they developed into means of viscerally reacting to people and practices distinguishing ingroup membership from outgroup: disgust at the neighboring group's diet or sexual practices is a pragmatically powerful way of driving a wedge between ingroup and outgroup. Groups differ, of course, in their disgust reactions; most of us would be disgusted at a diet of bugs and worms, although that was the preferred diet of our ancestors who developed these moral projects; some contemporary Americans are disgusted at the idea of homosexual relations, whereas for others they are the preferred kind and for yet others are natural and acceptable if not to their own taste.[10]

We can integrate the Axial Age and moral projects hypotheses. The new Axial Age religions radically universalized the first two moral projects. Protective emotional response to harm to a member of the ingroup became a commandment to love and have compassion for all people (for all sentient beings in the case of Buddhism, even for enemies in the case of Christianity). Reciprocity within the ingroup became a commandment for justice for all peoples and a universal obligation of righteousness. Ingroup affiliation itself became subordinated to membership in the human race and to some kind of individual relation to ultimate conditions. Respect for authority structures became desacralized and were made pragmatic, often with roots of suspicion implanted about hierarchical institutions. And visceral disgust reactions regarding impurity and purity were recognized as culturally relative ("When in Rome . . ."). At least these transformations became the *ideals* for the Axial Age religions.

But in point of fact, the ideals of the Axial Age religions, however beautifully stated in their sacred texts, were laid down tenuously on top of the tribal religions and even to this point have not taken secure hold. Christianity as an Axial Age religion, for instance, heir of the prophets as well as Greek philosophy, holds that we should go so far as to love our enemies, and yet it has been a bellicose crusading religion in many occasions in which it has had the wherewithal to do so. Christianity commends universal justice and yet throughout its history often has exploited other peoples and members of its own group when profit or power would result. Priding itself on extending the ingroup divine promises from Israel to all the gentiles, Christianity, in the greatest irony of all, has made membership in Christianity itself a new ingroup, with "acceptance of Jesus as Lord and Savior" functioning as a badge of membership. The various Christian ingroups have very often established themselves as authoritative cultures with hierarchies distinguished from others. Disgust reactions typical of Christian cultures have been deemed normative. What is true of Christianity has generally been true of the other surviving Axial Age religions. Thus, there is a terrific and often volatile tension between the Axial Age dimensions of our religions and the strongly entrenched tribal dimensions within those same religions.

In fact, Haidt and his associates have done social-psychological studies of populations of people in America, the United Kingdom, and Latin America, asking them to characterize their attitudes toward a variety of issues on a scale from very conservative to very liberal. They have found that toward the very conservative end of the spectrum, people tend to give more or less equal weight to the five moral projects—love, justice, ingroup identity, authority, and purity. Toward the very liberal end people tend to give very great weight to the first two and much less importance to the last three. Of course, most people fall between the extremes, and individuals are not always consistent. But Haidt's instruments allow for the mapping of just how conservative or liberal people are in various parts of the country on various issues.

My proposed new framework for understanding the future of liberal theology picks up at this point. My hypothesis is that conservative people tend to have more affinity with the Pre–Axial Age, tribal, dimensions of our religions, whereas liberal people tend to have more affinity with the Axial Age ideals. Conservatives tend to be more sensitive to ingroup/outgroup identities; quicker to limit love toward the others, particularly enemies; willing to sacrifice expensive justice for outsiders when the ingroup might be at a disadvantage; highly conscious of the markers that distinguish the ingroup from outgroups; more patriotic in defending ingroup culture and condemning those, such as sexual minorities, of the outgroups; and more visceral in their reactions to what they regard as impure. Liberals, of course, are also imperfect in the universality of their love and justice, in their sense of humility regarding their group identities, in their treatment of authority structures as merely pragmatic arrangements, and in their tolerance of disgust reactions other than their own. Nevertheless, the liberals feel a moral bite in their commitment to the Axial Age ideals and to the deconstruction of tribal ingroup/outgroup distinctions they entail.

The unifying task I propose for liberal theology is the articulation and promotion of the completion of the Axial Age religious cultures of the world. This of course means many different, though perhaps relatable, things in various parts of the world. Nevertheless, there are two central questions for liberal theology in Christianity as well as other religions, each something of a paradox. The first can be called an "ecclesiastical" paradox, the second a "responsibility" paradox.

The question at the heart of the ecclesiastical paradox is how to develop the discipline and culture of Axial Age religion without turning that discipline and culture into an ingroup over against the outgroups that lack that particular discipline and culture. To develop attitudes and practices of universal love, including that directed to enemies, and universal justice, including policies that put justice to others ahead of one's own advantage, requires serious discipline.

The need is obvious for social institutions such as churches, synagogues, mosques, temples, and so forth, to organize communities to articulate the religious practices, teach them with mutual reinforcement, educate the young, and apply the ideals to specific circumstances. The scriptures and music of the "old-time religion" are as important for conveying the weight of commitment for liberal Axial Age religion as they are for developing exclusive, tribal, ingroup communities.

Moreover, liberal theology needs to contribute to the discipline of liberal anti-ingroup religion by providing a worldview that connects its ideal practices with all things ultimate. That worldview needs to make connections with the sciences, the secular cultural realms, and the plurality of religions, for all of these are important for universal love and justice. Even more important, however, is that the worldview needs to show how all of these things are conditioned by the ultimate, by God, Brahman, the Dao, or the interactions of Heavenly Principle and Earthly Material Force (the Confucian ontology). It was a great mistake of late-nineteenth-century liberal Christian theology to attempt to hold on to a Christian moral agenda while allowing its connection with the ultimate conditions to slip away, just because those connections seemed to involve superstition and supernaturalism. Without those connections, liberal religion dies as a religion, and its moral commitments lose their ultimate obligatoriness. But to sustain those connections requires a seriously metaphysical worldview. The liberals' mistake of moral reductionism was a failure of metaphysical imagination rather than some special allure of religious ethics.[11] Contrary to much Kantian-influenced liberalism, but in accord with Tillich, Boston personalism, and process theology, liberal theology has great need of contemporary metaphysics.

Finally, the ecclesiastical paradox of developing Axial Age religious discipline without setting up a disciplinary culture as an exclusive, tribal, ingroup requires fostering transcendent religious experience. "Religious experience" has many valid senses, and many if not most of these are not "transcendent" in the sense that they transcend communal, personal, and conceptual practices. Experiences of worship in church, of personal prayer, of music and art, all are important kinds of religious experiences. But by "transcendent" religious experiences I mean those that break, or undermine, or relativize, or run orthogonal to the experiences deeply mediated by tradition, communal organization, and habit. All experiences are semiotically mediated, of course, but transcendent mystical experiences are mediated with apophatic destructiveness or ecstasy, as Tillich put it. Transcendent mysticism is not so much a tradition in itself as it is the underside of religious traditions that are organized around being faithful to ultimate conditions. Religious organizations have rarely been comfortable with mystics. Nevertheless, the fire in those transcendent experiences is what gives life to disciplined religious life and practice. Mystical geniuses can articulate this fire for a generation. But nearly everyone can be awakened in mini-mystical experiences to the ultimate that lies behind and beyond our mediating categories. A crucial part of liberal ecclesiastical discipline needs to be the valorizing and nurturing of transcendent religious experience that knocks traditional discipline askew and at the same time legitimates it as a way of living before that which cannot be fully captured in human terms.

To sum up the ecclesiastical paradox, liberal theology needs to articulate and guide Axial Age religious practices, evolving worldviews that connect everything, and transcendent religious experiences in order to give vitality to the project of fulfilling Axial Age religion in its commitment to universal love and justice understood in terms of a single world with universal humanity under unified ultimate conditions.

The responsibility paradox for liberal theology can be stated much more simply. How can liberal religion adhere to the Axial Age deconstruction of sacred justifications for ingroup/outgroup distinctions while also articulating the responsibilities we have for particular groups? For all the concern about universal love and justice, we also have responsibilities to our families and communities. These responsibilities include organizing our personal, social, and political lives in such ways as to assure that love and justice are carried out in the local groups of which we are parts. It is easy to say that these local arrangements for the fulfilling of responsibility should be made with an eye to practical consequences rather than some divine authority. But it is hard to accomplish that in fact. It is an important task for liberal theology.

To summarize the argument so far, I recommend that liberal theology conceive its work in the framework of the historical project of bringing Axial Age religion to fruition. Under the aegis of that first recommendation, several other recommendations for the future of liberal theology follow, some of which have already been mentioned.

PRAGMATIC INQUIRY

The second recommendation concerns the methodological frameworks of liberal theology and is that liberal theology ought to embrace a pragmatic approach to theological knowledge. Pragmatism insists that all knowledge is fallible and subject to correction. In fact, the most plausible hypotheses are those that have been made most vulnerable to correction. But that an hypothesis is fallible does not mean it is wrong, or only possible. It means that most everything we know makes it appear to be true, even though something might come up to require its modification or rejection. Religious thinking and experience rests on many cubic acres of tested engagements with ultimate realities as well as the non-ultimate ones. We should not say that our claims to universal knowledge are only possible, or even probable, although alternatives might be possible and we should be happy that our claims are more probable. The claims rather should be regarded as true until proven otherwise.

Of course, we should go on to make such claims with appropriate arguments. The appropriate arguments for theological claims are enormously complicated and varied, as liberal theology and its critics have learned. I distinguish four main families of arguments for theological claims, those oriented to imagination, assertion, system, and practice.[12]

Arguments oriented to imagination pertain to sorting and assessing the development of religious symbols expressing religious claims and presuppositions. Here is where appeals to scripture, to ancient stories, to rituals, music, and other cultural forms that articulate the religious imagination are important. Broadly construed, the disciplines of biblical studies and ritual studies are central here, as well as the social sciences that give thick descriptions of how religious imagination plays out in life. The concern with imagination is not so much with whether specific claims are true, but rather with whether the imaginative terms pick up on what is important religiously (which is not disconnected with the concern with what is truly important!).

Arguments about theological assertions, by contrast, are aimed to discover their truth or falsity. Following from pragmatic semiotics, we know that assertions are interpretations within some particular context or contexts, and what might be true in one context might be false or misleading in another. We know that assertions interpret their subject matter in certain respects and not other respects; identifying the respect of interpretation is crucial to assessing validity. Assertions refer in at least three modes of reference. All assertions refer symbolically and therefore need to be understood in terms of the symbolic systems involved; confusions occur when a symbol from one system is construed as being in another symbolic system. Many theological claims are asserted to refer iconically, claiming that the reality is *like* what the symbols say. Many other claims, however, do not refer iconically:

God is not really *up*. The third mode of reference is indexicality, where the function of the assertion is to point to subject matter from which the interpreter is otherwise disconnected. Religious assertions, for instance, doctrines, sometimes have to "work on" people for many years before the people are transformed enough to pick up on what the assertion refers to. Finally, the interpreter must be ready for the assertion to be meaningful, for instance, not too young, not psychologically prevented from engaging the reality through the assertion. The families of arguments about theological assertions need to sort and assess context, respect of interpretation, mode of reference, and the readiness of the interpreter to determine the truth or falsity of an assertion.

Yet another family of arguments about theological claims has to do with putting assertions in systematic perspective. What was just said about assessing theological claims as assertions about their subject matter means, in effect, attempting to look at them from all angles. "All angles," of course, means system. But systems are constructions with their own claims that need to be made vulnerable to correction. Here is where the preceding remarks about connecting theological claims to the sciences, arts, the plurality of religions, and to metaphysics come in. Metaphysics arose as part of the intellectual work of the Axial Age religions, not as some nonreligious parallel process in philosophy. Metaphysics is crucial for the systematic element in theology.

The fourth family of arguments for assessing theological claims concerns how the claims guide practice. This is a double-edged sword, as the pragmatists liked to say. On the one hand, it means that the theological claims, more or less systematically integrated, need to make a difference to the practice of life. Their very meaning lies in the difference they make to how we experience and act within the world. If they do not make a difference, they are not worth much. On the other hand, the guidance of practice is part of the way we can assess our theological claims, perhaps in the long run the most important part. If not individual theological claims, then assemblages of such claims that shape lives do so in such a way as to bear "spiritual fruits," among other outcomes. This is because those claims shape lives to be more or less in accord with what is ultimately important. To be sure, articulating what is ultimately important is part of the theology and is thus defined in loose circles with the theoretical and practical considerations. Nevertheless, a theology preaching peace, justice, joy, and love must contain an error somewhere if its consequences are violence, exploitation, rancor, and bigotry as exhibited by so much religious practice today.

The pragmatic method of theological inquiry I am recommending does not reduce to "believing what is practical." It is at least as complicated epistemologically as these four families of argument types.

PRAGMATIC REALISM

Part of the sensibility against which pragmatism struggles comes from what is now widely regarded as the "social construction" of reality, and of religious experience and theology. I recommend that we recognize a truth in social constructivism but defend instead a kind of realism consonant with the pragmatic theory of religious engagement. The liberal fascination with the social sciences at Chicago illustrated by Shailer Mathews and Henry Nelson Wieman was an early manifestation of the social constructivist impulse. Michel Foucault, twisting the hermeneutical efforts of Gadamer and Ricoeur in a particular direction, followed by forty thousand Frenchmen and most American postmodernists, developed this into a mind-set that makes it seem as if reality does not measure our representations of it. Against this, pragmatism argues that, despite the fact that all signs arise as cultural constructs, they exist in living experience as directing us to discern realities that, if not discerned rightly, bite us. Signs might be socially constructed, but they are useful and survive only if they pick out what is important in reality.

Although the social constructivist movement has made us aware of the semiotic particularity of our signs, and hence of their cultural contextuality, its truth has reached its limit. I point to advances in the natural sciences, including evolutionary biology, that restore some of the experiential claims of the old liberalism. We can admit with postmodernists that scientific projects have their own traditions that are local and biased. Nevertheless, over the course of time experimental methods allow for correction by reality rather than only by the next conversational move, even when reality is expressed in a conversational form.[13] So we know (fallibly), for instance, that all cultures have music, speech, and religion. The semiotic content of those three differ by cultures. But music is necessary for early development, and in all cultures surveyed, people sing high and slowly, relative to their other songs, to infants. If infants don't get that, they cannot fully develop the capacities to distinguish pitch and meter in speech and have difficulty there. By the age of two or so, properly musical brains can begin to discern speech patterns. By adolescence, when the brain has developed to deliver dopamine to certain areas important for religious commitment, religion develops in a solid way; if the brain and the culture do not present the right opportunities during adolescence, the mature adult brain, which delivers dopamine differently, has a very hard time recognizing religious realities and engaging them appropriately.[14]

Contrary to the cultural relativism concerning even mystical religious experience that comes from a Kantian social constructivist such as Steven Katz, science is showing that several kinds of religious experience have their base in humanly common brain structures and (through evolution) anthropologically common human situations. None of this can be used to "prove" theological doctrines by appeal to direct experiential revelation or other certifying experiences. Nevertheless, it shows that the significance of religion comes not only from human signifiers but from a robust reality about which we might be wrong.

Under the influence of social constructivists from Durkheim to historicists, we have come to believe that religion is not buoyed up and given credibility by experience that engages religious realities. And yet, I claim that the heart of the human condition in every culture is, on the one hand, a desolate prospect on nothingness that is balanced, on the other hand, against an overwhelming river of abundance. Religions attempt to domesticate this extraordinary contrast with a blunting of the experience of nothingness and a setting of controls over abundance. Nevertheless, this primal experience, always parsed in particularistic cultural terms, is what gives life to the socially organized and constructed practice of religion. Where that existential experience is not acknowledged, religion becomes a performance. Liberal religion is in danger of being a performance, as its critics have claimed. This is to say, when liberal religion becomes ethics and fellowship, without the underbelly of vital religious experience, it's more fun and effective simply to be a Democrat. Deep religious experience is at the center of religious liberalism, however, if we have the epistemology and metaphysics to acknowledge it.

RELIGIOUS EXPERIENCE

The rescue of religious experience from the social constructivists cannot be accomplished just by reasserting it, however, because all experience is mediated by contextually cultured semiotics. So I recommend that liberal theology invest heavily in cross-cultural comparative religious studies that can examine in detail just where different expressions are similar, different, contradictory, complementary, incommensurable, or simply estranged from any real experience. A pragmatic emphasis on direct but mediated experience needs supplementation by cross-cultural studies to handle the issues of contextualism.

Cross-cultural comparative theological studies are fraught with the perils of colonialist bias. The history of comparative religions in the West for the last three centuries has been that of a gradual awakening to the biases in its comparative categories. Hence, it is necessary that a pragmatic method of inquiry be employed for comparison that makes the comparative categories themselves vulnerable to correction as they are used to sort comparative elements. Comparativists need to be resistant to hasty generalizations, as well as cognizant of precritical generalizations that guide their inquiry. All this is possible, and very rewarding for the pursuit of liberal theology's understanding of the relations, conceptual and otherwise, among the world's religions.[15]

METAPHYSICS AND APOPHATIC THEOLOGY

My fifth recommendation refocuses two points already made, namely, that liberal theology needs to develop its own metaphysics and that it needs to do so in conjunction with apophatic theology. Metaphysics in the pragmatic tradition is the development of hypotheses that allow for a view of the whole. Since "the whole" is not obvious, metaphysics needs to construct connections between domains of experience, reality, and knowledge that are otherwise out of connection, or connected with destructive bias. I have argued that this means, among other things, connecting theology to the sciences, arts, and secular culture, as well as connecting all religions to the domain of theological reference. As hypothetical and vulnerable to correction, such an approach to metaphysical inquiry gets around Kant's objections to metaphysics. That some liberal theologians have inclined more to historiography than to metaphysics has served to undermine liberalism. Without a metaphysics that makes history theologically interesting, honest history has no theological dimension and reduces to social studies.

If the ultimate is worth getting excited about, it would have to be bigger than what we can get our signs around. To say this is to say that theology ultimately is apophatic. Concerning the importance of embracing negative theology, metaphysics has a special function. As Duns Scotus pointed out long ago, the negation in negative theology requires some positive affirmation that justifies it. Of course, we all know that all our concepts are but faint glimmers that do not do justice to the really big issues in theology and philosophy. But negative theology is not just modesty about our concepts. It is the assertion that there is something beyond our grasp, and that the grasp at hand is in some important sense false to what is beyond. Only metaphysics can say how this can be so. Metaphysics has not been absent from liberal theology, as mentioned earlier, despite the pervasive influence of Kant. My recommendation is that we embrace the metaphysical task within liberal theology, and do it better than it has been done so far.

Permit me to summarize the recommendations I have made here for the future of liberal theology. First, I have claimed that we should abandon the defensive posture of some liberal theology that sees itself as leading religion's retreat from cultural dominance in the face of skeptical science. Rather, we should instead see liberal theology's purpose as positive, namely, to complete the Axial Age revolution in religion. All the customary ways of looking at liberal theology listed at the beginning of this essay have positive functions within this project of completing the Axial Age revolution. Second, I have recommended a strong embrace and development of theology as a kind of symbolic engagement with ultimate realities according to the epistemological outgrowths of pragmatism. Third, I have recommended that the forces of social constructivism, postmodernism, and historicism be limited by the kind of realism that pragmatic engagement provides. Although all our interpretation of ultimate matters is mediated by signs, that mediation employs signs in direct engagement with those real matters, and the signs are corrected in the process. Realism in religion, mediated by metaphysics, allows liberal theology to regain its strong hold on religious experience. Moreover, liberal theology will find that the natural sciences will be allies in laying out some of the universal traits of religion to which Axial Age liberal theology is committed. Science is the friend of religion, liberally conceived, rather than the threat that forced liberalism into a retreat. Fourth, I have recommended that liberal theology take place within a comparative theological context, with special attention to comparative theology. An implication of this is that liberal theology should not be only Christian theology, but also Jewish, Muslim, Buddhist, Hindu, Confucian, Daoist, and so forth, in all the respects in which theology can learn from those imaginative bases. This is not to say that a theologian's practice of religion needs to be more than one consistent religious tradition, suitably liberalized in an Axial Age direction. But it is to say that theology, even if aimed for one religious group, needs the comparative and universalizing context of liberal theology if it is to guide that group toward an Axial Age, rather than tribal, identity. Fifth, I have recommended that liberal theology embrace the tasks of metaphysics not merely to bring together a coherent worldview, connecting theological matters with all the rest of experience. It should also embrace metaphysics to justify and insist upon the apophatic moment in theology. For only such a theology can play host to the experiences that lie at the root of religion, the experiences that, in one way or another, balance on the cusp of existential desolation and ontological abundance.

NOTES

1. This is a positive way of putting Gary Dorrien's way of characterizing the "essence" of liberal theology: "it is the idea that Christian theology can be genuinely Christian without being based upon external authority." See his *The Making of American Liberal Theology: Imagining Progressive Religion, 1805–1900* (Louisville: Westminster/John Knox Press, 2001), xiii. I put the point in a positive way because what seems at one time to be a lack of external authority later turns out to be an external authority of a different sort, as in the switch from ecclesiasticism to scientism in some liberal quarters. When scientism itself is discovered to be implausible, the plausibility conditions drawing theological inquiry move on. Dorrien also limits liberal theology to liberal Christian theology. This is likely because he is a faithful historian dealing with the historical phenomenon of liberal Christian theology (in America). I write as a theologian and philosopher, however, and thus delimit the phenomenon with an eye to the norms that define how liberal theology should move, as best we can ascertain them in our situation. Liberal theology, I argue, should seek truth wherever it might be found, which means that Christianity should attempt to learn from other religions, among other sources. So it is needlessly limiting to say "liberal Christian theology" when the movement has already embraced liberal Jewish theology and anticipates the day in the near future when it is joined by liberal Muslim theologians. The goal of liberal theology, as discussed in this chapter, is to be "genuinely true, including true to tradition," rather than simply "genuinely Christian." Dorrien's volumes on liberal theology amply demonstrate this. See also his *The Making of American Liberal Theology: Idealism, Realism, Modernity, 1900–1950* (Louisville: Westminster/John Knox Press, 2003) and *The Making of American Liberal Theology: Crisis,*

Irony, and Postmodernity (Louisville: Westminster/John Knox Press, 2006). On the identification of liberal theology through plausibility conditions, see Wesley J. Wildman's *Fidelity with Plausibility: Modest Christologies in the Twentieth Century*, with a foreword by John B. Cobb, Jr. (Albany: State University of New York Press, 1998), part 1.

2. See, for instance, the discussion of the Chicago School in Dorrien's *The Making of American Liberal Theology: Idealism, Realism, and Modernity*, chapter 4.

3. Consider, for instance, the impact of Ernst Troeltsch and Max Weber, or of Gordon Kaufman in our day. See Kaufman's *The Theological Imagination: Constructing the Concept of God* (Philadelphia: Westminster Press, 1981) and *In Face of Mystery: A Constructive Theology* (Cambridge: Harvard University Press, 1993).

4. This has been a liberal theme from Schleiermacher through Bultmann to Tillich. My own contribution is in *The Truth of Broken Symbols* (Albany: State University of New York Press, 1996). See also my critique of anti-symbolic liberal naturalism in the following chapter.

5. Associated with Ritschl, this theme has also been important for liberal anti-Ritschlians such as Reinhold Niebuhr and the Boston personalists.

6. This is the main thesis of my *On the Scope and Truth of Theology: Theology as Symbolic Engagement* (New York: T&T Clark, 2006).

7. This framework is definitive of the current Boston University theological project, finding a significant moment in the Comparative Religious Ideas Project (1995–1999); see its volumes, *The Human Condition*, *Ultimate Realities*, and *Religious Truth*, all edited by Robert Cummings Neville (Albany: State University of New York Press, 2001).

8. See Karl Jaspers, *The Origin and Goal of History*, translated by Michael Bullock (London: Routledge and Kegan Paul, 1953; German original 1949). See also *The Way to Wisdom*, translated by Ralph Manheim (New Haven: Yale University Press, 1951; German original 1950).

9. See Haidt's summary article, "The New Synthesis in Moral Psychology," in *Science* 316 (18 May 2007), 990–1002. See also Jonathan Haidt and Jesse Graham, "When Morality Opposes Justice: Conservatives Have Moral Intuitions That Liberals May Not Recognize," *Social Justice Research*, forthcoming; and Jonathan Haidt, Silvia Helena Koller, and Maria G. Dias, "Affect, Culture, and Morality, or Is It Wrong to Eat Your Dog?," *Journal of Personality and Social Psychology* 65/4 (1993), 613–628.

10. See Haidt's discussion in his *The Happiness Hypothesis* (New York: Basic Books, 2006), chapter 9.

11. Too many nineteenth-century liberal Christian theologians were moved by Kant's supposed refutation of the possibility of metaphysics. See my "Religion and Metaphysics in Late Modernity," in *Metaphysik und Religion: Die Wiederentdeckung eines Zusammenhanges*, edited by Hermann Deuser (Guetersloh: Guetersloher Verlagshaus, 2007), 89–101.

12. The four families of arguments summarized here are treated at length in my *On the Scope and Truth of Theology* (Albany: State University of New York Press, 2006).

13. It should be clear that the kind of pragmatic theory of inquiry I am advocating differs from the neo-pragmatism associated with Richard Rorty. See his *Philosophy and the Mirror of Nature* (Princeton: Princeton University Press, 1979) and my "A Paleopragmatic Philosophy of History of Philosophy," in *Pragmatism, Neo-Pragmatism, and Religion: Conversations with Richard Rorty*, edited by Charley D. Hardwick and Donald A. Crosby, American Liberal Religious Thought (New York: Peter Lang, 1997), 43–60.

14. On this interesting point, see Candace S. Alcorta's "Religion and the Life Course: Is Adolescence an 'Experience Expectant' Period for Religious Transmission?," in *Where God and Science Meet: How Brain and Evolutionary Studies Alter Our Understanding of Religion, Volume 2: The Neurology of Religious Experience*, edited by Patrick McNamara (Westport: Praeger, 2006).

15. These traits of cross-cultural comparative theology are precisely those embodied in the Comparative Religious Ideas Project at Boston University in the late 1990s that resulted in the three volumes, *The Human Condition, Ultimate Realities*, and *Religious Truth*.

Chapter 12

NATURALISM
So Easily Wrong

INTRODUCTION

One of the things right about naturalism as an ideology is its rejection of authoritarianism and its insistence on experiential inquiry. One of the things often wrong with some naturalist positions is their insistence that only natural science constitutes valid inquiry. Another of the things right about naturalism is its rejection of literal supernaturalism as having explanatory or hermeneutical power. And yet, one of the things often wrong with some naturalist positions is tone-deafness with respect to the symbolic power of supernaturalistic thinking, resulting in a religiously flat grasp of ultimate realities.

My purpose here is to present a particular naturalist Positive Thesis, plus two corollary theses, about ultimate reality through a form of hypothetical, empirical inquiry that is not supernaturalistic. It is empirical, but not limited to the natural sciences. In fact, the sciences at most provide interesting symbols for ultimacy and are in danger of being reductionistic in a bad sense. I call this corollary of my Positive Thesis the "UnFrankenberry Thesis" because our colleague Nancy Frankenberry has sometimes been taken to believe that science has the last word about the world. My Positive Thesis includes the claim that ultimate reality, although not knowable in an iconic sense, is indeed knowable in indexical senses that elaborate fundamental symbols or metaphors for that which is beyond iconic reference. I call this corollary of my Positive Thesis the "UnWildman Thesis" because our colleague Wesley Wildman is so irritated by supernaturalistic theological claims that he rarely allows them to sing. Frankenberry and Wildman will surely dissociate themselves from the negative criticisms in my remarks and tease back.[1]

THE POSITIVE THESIS

The Positive Thesis has two basic parts. The first is the observation that anything in the world is determinate in some respects, determinately different from other things, and determinately what it is rather than nothing at all. The second is the observation that determinate things are possible only as the end products of an ontological creative act. The creative act, including what it creates as its end products, is the ontological ultimate reality and is what I think we should mean by "nature." I shall explain why this is a naturalistic philosophical theology after glossing the two observations.

The first observation sets the level of discussion at the most abstract and universal level possible, that of the nature of determinateness itself.[2] At this level it does not matter what the world contains, so long as what it contains is something rather than nothing. To put the point another way, this theory of determinateness tolerates all possible conceptions of the world and what it is to be a thing. The theory articulates the conditions for all distinctions, including those such as earlier and later or hotter and colder. So, the possibility that the Big Bang happened is conditional upon the nature of determinateness.

To be determinate is to be something, to be anything that is "this" rather than "that." One thing can be determinate only with respect to some other things, the "that's" to its "this." Therefore, if there is anything determinate, there must be a plurality of things that are determinate with respect to one another. If there is a plurality of things determinate with respect to one another, then each must have components that are conditions given by the other things; call them "conditional components." But each must also have "essential components" of its own to be external to the others and not wholly swallowed up in them. Therefore, each determinate thing is a harmony of at least two kinds of components, conditional and essential.

A "harmony" is just the way the components fit together. This is the most basic aspect of determinateness—a plurality of fittings together. If the harmony were some sort of Aristotelian "third term" that sits atop and unifies the components, it would be just another determinate thing, another determinate harmony with its own conditional and essential components. Then there would have to be a determinate harmony that integrates the top with the original components, and so on.

Harmonies are subject to four kinds of analysis. (1) They have forms or patterns by which their components are together and these most likely are complex hierarchies of patterned arrangements. (2) They have the components that can be analyzed on their own. (3) Because determinate harmonies have conditional components relative to other determinate harmonies, they are located relative to the other harmonies in what is best called an "existential field"; the field is the networks of relation among things constituted by the mutual determinations of the conditional components. (4) Any harmony has the actual identity of getting its particular components together in its particular form at its particular location in the existential field relative to other things. Because of the hierarchical character of form or pattern, anything with a form has a value, although this is not a point I will argue here. The achievement of an actual identity is thus the constitution of a value-identity. Determinate things are harmonies having (1) form, (2) components including both conditional and essential kinds, (3) existential location relative to other determinate things, and (4) value-identity. To illustrate the points about form, components, location, and identity would take us too far from the abstract metaphysics of determinateness as such in the direction of a defensible philosophical cosmology.

Let me cut back then to my second observation, namely, that determinate things are possible only as the end products or results of an ontological creative act. Here is the problem of the possibility of a plurality of determinate things. How are the many determinate things together? They are obviously together in terms of their mutual definition of the existential field through which they relate to one another conditionally. But no determinate thing is only its conditional components. It is a harmony of the conditional components with its essential components. If its essential components are not together in some nonconditional way with the essential components of the other determinate things, the determinate things do not have externality or independence from one another. Otherness is not possible without things being together in such a way that each has its essential components harmonized with its conditional ones. Whereas the togetherness constituted by the mutual relations of conditional components can be called a cosmological context of mutual relevance, the togetherness of the plurality of things with their essential and conditional components harmonized can be called an ontological context of mutual relevance because it is the condition for the very possibility of determinate being, and hence of the possibility of the cosmological context of mutual relevance.

What might be the ontological context of mutual relevance? If it were something itself determinate, then there would have to be an even deeper ontological context of mutual relevance making possible its togetherness with the other things. But what could be an indeterminate context of mutual relevance? The only thing that could be this is a creative act that has no nature of its own except its creating all the determinate things together. Without the actual creating, there would be nothing, no world, nothing determinate. With the actual creating, the ontological creative act has the determinate character of being creator of this world. But the act is not anything determinate apart from actually creating something determinate, and its own determinate nature is among the determinate things created.

This is all very abstract, as you must have noticed. But some important religious implications follow immediately. First, absolutely everything determinate in any way is created. Determinateness as such is created, as is intelligibility, possibility, space-time, dynamic creativity, and motion within time, all ideals and standards, all aspects of agency and intentionality. All these things are determinate and hence are created products of the ontological creative act. Second, this conception of the ontological creative act as indeterminate apart from its creatures rules out any more specific conception of a determinate creator God, such as one having intentions, agency, morality, knowledge, goodness, unity, beauty, truth, or fullness of being as in the Neo-Platonic One prior to the Dyad or the Thomistic Act of To Be. No possibility exists for any literal personal theism or supranaturalism in the character of the ontological creative act. Any positive characterization of the ontological creative act apart from or as a source of creation would have to be at best metaphorical, a point to which I shall return in my UnWildman Thesis.

The thesis that everything determinate is created by an ontological creative act has scientific as well as religious consequences. Some scientists, such as Lawrence M. Krauss, attempt to answer the question "why is there something rather than nothing?" by accounting for the origin of determinate things within the process of nature, especially that part of the process associated with the Big Bang.[3] But the very distinction between an earlier, perhaps indeterminate, state of affairs and a later determinate one, say a time of very great heat following upon a heatless universe, is a determinate distinction. Any differences that science might note to explain the evolution of the "something" of the universe would have to be determinate and therefore themselves dependent on the ontological act of creation.

What then does this Positive Thesis say about ultimate reality? Ultimate reality is the world of determinate things as together in the ontological creative act. What does reference to the act add to the world of determinate things? This frequently asked question usually supposes that any possible answer would have to cite something determinate (in order to be "additive"), which would disqualify the act as the ontological context of mutual relevance. The creative act does not add a thing. What it adds is the existence of all determinate things. But then is the ontological creative act nothing more than the world, a kind of pantheistic conception? No, because the world of determinate things would not be possible if they were not together in an ontological way that goes beyond what each of them separately could provide. We can very well look at ontological ultimate reality as the collection of determinate things, so long as we recognize that they could not be determinate without being together and that the possibility of their togetherness requires an ontological creative act that makes them together. From this perspective, the ontological creative act is not something separate from the world but is what some philosophical theologians such as Paul Tillich call the "depth dimension" of things that grounds the being of things in mutual determination.

On the other hand, ultimate reality can be characterized from the standpoint of the act, noting the dynamism and novelty making, that is involved in creating the determinate things. The creative act cannot be separated from its creatures; they are its end products. There would be no creative act without the things created. The phrase *natura naturans*, made famous by Spinoza, is a good image for the ontological creative act, so long as we recognize that *natura naturata* is inseparable from it and in fact is the determinate character of *natura naturans* doing its thing. I recognize that our colleague Robert Corrington employs the concept of *natura naturans* but in a sense that separates it from *natura naturata*, something that would ruin the point I am making here.[4]

Albeit indeterminate apart from creation, the ontological creative act has all sorts of interesting, if abstract, characters that come from its actual creating. First, it is singular in the sense that all plurality among determinate things is contained in its end product. The act does not create each thing by itself, because each determinate thing is defined conditionally in part by how it is determinate with respect to all the other things. So, the realm of determinate things is created as a singularity. Second, the ontological creative act is eternal in the sense that time and space are determinate creatures. There is no time at which the creation takes place—all temporal as well as spatial location is a function of the existential fields constituted by the conditional connections of determinate things. Third, because the ontological creative act creates determinate things (that's what creation of things means), the act can be characterized by the transcendental traits of determinateness. Thus, the ontological creative act is the source of form, plurality to be formed into components, existential location, and achieved value-identity. Those four transcendental traits of determinateness can be called "cosmological ultimate realities" because they must obtain and be ultimate conditions in any possible created cosmos.

Earlier I said that this positive thesis about ultimate reality is an empirical hypothesis, and yet I doubt you have ever heard a more conceptually dialectical argument except maybe from me on other occasions. What is empirical about it? Let me answer on two levels.

First, the hypothesis is confirmed by any possible evidence because that evidence would have to be determinate. It is also confirmed by the counterfactual of any possible evidence, because that too would have to be determinate. So no matter what you say the world is or is not, this is evidence for the thesis about determinateness and its necessary contingency on the ontological creative act. Of course, the dialectical analysis of determinateness and the inference to the ontological creative act as that upon which it is contingent might be mistaken. As an hypothesis it is fallible. But then the objection would have to be made that determinateness is something significantly different from what I have said, which would have to be a counterdialectical argument, not an appeal to different sorts of determinate things.

Second, and more deeply, the issue of empirical status for the hypothesis pertains to two kinds of reference for hypotheses. Peirce distinguished iconic from indexical reference. Iconic reference is when the interpretation asserts that the object is like what the signs in the interpretation say. Iconic reference asserts a kind of modeling or formal correspondence between sign and object, as in a description, or in a scientific theory that says the relations among things in the world are like what the mathematical formulation lays out, or as a map is an icon for territory, or as a metaphor in the sense of a simile. Although all the determinate things in the world can be modeled iconically because of their form, the ontological creative act apart from its creatures cannot be modeled because it has no form except what it creates. Charles Hartshorne insisted that all philosophical explanation necessarily is iconic because it refers to first principles. First principles, for him, are the only kinds of things that explain because explanatory reference must be iconic. Indexical reference, however, explains by pointing so that a new relation between the object and interpreter is established, like getting a person to look in a new direction. A dialectical argument is a kind of philosophical index, causing a person to get into a relation with the logical object so as to pick up on it. My argument that the ontological act is required for anything determinate to exist aims to persuade people that the act of creation, not what is created, is what explains. Creative decision-making is not the same as before-and-after snapshots of a creative process; the latter can be an iconic map of a creative process. The actual creating needs to be grasped indexically, encountered, perceived in some sense. So my dialectical argument is empirical in the sense that it attempts to conjure up the perception of creative making, not only what is made, a perception of determinate things as being created. This is an empiricist's appeal to brute experience rather than a rationalist's appeal to first principles.

In what sense, finally, is this positive thesis a naturalistic one? Clearly, it is not supernaturalistic or supranaturalistic in the sense of claiming that there is a determinate being that creates the world or that is ultimate reality. On the other hand, it is not a naturalism that limits religious interest just to the things of nature taken by themselves. Rather it reconceives the things of nature as being unified with one another in the ontological creative act. Things do not exist by themselves but are ontologically defined by conditioning mutuality as well as by their essential otherness and independence. We are who and what we are only insofar as we are with all other things as elements in the end product of the singular ontological creative act. This is enough now for the positive thesis of my naturalistic philosophical theology.

THE UNFRANKENBERRY THESIS

My UnFrankenberry thesis takes its title from a conversation at last year's IARPT meeting on the deck of Creighton Peden's house under the influence of his wine. Nancy Frankenberry said to me in an incredulous tone, "Bob, you don't really believe there is more to nature than science in principle can or will know, do you?" Bill Dean, standing at her right hand, vigorously nodded agreement to the implication of her rhetorical question. We had been talking about the explanatory power of metaphysics and theology regarding whatever is to be known about the existence and nature of the world. I responded by saying that I do believe there is more to nature than science can know, blurting out a brief vinous version of my Positive Thesis. But her question deserves much more serious reflection, which gives rise to my UnFrankenberry thesis.

By science Nancy meant what we know as the natural and perhaps social sciences, subject to their own self-correction and development. The virtue of those sciences, at least in their ideal intent, is to be reductive in a proper Kantian sense. That is, a science understands its subject matter by reducing it to what can be registered by the science's theories, experimental instruments, special skills in experimental design, the tastes and specific ambitions of that science's community, the processes of peer reviewing, and the like. The objectivity of the science consists precisely in that it does not make claims about the subject matter in itself beyond what is so reduced, but only about the subject matter as reobjectified in the science's own terms. Kant drew out the full implication of this. The world as knowable by science is an objectified construction of the science itself, not the world in itself. Strictly speaking, science makes very modest and humble claims and is ready to admit that the subject matter in itself might have all sorts of content that cannot be registered in that science's terms. For many of the natural sciences, the objective world is whatever can be registered in mathematical languages, and all those aspects of the world that cannot be so registered may well be real but do not show up as objects of their specialized scientific knowledge.

Pragmatists of the sort likely to be found in our group (IARPT) have a more realistic, non-Kantian, interpretation of the sciences as engaging the real objects in themselves but only in the respects in which the sciences' signs can interpret those real objects.[5] Always there are other respects in which those objects can be interpreted, and these might be much more important than the ones amenable to the science. For pragmatists, the respects in which things are interpreted are functions of the semiotic habits of inquirers as well as their purposes. Dewey sometimes interpreted scientific knowledge as whatever is "instrumental" under controlled inquiry for satisfying human purposes. Peirce emphasized another side, namely, that the more we learn about the world, the more we learn what purposes are really worth having, those that engage things in their most important respects. Pragmatists are enthusiastic about the special sciences that exercise controlled responsibility for what their categories and disciplined modes of inquiry can know. But they also ask about what is left out when reality is engaged with those special sciences.

How in fact do and should we ask about what is left out of a properly reductive analysis? The obvious first answer, one that is perfectly compatible with the assumptions in Frankenberry's rhetorical question, is that relative to any one science we can check out what the *other* sciences have to say. Suppose our subject matter is religion and we learn enormously from Durkheim about the respects in which religions are social phenomena.

Sociology of religion leaves out a lot that can be learned about religion from the anthropological treatment of it as a matter of culture. It also leaves out what can be learned from psychology of religion, or rather from the very many different disciplines within the psychology of religion. Now we have religion studied by evolutionary biologists, neuroscientists, and cognitive scientists of many stripes. Perhaps we should count among the sciences studying religion the various traditions of historical research on religious traditions. Of course, the sciences themselves are developing and changing their boundaries, drawing on one another in new ways and finding ways of increasing certain kinds of irrelevance: recent developments in cognitive science are regrouping psychology, biology, and anthropology and making sophisticated theology irrelevant. But if you put the sciences together and allow them their self-controlled critical development, it is possible to say that what one science leaves out some other science will take up, so that the nature of religion in principle can be studied exhaustively by "science" in the general sense Frankenberry meant it.

While all to the good, this is not satisfactory, however, in relation to what is left out in scientific reduction. What the sciences have in common, excepting perhaps the quasi-humanistic ones in history of religions, is the reductive ideal of finding a theory or set of categories, or ideal language, which is itself unified and intelligible and that "explains" many things as different instances of the same category. Early modern physics tried to explain all motions as instances of Newton's Laws of Motion. Evolutionary biology tries to explain the origins of religion in terms of the adaptive advantages of either what it identifies as religion or of human traits that go into religion but are not themselves necessarily religious. In fact, for many scientists the very meaning of "explanation" is showing how the subject matter illustrates some underlying theoretical generalizations, such as in mathematical physics or evolutionary theory. What is unsatisfactory about this is that it limits our understanding of things to the universal properties of which they might be instances. What about those aspects of things that are singular and unrepeatable, that are important precisely in their particularity? My friends surely move according to some updated version of the Laws of Motion, have biochemical brains of the sort that allow for friendship, and exhibit psychological traits found in friends, but for me to understand their friendship and grasp it with friendly responses that define my own identity requires attending to their singularities and the particularities of our interactions.

The humanities and arts in general are ways of getting at those aspects of things that are not most importantly understood as instances of more general categories. Hence the importance of narrative, of the immediacy of materials in painting and sculpture, of the difference between a particular hearing of a piece of music and its score, or even a CD that makes the same notes each time it is played. A poem by Gerard Manley Hopkins can be an index leading us to see haecceity, "explaining" thisness, in an imagined this.

The most culturally problematic limitation of the sciences is that most of the base languages to which they would reduce what they claim to know are not capable of exhibiting value. This is particularly true of the mathematical languages that are favored by so many sciences. Sometimes the beauty in the explanatory theory is exhibited, but the first-order beauty in the particular things is not explained. Because modern culture easily forgets that science is explaining things only in their universalizable respects, it assumes that the real world does not have value, or that experienced values are mere subjective projections onto the subject matter, or that the objects of science, including people, can be treated just as objects. Elie Wiesel's *Night* is about the horror of nature conceived as valueless facts intelligible as instances of more general theories.

The cultural motives for the humanities in this age of science include a strong imperative to deconstruct scientific reductions so as to recover the particular value-identities of things and to respond appropriately. I take it that one of the main functions of philosophy is to track the significance of scientific reductions and humanistic counter-exhibitions of important aspects of things, a truly dialectical process. This is not philosophy's only function, but it is important, and in our time, is closely associated with postmodernism. Philosophy also has a systematic function, to provide a kind of framework, with properly defended parts, in terms of which things can be seen in something like their wholeness, with the deliverances of the sciences and humanities integrated.

Underlying what I have said here is an appreciation of a pragmatic approach to explanation or understanding, namely, through interpretive engagement with the subject matter. In the long run, all the elements of knowing help us perceive or feel the subject matter with greater depth and discrimination. We engage religion with greater acuity when we see the underlying functions of neurobiology in it and when we sing its songs ecstatically. The central metaphor for the ideal of explanation or understanding is perception: we aim to perceive better and then act in accord with what we perceive.

Let me conclude the UnFrankenberry thesis by pointing out the importance of indexical reference in explanation. Our categories, theories, poems, and dances are aimed to shape up our interpretive abilities so that they are pointed to the right things in the subject matter and engaged with them. The bottom line for explanation is not grasping things as instances of first principles or of a base language but rather the encountering of them with proper discrimination. I claimed in my Positive Thesis that the ontological act of creation of the world is grasped best by a dialectical argument that is an index formative of an experience of it. I now want to claim in my UnFrankenberry thesis that understanding anything in the world involves a similar kind of perceptive encounter shaped by the many respects in which our disciplined and highly imaginative signs indexically guide the engagement. A viable naturalism needs to hold that understanding nature is more than the grasp of it by ideal sciences. I wish I had thought to say that to Nancy and Bill at the party.

THE UNWILDMAN THESIS

My UnWildman thesis takes its title from a conversation in Highlands at our annual meeting five years ago late at night when Wesley Wildman, Gordon Kaufman, and I shared a cottage. For about three hours the two of them ganged up on me to protest my continued use of biblical and other religious symbols to express what I believed to be religiously true. I agreed with them, of course, in rejecting supernaturalism and the literal meaning of most of the religious symbols. They argued that in my writing and preaching, however, most people would assume that I did intend those symbols to be taken literally. They argued with great force and repetition that the continued use of those symbols was, in practice if not in theory, extremely hypocritical and counterproductive to fostering our common theological naturalism. To be beaten up by two of America's best theologians for so long a time was one of the best experiences of my life. But now I want to argue again that a proper naturalism should be symbolically musical.

In my Positive Thesis I argued that the ontological act of creation cannot be modeled except in its end product, the created world. Nevertheless, it is the ultimate ontological reality of the world we live in and so people do have to refer to it if they are alert to their surroundings; if they have studied enough pragmatism, they know the reference is indexical and not iconic. Even if their education has been lacking in that regard, they still say that their references are metaphorical and should not be taken literally when push comes to shove.

There are three main symbol systems by which various religious cultures have attempted to elaborate metaphors for referring to and thus engaging what I call the ontological creative act. These symbol systems take something important in ordinary life and push it, stretch it, and transform it until it is not so obviously false about that which gives rise to everything determinate. One of these is the notion of person, most familiar in the West, that has been metaphorically developed in religious theisms. Gods are like persons but with greater powers, with fewer limitations, and the like. Many theists conceive of God the creator as having agency and intentions for human life, and a good will, and perhaps also a touchy, judgmental disposition. By the time sophisticated theologians push the concept of person to the high transcendent level so as to articulate creation of everything contingent, say in the Neo-Platonic conception of the One beyond any duality or in the Thomistic conception of the pure Act of To Be, or my conception of the ontological creative act, such a God cannot be conceived to be in relation to anything else the way a person must be. But there is a history of the transformation of the concept, and Thomas's doctrine of analogy allowed him to say that finite things are significantly like the pure Act of To Be such that, on the one hand God is simple, pure, indeterminate, and unrelated to the world and on the other hand that the Blessed Virgin is His Mother; there are quite a few steps in between those points.

Another basic metaphorical system for referring to ultimate reality is built on the experience of consciousness. Anyone can sit quietly and distinguish somewhat between the objects of consciousness and the being conscious of them. Techniques for improving such contemplation have proliferated for millennia with many different theories about what is going on. In Upanishadic forms of Hinduism, consciousness is conceived as an underlying self or atman, which is identical in all people and itself is real in being Brahman, first with qualities and then without qualities. Of course, Brahman without qualities has no qualities of consciousness, but the progressive transformation of the metaphor maintains a conceptual continuity that is related to disciplined experience. Buddhisms do different things with the consciousness metaphor, denying the deeper self of atman or the fundamental reality of Brahman and emphasizing instead the creative powers of empty-conscious enlightenment. In the Lotus Sutra, for instance, the manifest qualities of the plural worlds are the direct creation of the enlightened Buddha-mind. In the symbolic systems based on consciousness, intentionality and agency are precisely what is removed from the ultimacy of consciousness, quite the opposite of what happens with the personification metaphors.

A third symbolic system for the ontological creative act, more common in East Asia, is based on spontaneous emergence—buds opening in the spring, water gushing out of the ground, instances of spontaneous personal creativity. Multiple conceptions of the Dao, and of the interaction of Heaven and Earth, have been developed, leading to versions of the Neo-Confucian and Daoist insights that everything comes spontaneously from nothing.

None of these symbol systems can literally be true of the ontological creative act, and sophisticated theologians in just about every Axial Age tradition have affirmed an apophatic moment to recognize this. Nevertheless, these systems have been elaborated in rich cultural ways to frame up the underlying philosophy of a glittering array of religious practices. Every religion I know of develops symbols for engaging at least five problematics: (1) the shock and glory of the existence of the world itself, (2) the ground of basic obligation, (3) the project of human wholeness, (4) engaging others as others, and (5) articulating meaning in life. You will have noticed that these five correspond to the ontological ultimate reality of the creative act and the four cosmological ultimate realities of the transcendental traits of determinateness. These are the ultimate boundary conditions of any determinate world and are engaged by any religious sensibility with a complex intellectual history. All these symbols guide religious living.

Of course, religious living has done some very terrible things. Surely, it is important to inquire robustly into the truth of the religious symbols that guide engagements. The symbols by themselves are not true or false. They have truth value only when involved in an interpretive engagement. The question of their truth consists in whether they carry across into the experience of the interpreter what is important and valuable in the things interpreted in the respects in which those symbols stand for the things. Iconic carryover is fairly obvious; assessing indexical carryover requires triangulating in from different directions. Religious symbols in the myriads of cultures engage people with life's predicaments and carry ecstatic fulfillments.

Now my UnWildman thesis says that naturalism goes very wrong if it insists on only literal and nonsymbolic engagements of things. Rather, naturalism needs to cultivate the arts of critical symbolic musicality. Let me illustrate with a brief discussion of the Twenty-Third Psalm, which you all know. This psalm has been one of the most moving pieces of spiritual life for nearly three millennia in at least three major religious traditions, and it even moves secular atheists to tears. In the classic English King James translation:

> The Lord is my shepherd; I shall not want.
> He maketh me to lie down in green pastures: he leadeth me beside the still waters.
> He restoreth my soul: he leadeth me in the paths of righteousness for his name's sake.
> Yea, though I walk through the valley of the shadow of death, I will fear no evil: for thou art with me; thy rod and thy staff they comfort me.
> Thou preparest a table before me in the presence of mine enemies; thou anointest my head with oil; my cup runneth over.
> Surely goodness and mercy shall follow me all the days of my life: and I will dwell in the house of the Lord for ever.

The psalm literally says that God is a shepherd and that we are sheep. Surely, no one past the age of ten ever has believed that literally. A literal interpretation is nonsense.

The age-old tradition of interpretation is metaphorical in the iconic sense of simile. *Like* a shepherd who cares for his sheep, God supplies what we need: life in pleasant places, peace, tonics for the soul, a righteous life, no evil even in death, comfort, gloating repasts in the face of enemies, anointing oils, overflowing cups, a life attended by goodness and mercy lived in the constant presence of God. Each of these divine beneficences is itself a metaphor for thousands of other benefits from the benevolent God. The Twenty-Third Psalm is a classic because everyone understands this metaphoric meaning and is in love with the vision it sings.

But it is false! Life is full of trouble and grief, want and desolation, humiliation and defeat, and always death. To think God is like a provident shepherd is just perverse in the face of life's realities. Sure, life has many good things, including occasional triumphs and the comforts of the overflowing cup—but all these things pass, and many people get none of them. The ancient Israelites knew this as well as anyone.

How then do we understand the extraordinary moving power of the Twenty-Third Psalm when it is literally nonsense and metaphorically false? Both literal and metaphorical intentions are claims that God and life are *like* what the psalm says, in different but related senses of *like*. The deeper meaning of the psalm, however, which nearly everyone somehow gets, does not have to do with likeness at all. It concerns becoming connected with what I call, so unmusically, the ontological creative act. If we shape our souls with the images of the psalm, even though it is literally nonsense and metaphorically false, we become connected with the ground of our being and our own lives so as to be transformed into gratitude with peace that passes understanding, a truth far more profound than satisfaction with the good things of life. In fact, it is precisely because life is filled with trouble and grief, want and desolation, humiliation and defeat, and always death, that we move beyond the historical to the depth dimension of our relation to our ontological creative ground. Because we know that the life of a happy sheep is a lie (remember *why* shepherds keep sheep!), we come to realize that the genuine comforts of God are not like that. But letting the Twenty-Third Psalm work in us to shape our soul causes us to connect with ultimate reality beyond that superficial metaphor and to take overwhelming comfort in the Abyss out of which the maelstrom of life arises. The depth meaning of the psalm is not in its likeness to anything: it is not an icon. The depth meaning is in its transformative pointing and connection: it is an index, like a pointing finger whose direction we follow until we connect with something otherwise inaccessible. That transformative depth meaning has worked for centuries with astonishing indexical power regardless of people's literal or metaphorical thoughts in the matter. By "working" I mean that the psalm has carried over a profound truth about how we rest in the ontological creative act, the grasp of which is a kind of ecstatic fulfillment even in the worst of times.

When I argue that theological naturalism so easily goes wrong if it fails to be musical about religious symbols, I do not mean that we can ignore the ways those symbols have been abused and interpreted mistakenly. The new atheists have their point. Preachers have an extraordinary responsibility to interpret the symbols appropriately, hedging against their misuse while sounding their resonances. I also do not mean to suggest that literal naturalistic, anti-supernaturalistic, metaphysics is for the sophisticated, whereas symbolic religion is for popular employment. I mean to say rather that the whole of religious truth requires both the metaphysical and the symbolic. My UnFrankenberry thesis is that there are dimensions to truth about the real that the sciences, even under ideal conditions in the infinite long run, cannot register. My UnWildman thesis is that ontological ultimate reality cannot be grasped iconically but only through the indexicality of dialectical metaphysics and non-iconic symbolism.

Where naturalism in religion so easily goes wrong is when it flattens its representations of how we can engage ultimate matters by assuming the sciences to define the only serious paradigm of knowing and, perhaps as a correlate of that, insisting that non-iconic symbols cannot truthfully carry across what is important to know about ultimate reality. The emphases on the importance of knowing for practical life and the bodily embeddedness of knowing fostered by the American pragmatic tradition are counterforces against the error so easy within naturalistic thinking of letting the living waters of religion slip away. Pragmatic philosophical theology needs to be bold, however, in engaging the ultimate realities important to religion. I have not argued from a theory of inquiry, scientific or symbolic, to what can be known about ultimate reality. I have argued instead from a theory about the nature of ultimate reality as to what knowing it would need to be.

NOTES

4. This chapter began as an address at the June 2012 annual meeting of the Institute for American Religious and Theological Thought. The meetings of the institute have constituted an ongoing conversation for many of its members, into which the newer members are being introduced with rapidity. This accounts for the informality with which I refer to Professors Nancy Frankenberry and Wesley Wildman, and subsequently to the late Gordon Kaufman. Professor Frankenberry's article, "Does Evolutionary Biology Refute Every Form of Theism?," quotes a paragraph from the present chapter to indicate her response in a teasing way. Professor Wesley J. Wildman's "The Ambiguous Heritage and Perpetual Promise of Liberal Theology," *American Journal of Theology and Philosophy* 32/1 (January 2011), 43–61, argues that when liberal theology is honest, literal, and unmusical, it is religiously deficient with regard to the support of religious communities. At the meeting, Frankenberry asserted vehemently that she loves and supports the humanities, not only the sciences; Wildman himself does sing, especially in his sermons.

5. The arguments in the rest of this section summarize a systematic position I have developed over many years. See my *God the Creator: On the Transcendence and Presence of God* (Chicago: University of Chicago Press, 1968; reprint edition with a new introduction, Albany: State University of New York Press, 1992), part 1; or *Symbols of Jesus* (Cambridge: Cambridge University Press, 2001), chapter 1. The most complete presentation of this

thesis is in *Ultimates: Philosophical Theology Volume One* (Albany: State University of New York Press, 2013).

6. See Lawrence M. Krauss's *A Universe from Nothing: Why There Is Something Rather than Nothing*, with an afterword by Richard Dawkins (New York: The Free Press, 2012).

7. See Corrington's *Ecstatic Naturalism: Signs of the World* (Bloomington: Indiana University Press, 1994).

8. "Our group" refers to the Institute for American Religious and Philosophical Thought, at whose annual meeting this conversation took place and at another meeting of which a version of this chapter was delivered as a paper.

Part IV

PHILOSOPHICAL THEOLOGY

PRELIMINARY REMARKS

The four chapters of this part deal with large and basic issues in philosophical theology, although in different ways. Chapter 13 structures a debate between process theology's conception of God and my conception of the ontological creative act. Its form is a long letter to David R. Griffin in response to a chapter he wrote about my work in a book identified in my letter. His chapter itself was a response to a book I published in 1980 that was critical of process theology. Our debate has long legs. This chapter could have been grouped in part 5 of this volume because it is a debate with a friend; but it fits here better because the real focus is the concept of the ultimate, not his work or mine. Chapter 14 also could have been located in part 5 because it too is a discussion of the work of a friend, Joseph Bracken, S.J. But its focus is on the issue of creation *ex nihilo* against which Joe argues with his own original form of process philosophy. Chapter 15 discusses a crucial aspect of apophatic theology, namely, what to do existentially when one's worldview finally cracks, as apophatic theology predicts. Chapter 16 returns to the theory of five ultimate realities, this time from the perspective of how they might be studied in various disciplines.

Chapter 13

A RESPECTFUL ALTERNATIVE TO PROCESS THEOLOGY
A Letter of Grateful and Affectionate Response to David Ray Griffin's Whitehead's Radically Different Postmodern Philosophy: An Argument for Its Contemporary Relevance

July 10, 2007

Dear David,

I was surprised and deeply grateful to receive several weeks ago the autographed and personally dedicated copy of your new book with its long chapter about my discussions of process theology. Of course, we all appreciate people who pay attention to our work, and I have been fortunate to have serious orthodox process conversation partners in John Cobb, Charles Hartshorne, Lewis Ford, Marjorie Suchocki, Joseph Bracken, and many others. But yours here is the longest, most sustained, and most detailed response, for which I thank you. We have been friends for many years, interweaving through conferences and publications as close colleagues do. I had not realized that we are the same age until reading, in this book, the date when you will turn seventy, about two months after I do, *deo volente*. You have unparalleled intellectual precision, energy, and wit. I am honored to receive this book and thank you with appreciation, gratitude, and the affection borne over a long friendship.

The book as a whole is a *tour de force* of defenses of Whitehead on a variety of controversial fronts, where you have mastered the literature in each field: phenomenological consciousness, ecology, truth as correspondence, physical and lived time, moral theory, and relativity theory in relation to Whiteheadian theism, as well as my anti-Whiteheadian theism. The book deserves reviewers in each of these different fields, for I doubt that anyone exists other than yourself who is comfortable with the state of the art in all. Here I mean to respond to the chapter focusing on my criticisms of Whitehead.

Let me express a special kind of gratitude here. Your discussion in this book tries to take very seriously the fact that I have a philosophical-theological alternative to Whitehead. Process theologians have been generous in paying attention to my work—there are so few of us metaphysical types that we know we should stick together. But most of the time they have been interested only in my criticisms of Whitehead, not in whether my own view has merit. In this book you take care to contrast my theological views, and indeed my religious sensibilities, from those common in process theology, for which I especially thank you. There is more to my philosophy than the parts you mention, and I'll have occasion shortly to bring some of that up. Most followers of Whitehead, beginning with Hartshorne and Wieman, have modified his philosophy to address problems, still considering themselves Whiteheadians. A number of other philosophers of our generation, for instance George Allan, Robert Corrington, Frederick Ferré, and Joseph Grange, as well as some of our students, have developed alternative philosophical systems that learn from Whitehead without identifying as Whiteheadians. It would be good to cultivate a dialogue among these systems, would it not? My response here is an attempt at advancing the dialogue between your system and mine, not just to answer your criticisms of my criticisms.

Before turning to your arguments about my critique, however, let me wish you well in your ongoing struggle to claim the term "postmodern" for Whitehead. You are right to point out that Whitehead himself was one of the first to use the term "post modern" when he wrote *Science and the Modern World*, objectifying modernity's metaphysical assumptions in science, criticizing their limitations, and offering a better metaphysical system. Dewey, Heidegger, and in his way the "Later Wittgenstein" attempted similar moves. You have an uphill battle, however, because in the current situation the term "postmodern" has come to be the adjective form of "postmodernism." Modernism is not the whole of modernity or Whitehead's Modern World. Modern*ism* refers to the drive for foundational certain starting points, say with the rationalists' intellectual intuitions, the empiricists' sense data, or the Kantians' a priori transcendental philosophy. In culture, modernism manifested itself in the drive to abandon references to the past, to simplify, and to make form follow function. Modernism seeks a clean, well-lighted place where everything simply is what it is without depending on larger contexts for meaning.[1] For common postmodernists, this has required an all-out attack on any hint of supposition of a clear and unique logocentric story of Western culture, especially philosophy. Although Whitehead would agree with the common postmodernists that reality is very ambiguous, multivalent, and filled with things, including ideas and populations, that don't fit into the larger dominant pictures, even his own metaphysical worldview, he was not preoccupied with attacking modernism.[2] He sought instead to enlarge his theory to take into account evidence other theories marginalized.

Modernism is but one current within the river of European modernity. The headwaters of modernity, I think, flow from the conviction that we should learn from experience. This entails setting aside tradition's and religions' claims to absolute authority, not rejecting tradition and religion as such, only their claims to authority that trumps what might be learned from experience. Modern science, for Whitehead, was the epitome of the method of learning from experience, where reality corrects our ideas. The intellectual puzzle, to him, was that the typical modern metaphysical assumptions about reality made it difficult to understand how mathematical science could apply to reality. His alternative metaphysics, with its causal theories of perception and judgment, was intended to show how real entities might bear the mathematic relations science discovered there.

With regard to the modern principle of learning from experience, Whitehead was thoroughly modern. He was highly critical of the modernist philosophies, especially of Kant's, and followed rather in the line of modern thought that ran through the Scottish commonsense philosophers to Peirce, James, and Dewey, all of whom were fallibilists, like Whitehead. Like the pragmatists, he treated the big theories of the modern philosophers, Descartes, Leibniz, Spinoza, Locke, Berkeley, and Hume, as if they were hypotheses that had something but not everything going for them (say, in *Process and Reality*, part 2). He treated his own metaphysics as an hypothesis to be proved, amended, or disproved through engagement with the "broad experience of mankind."

In respect to the fact that most common postmodernists try to sever any putative connection between discourse and the real, denying that anything except more discourse can correct our thinking, Whitehead, the pragmatists, I myself, and even you, dear David, are alternative late-modern thinkers. We are not "post" the conviction that inquiry can learn from reality, even if we never believed that such learning needs to be based on certainty. The conviction that inquiry can learn from reality is an enduring and highly valuable contribution of modernity, which need not be identified with its foundationalist or modernist current. We should be proud to be "late-moderns" in this sense.

Now Whitehead was against, and therefore "post," the assumed metaphysics of early modern science. In this sense he was postmodern, and you are right to claim him here. He identified the fault of this scientifically assumed metaphysics as the fallacy of "simple location." But he also looked to the great modern philosophers, especially Leibniz with his mirroring monads and Spinoza with his modes, as well as the others I just mentioned, for clues to build a metaphysical alternative to simple location, a better metaphysical hypothesis. So he viewed the metaphysical adventure of the modern age to be a collective groping toward a metaphysics in which the relations postulated by mathematics in science could be ingredient in the *rei verae* of the universe. I think he saw himself not as "post" the metaphysical speculations of the great modern philosophers, but as their culmination. Again, he was a late modern rather than a rejecter of the modern.[3]

So what is at stake in your valiant effort to claim Whitehead for postmodernism, or postmodernism for Whitehead? You argue neatly in your introduction that people who want to deny that Whitehead was postmodern commit the fallacy of confusing a species for the genus: postmodernism is the genus, for you, and your constructive postmodernism is the good species and reductive postmodernism the bad one. I've turned that argument a bit on its head. For me, modernity is the genus with foundationalist modernism as one species (bad) and nonmodernist late-modernity as another (good). Postmodernism is the rejection of foundationalist modernism (throwing out the root modern connection of thinking with experiential learning), and process philosophy is one of the culminations of nonmodernist modernity.

I think what is really at stake for you in this war for claiming names is to point out, as in your title, that Whitehead Is Radically Different from just about everybody. He was so creative and original that he was radically different from all the great modern philosophers he discusses, even when he finds unusual anticipations of his ideas in them. He was radically different from all forms of foundationalist modernism in his breathtaking *hypothesis* about cosmology. He was radically different from the pragmatists and others who shared his scientific realism because he was far more sophisticated with metaphysical abstractions. He was radically different from the analytical philosophers and logicians of his time and ours because of his philosophically systematic investigations of first-order questions of human life. Why is this radical difference not noticed and universally applauded?

Why, because Whitehead is so very hard to read and understand! Most people get bogged down and try to assimilate Whitehead to something they already know without understanding the extent to which he is radically different. So you are calling on people to recognize Whitehead's philosophy, not as something they already expect, but as something radically different, which solves or dissolves all sorts of problems with a radically new vision of reality. In this you are exactly right. If claiming a popular label helps make this point, more power to your campaign to get Whitehead recognized as a postmodern philosopher. For my part, I'll let postmodernism fade away as the modernism on which it is parasitic fades away.

ONTOLOGY

With regard to your discussion, in the ninth chapter, of my criticisms of process theology, let me begin with a confession. The confession is that you are right to chastise me, as you do in many places, for caricaturing, exaggerating, or otherwise distorting positions. I also get carried away sometimes by a felicitous turn of phrase and sacrifice nuance for punch; you nail me there. Most of your discussion focuses on my book, *Creativity and God: A Challenge to Process Theology*, published over a quarter century ago. That book consists largely of reviews I had written when in my twenties and thirties, lightly edited with a few new chapters to form a "sustained critique." In those days, I knew a lot more than was to be known. But even then, I had sense enough to write in the preface:

> So, from the private side, a "sustained critique" inevitably has a polemical odor. As mentioned, my personal stimulation for this essay was the intriguing divergence of process theology from my own. Where this has led the text to draw unnecessarily harsh contrasts or to represent process theology in a poor light without evidence, let my apology be an object lesson about the failure to transcend the privacy of selfish thinking. But from the public side a "sustained critique" itself exemplifies the partiality of individual thinking and serves to take process theology seriously as it cannot be taken seriously by itself and from within.[4]

You are right to point out the enthusiastic immaturity of so much of my argumentative rhetoric. I confess to that fault and hope that the other point, that a critique from a sympathetic outsider contributes something insiders cannot, helps to make amends. Confucius said that when he was seventy, he could trust his heartfelt enthusiasms not to be immature or require further deliberation; we have only two years to go, David.

The first point you bring up about my critique of process theology is what you rightly call the "ontological issue."[5] You have an extraordinarily fair and thorough discussion of my various arguments and interpretations of Whitehead, noting ambiguities of interpretation in the larger field of Whitehead scholarship, and developing your own interpretations with care. The short version of my argument is that Whitehead's ontological principle should apply not only to explaining temporally contingent things but also to explaining why there is any complexity at all. I argue that all complexity, including the category of the ultimate, the relation between God and the world, and even the metaphysical principles (as in *Process and Reality*, chapters 2–3), needs explanation by some kind of creative decision. In my view, that creative decision requires a God who is quite different from the process God who is finite relative to the world. I think the nub of your argument is the set of issues around your defense of the Hartshornean version of Whitehead that equates necessity with eternity, and the continent with the temporal. For your interpretation of process theology, in this instance a mainstream interpretation, the fundamental eternal metaphysical structure of God and world, including the category of the ultimate, does not need explanation because it is eternal and therefore necessary. What is necessary does not need explanation, and so the ontological principle does not apply. I think you are right about Whitehead's and Hartshorne's views, and I understand yours.

My own line of reasoning about ontological matters started (in my dissertation, which became my first book, *God the Creator*) from a consideration of the question of Being.[6] Unlike Heidegger, who wanted Being somehow to appear across the open to him in a phenomenological show, I approached the problem of Being through the ancient and nearly ubiquitous problem of the one and the many. Suppose, I asked, following the main line of the Western tradition, that Being somehow is the One for the many. Is Being as the One determinate or indeterminate? That is the crucial first question. In a series of arguments (apparently too detailed for any but graduate students to read), I argued that Being cannot be determinate, for if it were it would be just one more of the many, requiring yet a deeper ground for unity. In the course of this argument, I developed a theory of determinateness that I'll sketch shortly.

If Being is not determinate, however, how can it function as a One for the many? After considering many alternatives, I argued that only a singular, eternal, ontological act of creation could function to create each determinate thing with both the internal unity it needs and the relational interdefinition with other things it needs so as to be determinate over against them and also in continuity with them. There need be no overarching determinate unity, a totality, or a One: only the singular ontological creative act that creates just the kinds and degrees of unity and diversity we find in the world. The character of the cosmos created could be anything that philosophy, science, and other modes of inquiry might determine. Temporal flow might be partly indeterminate so as to account for human freedom, as I believe it is, following process philosophy in this.[7]

Following a main line of the Western tradition, especially in its Neo-Platonic moments, I identified God with Being as the ontologically creative act. Like Plotinus's One, or Thomas's Act of Esse, God as creator is not determinate in itself, but only as creator of this determinate world, whatever that might turn out to be. I do not say that God is an indeterminate something, only that apart from creating God is not determinate, is nothing. Given the creation, God is the determinate creator of this world, whatever that turns out to mean. Because time and all other dimensions of extension are created, God is not in time or space. The creative act is not temporal, not before, nor simultaneous with, nor after anything. All temporally ordered things are created. In my theology, I have elaborated a theory of transcendentals for the created world that functions as a logos theory.[8]

You see now, David, why I am not impressed with the claim that everything eternal is necessary and only the contingent is created and needs an account. If everything determinate is created, as I argue, then all those "necessary" metaphysical principles—the reality of God and world, the functioning of the category of the ultimate, among others—are contingent upon the ontological creation. It doesn't matter if all the metaphysical principles are eternal and necessary for contingent things to happen (not just functions of our cosmic epoch but always and everywhere—you make nice distinctions here): if they are determinate, the ground of their being lies in being created together. It doesn't matter if the metaphysical principles are true as a result of the principle of noncontradiction (even Hartshorne does not claim that): if they exhibit one-many complexity, the ground of their being lies in being created together. It doesn't matter if we cannot imagine an alternative to intelligibility itself: if intelligibility involves the complex dyad, as Plotinus would say, it is ontologically contingent. The distinction between necessity and contingency is contingent upon the creation of a world that conceivably exhibits such modalities.[9]

The general observation behind nearly all my metaphysical criticisms of process theology is that it does not adequately address the problem of the one and the many. You argue in effect that the problem of the one and the many applies only to things within temporal process. But the problem needs to be solved wherever there is a many of related things, which includes your eternal principles. Whereas the eternal metaphysical principles might be necessary for the temporal world, they are not necessary in the sense of exhibiting a solution to the problem of the one and many with regard to themselves.

Of course, it is possible for a philosopher or philosophical theologian just to ignore the problem of the one and the many. In effect, that's what I said Whitehead had done. Our friend Wesley Wildman argues that whether one deals with the problem of the one and the many is something of a matter of taste.[10] Surely, we all take up our philosophical agendas based on taste and accidents of learning, as well as on the public structures of philosophical agendas. No reason exists why every philosopher should take up the problem of the one and the many—there are so many other interests. Nevertheless, when a philosopher or philosophic school finally does get around to considering the problem of the one and the many, my main argument is that it will have to abandon any claim that the basic ontological category, Being or God, is determinate: the analysis of the one and many shows that the One cannot be one more of the many. If any philosophy is asked to address the problem of the one and many, it will have to abandon any claim that some special determinate things, for example, necessary metaphysical principles, do not themselves need an ontological grounding cause. They need such a cause because of their very determinateness, a cause I parse as God the creator. This is why, despite my great admiration for Whitehead's cosmology, I think his theology needs to be abandoned when you get around to the issues raised by the problem of the one and the many.

But notice how close my theological position is to process philosophy in other respects. God, I claim, is the ontological act creating everything determinate, including whatever temporal and otherwise contingent relations might exist and however long and extensive it takes them to unfold, perhaps an immense eternity. How can we understand the ontological act?

I say that understanding the creative act requires three related notions. First, the act itself is productive of novelty, a sheer making. Second, the end product of the act, its terminus, is the world created; the world is the act itself made determinate in its conclusion, something like Spinoza's *natura naturata* being the determinate end product of *natura naturans* (though I don't think *natura naturata* needs to be deterministically determinate, as Spinoza did). Third, the act itself does not arise out of a primal nature that determines anything about what the act creates: it is indeterminate as the creator of the one-and-many world except insofar as the act itself gives it the character of being creator of this world. For this reason, the ontological act (God) is not another determinate thing to be added to the many and hence does not need a further ground to connect with the world. This seems to be a far cry from Whitehead's conception of God with its primordial nature and perhaps primordial creative act of determining eternal objects: you deal very nicely with these issues.

Consider, now, an analogy with a Whiteheadian actual occasion. Its creativity consists in prehending past occasions and integrating them into a new definite entity. Its own share of novelty-making creativity might be very small. Yet, each occasion adds something novel to the realities that existed before it, "increasing the many by one." In the case of God as I conceive the creator, there are no antecedent things to be prehended. The creative act is totally one hundred percent novel. Whitehead was exactly right that creativity involves the making of something novel. It is not only the rearrangement of old things, or the repetition of an old arrangement (a *re*arrangement would be novel). The entire divine nature, I argue, is the result of the creative act. Just as we human beings in some small ways make ourselves, or at least our own moral nature, by adding novelty in response to what is given in our lives, so God makes the divine nature in a total way with the total novelty of creation. God has nothing antecedent to respond to, or with. To put my point in Whiteheadian language, God the eternal creator is like an actual occasion but with all novelty and no prehensions. God's actualization or concrescence results in the whole world, including the whole of spatiotemporal dimensionality as this then gets played out moment by moment within time. God's creative act is eternal because there are no prehended antecedents and no consequent occasions after the divine act (all created occasions are determinate and hence fall within the creation, not after it). Yet God as creative act determining the divine nature along with the created world is a singular act; so, I can call myself a theist without believing in a determinate God apart from the world. Singularity, not primordially determinate individuality, is what theism requires; the Dao, too, is singular.

This process-based conception of God as singular, eternal, ontological creator is a reversal of the more common analogy between human beings and God. The common analogy is to say that, just as we have given natures out of which we act in character, God has an essential divine nature out of which the creation comes. Both Plotinus and Thomas assume that the God (or One) behind creation has an ontological actual fullness, so that creation is the mere introduction of negations into an infinite plenitude of being. But neither of them drew the full implication of indeterminateness for the problem of the one and the many. There can be no antecedent fullness of being in God, or goodness, or supernal unity or truth. If any of these antecedent things have meaning, this would make them determinate, rendering God just another one of the many. Nothing is antecedent in God: all is consequent on the eternal ontological creative act. Thomas Aquinas and many other philosophers approved the slogan "out of nothing, nothing comes." But this is a great mistake. If anything (new) comes, it has to be at least partly out of nothing, not entirely out of something old. As Whitehead saw so well, for an actual occasion to come to be, it needs to add something to the primary data prehended; if it did not, there would just be the old data and nothing would arise as a new thing. With Whitehead, I reject the view that an actual thing arises as the unfolding of the act in the past; rather, an actual thing arises by its own present, concrescing, creative energy making the past relevant and adding novelty to bring about a new definite singularity. I take this model, which so supports human freedom, to analogize to God, who is all novelty-making and no prehension-receiving.[11] So whereas Whitehead was wrong about God in particular, his great point about the novel productivity of creativity offers a better way of thinking about God.

Your defense of Whitehead (and Hartshorne) against my ontological criticisms, David, takes the form of showing that on their own terms they do not have to take up the problem of the one and many that would ask for a ground or cause of necessary principles, or of God's primordial necessary nature. But are their own terms adequate? My many little arguments against process theology argue that the problem of the one and many lies unsolved in this or that interstice of the system. Your answers often admit that, but then claim that the one and many problem is not applicable. How can it be not applicable, especially if everything determinate, including metaphysical principles, requires a grounding unifier to connect it with any things with respect to which it is determinate? The problem of the one and many lies at the very heart of intelligibility.

INTIMATE RELIGIOUS SENSIBILITY

One of the most important dimensions of your chapter, David, is its extraordinary sensitivity to religious sensibilities as well as to dialectical argument. I've never seen a finer process exposition of the intimacy of relations between God and a person than you give here. The typical process exposition notes that God must be past to be prehended by us, and we must be finished and objectified to be prehended by God, emphasizing the solitariness of our response to God and the total otherness of God's response to us. (I'm glad we agree that Hartshorne's social God is an improvement on Whitehead's with regard to God's availability to be prehended, and temporal readiness to prehend things in the world.) You point out, by contrast with the typical representation, that the back-and-forth series of prehensions consists of minute occasions and that any humanly experiential terms are themselves functions of long societies of interactions. Experiencing God, we cannot notice the itsy-bitsy backs and forths of solitariness and otherness. So God can be as intimately present to us in the specious present, or presentational immediacy, as any person could be. This is an important argument for showing that the process God, as an independent entity with its own subjectivity, is yet still so intimately connected with us by prehending and being prehended that a truly personal relation to God can be conceived, like a relation to ordinary persons. (Of course, much more needs to be said about the sense in which the process God is "personal.")

You raise the question of intimacy, in religious sensibilities, in connection with my claim that the process God is an Other, whereas my sense of divine intimacy finds God deep in the soul, closer to us than we are to ourselves.[12] Let me say more about what is at stake here. On my understanding of determinateness, to be determinate is to be a harmony of many features, of at least two kinds. One kind of feature is conditional, by virtue of which the thing relates to other things. A prehension is a conditional feature according to the process model. Another kind of feature is essential, by virtue of which the thing integrates the conditional features into the harmony's own existential location. In Whitehead's model, the subjective contributions to concrescence would be essential features. This theory of determinateness is more abstract than the particular model in process philosophy. It should apply to an Aristotelian model, such as Paul Weiss's, or to any other model, such as Justus Buchler's notion of natural complexes. One advantage of this theory of determinateness is that by acknowledging the necessity of conditional features it trumps all atomisms, which fail because they admit no internal relations between things or with the space-time container for atoms. Another advantage is that by acknowledging the necessity of essential features it trumps all idealisms, which fail because they take relations to swallow up all terms to be related. In addition to the requirement that all harmonies have essential and conditional features, there are four more transcendental traits of harmony. There is a form (perhaps dynamic, as in music, not static) by which all the features of both kinds are integrated. The features are the components formed, and sometimes the components have greater value in themselves than they do in the roles they play in the given harmony's formal pattern. The form and components are together in ways that define an existential location for the harmony, relative to other harmonies. Getting these components together with this form in this existential location has a value; the harmony would have a different value if its form were different, or it had some different components, or were elsewhere.[13] Form, components, existential location, and value are transcendental requirements of determinate harmonies.

Now the primary religious sensibility regarding God, I believe, is that we discover ourselves, as harmonies, to be parts of the end product of the divine creative act. Because we have conditional features, however, we discover that what creates us, and is present in us as the creative act, also creates the things with respect to which we are determinate, connected by conditional features. So we experience ourselves as part of something larger, the scope of that being determined by our imagination of our conditions. At the same time, we experience ourselves as unique and "other" than the things with respect to which we are determinate. For, we are harmonies of our conditional features (shared with others) and essential features (shared with no others). In fact, the very reason for saying that God creates harmonies together is that the essential features of one thing need to be together with the essential features of another thing if the two harmonies are together as mutually determinate. The togetherness of harmonies by virtue of their conditional features is a function of cosmological relations, as described, for instance, in Whitehead's cosmology. But the togetherness of the essential features of two harmonies, by definition not cosmological, requires an ontological context in which the harmonies might be mutually relevant. The harmonies are together with one another as harmonies of their (perhaps mutual) conditional features as well as their existentially exclusive essential features. You don't have a harmony without both essential and conditional features. Therefore, one harmony cannot relate to another unless both involve their essential as well as conditional features. What is the ontological ground in which their separate essential features can be together, so that the whole harmonies can be together? I answer that it is the ontological creative act that creates both (or all) harmonies together, exhibiting their conditional relations and essential differences. Therefore, the intimacy of religious experience includes an astonishment at the otherness of the other, vis-à-vis the other's essential features, as well as the warm feeling of solidarity with the others through conditional features.

Religious experience is vastly too complicated to discuss here in detail, although you are right, David, to see my opposition to process theology as deriving in part from my own kind of experience. Much of the complexity of religious experience comes from the fact that people have multitudes of historically conditioned symbols, often different and incommensurate, to articulate their experiences, and these experiences vary over time, place, culture, and personal maturation. But a scheme can be derived from the theory of determinateness and the conception of God as creator for the nodal points of religious experience.

Permit me to mention six ways of focusing the experience of God as creator. First, for those whose focus of religious attention is on the connection of things (the conditional features), experiences close to the heart of nature-romanticism, and feelings of oneness, overall unity, and the dropping away of distinctions are common. Second, for those whose focus is on the astonishing otherness of things, particularly other people, religious experience of the depth of reality, particularly personal reality, is common, say, as made popular by the writings of Levinas. Third, to focus on the harmonies of essential and conditional features in other things calls attention to their "suchness," as the Buddhists say, their unique singularity. Fourth, to focus on one's own essential features is to have the existentialists' experience of interiority and will. Fifth, to focus on one's own conditional features is to feel oneself as particular and yet as deeply connected with other things, not in featureless bliss but in self-identifying connection. Sixth, to focus on the harmony of one's conditional and essential features is to experience one's own uniqueness and singularity as a creature of God, relative to other things. These are six modulations of religious experience that come from focusing on some node or other of the structure of determinateness. They all involve discovering God as the creator of us determinate beings.

The "discovering God" part itself has its modulations, of which there are at least three. If we focus on any of these ontological experiences of determinateness as they are apprehended as terminal elements in the divine creative act, we experience their contingency. Schleiermacher's "feeling of absolute dependence" comes to mind as a classic articulation of this. If we focus on any of these ontological experiences, however, not as the termini of the creative act but as the bearers of the creative act itself, the religious experience is of the power of divine making, of existence itself as existing. One thinks of the Scotistic poetry of Gerard Manley Hopkins. If we shift the focus from the created loci of divine creativity to the creative act itself, the act giving rise to determinateness, we make the mystic's move to the Abyss of non-being whence come the fires of creation, to use the language of Eckhart, Boehme, and Berdyaev.

I would suppose in the lives of religious people attuned to experiences of God that at no time does one experience God in all these loci and with respect to contingency, existential power of being over non-being, and Abysmal Depths all at once. Perhaps some people are adept at certain modulations and tone-deaf to others. Whatever, this is the kind of complex religious experience I have in mind in calling for a philosophical theology that expresses intimacy. These are all senses of intimacy that involve the experiencer in wholeness and the divinity as wholly containing and sustaining the experiencer and the world. Without for a moment denying the quality of intimacy you defend in the process view, David, there is a depth and pervasiveness to the quality of intimacy in my way of thinking that is different and worth articulation in its own right. It is far deeper than interaction with an Other, even when that other supplies one's initial aims and has to prehend one no matter how bad one is.

CONCEPTIONS OF GOD AS RELIGIOUSLY AVAILABLE

Having said this, however, it is important to come to terms with the common experience of religious people to relate to God in highly personal symbols, using biblical imagery. This is true not only of the monotheistic faiths but also of most others. We found in the Comparative Religious Ideas Project that most traditions have symbols of the ultimate that range along a spectrum from highly personifying imagery to highly abstract.[14] This is as true for the Chinese, whose rhetorical center of gravity tends toward nonpersonal abstractly described ultimates, such as Dao and Heaven, as it is for the monotheistic religions whose center of gravity is toward the personifying end. On the personifying end, the Chinese believe in the mandate of heaven, that is, the will of Shangdi the storm god, just as on the abstract end Christians think of God as the One beyond determinateness or the Act of Esse. A theology must position itself so as to deal with the religious accessibility of the whole spectrum, especially as this relates to the defining vocabulary of scriptures.

One of the advantages of process theology's conception of God regarding "religious availability" is that it is abstract enough to address some of the issues that force theologians toward the abstract end of the spectrum (although not the issue of the one and many!) while depicting God as a being whose metaphysical foundation for consciousness is rather like our own, prehending, using concepts, intending valuable satisfactions, and the like. Some process theologians, including yourself but perhaps most especially our friend Marjorie Suchocki, construe the process model of God as a metaphysical scaffold for hanging religious notions on that depict God as a personal being. This is taken to justify the liturgical and personal piety of treating God as a person to whom we can relate in gratitude, petition, and ongoing development as persons ourselves. Although the biblical and liturgical personifying images of God are obviously metaphors, they are metaphors whose referent is abstractly personal in the way the images are concretely personal. Whitehead and Hartshorne did not say very much about a rich metaphysical sense in which God is personal, but then neither did they say very much about how human beings are concretely personal. I've found both pragmatism and existentialism necessary supplements to the process model of human personality.

For your chapter, this issue comes up in the form of the problem of how God can act in the world. Neither of us wants to say that God acts in the world in miraculous, personal interventions, as some evangelical theologians want to say. So we are both unfriendly to interpretations of Christianity that stress a narrative character for creation and redemption, focusing on the human story. We are not moved by Barth's sophisticated version of this, nor by the Dispensationalist version made popular by the "Left Behind" series of books. You want to defend, rather, the Whiteheadian position that God is universally and by necessity a component of the initial data for each occasion in the form of a lure for satisfaction, an initial aim. Thus, God is intimate in this sense to every actual occasion, including the zillions that make up a human intentional act or duration of consciousness. This by no means suggests that God correlates three or four zillion initial aims so as to influence the Israelites to escape Egypt and invade Canaan, or otherwise to play a role in a divine-human drama, understood on the scale of human events. You and I would agree that a lot of faith-based special pleading (remember the perspectives of the Egyptians and Canaanites!) would be necessary to suggest that Whitehead's God behaves like Yahweh, anthropomorphically understood. Remember Don Sherburne's attempted *reductio* of the process God, asking whether God could provide enough powerful initial aims in the air—actual occasions to deflect a piano falling off a mover's crane at the top of a building to prevent its crushing a small child directly below.

My objection to the Whiteheadian notion of God's action or presence in the world through initial aims was that it is an unnecessary abridgement of human freedom. For a given actual occasion, the divine lure is one of the very many things prehended. Each of those initial data, including the divine initial aim, has its own value and hence appeal to be objectified in the occasion's satisfaction. My objection was that the bigger and more important the divine initial aim, the more it forces itself over against the competing initial data. You rightly answer that human (or any occasion's significant) freedom consists in how the occasion grades the divine initial aim, in what importance the occasion bestows on it relative to the other initial data. Point well taken. But my point was that freedom requires at least some indifference to the given initial data, at least some wiggle room to grade things in different patterns. So the more powerful the claim of the divine initial aim, the more it functions as an overwhelming claim on importance, like an addiction or a moment of frenzied lust; an addict or a person lost in lust simply has less freedom than people without those compulsions. To the extent that an initial aim is strong like a compulsion, to that extent a human being is nudged too much by God relative to the freedom to reject God. To the extent that the initial aim is weak and easily graded up or down by the occasion, to that extent is God's presence made impotent, however intimate. So I stand by my objection that the power of God in initial aims is inversely proportional to the human freedom to respond to that power, and hence a compromise of freedom, for Whitehead's theology.

Now technically, on at least one reading of Whitehead, the function of an initial aim from God is not so much to influence moral or aesthetic life but rather to determine which occasions can function in the subjective unity of an occasion at the beginning of its concrescence. This is to say, God chooses through the subjective aim which occasions are past relative to the concrescing occasion. This might seem counterintuitive, because the past is the past, and all the occasions that are finished at the potential emergence of the concrescing occasion are in its past. Nevertheless, for Whitehead, at least in some moments (and for Hartshorne surely always, as well as for John Cobb), the past data do not exist simply as past but only as prehended from the standpoint of a prehending subject. One function of God is to give all fully concresced occasions a place to exist as objectified. And so, God can suggest to a new occasion about to concresce that a certain field of occasions constitutes its past. The divine initial aim, in this context, is not one among many data prehended but the determiner of what can function as data at all. I don't understand Whitehead to have an evolved theory about how the initial aim constitutes subjective unity for an occasion, because it cannot do so by being prehended—the possibility of prehension in the concrescing occasion depends on already having subjective unity. I solve that problem, insofar as my cosmology is like Whitehead's, by saying that God creates the occasion with its subjective unity whence concrescence follows; Whitehead rejects this notion of creation.

The real punch of your argument about God's action through initial aims is its critique of my own position. If I say that God creates absolutely everything, including all the novel spontaneous steps within the genetic analysis of an occasion, then God is the absolutely overwhelming determiner of human thought and action. No freedom from God at all is possible, you claim, for my view. Like Calvin's, my conception of God lets God's sovereignty run over human freedom like a bulldozer. Yes, I am a Calvinist with regard to God being the author of absolutely everything.

Yet I am not a Calvinist with regard to human freedom, that is, not a determinist. I wrote *The Cosmology of Freedom*, my second book, precisely to answer this criticism that you detail so nicely. There I argued that freedom has several dimensions or senses, including freedom of external liberty (not being in chains), freedom to act on the basis of intention (as opposed to being unable to get our act together), freedom to choose between real alternatives (as opposed to there being only one possible course of action, and as opposed to us being unable to make a decisive intervention), freedom to choose on the basis of standards or norms (as opposed to randomly), and freedom to evaluate and take responsibility for our standards and norms; I analyzed social dimensions of freedom as well. In each of these dimensions of freedom, it is an empirical question just how much freedom we have. In each case freedom is something that needs to be learned and perfected, including the construction of a society that fosters external liberty, competent action, the exercise of choice, intelligent analysis of value and norms, and responsibility for good normative thinking. I argued that these dimensions of freedom, plus the social dimensions (and religious ones analyzed in *Soldier, Sage, Saint*) together flesh out a model of free human agency, free within limits.[15]

God the creator can, and did, create a world in which all these dimensions of freedom are possible. Within time, each of us has a certain range of possible action, makes choices among real options based on values more or less well justified and acts so as to affect the outcome of affairs. From our position within time, the future might well be open to significant options; God, not being in time, does not know the future from a position within time (I agree with you there). At a decisive moment within time, we might significantly make a choice that issues in action, affecting our moral character. If we do so choose and act, that is a spontaneous novelty on our part, working with what is given to produce something not in the past. In this sense, we determine our moral character by what we choose. Although we always have some moral character based on the past, including our past choices, that character alone does not determine our action in the present. If it does, then we are more like automata than free people. Rather, when free, we spontaneously make a choice, the rationale for which then becomes our motive and hence our moral character. Like God, who is what God does and makes up the divine character in the productive novelty of creation, we make our moral character in the thousands of small decisions that add to what we are given, moment by moment. When and how we do this is a matter to be determined empirically.

In one sense, every one of our spontaneous free decisions is part of the terminus of the divine creative act. God is the ontological source of everything, including the determination of free options within human time. In a completely related sense, every one of those spontaneous free decisions is our construction of our own character within the limitations of what we are given. Of course, the matters of decision and action are much more complicated than this—most of our actions are conjoint actions with others and have meaning only in semiotically shared space. Nevertheless, I am quite comfortable saying that there are two authors of every free human action: God and the self-determining actor.

This two-author theory would not be plausible if God is a different being from the human author. That would require a kind of co-creation of shared influence theory that I suspect bedevils process theology: the stronger one of the co-creators, the weaker the other. But on my theory of God as creator, God the author of a person's spontaneous exercise of freedom is not another being but a deeper part of the person, one connecting the person cosmologically and ontologically with the others with regard to which the action takes place. There is only one author of the world, and in that world human beings (and perhaps others) are made to be authors within their limited sphere.

It is obvious to everyone who thinks about it, not only you, David, that I must give up the claim that God is not responsible for human evil and suffering. In the deep sense in which God is creator of everything, God creates a universe where planets have shifting plate tectonics causing earthquakes and tsunamis that bring human suffering. In that same deep sense God creates people who choose selfishly and maliciously, causing great harm to others, but those selfish and malicious choices are part of the freedom that determines the moral character of reprobates. I cannot say, then, that God in the divine aseity is good. Rather, God creating out of the divine aseity is awesome, terrible, glorious, and wild, not domesticated to take pains with the human scale of things. This is a powerful biblical theme. But then, I do not want to say that God in the divine aseity is good, as you do, for that would be to make God determinate apart from creation, requiring a deeper ground, and so forth.

My point is that God's character comes from the creation created. I agree with the Whiteheadian cosmology that to be a thing, a harmony, a "contrast," is to have value. Each harmony has its own value, even if that value is destructive of other harmonies. So in this sense, hoping that a value-laden cosmology is true, God is the creator of a world of goods, even when they conflict. Because of conflict, God is also the creator of ills, ills derivative from the conflict of goods. This conception of divine creation accords with the biblical notion that God creates the world "and sees that it is good." Relative to human life, our options are filled with competing values and the nuances of our choices give us what moral character we have. With Job, however, we should see that we have no standing to judge whether God creates with a moral character. We have no sufficient sample of the cosmos, and do not know how to evaluate goods outside the human sphere. Moreover, norms apply to our choices because our choices take place within a given environment that determines the relevant values. God creates in no environment, and therefore has no norms for creation. Norms apply only within creation. Such is the glory of God, and the moral character of human freedom. Divine freedom does not have a moral character.

Many people, supported by process theologians, believe that we need a conception of God as a moral agent, wishing us to do good and somehow rewarding us according to our merit, for us to face the rigors of moral life. Without this belief in God as a fellow sufferer, coach, and umpire, we would not have the courage to do what is right in the face of opposition and difficulty. We could not do the good for the sake of its own goodness. Much popular religion is organized around the program to show that by doing the moral thing we are doing God's will. Perhaps this point of view expresses what truly counts for success in this world. But I see it differently and agree with Kant that the only really good justification for doing the good is that it is good to do, and we make ourselves morally deficient by not doing the good. This removes religion as a moral prop, in some senses, for the moral life. But it also recognizes the need for human beings to take responsibility for themselves with regard to morals, not attending to the good because we believe it is God's will or that we will be rewarded. Here lies a kind of human moral maturity, with regard to which the view of God as a moral agent guiding and striving with us tends to hold us back in immaturity.

Now you see, David, something of what is at stake for me in the issues about how God and human beings relate in the world relative to freedom. It's not just a competition between metaphysical models of God as contributor of initial aims versus God as the ground of being. My position seems to you and many others to be a paradox. On the one hand, mature human freedom needs to take responsibility for choices, irrespective of whether God is a superagent on our side (or against us when we are bad). On the other hand, because we are parts of the ontological divine creative act, we participate with those other parts in constituting the cumulative value of the cosmos. That God's creation includes the whirlwind, earthquake, and fire means we are in those wild things too. Those monsters of creation, those vast expanses of swirling gasses that have no regard for human life, those are our heritage, part of our blood. So, while we are always obligated to do the best in our circumstances, we also need to take responsibility for being monsters of the deep as well. Calvin knew a bit about this too. From a religious point of view, I think that becoming reconciled to being creatures of the wild God is more important than figuring out how to do our duty. The guilts for which we are not personally responsible are more significant religiously than those for which we are personally responsible.

You see why the process model of God as the benevolent poet co-creating the world with us seems religiously shallow to me. As you point out, David, I am a Methodist from Missouri with a strong Wesleyan sense of prevenient grace (your page 201). The world is filled with things of value that give rise to and facilitate our lives and moral obligations. But the world is also filled with things that make the value of our current lives problematic, and that give ontological depth and ambiguity to our moral obligations. As Tillich said, the normal thing is for us to be alienated from our deep ground in God's whole eternal act of creation, often because of the blood guilt involved in just being a creature within God's world, irrespective of personal responsibility. Reconciliation with that ground, with God and creatures, especially enemies, is a spontaneous free choice for us, and is also part of God's creating us, or certain of us. That God is the ultimate author of reconciliation, rather than our choosing over against a determinate-entity God, is my Missouri Methodist version of the justification by faith rather than works.[16]

You say that my Methodist friends in Missouri would probably all believe that God is only good and would agree with Charles Wesley that God is "pure, unbounded love." I think that is likely true. That belief is part of one version of what Peter Berger would call a Christian "sacred canopy," a complex fabric of beliefs that provides the background for daily life and worship in Christian communities. Beneath that sacred canopy, the process conception of God fares rather well regarding the problem of evil, as you point out, as well as regarding being a model and coach for human behavior: as God loves us, so ought we to love one another. I prefer this Christian sacred canopy to others that emphasize guilt and punishment. Much of our teaching in theological seminaries is to equip prospective ministers to articulate this sacred canopy for all the nuances of ministry in the life of a community. Nevertheless, the maintenance of the sacred canopy, and the interpretation of life it affords, is limited by the wildness of reality that rends it unexpectedly. Sometimes things happen that render the canopy implausible, as the rise of modern science did to a certain kind of late-medieval Christianity, or as the holocaust did for many people who believe God gives us what we deserve or rules the world with kindness and justice. Horrors seem to make the customary God-is-good sacred canopy somewhat unhelpful, uncomforting, irrelevant, and untrue. Precisely when the customary sacred canopy is rent is when real theology needs to kick in. Real theology is not just the articulation of the canopy, but rather is the acknowledgment and articulation of those arbitrary wildnesses that relativize all canopies. Real theology lives on the edge of the apophatic, of the "yes but not really" affirmation of the canopy's sacred symbols. Now, I think this is true of Missouri Methodists, that the liberal Protestant sacred canopy is fine for ordinary life and the common speech of congregations, but that something deeper and more mysterious peeks through the torn holes of the canopy all too often. Missouri is tornado and earthquake country.

I love Charles Wesley's affirmation that God is "pure, unbounded love" and give it a rather metaphysical interpretation as God's free and fecund creating. To love in the purest sense is not to have a sentiment about something but to make something good, or, in less pure contexts, to make something better. God, on my view, does not create the world for a reason. God creates in an act of pure, unbounded love that provides its justification in the things created. God does not love us because we are lovely—quite the opposite—nor does God love us because we are unlovely. God creates us with our own loveliness, and this creation is God's pure, unbounded love. The unboundedness of love means that one thing's loveliness is another's devastation—think of the lovely tornados, cancers, and nuclear weapons. I think my conception of God as creator captures the wildness and arbitrariness of the cosmos better than the process conception according to which God is necessarily good, but bounded by the rest of the cosmos.

Your conviction that God is purely good, David, lies behind two other problematic questions you pose for me (203ff.). One is to ask how I would account for the introduction of novelty in process. You suggest that if all the lures for novelty come from conceptual prehension of past data, then we would be in a Nietzschean universe of eternal recurrence. I made that remark about conceptual prehensions of past data in something of a complaint about Whitehead's theory of divine initial aims, because they too are prehended among the initial data. In my own theory, the novelty that God creates in eternity unfolds within time as it comes up. So I would say that subjective spontaneity in a concrescing occasion adds novelty to what has been prehended before, and that this spontaneity is both divinely authored and is part of the self-authoring of the occasion.

Your second question of this series is similar: where does the order of the cosmos come from, if not from divine initial aims? I answer that it comes from the divine creative act, as does everything else. But I would insist that we limit our claims about order to the actual order that we find, and I do not suggest an order of progress or an order of justice based on our antecedent assessment of a divine character. I'm especially nervous about fudging the scientific evidence about the cosmic future with some claim that the cosmos must continue forever to preserve Christian values, and I think we do not disagree on this.

You raise a somewhat related question in another place (212–214), concerning my critique of Hartshorne's social conception of God. My original question to Hartshorne, which I think he cannot answer, had been how the divine abstract necessity in one member of the divine society could bind some subsequent occasion also to be a successor divine occasion. If one emphasizes the concrete particularity of the given divine occasion, saying that the necessity is only abstract and partially instantiated in that occasion, there is nothing to oblige another occasion to be divine. If on the other hand one treats the necessity in the divine occasion to be transcendently powerful enough to command a series of divine occasions into being, I said that transcendent necessity would be more worshipful, that is, more divine, than each of the members of the divine society. You answer by taking the second horn of the dilemma; you claim that the transcendence of the necessary metaphysical principles obliging a society of occasions still does not make them God, rather than the concrete society. But with the second horn of the dilemma, you would have to show how the transcendent metaphysical principles could in fact oblige a succession of occasions to exhibit them, which means showing how they could act in some sense over and above the action of a single member of the divine society in which they are ingressed. I bet you won't find a better theory of divine action giving rise to metaphysical necessities that oblige a world than my theory of God as ontological creator. Certainly, Hartshorne's theory won't do, because all occasions subsequent to a given member of the divine society might simply negatively prehend the metaphysical principles required to make them divine.

RELIGIOUS LANGUAGE AND METAPHYSICS

Let me conclude my response to your chapter with some remarks on the difficult problem of relating our metaphysical theologies to religious language, often biblical and anthropomorphic. The strategies of process theologies, worked out with different models and nuances among different thinkers (compare Suchocki and Bracken), pertain to offering the metaphysical model as a kind of framework on which to hang various culturally specific images. So, for instance, the process God can be personified because of the structures of intentionality in concrescence, of which God has one big version (Whitehead) or a society of versions (Hartshorne). As a consequence, as I argued earlier, the process God has an interior subjectivity over against and in relation to the world that makes this God a determinate entity requiring a deeper ground in order to be related to the world in the first place.

My alternative strategy is to identify God with the most abstract pole of the spectrum and to treat the other rhetorical stopping places as symbolic imaginative constructions. From the point of view of my ontological arguments, the finite God of process is much too finite to relate to the issues of transcendence and the one and many that have pushed theologians to the abstract pole. With all apologies for using the polemical term "idolatry," as you say so well, David, I think that to give some less than ultimately abstract concept a literal translation within the spectrum is to commit idolatry. This is to say, it would be arbitrarily to cut off the further arguments that would push toward the end of the spectrum that houses the problem of the one and many.

My preference is to move metaphysics all the way to the abstract side, appreciating Whitehead's abstract metaphysics and trying to advance upon that. One of the supplementary agenda items, then, of philosophy of religion or philosophical theology would be to develop a theory of religious imagination that shows how the more personifying images of the ultimate, in Christianity and the other religions, do sometimes function to engage people truly with the ultimate without needing to claim literal forms of reference. Whitehead's theory of symbolism does not take us very far when trying to make sense of how religious symbols can sometimes be true even if they are not literally descriptive. I've found Charles Peirce's semiotic theory much more helpful. He distinguishes iconic reference, that is, the supposition that the object is like what the sign says, from indexical reference, that is, the supposition that the sign connects the interpreter causally with the object so that the object can be directly engaged. Living with profound religious symbols transforms people so that they become open to engaging dimensions of reality that are otherwise opaque to them. These symbols do not have to be true literally to play that function. I've worked this out in some theoretical detail in my *The Truth of Broken Symbols*, and I have illustrated it with the analysis of Confucian symbols in *Boston Confucianism* and of Christological symbols in *Symbols of Jesus*.[17] I believe that the approach to religions' practices through the study of their symbols facilitates a much richer and more fluid appreciation of the nuances of religious belief and commitment than attempts to match up the main symbols with metaphysical models. Marjorie Suchocki has pushed the latter enterprise about as far as it can go in her *God/Christ/Church*. That is a brilliant book that I use regularly in classes. Nevertheless, the religion it enables is only a morally earnest liberal Protestantism, with little to say for the baroque extremes of Roman Catholicism or Eastern Orthodoxy, let alone Tibetan Buddhism or the dancing Shiva. Of course, I myself am only a morally earnest liberal Protestant, like you and Marjorie, which leads me to appreciate her book as I do. But the task for philosophy of religion is to deal with religions more broadly.

Permit me to raise a topic that you did not. I take it that my most important criticism of process philosophy is that its account of process cannot explain how time flows. To understand how time flows, assuming the process account as far as it goes, additionally requires acknowledging an eternity (nontemporal reality) in which the past, present, and future are together, but not temporally together. My first systematic statement of this criticism was in my contribution to Charles Hartshorne's Library of Living Philosophers volume and it was elaborated much more fully in reference to its implications for morality and the divine nature in *Eternity and Time's Flow*.[18] The root claim I make is that time's flow requires that the present, past, and future be together and mutually implicated in some real sense. One interpretation of process philosophy is that the past has no reality unless it is prehended within some concrescing occasion; likewise, the future is unreal except as representatively anticipated in some concrescing occasion, hence only emergent concrescence is real and there is no flow of time through future, present, and past. Lots of technical arguments go into making my case.

To understand eternity, on this view, is to see it as the concrete reality that contains all things as past, present, and future, mutually relating to each other so that within the dimension of time's flow, temporal unfolding takes place. Temporal flow is an abstract part of the larger eternal togetherness of the conditions of time. My exposition of this starts with the conceptions of the past, present, and future as harmonies with essential features of their own and conditional features that they get from one another according to which time flows. The essential features of the present have to do with spontaneity and decisive creativity; those of the future have to do with formal unity; those of the past have to do with the fixity of actualized things. From the past, the present gets conditional features that provide it with actual potentials to be spontaneous with and decisive about. From the future, the present gets conditional features setting logical possibilities of patterns for integrating the past. From the present, the past gets the conditional features of ever-new accretions of actuality, so that actual structures and events grow and sometimes change in value. From the future, the past gets conditional features of structural possibilities that carry value (the value of having these components integrated with this form in this existential location). From the past, the future gets conditional features of actual diversities of things to provide unity for, so that the future is patterns of possibilities for determinate things, not pure unity. From the present, the future gets conditional features of a constantly shifting field of possibilities as present decisions alter what needs possible integration. All of this is congenial to process philosophy, I think, although the mention of eternity is very different from a process focus on eternal objects.

The theological significance of this view of time and eternity is that, because God creates a temporal world in which time flows, the eternal act of creation includes the eternal togetherness of the modes of time. Notice how dynamic they are. The present is dynamic in the customary process sense of spontaneous creativity. The past is dynamic in the sense that any given actual accomplishment is immediately added to by subsequent actual developments. The future is dynamic in that every present moment shifts the possibilities that had obtained for a world just prior. From our perspective as temporal creatures, only the present seems dynamic, but our temporal lives presuppose the full dynamism of eternity. Given the dynamics of present, past, and future in eternity, it is entirely legitimate to call this the divine life. The divine life is not in time. Rather, it is the eternal reality within which temporal life flows. But the divine life is far more dynamic than our limited temporal lives.

Our temporal lives are more than we sometimes think, however. Right now, I am in my sixty-ninth year, with today's events present to me, including the minimal decisive creativity of writing this letter to you. All my previous moments are now fixed and past. Perhaps I have several years of moments that are future. In eternity, however, every one of my moments, however long I live, is present, past, and future together, for my time to flow. When my first day was present, all the other moments were future, with rather vague structures of possibilities. As I grew through adolescence, a lot of childhood experiences had determined much of my character and gave my future more definition; moreover, I learned to take some responsibility for the choices I made. When I was middle-aged, with a growing family and demanding jobs, it seemed that all my decisions were hedged in by responsibilities. Some of those responsibilities came from past commitments, for instance, to pay my mortgage; others came from anticipations of the future, for instance, to pay for our daughters' educations (middle-aged responsibilities have a lot to do with money, don't they?). Now the next generation of my family is middle-aged (almost) and my career has a definite path, mostly trodden. I think I have a few more books to write and classes to teach and look forward ambiguously to a happy senility. I'm sure my future will contain a lot of reflection on my past. At every stage of life certain dates have become past, others are present, and yet others are future. Who is the real me? Not the infant, the adolescent, the middle-aged entrepreneur, or the old philosopher. I am all these dates as future, all as present, and all as past. This is my eternal identity. Within time, I am only one present date at a time. But even in this temporal present, I eternally am the one who years ago contracted the mortgage and thus now am obligated to pay it. Right now,

I still have obligations to the future (we just refinanced!). Within the divine life, my eternal life is whole. Because each of us lives in necessary interconnection with one another, we are eternally together. Because we together live in a larger natural environment, what we do with our days relative to our social and natural environments defines eternally who we are.

Participating in the divine life is not like a drop merging in an ocean of divinity, although that anticipatory experience is one way of appreciating our solidarity with all things. Nor is participating in the divine life a future kind of temporal life. We'll just have to see what the cosmic future brings; actually, you and I won't see it. Every religion has tried to schematize our finite temporal approaches to the immense and eternal ground of being with images of afterlife and a geographical heaven. If we take those images literally, they fall apart. Iconically, the heavenly afterlife imagery is false. But indexically it can be true in the sense that it orients us to the divine creator in whose eternal life we live and move and have our being. Very ordinary religious symbols can suffice to orient us productively and truly to the divine eternal reality within which time flows and our lives pass their days.

David, as you can see, this theological vision, emphasizing eternity as the ground for temporal flow, is very far in many respects from the process vision. You see how close I am to Whitehead on many levels of cosmological understanding. Yet I think the religious and theological implications of process thought require a more mysterious, apophatic, and temporally transcendent vision of God than process theology offers. To my mind, the process emphasis on temporality as the most inclusive and concrete reality is an unfortunate holdover of Kantianism. It leads, as Kant saw, to the reduction of the moral and religious dimensions of human life to the thin sphere of affairs of personal responsibility. We are much worse, and better, and deeper than that. God, too, is much worse, better, and deeper than "the great companion—the fellow-sufferer who understands."

In gratitude for your splendid and detailed discussion of some of my criticisms of process theology, I've taken the occasion of this reply to lay out some of the dimensions of the systematic perspective from which my criticisms have come. I hope that you enjoy this alternative and look at your own perspective in its light, at least for a few moments.

With respect and affection,

Robert

NOTES

1. See, for instance, Lawrence Cahoone's anthology, *From Modernism to Postmodernism* (Oxford: Blackwell, 1996).

2. Who but Whitehead would read Descartes as the great empiricist (because of the subjectivist principle, which you treat so nicely in the appendix) and Locke as the great metaphysician (because of the idea of force or power)?

3. For a more extensive discussion of this, especially regarding Whitehead, romanticism, and speculative metaphysics as condemned by postmodernism, see my *The Highroad around Modernism* (Albany: State University of New York Press, 1992).

4. *Creativity and God: A Challenge to Process Theology* (New York: Seabury, 1980; new edition, Albany: State University of New York Press, 1995), xi.

5. David Ray Griffin, *Whitehead's Radically Different Postmodern Philosophy: An Argument for Its Contemporary Relevance* (Albany: State University of New York Press, 2007), 189–198.

6. *God the Creator: On the Transcendence and Presence of God* (Chicago: University of Chicago Press, 1968; revised with a new introduction, Albany: State University of New York Press, 1992).

7. See my elaborate use of Whitehead, with a few significant "corrections," in my *The Cosmology of Freedom* (New Haven: Yale University Press, 1974), especially part 2.

8. See my *A Theology Primer* (Albany: State University of New York Press, 1991) where the transcendental elements of harmony—form, components, existential location, and value—structure a systematic treatment of Christian theological topics. See my *Symbols of Jesus* (Albany: State University of New York Press, 2001) for a complex logos Christology based on the theory of transcendentals of harmony. To be a determinate thing is to be a harmony in connection and distinction from other harmonies, I argue, so that Christology is a Christian consequence of creation.

9. One of my earliest articles, "Some Historical Problems about the Transcendence of God," defended Descartes's claim that the reason A is not non-A is because God makes it so. This was over against Leibniz's view, close to process theology's, that God has a necessary nature and can make only the things that nature obliges God to make, for instance, the best of all possible worlds. The article was published in *Journal of Religion* 47

(January 1967), 1–9, and republished with modifications in *Realism in Religion: A Pragmatist's Perspective* (Albany: State University of New York Press, 2009) as chapter 13.

10. See his essay, "Neville's Systematic Theology of Symbolic Engagement," in Amos Yong and Peter G. Hetzel, editors, *Theology in Global Context: Essays in Honor of Robert Cummings Neville* (New York: T&T Clark International, 2004), 3–27. See also John B. Cobb, Jr., "A More Radical Pluralism," in the same volume, 315–326, which takes me to task for abandoning the Whiteheadian pluralism of acknowledging both God and creativity as religious ultimates.

11. I have developed this point, over against Keith Ward's Thomistic analogy, in the first chapter of *Symbols of Jesus*.

12. This distinction is the main point of Paul Tillich's famous essay "The Two Types of Philosophy of Religion," in Robert C. Kimball, editor, *Theology of Culture* (New York: Oxford University Press, 1959), chapter 2. He distinguished two "ways of approaching God: the way of overcoming estrangement and the way of meeting a stranger. In the first way man discovers *himself* [italics original] when he discovers God; he discovers something that is identical with himself although it transcends him infinitely, something from which he is estranged, but from which he never has been and never can be separated. In the second way man meets a *stranger* when he meets God. The meeting is accidental. Essentially they do not belong to each other" (10). Clearly Whitehead's God is not quite a stranger in Tillich's sense because of the mutual prehension of God and a person, the divine provision of a lure, and so forth. But Whitehead's (and Hartshorne's) God is only a part of a person and has its creative reality outside the person. Tillich's alternative of meeting God as one discovers oneself says that the whole of the person somehow is in God who extends to more as well. Tillich called the overcoming estrangement model "ontological" and associated it with Augustine; he called the meeting a stranger model "cosmological" and associated it with Aquinas. That works better for Augustine than it does for Thomas, I think.

13. On essential and conditional features, see *God the Creator*, especially chapter 3. On the transcendentals of harmony, see *A Theology Primer*. On value, especially in relation to Whitehead, see *The Cosmology of Freedom*, part 1.

14. See my edited *Ultimate Realities* (Albany: State University of New York Press, 2001), especially chapter 7 by Wesley J. Wildman and myself.

15. See *Soldier, Sage, Saint* (New York: Fordham University Press, 1978) for the explication of dimensions of religious freedom. You cite the summary metaphysical chapter in this book, but not those discussing freedom.

16. For a defense of atonement theory, a strange project for a liberal theologian such as myself, see chapter 2 of *Symbols of Jesus*.

17. My *Religion in Late Modernity* (Albany: State University of New York Press, 2002) contains several essays on issues of personification in symbols of ultimacy.

18. See my "Time, Temporality, and Ontology," Lewis Edwin Hahn, editor, *The Philosophy of Charles Hartshorne*, volume 20 of the Library of Living Philosophers (LaSalle: Open Court, 1991), chapter 19, and *Eternity and Time's Flow* (Albany: State University of New York Press, 1993).

Chapter 14

THE TRIUNE GOD AND CREATION *EX NIHILO*, OR "THE ONE AND THE MANY" STRIKES AGAIN

CREATIVITY ACCORDING TO JOSEPH BRACKEN

Joe Bracken and I have been friends and interlocutors for decades. I provided a foreword for his *The Divine Matrix* and he has discussed my ideas there and elsewhere, such as in *The One in the Many*.[1] We share many philosophy-shaping intentions. One is a strong conviction of the importance of comparative theology: the public for which theology should be written includes thinkers from any tradition that might have an interest in the topic. A second is a conviction that philosophy is the venue within which most theological topics are best discussed, in part because philosophy builds on an indefinitely long dialectic of checking up on what has just been said. A third is a conviction that philosophical theology needs to be friendly to, conversant with, and shaped by scientific knowledge. A fourth is a conviction that the philosophy of Alfred North Whitehead is the best place to start because of the originality of its theological ideas, its usefulness in comparative theology, and its responsiveness to science. A fifth is a conviction that the philosophy of Alfred North Whitehead is not the place to stop and that Whitehead's fundamental theological ideas are simply not adequate. While employing many of Whitehead's cosmological ideas, both of us extend them, amend them, and sometimes reject them. We have our own philosophical theologies that are different from Whitehead's and so the orthodox Whiteheadians treat us as strange puzzles.

Bracken and I also differ in some philosophy-shaping intentions. He is a Roman Catholic who is comfortable talking about the Trinity in purely philosophical ways whereas I am a Methodist pietist who rarely talks about the Trinity without reference to Jesus. For the same reason, he writes with an undercurrent of worry that one of his bishops might read his not-so-orthodox books whereas I am confident that my bishops would never do such a thing. Bracken is a close reader of his dialogue partners, is always generous in his interpretations, and tries to find common ground before expressing differences; I, on the other hand, tend to be polemical with others and preoccupied with developing my own views. We have also come to positions that, while sharing much of a common vocabulary and set of historical traditions, differ quite sharply on outcomes concerning the nature of God or ultimate reality. His philosophical theology articulates a Triune God interacting with creatures in time whereas mine articulates God as an ontological act of creation that creates, ex nihilo, everything determinate, including time, process, and activity. The ground over which we argue is the problem of the one and the many, and in this essay I want to explores some of our differences.

Bracken's great originality is in reshaping the question of the one *and* the many into his theory of the one *in* the many. For Whitehead, every actual entity, including God, is a one that unifies the many it prehends while also leaving that many over against it. Thus, every creative act of unification adds a new one to the previous many. The problem with this view is finding the context (or unity?) within which each one can be together with its many without one of the poles dissolving. Whitehead's student, Paul Weiss, rang the changes on this problem in his *Modes of Being*. Many Whiteheadians (to be discussed more later) dissolve the prehended many into the prehending unifier, saying that past actual entities cease to exist except insofar as they exist within the newly concrescing unifier. Thus, only the present exists and, alas, time and change cannot flow (paradoxical for "process" philosophy!). Also, it is hard to understand how completely actualized things can cease to exist because ceasing is a change and what is completely actual cannot change. Bracken has a different solution.

His fundamental idea is that creativity is an ontological activity that is infinite and everlasting in scope. It is not reducible to instances of creativity in actual entities as Whiteheadians commonly say (it's not clear what Whitehead thought about this). Although creativity receives articulation only in actual entities in time, it has a unity as a fundamental activity that is the creative ground of the creativity in actual entities. Nevertheless, precisely because the underlying ontological creativity is determinate only in actual entities, and the determinateness of actual entities comes from prehending other actual entities, the extensive continuum constituted by the mutual prehendings is equiprimordial with ontological creativity. They are not the same, but they cannot exist without each other. The ontological creativity is the one and it is in the many constituting the extensive continuum. The one is not over against the many as one actual entity; for instance, Whitehead's or Hartshorne's God is over against the finite actual occasions of the world. Nor is the many reduced to something that is in the one, as is the case with Hartshorne's panentheistic view.

Given this move by Bracken, Whitehead's notion of societies becomes much more important for Bracken than it seems to be for Whitehead. For Bracken, societies are not reducible to their member actual entities prehending one another in order with a common reiterated pattern, although they are at least that. In addition, Bracken emphasizes an overall shape to a continuous society such that all the member entities relate to that overall shape as well as to what they would reiterate from their predecessors. As Whitehead himself said, all the really interesting enduring entities, including agents that change in response to their environments, are societies. Bracken adds to this a special theological conception. In the primordial state, the underlying ontological creative activity and the extensive continuum are shaped by three divine societies, which he identifies with the Christian Trinity. Each divine society has its own nature to which all of its parts relate. But each also relates to the other two and their distinctive natures so that there is a perfect mutual indwelling. And the divine nature common to all three divine society Persons is the mutual relating that the three Persons have with each other. So, the primordial situation is the one ontological creativity expressed through the extensive continuum of the three divine Persons such that each moment in each Person is attentive (1) to the peculiar nature of the Person's society, (2) the peculiar nature of the other Persons' respective societies, as well as (3) to the other moments within its own society and in the other Persons' societies. This whole shebang is God, whose nature is the Trinitarian Persons and whose being is the activity of creativity throughout the extensive continuum. This whole God can then go on to create the finite actual entities, in Bracken's theology, a topic I'll not pursue here.

THE PROBLEM OF THE ONE AND THE MANY

The question I do want to pose is whether the notion of creative activity is sufficiently fundamental with respect to the one and the many. Suppose for the sake of argument that Bracken's account of God as such a creative activity with an appropriate extensive continuum, and the determinate nature of which is three divine Personal societies, is internally valid and metaphysically helpful in a host of ways. As an activity, it has earlier parts and later parts. These temporally distinct parts might involve continuities in many senses, including those Bracken and Whitehead discuss. But the temporally distinct parts need to be external to one another in some crucial sense as well. For, if they are not external as well as connected, then they are not genuinely different, which is to say, they are not many. A temporal activity is one through its continuities and many through its parts that constitute or occupy different moments of time.

Let me press this point deeper. One way of interpreting Whitehead, Hartshorne's, for instance, is to say that an actualized entity has no reality in itself except insofar as it is taken up within the concrescent process of an actualizing entity. Insofar as it is so taken up in a "present" moment it has lost its own subjective reality, its own external existence. Finite actual occasions take up actualized occasions from their past and include them in modified or perhaps negatively prehended form within their own satisfaction. But those past occasions do not retain their own identities external to subsequent occasions that prehend them. This is true for God as well, on this interpretation of Whitehead. Suppose that Hartshorne is right that God is a society of occasions. Each divine occasion in that society prehends all the previously actualized finite occasions as well as the previous divine occasions, "surpassing" all, including its own divine predecessors, as Hartshorne claims. Those previous occasions, worldly and divine, maintain their plural identity within the concrescing divine occasion but only as elements of that divine occasion's concrescence, not as having any external reality of their own. Hence there is no activity or process with earlier and later parts, even in the divine society. There is a relation of before and after within a divine occasion of concrescence, something that Whitehead would describe through a "genetic" analysis of an actual occasion as in part 3 of *Process and Reality*.[2] But there is no process or activity within a concrescence with earlier and later parts, only the logical ordering of the coming-to-be of the satisfaction in the novel occasion. As I said earlier, it is somewhat paradoxical that this kind of "process philosophy" denies any process or activity within time. For Hartshorne's line of interpretation, the only real things are the concrescences of "present" occasions as they occur. This is why Hartshorne stresses the theme of panpsychism, the view that everything that is real is "mental" in the special sense that Whitehead attached to genetic concrescence in contrast to the "physical" of finished actual occasions. Hartshorne's line of interpretation rejects the equiprimordiality of the physical with the mental and acknowledges a reality for the physical only as a component of a mental concrescence.

Bracken decisively rejects this line of development of Whitehead's thought in his emphasis on divine activity. This is implicit in his rejection of the interpretation of creativity as exhausted in the finite (and divine) actual entities or occasions. For Bracken, the divine life is an activity with earlier and later parts and with continuity in relation to the temporal history of the creative world as well as internally to itself in the fellowship of the three Persons. How, then, can the externality of the earlier and later moments of the divine activity be accounted for?

Grant for present purposes whatever continuities are appropriate. In the general Whiteheadian view these would include the prehension of the earlier by the later and the reiteration of eternal objects from one occasion to the next; Whitehead would also stress superjective continuities of the concrescing occasions with the future. What would give a past occasion, say, the integrity necessary to sustain an external relation (however much also internal) to a subsequent occasion that prehends it? Whitehead said that an actual occasion is subject to two kinds of analysis. Morphological analysis describes the shape of the occasion within the concrescence of another occasion as Whitehead argued in part 4 of *Process and Reality*. Genetic analysis describes the logic of the subjective genesis of the occasion rendering initial data into a harmonized definite satisfaction. If the past occasion is both morphologically continuous with its subsequent prehender as well as genetically subjective in itself, then its subjective genesis would give it external integrity. That subjective genesis, however, is past and gone from the standpoint of the subsequent prehending entity. So, from that subsequent perspective, the previous occasion is nothing more than what is left of it—its morphological nature—in the later occasion. This is the powerful pull of the Hartshornean interpretation.

If Bracken is to defend real ontological temporal activity, then it is necessary to establish how the earlier occasion can have its own integrity, with the subjective as well as objective sides, relative to the later occasions that prehend it. We are talking about ontological activity within the life of God here, although the point holds for the entire extent of whatever is cosmologically real. What is the context, what is the "one," that allows for the earlier occasions to be together with the later ones so that both have their integrity over against each other as well as their continuities? Whitehead's approach to the problem of the one and many, as said, is that only occasions can be ones for the manys they prehend, and this loses the externality needed for activity or process in time. Bracken's approach is to supplement Whitehead's with the ontological activity of creativity within the many but not reduced to locations in actual entities. But the one of ontological creativity in Bracken's view has the unity of its continuities and still needs a deeper way to keep its earlier and later elements together as partly external to one another.

ETERNAL CREATION

My suggestion is that temporal activity is dependent on an eternal context that allows the earlier and later moments to be together in their own integrities, partly external to one another. "Eternity" here does not mean static form, as in Whitehead's conception of "eternal objects." It rather is defined negatively at this point as a kind of ontological togetherness that embraces but is deeper than the cosmological togetherness within time. Within the temporal order, as we have seen, the past has no reality external to the present (and the same can be said of the future), and so the temporal order, so understood, has no flow or activity. But time does flow, and there are many kinds of activity, perhaps even the divine one described by Bracken. Therefore, there must be an ontological context in which earlier and later moments of temporal activity can be together so as to be both external to one another and connected. I call this context "eternal." What can it be?

To answer this question, permit me to move the discussion from the details of Whiteheadian, Hartshornean, Brackenian cosmological debates to a more abstract level. What is the nature of being determinate, where "determinate" might refer to a process actual entity, a Buddhist dharma arising and ceasing, a yin/yang change, a supernova, a quark, or whatever? To be determinate is to be something rather than nothing and to be something rather than something else. It is to be this rather than that (whatever this and that might be). Putting a finer point on it, to be determinate is to be determinate with respect to some other things, which is what is meant by saying a determinate thing is this *rather than that*. So, a determinate thing has some components that register the other things with respect to which it is determinate. I call these "conditioning components" because they are the ways determinate things condition one another so as to be determinate with respect to one another. In Whitehead's scheme, the initial data of a concrescing occasion are the conditioning components (and God's divine lure functions as an initial datum). But a determinate thing cannot be only conditioning components; if it were, it would reduce to nothing but those other things. A determinate thing needs essential components as well that integrate the conditioning components and give them an integral reality constituting the determinate thing itself. If a determinate thing were only its essential components, it would not be determinate with respect to anything else; it would not be this rather than that and hence would not be something rather than nothing. Both conditional and essential components are necessary for a thing to be determinate. The essential components are no more necessary than the conditional ones.

The result of this analysis is that determinateness requires a plural world of many things that are determinate with respect to one another. To do this, they need internal relations within themselves that integrate their various components, and these are constituted by their essential components. But they also need external relations among one another so that none is swallowed up in another with respect to which it is supposed to be determinate. As we have seen, on the Whiteheadian cosmology, the past is swallowed up in the present (and the future a mere projection), and so determinate activity through time is impossible. If all relations were internal, there would be only one thing, as F. H. Bradley observed. If all relations were external, the atoms that constitute the termini in the relation would not be determinately different from one another and thus could not really be termini. A determinate thing is a harmony of conditional and essential components, necessarily in a field with other such harmonies with respect to which it is determinate and relative to which it has conditional components.

What is this "field" or context in which things can be determinate with respect to one another, connected but also in a certain respect external? It has two dimensions. One, which I call cosmological, is the matrix of ways by which the determinate things condition one another by the conditional components they give one another. Space-time causal connections are elements in such a matrix, but there are many other kinds of conditioning: the decades-long conversation between Joe Bracken and me is a rich matrix of intellectual and affectional conditionings. In Whitehead's cosmology, the cosmological context of interactions is constituted by the prehensive relations among actual entities with all their elements such as eternal objects, and so forth.

But the limitation of the cosmological context is that within any given determinate thing another thing with respect to which it is determinate functions only as a conditioning component, leaving out the other thing's integrity given by its essential components. The other thing becomes merely an object, as Whitehead would say. The past occasion, for instance, does not have its essential subjectivity, only the objective outcome of that subjectivity, insofar as it exists as a conditional component in another occasion that prehends it. Continental philosophers from Buber to Levinas have sensitized us to the problem of the Other: to relate to others only as elements in our own experience is to reduce them to objects for us, marginalizing or denying their subjectivity that would make them genuine Others. For the less dramatic concerns of cosmology, from the standpoint of the present, the past is a mere object internal to the present, not a genuine Other that can hold down a separate position in an activity or ongoing process.

The second dimension to the context in which determinate things can be related must be one in which the mutually different things can be together not only with their conditional components but also with their respective essential components. Each thing is a harmony of its own essential and conditional components, and they must be together in an ontological context of mutual relevance that allows the externality of the essential components of each of the things to the other. From the perspective of any of the determinate harmonies, the others can be integrated as components of that harmony, but without the others' essential components. The ontological context of mutual relevance allows the separate determinate things to be together without any one of them to swallow any of the others. Moreover, there must be such an ontological context of mutual relevance if there is to be even the cosmological context in which things condition one another because such conditioning requires the independent integrities of the mutually conditioning things. The conditioning things must be real terms in their relations with one another, which requires that their independent essential components must be ontologically together even though they are cosmologically out of relation.

AN ETERNAL ACT OF CREATION *EX NIHILO*

What can this ontological context of mutual relevance be that allows for the cosmological context in which we so obviously observe things affecting one another and being determinate with respect to one another? One thing for sure is that this context cannot be another determinate thing.

For if it were, it would have to be a determinate harmony of conditional and essential components and thus would require an even deeper ontological context of mutual relevance to make possible its determinate relations with the other things it is supposed to contextualize. On the other hand, if the ontological context of mutual relevance were wholly indeterminate, it would do nothing to contextualize the determinate things. If it were wholly indeterminate, it would be indistinguishable from nothing; it would not be something rather than nothing.

I propose that the only thing that could be the ontological context of mutual relevance is a singular ontological act that creates everything determinate. The determinate things created are determinate with respect to one another as the termini of the act in whatever ways we empirically find them to be. The act itself is a pure making of determinate things. The only nature it has is what comes with the creating itself: it is the creator of this world. Apart from creating, the act is wholly indeterminate, hence nothing. But it is not apart from creating, it is the creating itself, the making of novel things. Every determinate thing is created by this act, in whatever relations with other determinate things are involved in its determinateness.

I call this ontological creative act "God" in accordance with a long tradition, a bit of which I shall rehearse here. But this act, which makes possible determinate things, including activities and processes of creativity through time, is deeper than Bracken's complex God involving creativity, the extensive continuum, and the Triune Persons. A few remarks will indicate how different my conception of God is from his.

First, because all determinate things are created, there is nothing out of which they are created, no primal stuff, no divine fullness. Therefore, the act can be called "creation *ex nihilo*" in accord with a long Christian tradition. Not many people talk about creation *ex nihilo* today and those who do, such as Catherine Keller in *Face of the Deep*, neglect this theory entirely.[3]

Second, because all determinate things are created, we cannot say that God is a determinate being. Rather, God is the ground of all determinate being in the sense of being the ontological creative act. Of course, we can take concepts from ordinary life such as that of a person and develop metaphors for the ontological act of creation, thinking of that act as an intentional agent, or a spirit, and as having purposes. Religions from South Asia tend to develop metaphors of consciousness for thinking about the ontological creation of determinateness, and religions from East Asia have elaborated metaphors of spontaneous emergence. However useful those metaphors might be in appropriate contexts, they cannot be taken literally. God is not literally a person, but the creative act. What God is, is the creator of the cosmos that we have and about which we understand such a small sample that it is difficult to generalize about the nature of the creator that comes from creating.

Third, the creation is gratuitous in the sense that there is no antecedent reason for it to happen, arbitrary in the sense that there is no antecedent reason why it is this way rather than another (as if God were antecedently good and has to create a good world), undeserved in the sense that whatever values are in this world do not cause their creation, and surprising in that the existence of each thing has no reason for being what it is save those involving its determinateness with respect to other things. The piety responsive to the gratuity, arbitrariness, undeservedness, and surprisingness of the creative act including its product is a kind of ontological love expressed in gratitude, appreciation of singularity, humility, and awe. This is different from the kind of piety responsive to God imaged as a person.

Fourth, because time and space (and any dimensions of extension) are determinate, they are created. God as the ontological creative act is therefore eternal in the sense of nontemporal and immense in the sense of unlocatable in spatial extension. God does not create at a time. Some theologies say that God creates at a first moment and that the cosmos unfolds from there. Others say that God creates in a kind of present totality that includes all times as if they were present. Others say that God creates through a kind of future telos that gives shape to things unfolding. These theologies miss the point that creation is of everything determinate. All elements of time are created.

A brief analysis of time in terms of essential and conditioning components, summarizing the much longer analysis I've given in *Eternity and Time's Flow*, can make sense of activity or process through time.[4] Time has three modes, past, present, and future. Each has essential components unique to itself. The essential components of the past have to do with fixed, finished, actuality. Those of the present have to do with spontaneous creativity. Those of the future have to do with pure unity or the principles of harmony. Each mode also receives conditional components from both of the others. From the past the future receives a plurality of actual things that have to be unified; hence, the future is not pure indeterminate unity but rather patterns of determinate possibilities, often containing alternatives. From the present the future receives constantly shifting demands of relevance, requiring that the future provide possibilities for decisive actualization relative to each present. Thus the future is an ever-changing kaleidoscope of possibilities relevant to every moment as it is present. From the past the present receives conditioning components in the form of potentialities to integrate in its creative selections, and from the future the present receives as conditioning components the possibilities for present creativity; the dynamism of the present is the creative novelty of deciding which of the alternate possibilities will be actualized in the integration of the potentialities acquired from the past. From the future the past receives as conditioning components the formal structures that are actualized, including the value in those structures; from the present the past receives ever-growing new actualizations so that the structure of the past, including its value and meaning, are constantly changing.

The past, present, and future are not together temporally but rather eternally in the ontological creative act that is God. Time's flow, the activities of temporal things, and temporal relations themselves are made possible by the eternal togetherness of the modes of time within God. Their togetherness exhibits an extraordinary ontological dynamism: the ever-growing edge of actualization, the dynamic spontaneity of each present moment that adds to the past and reshapes the future, and the kaleidoscopic shifts of future possibilities, including shifts in what values are possible. Every moment in the eternity of the ontological creative act is that kaleidoscope of future possibilities, the present of spontaneous creativity, and a complex past fact whose meaning and value are caught up in time's flow. The dynamism of past, present, and future together constitute what can be called "the life of God." But that life is not within time, with God living moment by moment. Temporal moment-by-moment life is an abstraction, caused by a prejudice for the immediacy of the present, from the eternal life finite things have in God as ontological creative act.

Fifth, this conception of God as the ontological creative act is anathema to the sensibilities of process philosophers, like scraping their fingers down a chalkboard. They look for models of God as a being within time, able to interact with things in the world as an intentional agent and free of responsibilities for evil. Joe Bracken is hesitant about these process sensibilities. I encourage him fully to abandon them and move from a commitment to an ontological activity of creativity to a commitment to the singular ontological creative act. That act allows for understanding how real activity through time is possible, with each of the earlier and later moments real in itself as future, present, and past from an eternal standpoint. In divine eternity, each moment is together with each other moment in its fullness as possibility, subjective creativity, and actual singularity, and so the passage of temporal activity is possible without past and future being swallowed up in the present.

From a temporal standpoint, the eternal creative act appears as creativity such as it is in a present moment; this is God creating now, and we are parts of it, determinate as we are so that it is our creativity too. But if we peer more deeply, we see the creativity of God in the past as the condition for our creativity now, and that divine creativity is gratuitous, arbitrary, undeserved, and surprising. If we look deeply into the future, we see the possibilities confronting us for our present creativity to be the creativity of the divine ontological creative act in a different guise. If we meditate on these three temporal loci of the divine creative act, we might grasp a bit of the sense in which God acts in time, having set up our present relative to past and future. But God's creative act really is in the creation of time and of our temporal positions relative to the rest of the world, and the vision of that surpasses any domestication of the ontological divine act into an ontological divine action in time.

NOTES

1. Joseph A. Bracken, S.J., *The Divine Matrix: Creativity as Link between East and West* (Maryknoll: Orbis Books, 1995), and *The One in the Many: A Contemporary Reconstruction of the God-World Relationship* (Grand Rapids: Eerdmans, 2001).

2. Alfred North Whitehead, *Process and Reality: An Essay in Cosmology*, corrected edition, edited by David Ray Griffin and Donald W. Sherburne (New York: The Free Press, 1978).

3. Catherine Keller, *Face of the Deep: A Theology of Becoming* (New York and London: Routledge, 2003).

4. *Eternity and Time's Flow* (Albany: State University of New York Press, 2003).

Chapter 15

PERPETUAL APOPHASIS AND THE EXISTENTIAL IMPLOSION OF WORLDVIEWS

This chapter has four parts: some remarks on the character of religion, the sketching of a technical theory of sacred worldviews, a brief analysis of an apophatic character of theology, and some queries about how to handle the existential implosion of sacred worldviews.

ON RELIGION

I recommend that we understand religion as human engagement of ultimacy expressed in cognitive articulations; social patterns of life, especially ritual; and personal and communal existential responses to ultimacy that give ultimate definition to the individual and community. Some of the reasons for this recommendation will be apparent in the discussion to come, although we all are aware of the complexity of the conversations among philosophers, theologians, and religion scholars about how to define religion.[1] You will have noted in the definition the reference to three kinds of expressions of religion, the cognitive, the social, and the existential. These vague categories overlap and interact, and are themselves broad enough to host the important ongoing discussions in religious studies, philosophy, and theology of various kinds of cognition, ritual, and social organization, and of existential choices and commitments that define personal and communal identity in various ways.

The reason a definition of religion is heuristically necessary is for us to be able to tell what is left out in the study of religion by a reductive analysis. A proper reductive analysis, say, in psychology or sociology of religion, or neuroscience, is careful to say that its conclusions are only what appears of the phenomenon when it is reduced to what can be measured by the discipline's instruments and expressed in its theoretical terms. But then it is no longer speaking about religion, rather about religion *as reconstructed as an object within the discipline's apparatus*, something that guarantees objectivity in the Kantian sense.[2] A definition of religion is needed to specify what is left out in this reduction, a question that cannot be addressed by the reductive discipline itself (although it might be addressed by the discipline's practitioners who move into philosophy to do so). This vague reference to cognitive, social, and existential expressions of religion is enough in a working definition to serve as warnings about what is left out or pushed into the background in various reductionisms. We are warned that when theologians are concerned about cognitive matters, the first-order questions of truth, they are likely to leave out the social and existential dimensions (though not the *conceptions* of those dimensions). We are warned that scientists are likely to leave out the first-order intellectual truth questions as well as certain kinds of existential issues when focusing on what can be expressed and explained in social structures and linguistic, neurological, and psychological habits. And we are warned that gurus, preachers, and prophets are likely to leave out disciplined concern for the cognitive and social aspects of religion when focusing on the existential issues. Healthy disputes about just what the cognitive, social, and existential boundaries are help to vivify this part of the definition for purposes of understanding the costs of reductive analysis.

My definition identifies religion with human *engagement* of ultimacy.[3] Engagement is a term with roots in pragmatism, something like Dewey's terms "interaction" and "transaction," with overlays of habit and intentionality.[4] By identifying religion with engagement expressed in cognitive, social, and existential ways, the definition precisely does *not* identify religion flat out with belief, social practices, and existential issues, which many other definitions do. Religion is engagement of ultimacy as expressed in those three ways, not just the expressions themselves.

To define religion as the engagement of ultimacy is a significant move. By and large, the field of religious studies for the last century or more has accepted the vaguely Neo-Kantian point that religions are social constructions, and that by studying the social constructions we can exhaustively understand religion. The prevalence of the Neo-Kantian impulse has led to deep skepticism about the category of "religion" itself, pointing out that it is but a social construction that comes from the West and biases the study of religion.[5] More recently, however, studies of religion in the cognitive sciences and evolutionary biology have treated certain aspects of religion as universal characteristics of human development and life engaging common realities.⁶ To be sure, different cultures give these different expressions, and these expressions should be studied as social constructions. But these social constructions are diverse expressions of the engagements, many of which are humanly pervasive and universal. The social constructivist approach reduces out the universal elements that are found by ways other than comparing social constructs. The pragmatic approach through engagement calls attention to them and opens the field for much more empirical and less reductive studies of religion as "religion" is expressed in various "religions."

An important aspect of the engagement model for the defining of religion is openness to the supposition that "reality" pretty much is what it is for all human beings and that all need to develop cultures that cope with that reality. Of course, cultures themselves are important parts of reality for human beings, and cultures are different; so, each culture needs to cope with the particularity of its own conventions, often relative to other cultures, as parts of reality. Important geographical and other physical variations also are real, and each variant is likely to be important for its culture rather than for others.⁷

I recommend defining religion as engagement with "ultimate reality," or "ultimate realities," or "ultimacy," or "ultimate dimensions," and such cognates that I shall discuss shortly. Relative to ultimate matters, cultural differences are often proximate. Therefore, we can expect all religions to have to find cultural ways of engaging pretty much the same ultimate realities. Or at least this becomes an open empirical question. Paying attention to the semiotic differences and uniquenesses of religious cultures, we can ask just what aspects of ultimacy they are engaging, how they do so, and whether they are similar or different when viewed as ways of engaging ultimate matters.

The engagement of ultimate reality is always *symbolic* engagement, as is true of any interpretive engagement. Pragmatic theories of engagement stress the roles of signs in guiding engagements. Signs interpret their objects in certain respects, and the contexts and purposes of the engaged interpretation determine which respects, within the resources offered by the semiotic systems within which the signs lie. This necessity for signs is why religion's engagements of ultimacy are expressed in cognitive, social, and existential ways. We intellectual types think first of the cognitive signs as embodied in concepts and explicit symbols. But social structures, particularly rituals, and semiotically shaped existential matters can also function as signs for engaging ultimacy. Symbolic engagement of ultimacy is "embodied" just like so many other engagements.

The importance of ultimacy in the definition of religion cannot be overestimated. The topic has kept theologians and philosophers well employed for millennia. I shall approach it here through a discussion of sacred canopies and worldviews.

SACRED WORLDVIEWS

Peter Berger popularized the phrase "sacred canopy" in his book with that name to indicate a cluster of socially constructed symbols that articulate the boundary conditions of the world.[8] Working within his imaginative sociological theory of knowledge, Berger was concerned with the way in which societies or cultures subjectively construct symbols of those boundary conditions and then project them onto their objective understanding of the world. As objective conditions of the world, the symbols of the sacred canopy feed back into subjective experience, perhaps being corrected, and prompting new projections that get corrected by objective reality. I am not concerned to limit the symbolizing activity to social entities and am more interested in how individuals symbolize their boundary conditions, although of course recognizing the social elements in nearly all semiotic behavior. As a social scientist, Berger was scrupulous not to comment on what the *real* boundary conditions of the world are, and so limited his inquiry to how the sacred canopy articulates a socially constructed set of symbols of how those boundary conditions are imagined. I, by contrast, take the symbols in the sacred canopy to be the signs by which the real boundary conditions are engaged, felicitously or not, truly or not. Religions, including their metaphysical parts, carry sacred canopies of various sorts to engage the boundary conditions, or ultimate realities.

Permit me to go beyond Berger's analysis to provide a more technical theory of the boundary conditions. What are basic dimensions of the world as experienced? Here are some examples. The world has form and human beings face this as possibilities to be actualized, possibilities that are actualized, and those that have been actualized. The existence of form is a boundary condition. Form bears value. Given the same components, different forms yield different values for harmonizing them, and an account of form such as Whitehead's discussion of contrasts, and of vagueness, triviality, narrowness, and width exhibits how this is so.[9] Therefore, value is a boundary condition associated with form, and insofar as human beings face choices about which possibilities to actualize, they lie under some kind of obligation. This ground of obligation is a kind of boundary condition; or rather form as possibilities, values, and obligation together constitutes a complex boundary condition.

Things in the world are harmonies with components, and the ways by which things comport themselves toward those components constitute how they are grounded in them.[10] For human beings, questions about wholeness arise out of the boundary condition of having to comport ourselves toward the important things that make us up. Things in the world exist and interact with one another in an existential field; within this field they mutually determine one another in various ways and yet are "other" to each other. The existence of an existential field for interaction is a boundary condition. So is the fact that things in the world have the value-identity that they achieve cumulatively by harmonizing their components with their forms in their existential location.

Most of all, the very existence of any of these boundary conditions is a boundary condition, because there might not be anything determinate at all. The first four boundary conditions mentioned—form, components, existential location, and value-identity—are conditions the cosmos has just because it contains determinate things. They all bear upon human life in ultimate ways. But the existence of the cosmos of determinate things is an even deeper boundary condition. I have argued in many places that this boundary condition is ontological, whereas the others are cosmological, and that it consists in an ontological act of creation that itself has no nature except what comes from its creating the world; the world is the terminus of the act.

The proximate affairs of the world are the various existing things with their value-laden forms, components, locations with respect to other things, and the value-identities achieved. But the boundary conditions themselves—forms, components, existential location, value-identity, determinate existence itself—are ultimate. No going behind them is possible, at least on my metaphysical account. Ultimate reality consists in the boundary conditions. Sacred canopies directly and indirectly symbolize some or all of these boundary conditions as ultimate realities, or ultimacy. This is not to say that the sacred canopies symbolize the ultimate realities well, or truly, only that they provide symbols by means of which those realities can be engaged.

A more precise understanding of the ultimate realities as boundary conditions is made possible by a theory of finite/infinite contrasts. "Contrast" is Whitehead's term for a complex thing whose components at the highest level just fit together; they are not integrated by a higher order—they just fit, and he gave an aesthetic analysis of what this means.[11] An ultimate boundary condition is a finite/infinite contrast in which the finite and infinite sides just fit together. The finite side is whatever the condition itself is, for instance, form, components, existential location in a field with others, value-identity, and the sheer existence of determinate things as such. The infinite side is what reality would be without the finite side: no form or value, for instance, no integration of components, and so forth, including no world of determinate things. Of course, the infinite side is a counterfactual, because there really is form, components, existential location, and value-identity in every determinate thing, and there are in fact determinate things. The finite side is indicative, the infinite side subjunctive. The fact that the ultimate realities are boundary conditions is registered in the contrast between the facticity of the finite side and the what-if-there-were-no-finite-side of the infinite side. Insofar as the religious symbolizations of the ultimate realities allow for it, the felt contrast of the finite and infinite sides is how the ultimate realities are registered as ultimate. The symbols of ultimacy sometimes engage the ultimate realities with feelings of their ultimacy as sacred, numinous, and mysterious, and this comes from feeling something of both sides in the finite/infinite contrasts.

As clusters of symbols for engaging ultimate boundary conditions in the form of finite/infinite contrasts, sacred canopies are parts of *worldviews*. A worldview as I wish to define it is a more or less coherent set of clusters of symbols for orienting various domains of human life. Engaging the ultimate in a sacred canopy is only one such domain. At the opposite pole from ultimate realities are the more proximate domains of how we live domestically, and work, and have neighborhoods. We treat people in the domestic domain differently from the way we treat colleagues at work, which is also somewhat different from the way we treat people in the community whom we barely know. Actions in each of these domains have their own immediate characters, but they also have larger meanings because of how they are oriented in and by that domain. Each domain gives meaning to the human affairs within it.

Moreover, the symbolic connections between the various domains within the worldview give extra meaning to the affairs within each domain, making the other domains relevant to matters in the domain at hand. Among the many domains that most worldviews have to include, between the ultimate and domestic ones, are those of the political society beyond the community, the economic system within which one's particular work is oriented to others' work, perhaps important historical circumstances, perhaps a larger sense of identity as a people, or as a nation, or as a human being in the natural environment. Worldviews differ significantly concerning the kinds of connections they make or fail to make among these and many other domains. But whatever their connections, people's affairs are given more or less meaning by being oriented and cross-connected within the worldviews' various domains.

A *sacred* worldview, in my usage, is one in which many of the important domains of life are connected with the domain of the sacred canopy in which ultimacy is engaged. For instance, families usually have meals together. In some worldviews, they would say grace or observe a ritual posture at the meals because something in the sacred canopy is connected with the domain of family meals. Insofar as a worldview does connect the sacred canopy to a mundane domain, so that orientations of affairs within that mundane domain are affected and partly shaped by the connection with ultimacy, that mundane domain can be said to have an "ultimate dimension" and the worldview itself to that degree can be called sacred.

Needless to say, worldviews differ radically in how they connect the ultimacy that is engaged with the symbols of the sacred canopy to the other mundane domains of life. Not every kind of connection is true and good. Nevertheless, the ideal for a worldview that allows for the engagement of ultimate realities is that it should be thoroughly sacred in the following sense. Every domain involves form and, most likely, possibilities for choice among different values; every domain affects how one's life is integrated; every domain involves engaging others; every domain involves some contribution to value-identity; and every domain is radically contingent to exist at all. Thus, every domain exists within the ultimate boundary conditions and thus has an ultimate dimension. Whether or not a given worldview registers this, it should, if it is to be thorough and true to the realities being oriented.

The function of worldviews is to provide *orientation* for the matters of life. Therefore, the bearings of the ultimate on the mundane domains need to have forms that serve for practical orientation. The metaphysics of ultimacy briefly sketched is so transcendent of most matters of life that it provides little if any practical orientation. More intimate symbols of the ultimacy of form, value, and obligation, for instance, are needed for practical orientation. Some sacred worldviews thus say that being moral in one's community is a command of a kingly God, or a way of being devoted to the virtues of the ancestors, or a way of non-acting in accord with the Dao. Transcendent symbols are truer to the real ultimacy of the boundary conditions. The metaphysical depth of this point is that the ontological ultimate, the ontological creative act on which all determinateness depends, as I view it, has no character at all apart from that deriving from its productivity. Therefore, all conceptions of the ontological ultimate as an independent determinate being are false, a very transcendent consequence. Intimate symbols are truer to the need for human orientation.

The tension between the pull toward transcendence and the pull toward intimacy in symbols of the ultimate is at the core of a sacred worldview that provides ultimate orientation for the mundane domains of life. That core is constituted by *interpretation*, a hermeneutical weaving that keeps the intimate symbols from implying something that contravenes the transcendent, and vice versa. For instance, appeal to a kingly God commanding justice should not be allowed to imply that the God guarantees justice, which would give rise to the problems of theodicy. Nor should a transcendent analysis of obligation to choose the better obscure the intimate symbols of moral ambiguity, of the tragedy of goods excluded for the sake of greater goods. The hermeneutic of relating the intimate and transcendent symbols of ultimacy is built into the great worldviews associated with deep and reflective religious traditions. The most obvious symbols in their sacred canopies are likely to be the intimate ones. But behind them are the transcendent ones. Long, often competing, traditions of interpreting between the two sides are somewhat hidden parts of sacred canopies.

Let me now turn to perpetual apophasis.

APOPHATIC THEOLOGY

Apophatic theology is the negative move that says that the positive theological claims at hand fall short of the mark. Nearly every religious tradition with a long history of literate reflection has an apophatic theological moment. Neo-Platonism, which was extremely influential within Christianity and Islam, and fairly influential within Judaism, is redolent with apophatic theology because the One is beyond the Dyad and hence beyond any conceptual determination. Mystics such as Meister Eckhart and Jacob Boehme, and more recently Nicolas Berdyaev, represent apophatic theology with their interests in cosmogony, the arising of God from the abyss of non-being, paralleling the opposite plunge of the mystic from the world into that abyss.

Many forms of Hinduism treat rational thought as but a ladder to reach the realization of that which is beyond conceptualization, Advaita Vedanta being the best known in the West. The great Chinese classic, the *Daodejing*, begins with the line, "The Dao that can be named is not the true Dao."

Apophatic theology is not merely the admission that all conceptualities fall short. Pragmatic fallibilism says that this is true of any interpretive engagements whatsoever, although trivial in most cases: despite falling short of complete knowledge, most of our interpretations are quite adequate for most of life. Apophatic theology says that some positive theological assertions, or symbolic engagements, are true in a way but that their truth blocks a greater truth. Apophatic theology negates some positive or kataphatic theology. Duns Scotus was among the most important thinkers dealing with apophatic and kataphatic theology to point out that no negation can be made except on the basis of some affirmation that calls for it.[12] He had in mind, among other things, Thomas Aquinas's claim that God is good, beautiful, actual, and so forth, *only by analogy* with human goodness, beauty, and finite actuality. Thomas would have to know something about God that is not analogous to know that knowledge of God is analogous. Thomas did, of course, claim to know that God is the infinite Act of To Be, although that still left a quandary about the distance between divine infinity and finite determinate virtues: is there anything left of the meaningfulness of goodness, beauty, and actuality in God? Scotus's real concern was with Thomas's claim that being itself is analogous, that God *is* divine infinity in a difference sense from that in which a finite thing *is* its nature. Scotus concluded that being itself is univocal, not analogous: because God *is* infinite in the same sense of *is* that a finite thing *is* its finite nature, we can know God to be infinite.[13]

Theology cannot be wholly apophatic, therefore. The negation in apophasis must have some justification in kataphasis. Kataphatic theology is the engagement of ultimacy with the positive interpretive symbols functioning as hypotheses about ultimate reality and the ultimate dimensions of things. The theology involved in the critical development of sacred worldviews, especially their sacred canopies, is kataphatic. It works by engaging ultimacy with discrimination according to the symbolic theological hypotheses involved. Apophatic theology, in its turn, is also an attempt to engage ultimacy, but through the denial of something positive. Apophatic theology is a rejection of kataphatic theologies as too limiting for the ultimate, in favor of engagement that is enabled by the negation. Apophatic and kataphatic theology necessarily go hand in hand. At its best, it would seem, apophatic theology depends upon a robust kataphatic theology, with the affirmation and negation dialectically related within the sacred worldview. In this circumstance, the kataphatic side is negated but then also recovered within the living worldview, as in the heyday of Neo-Platonism.

What happens, however, when sacred worldviews lose their plausibility? It would seem to be a victory for apophatic theology. But this cannot be the case if the kataphatic ground for denial is lost. In those instances in which the sacred worldview becomes implausible because it is based on too small a truth and a larger truth becomes apparent, the new confidence in the larger truth is a kataphatic justification for negating the old. A Daoist sacred worldview based on the view that the Dao is mellow and harmonious becomes implausible when it becomes apparent that the Dao is wild, especially in relation to matters of the human scale. The apophatic theology rejects the mellow Dao by the kataphatic evidence of lack of domesticated harmony in the Dao. If Daoist thinkers go on to embrace a cosmology that articulates natural movement in ways unscaled to human affairs, wildness can become a positive, that is, a new kataphatic, affirmation. Or a monotheistic theology based on a symbolizing of ultimate reality as a cosmically scaled just king who rewards the good and punishes the evil can become implausible in the face of overwhelming evidence that the world is not run justly, the standard problem of theodicy. An apophatic response would be to reject the symbols of God as a just king, prominent as they are in biblical texts and very important tools for intimacy of the ultimate in human life; the rejection would be based on the kataphatic observations of the unjust character of the world. The apophatic theologian might go on to develop a larger conception of God that embraces the injustice in natural and social processes, which would be a kataphatic construction, justified as a better hypothesis than the just king symbols.

So, one very important sense of apophatic theology is the perpetual task of improving sacred worldviews. Sacred worldviews are always vulnerable for revision as new knowledge is brought to bear, by science, by the interaction with other worldviews, by the occurrence of conditions that were never registered in the worldviews as orientable before. The experience of perpetual apophasis is in part the temporal process of having sacred worldviews challenged by new things so that they need to be revised or discarded in favor of some improved version. The image of the apophatic theologian as a pragmatic inquirer into the ultimate foundations of worldviews, however, seems to be a near miss.

EXISTENTIAL IMPLOSIONS

Let me come at the problem of apophatic theology from another angle, that of the existential implosion of sacred worldviews. By existential implosion I do not mean the improvement of worldviews so as to take into account new evidence with better form. I mean the existentially disastrous crumbling of a sacred worldview that seemed to work, that provided reasonable orientation, and gave meaning to life, and suddenly no longer does. Consider four kinds of examples.

1. Most traditional religious worldviews developed their symbology in antiquity whose cosmologies were very far from those of modern science. The inconsistency of modern science with those worldviews has led to successive implosions of traditional sacred worldviews, from the events of the Copernican revolution to Darwin. The contemporary bizarre defense of creationism gets its energy from the attempt to save an evangelical worldview from science itself. Many of my students are broken evangelicals who are wondering whether there is anything left that is credible in religion.

These examples have many dimensions, and among the most important are problems of inconsistency. A sacred worldview requires consistency if it is to be plausible. Can its symbolizations of ultimate reality make sense? Consistency means symbolic consistency within the sacred canopy itself, between the sacred canopy and the various mundane domains of the worldview, between the worldview itself and the actual situation that needs orientation, and between the worldview and its practical effects.

2. Many traditional Jewish worldviews say that God rules like a just king and that the Jews are divinely chosen people. This is hard to make relevant to a situation like the Nazi holocaust. The answer that several of the great prophets gave to the earlier destructions of Israel, namely, that God was still in charge and was using the conquering nations to punish Israel for breaking the covenant, cannot be made relevant to the vast suffering of innocents.[14] Most Muslim sacred worldviews say that God wills everything that happens, which is very helpful for orienting Islamic life when Islam is expanding successfully. But how can those worldviews be made relevant to the situation where Islam is beaten down by colonial powers? The sacred worldview implodes. Or think of the problems of a sacred worldview oriented to conditions of ancient peasant life when the actual conditions of life are modern, urban, and meritocratic, the situation of traditional Confucians in Boston.

These are examples of the problem of the worldview not having proper relevance to the actual situation. The worldview that used to be effective does not address the present reality. Plausibility in a worldview requires it to be relevant or appropriate to the situation that needs orientation.

3. Consider the problems of the interpretive connections between the transcendent and intimate symbols. Whereas the transcendent pole might have some relative metaphysical stability, what counts as intimate depends so much on local circumstances that hard and fast rules are probably impossible. The problem is bad enough when symbols of the absolutely transcendent creator have to be reconciled hermeneutically with symbols of such things as social and personal narratives. How much more difficult it is to sustain the truly ultimate connections in the sacred worldviews of downtrodden people who engage their worlds mainly in terms of negations, complaints, rejections! How can the anger that life is a bitch, surely the most intimate ultimate expression of experience and identity for many people, be interpreted salvifically in terms of the ultimate boundary conditions of human existence?

Theistic religions often create intimate symbols of the transcendent ultimate reality by personification. What interpretive scheme can connect the personal with the transcendent symbols? Thomas's hermeneutic of the analogy of being stumbles over Scotus's point. The avatar theory of some strains of traditional symbolism just repeats the problem. Finding intimacy within a cosmic narrative might make sense when the powers of good fight those of evil in one's neighborhood and one can be a player in the story. But the narrative of the expansion of the cosmos from the Big Bang to the Final Dissipation is difficult to make intimate because it is hard to place human beings in that scale. By and large, sacred worldviews with transcendent enough symbols to register the vast extension and deep intension of the natural cosmos have difficulty preventing human anonymity.

4. Fourth, look to the issues of ultimate authority. Authority is obviously an extraordinarily complex issue, and many different things can give authority to a sacred worldview: antiquity, convictions about revelation, reinforcement from a social group, perspicacity of some of its virtues, and aesthetic appeal, to name a few. A worldview implodes when its authority collapses for some reason or another. The development of historical methods for reading scripture was devastating for the authority of certain sacred worldviews. Learning that one's priest or rabbi is a pedophile can implode

the authority of a sacred worldview that derives from a community. Crises whose main locus lies in consistency, relevance, and the balance of intimacy and transcendence also can erode the authority of a sacred worldview that derives from its aesthetic properties.

These examples exhibit four conditions of plausibility: consistency, relevance, maintenance of both transcendence and intimacy in the symbols of ultimacy, and authority. When one or several breaks down, the sacred worldview becomes implausible and implodes, with varying effects. Such implosions are existential crises for individuals, communities, and sometimes whole cultures as my examples have illustrated.

The existential function of worldviews for individuals is to provide orientation for the various things they do in the multiple mundane domains of life. A person's life has more or less coherence, depending on the integrative structures of their operative worldview, such as it is. Whereas separate domains of life each might be somewhat well oriented, for instance, a structured sense of domestic meanings on the one hand and on the other a sense of the role of one's people in world history, those domains might or might not be coordinated with one another in the worldview. What happens in one might not bear on what happens in the other. If they are coordinated, it is always through the medium of some symbolic connection such as a containing narrative or metaphors of inclusion and exclusion.

When a sacred worldview implodes in a serious way, the result is a failure of orientation. The things of life that used to have meaning in a larger whole no longer do so. No boundary conditions defining orienting symbols can themselves be symbolized with authority. What can be done in this circumstance of radical disorientation? Permit me briefly and in conclusion to suggest a complicated response, on several levels.

On the first level, taking note of the fact that a sacred worldview has the logical form of an hypothesis, the obvious thing to do is to improve it. How can a broken sacred worldview be improved? What is broken about it needs to be acknowledged and analyzed. In all the examples just mentioned of implosions coming from inconsistency, irrelevance to the matters at hand, or breakdowns in the connection between transcendent and intimate symbols of ultimacy, the problem is with the intimate symbols, not the transcendent ones. So, the transcendent symbols need to be reaffirmed, strengthened, and expressed so as to be consistent with the findings of science, the events of history, the characters of the particular lives of individuals and communities, and all the other things that might have been inconsistent with the intimate symbols of ultimacy. If my earlier philosophical suggestions about ultimacy were right, this means finding ways of symbolizing: first, the ontological creative act that is not determinate apart from creating; second, the ultimate grounds of obligation that come from the finite/infinite contrast of form as such; third, the ultimate grounds for seeking wholeness that come from the finite/infinite contrast of having components; fourth, the ultimate grounds for engaging other people and things that come from the finite/infinite contrast of existential location; and, fifth, the ultimate grounds for value-identity that come from the finite/infinite contrast of actually harmonizing components with a form in a location. These are bare-bones conditions of ultimacy that stem from nothing more particular than the radical contingency of determinate things and the nature of determinateness. As so transcendent, they are consistent or compatible with any determinate state of affairs that might be found, a point that needs to be affirmed within any plausible sacred canopy.

But how can these ultimate conditions be resymbolized with the intimacy necessary to orient a repaired or newly invented sacred worldview? This is the second level of response to imploded sacred worldviews, far more difficult than the first level, which, after all, can be handled by philosophers in the Metaphysical Society and the Society for the Study of Process Philosophies. Without the intimate symbols, the hypothetical sacred worldview will be very hard to make relevant or appropriate to the things of life. The rub, however, is that with the implosion of the old sacred worldview, there remains no orientation for the development of intimate symbols. The course of least resistance is to provide new interpretations of the old intimate symbols, making them compatible with the transcendent symbols and relevant to the facts of life. But where do the new interpretations come from? A more creative response would be the poetic invention of new symbols, which is why the image of the pragmatic inquirer is a near miss.

I am tempted to say that religion manifests itself at its greatest depths when a sacred worldview seriously implodes. Some theologians say that in circumstances like this we simply have to wait for a new word, by which they mean a divine revelation. But the metaphysics of divinity with capacities for revelation is likely to be a casualty of the implosion. So perhaps we wait for a poetic word, for human genius. That word would have to provide its own orientation.

The deepest part of religion, I believe, is reached on the cusp between a broken sacred worldview and a new vision that is not in sight, a point with no orientation in itself. The existential victims of an imploded worldview desperately hoping, and perhaps working, for a new orientation, live at that cusp without orientation. The profound apophatic theologians know that we are in perpetual apophasis, that our sacred worldviews are always a little if not a lot wrong, always arbitrary and conventional, that the heart of religious life is to admit this while the improvement is not in sight, and to hold on to this feeling of being on the cusp. The ultimacy in that religious life is expressed in the feeling of a finite/infinite contrast: the finite side is the broken sacred worldview and the infinite side is the indeterminacy of what would fix it. To live on this cusp is an ultimate definition of human identity.

NOTES

1. One of the most interesting and subtle recent accounts is Barbara Herrnstein Smith's *Natural Reflections: Human Cognition at the Nexus of Science and Religion* (New Haven: Yale University Press, 2009). See also Gavin Flood's *Beyond Phenomenology: Rethinking the Study of Religion* (London: Cassell, 1999) and Karl Barth's *On Religion: The Revelation of God as the Sublimation of Religion*, translated by Garrett Green (London: T&T Clark, 2006). A still excellent compendium of the arguments about defining religion is Walter H. Capps's *Religious Studies: The Making of a Discipline* (Minneapolis: Fortress, 1995); its chapters treat successively the essence, origin, description, function, language, and comparison of religion or religions.

2. By the Kantian sense here I mean Kant's claim that objects are constructions of the manifold of sensibility according to the transcendental conditions of logic. They are subjective representations that also have order that is invariant as discovered by science, according to his analysis in the "Second Analogy" of the *Critique of Pure Reason*. Instead of aiming to conform our representations to things in themselves, Kant said that we should force nature to answer our questions. Objectivity consists in limiting our claims to the constructions of objects as they give themselves in answer to our questions.

3. For the discussion of symbolic engagement, see Neville, *On the Scope and Truth of Theology: Theology as Symbolic Engagement* (London: T&T Clark, 2006).

4. These important pragmatic themes are discussed at length in John E. Smith's *Purpose and Thought: The Meaning of Pragmatism* (New Haven: Yale University Press, 1978).

5. Talal Asad's *Genealogies of Religion: Discipline and Reasons of Power in Christianity and Islam* (Baltimore: The Johns Hopkins University Press, 1993) is a powerful statement of this point.

6. For an excellent overview, see the three volumes of Patrick McNamara, editor, *Where God and Science Meet: Volume I—Evolution, Genes, and the Religious Brain; Volume II—The Neurology of Religious Experience; Volume III—The Psychology of Religious Experience* (London: Praeger, 2006).

7. As Eskimos need to be subtler about snow than Bedouins, who need fine discriminations about sand. For a delightful study of this point, see Jared Diamond's *Guns, Germs, and Steel: The Fates of Human Societies* (paperback edition; New York: W.W. Norton, 1999).

8. See Peter L. Berger, *The Sacred Canopy: Elements of a Sociological Theory of Religion* (Garden City: Doubleday, 1967). See also Berger, with Thomas Luckmann, *The Social Construction of Reality: A Treatise in the Sociology of Knowledge* (Garden City: Doubleday, 1966).

9. See Whitehead's *Process and Reality*, corrected edition, edited by David Ray Griffin and Donald W. Sherburne (New York: The Free Press, 1978), part 2, chapter 4, "Organisms and Environment." My own analysis of form as bearing value is in *The Cosmology of Freedom* (New Haven: Yale University Press, 1974; new edition, Albany: State University of New York Press, 1995), chapter 3; *Reconstruction of Thinking* (Albany: State University of New York Press, 1981), chapters 5–8, which argues that form is a function of value rather than the other way around; *Recovery of the Measure* (Albany: State University of New York Press, 1989), chapters 7–9, which argues that form presents possibilities with alternative values for choice; *Normative Cultures* (Albany: State University of New York Press, 1995), which studies the value-ladenness of theories and norms for conjoint action; and *Realism in Religion* (Albany: State University of New York Press, 2009), chapter 8, which discusses the aesthetic means by which value is grasped and interpreted.

10. That things in the world are harmonies with form, components, existential location, and value is a systematic metaphysical position I have defended in the references in note 9. The most direct and thorough argument that to be determinate at all is to be a harmony related to other harmonies is in *God the Creator: On the Transcendence and Presence of God* (Chicago: University of Chicago Press, 1968; new edition, Albany: State University of New York

Press, 1992), part 1, and my more recent *Ultimates: Philosophical Theology Volume One* (Albany: State University of New York Press, 2013), part 3.

11. See his *Process and Reality*, corrected edition, 22, 109, 111, 114, 244, 249, and 255.

12. Scotus said, "Every denial is intelligible only in terms of some affirmation. . . . if we deny anything of God, it is because we wish to do away with something inconsistent with what we have already affirmed." In *Duns Scotus: Philosophical Writings*, edited and translated by Allan Wolter, O.F.M. (New York: Thomas Nelson & Sons, 1962), 15. Thomas Aquinas agrees with the general point; see his *Summa Theologica*, Pt. I, Q. 13, a. 2. For a contemporary analysis of Scotus, see Richard Cross, *Duns Scotus on God* (Aldershot: Ashgate, 2005).

13. See Neville, *God the Creator*, chapter 1.

14. See the extraordinary structuralist arguments of Gerd Theissen in his *A Theory of Primitive Christian Religion*, translated by John Bowden (London: SCM Press, 1999). Instead of seeing themselves and their God defeated by the Assyrians and Babylonians, the prophets proclaimed their God the only one, the God who used those aggressive nations to discipline Israel.

Chapter 16

ULTIMATE REALITIES FOR THE SCIENCES AND HUMANITIES

Two kinds of ultimate realities exist and have been symbolized in the world's religious and philosophical cultures, the ontological and the cosmological.[1]

ONTOLOGICAL ULTIMATE REALITIES

Ontological ultimate realities have to do with the contingency of the world as a whole. Why is there something rather than nothing? Stephen Hawking concludes *A Brief History of Time* with the following remark:

> Even if there is only one possible unified theory, it is just a set of rules and equations. What is it that breathes fire into the equations and makes a universe for them to describe? The usual approach of science of constructing a mathematical model cannot answer the question of why there should be a universe for the model to describe. Why does the universe go to all the bother of existing? Is the unified theory so compelling that it brings about its own existence? Or does it need a creator, and, if so, does he have any other effect on the universe? And who created him?[2]

Ontological ultimate reality (or realities) is whatever responds to the question of why there is the universe, of what its "cause" is, in whatever sense of "cause" might turn out to be appropriate. If it is suggested that the universe does not need a ground or cause, that it "just is," the ontological question is reformulated as why it just is rather than there be nothing at all.

Reflection on ontological ultimate reality is ancient and multifarious in the diverse cultures of the world. But ontological reflection is always and inevitably subject to two contrary pressures. On the one hand is the pressure to think of ultimate reality in terms that are intimate to human life, that make sense to people. From the standpoint of human religious needs, the ultimate reality or realities are the ultimate boundary conditions of existence—matters of the meaning of life and death. The symbols that relate ontological ultimate reality to life need to be intimate and familiar. On the other hand is the pressure to think of ontological ultimate reality in transcendent terms—after all, it is supposed to be the "account" or "cause" of the world and everything within it. So ontological ultimate realities cannot be like the things in the world of which they are to give an account. The pressure toward transcendence, fueled by a consciousness of the dangerous seductions of idolatry, pushes concepts, language, and analogies beyond determinate limits.

Philosophical/theological/cultural reflections on ontological ultimacy have thus appropriated fecund symbols and pressed them in two directions—toward intimacy and toward transcendence. Three great symbol systems have dominated the world's cultures: consciousness, emergence, and personhood. These are internally various and overlap in many ways but have their own logic.

Consciousness, its powers and objects, has been a powerful symbolic theme, especially in the cultures of South Asia, including those we know as Hinduism, Buddhism, and Jainism. Everyone can relate to consciousness, and everyone can engage in meditation in which we become conscious of objects of consciousness and capacities to empty and to control consciousness to some degree.[3] Some people are extremely adept at this, but everyone can relate to the symbols of consciousness intimately. Pushing toward the transcendent side, consciousness is symbolized as a thing in itself, separable from its objects. In some symbolic systems, the objects of consciousness are real on their own, too, resulting in various forms of dualism; in other systems they are not so real, resulting in nondualisms. Some systems, usually Hindu, say that the underlying personal consciousness (atman) is somehow (in a great many different possible senses) identical with Brahman, a kind of Primal Consciousness. Brahman is symbolized as with qualities (Saguna Brahman), in relation to human life and the creation of the world, and without qualities (Nirguna Brahman), beyond any connection with the world or any kind of multiplicity. Other systems, usually Buddhist, say that the underlying personal consciousness is truly empty so that an enduring self is an illusion, but one that allows for symbolizing ultimate reality as Buddha-mind in some denominations. South Asians do believe in gods, including some highly transcendent ones such as Shiva and Vishnu. But as persons the gods are subject to the laws of karma and hence are not truly ultimate. The symbols of Shiva and Vishnu (and other gods) are pushed toward ever more transcendent representations and then they switch from models of personal agency to models of consciousness, identifying with Brahman.[4] The diversity in the models of consciousness cannot be overestimated, and yet the thematic symbol has some coherence throughout the models.

The theme of emergence developed prominently in East Asian cultures and takes its metaphorical center from springs of water emerging from the ground, the emergence of buds in the spring, and the like. Its symbolic stress is on novelty, the development of the complex from the less complex or simple. The notion of the Dao is two-dimensional. One is the emergence within time of the later from the earlier, often with a stress on spontaneity. The other dimension is the emergence of the Dao that can be described from a deeper, unnamable Dao. The *Daodejing*, for instance, begins:

> The Tao (Way) that can be told of is not the eternal Tao; the name that can be named is not the eternal name. The Nameless is the origin of Heaven and Earth; the Named is the mother of all things. Therefore let there always be non-being so that we may see their subtlety, and let there always be being so that we may see their outcome.[5]

Wangbi, the great third-century commentator on the *Daodejing*, gave this interpretation of the lines just quoted:

> All being originated from nonbeing. The time before physical forms and names appeared was the beginning of the myriad things. After forms and names appeared, "Tao (the Way) develops them, nourishes them, provides their formal shape, and completes their formal substance," that is, becomes (or is) their Mother. This means that Tao produces and completes things with the formless and nameless.[6]

On the Confucian side, the eleventh-century Neo-Confucian philosopher Zhou Dunyi wrote:

> The Ultimate of Non-being and also the Great Ultimate (T'ai-chi)! The Great Ultimate through movement generates yang. When its

activity reaches its limit, it becomes tranquil. Through tranquility the Great Ultimate generates yin. When tranquility reaches its limit, activity begins again. So movement and tranquility alternate and become the root of each other, giving rise to the distinction of yin and yang, and the two modes are thus established.[7]

These texts and others indicate some of the sophisticated thinking about the emergence of determinate things "from nothing" or "the formless and nameless." The pull of intimacy on the symbols of emergence highlights common experiences of spontaneity and fresh starts.

Personhood is the third major symbolic theme developed in the great religions of the world, as well as in most of the minor ones, including the tribal religions that did not develop into the Axial Age traditions. Symbolizing the ontological ultimate reality grounding the world with the metaphors of personal agency, intention, and creativity is dominant in Western pagan and monotheistic religions. The symbols of personhood are highly various and run from anthropomorphic representations of gods as superhuman agents to the highly transcendent conceptions of God as not exactly personal, in the sense of being a limited Spirit with intentional relations to other things, but as somehow being "more than that." There is nothing at all personal in the Neo-Platonic conception of God as the One beyond all determinate difference, or in the Thomistic conception of God as the pure Act of To Be, or in the Kabbalistic conception of Ein Sof, but these highly sophisticated superpersonal conceptions are usually tied into a continuum with more personalistic images. The fundamental ontological employment of personal symbols is to articulate a conception of God as creator of the world.

This point about the widespread elaboration of conceptions of the ultimate as somehow personal should not be confused with the points that all cultures have at times believed in supernatural beings, that people tend to overextend the attribution of agency beyond what can be justified on thorough analysis, and that all children at some time believe in supernatural beings who can read their thoughts.[8] Belief in supernatural beings need not have anything to do with the symbolism of ultimacy, or with religion; rather it is among elementary scientific beliefs, beliefs about what things there are in the world and how they work. Only some supernatural beings have been identified as symbolic of ultimacy. For instance, in many Hindu and Buddhist cultures there is widespread belief in supernatural beings of many kinds, but all are subject to karma and hence are not ultimate.

In cosmologies believing in reincarnation, a given soul might move from animal to human to various kinds of supernatural demonic or divine bodily forms. Only when these supernatural beings are tied somehow with the ultimate boundary conditions for how or why there is a world would they be religiously interesting. Nevertheless, the symbolization of ultimate ontological reality with themes of personhood is so dominant that many people in the West commonly think of religion as belief in God, where "God" means something personal. Taking a broader, more comparative, perspective, the symbolic systems of personhood comprise only one of at least three families of symbolic systems for engaging ultimate ontological reality.

From these considerations, an important set of research projects is the comprehensive multidisciplinary task of comparing how these families of symbol systems variously articulate ontological ultimate reality. One focus of these projects would be on the normative questions of what can be known of the ontological cause of the world, and another focus would be on how these symbols function intimately in religious and cultural life in various traditions.

COSMOLOGICAL ULTIMATE REALITIES

Cosmological ultimate realities constitute the boundary conditions for the world and human life that come from the characters of what it is to be a "world" or "thing in the world" at all. Of course, there have been many models of cosmologies that depict basic structures of the world, from the yin/yang cosmologies of East Asia to the causal *pratitya samutpada* cosmologies of South Asia to the substance cosmologies of West Asia. Such cosmologies have been given ancient expression as well as contemporary expressions that relate to the mathematical language of science. One of the most exciting intellectual adventures of the twentieth century was Alfred North Whitehead's criticism of substance models of the cosmos as being unable to allow for the kinds of relations mathematical physics imputes to things. He constructed an alternative cosmology based on relational connections developing in process.[9] But all of these and any other possible cosmologies suppose that whatever is proposed as real and basic to the cosmos is *determinate*. Any thing is determinate in that it is what it is and not something else, and it is what it is rather than there being nothing at all.

Although an analysis of determinateness as such is about as abstract a philosophical endeavor as can be imagined, it is extraordinarily fruitful in articulating ultimate boundary conditions for the world and for the human symbolization of the world. Any determinate thing has four features, each of which is a "cosmological ultimate reality" and evokes symbolization in reference to human life. The four traits are *form* or pattern, *components formed*, *existential location* relative to other things with respect to which the thing is determinate, and the meaning or *value* of having these components together in this form in this existential location relative to others.

That things have form (in some sense of form) means that they are actualizations (in some sense of actualization) of possibilities (in some sense of possibility). Since there are many things in existential fields, their possibilities are coordinated in something like a field. From the standpoint of human beings, sometimes there are alternative possibilities whose actualization depends in part on human choice. Whenever there is decisive actualization, by human choice or not, the actual includes the exclusion of the possibilities that are not actualized. Often the alternatives for choice differ in value. Many different accounts of value have been given, not all of which consider value to be a function of form—it might be the result of divine will, for instance. The mathematical language of some science obscures the value dimensions of the world, but even the most mathematically sophisticated of scientists faces problems of choosing well.

In all cases, however value is constituted, where there is a difference in value among alternatives for choice, the chooser lives under obligation. To choose the better is to be the better chooser, and to choose the worse is to be the worse chooser. Choice determines moral worth in the case at hand. Something like this is the root meaning of being obligated. Of course, the situation regarding obligation is extraordinarily complex. For instance, most decisive actions are conjoint ones involving more than one person. Choosing does not automatically address the real alternatives that are possible, but only those that are known, or potentially knowable.

Nevertheless, facing alternatives for choice with different values is a universal human condition, built into the cosmological trait that all things have form. Every culture and every religion has ways of articulating morality or righteousness, often with complex procedures of moral deliberation. Some social psychologists such as Jonathan Haidt claim that fundamental moral instincts have evolved so that humans act on the instinct before reasoning much about the choice, and that this evolution is because this kind of attention to choice is adaptive for passing on genes within individuals and groups.[10] Cultures differ fairly radically in their moral codes and the ways in which they articulate value and choice. But all cultures address the issues of choice among alternatives of different value. As they attempt to symbolize what the ultimate boundary conditions are that set up the situation of living under obligation, they develop symbols of the ground of obligation. The ground of obligation is a cosmological ultimate.

Any determinate thing has components that are put together in the form or pattern that it has. Cosmologies differ greatly in the kinds of things hypothesized to be components. Whatever the components of a thing are, they themselves are determinate and therefore have form, components, existential location, and value. Paying attention to the form of a thing focuses on the thing's unity. To focus on its internal multiplicity is to pay attention to proper comportment toward the character and value of its components. Only for sentient beings is comportment toward components a likely problem. The components of different people's lives vary widely. But all people have bodies and can comport themselves toward their bodies with care or neglect; special things are important for some bodies, for instance, caring for disabilities and disease conditions. All people have communities, usually families. Albeit people can rebel against their family and its culture, that is a way of comporting toward them. People have social and historical circumstances that are parts of their lives toward which they should comport themselves. Part of people's realities is how they impact their natural environment. Spiritual matters, including spiritual maturation, constitute important components of life, although different cultures conceive these in sometimes competing ways. Put in abstract terms, people are well grounded when they comport themselves toward their important components well, and ill grounded when they do not. The abstract fact, derived from being determinate, of having components toward which comportment can be differential means that having the task of well-grounded wholeness is an ultimate condition of human life. Symbols of ultimate reality include those for well-grounded wholeness, and all religious traditions have some such symbols.

Existential location is a trait of anything determinate because each determinate thing is determinate with respect to some other things. To be determinate is to be in relation. Therefore, a determinate thing has two kinds of components, conditional and essential ones. The conditional components are the ones that a thing has by virtue of being conditioned by or conditioning some other thing, as in cause and effect, thinking or thought of, here relative to there, half of and the square root of, and so forth. If a thing had no conditional components relative to other things, it would not be determinate with respect to them. On the other hand, a thing needs essential components to integrate its conditional components. If it were only conditional components, it would not be able to be a term in the relations of conditioning. Each of the other things with respect to which a thing is determinate also needs to have its own essential features so that it could be a reciprocal term in the conditioning relation.

An existential field is a matrix of conditioning relations by virtue of which things are determinate with respect to one another. These fields have been understood in very many ways, from large-scale cosmological pictures such as the expansion of the cosmos from a golden egg to a geography of levels of reality to fields of consciousness. A given thing might participate in a great many existential fields, giving it a complex sense of existential location.

The cosmological significance of location in an existential field is that a thing necessarily engages with the others in the field. On the human level, if not others, the engagement of others is often problematic. The others—other people, social institutions, various structures and ecologies of nature—have natures and values of their own. Perhaps the default position is for people to treat others only in ways consonant with their own needs and interests. But the Axial Age religions point out that this is unrealistic. A realistic engagement with others treats them according to their own nature and value, with respect. This is enormously complicated and incapable of being carried out completely because of the competition of so many things for attention. But most religious traditions have some symbols for the need to be compassionate, loving, just, and so forth. Engagement with others is a cosmological ultimate condition for human life.

Most things that happen in human life involve relating to all three ultimate conditions. Every action involves choice among alternatives with different values, all choices arise out of the state of well- or ill-grounded wholeness of the chooser, most involve engaging other things, often other people. The ultimate dimensions of obligation, wholeness, and engagement of others overlap and feed back on one another.

The value identity of a thing comprises both the value achieved in itself and the values it affects in other things that those other things integrate with their own essential features. The value of a human life achieved over a lifetime and in a lifetime's movement throughout various environments is very hard to conceptualize. For some traditions with personifying symbols for ontological ultimate reality, having a value-identity is like standing under judgment or having a divinely bestowed purpose. For other traditions, the forces of karma bear the meaning and value of a life, from one lifetime to another, and for many traditions the meaning of life involves escaping karma. For yet other traditions, the meaning and value of life are read in terms of participation in the larger harmonies of the cosmos, or in the smaller harmonies of the local community, clan, and land. Everything a person does contributes to the value identity that the person achieves, and much of that also is a contribution to the values (or disvalues) of other things with respect to which the person is determinate. The fourth cosmological ultimate reality is the fact that everything has a value identity with others in its existential field. This is what is usually meant when the question of life's meaning arises.

A very great portion of life is lived in reference to proximate, not ultimate concerns. We worry about what choices to make, not about how and why choice is a part of life; we do things to get ourselves together without worrying about how human life is the integration of components with form that requires a sensitive comportment toward the components. We treat others in pragmatic ways, hopefully with sensitive appreciation, without worrying much about the sheer ultimate fact of otherness. We attend to achieving important projects in life without thinking about the meaningfulness or value of our lives as such. But there are occasions when the proximate concerns are pushed back toward their ultimate conditions, and that is when those concerns take on an ultimate dimension. Living under obligation with a need for well-grounded wholeness and the open engagement of others according to their own worth, adding up to a value-identity that defines who we are and what our life's meaning is—these are the orientations toward the cosmological ultimate realities with which religion is concerned.

TOPICS FOR RESEARCH

With this philosophical framework of one ontological and four cosmological ultimate realities in hand, it is possible to lay out in somewhat systematic fashion a program of research topics that calls upon the collaborative efforts of the sciences and humanities, paying attention to the state of the art about the various topics. The following is a brief, suggestive, formulation.

1. Address the question from Stephen Hawking with which this essay began: Why is there a world to which scientific, particularly mathematical, theories apply? This project would obviously involve scientists who could

supply a deeper understanding of what the theories assert than an amateur reading would give. It would also involve philosophical dialecticians who could watch for the criteria of proper explanation for the existence of the world as such. Moreover, because the dialectical considerations of the existence question come from so many different traditions, the dialecticians would have to represent or be grounded in those various traditions.

2. Test the hypothesis in the philosophical introduction that there are at least three families of basic symbol systems for articulating and engaging the ontological ultimate reality: consciousness, emergence, and personhood. For this, both historians of religions as well as experts in symbolic religious hermeneutics would be required. One of the principal needs of this project is to reset the default position of most discussions in the West, particularly in the scientific community, which has a mainly Western ideology, that the ontological ultimate reality is to be understood as a divine being with personal characteristics. The comparative balance with consciousness and emergence symbols is crucial. Therefore, important experts in the religions with the nontheistic notions of ultimacy would need to be involved so as to rebalance the assumptions.

3. Building on but perhaps as part of number 2, ask what interpretive frame would be put on the scientific explanations of the world within those nontheistic approaches to symbolizing ontological ultimacy. Within the theistic West, the interpretive frame has been that the rationality and explicability of the world comes from the perfectly rational mind of God its creator. Whitehead, in *Science and the Modern World*, pointed out that this was the underlying assumption in the modern scientific community long after many scientists had given up belief in a real creator God; he called it a faith that the world has a rational base. Perhaps the interpretive frame for science that could be developed out of the traditions of consciousness would put greater emphasis on the contributions of human consciousness to the order supposedly found in the world than on an underlying realistic order. Perhaps the interpretive frame for science that could be developed out of the emergentist traditions would see rational order as itself evolving not the explanatory cause of phenomena but that which itself most needs explanation. The theistic interpretive frame usually associated with Western science is often not noticed unless it is put in comparative contrast with the frames associated with nontheistic approaches to what is ultimate. Scientists, philosophers, and scholars of religion would be crucial to this project.

4. Because each of the three families of ultimate ontological themes—consciousness, emergence, and personhood—is internally so complex with divergent and reintersecting streams, each should be studied on its own to work out the diversity of contexts and logics of the streams. Obviously, scholars of each of the many streams within each of the families would be needed to collaborate in this project. But the thematic families are not associated too much with separate traditions. The consciousness themes so important in South Asia show up in Chan Buddhist and Neo-Confucian meditation practices in East Asia and in contemplative monasticism in the West. Themes of emergence are important for the South Asian preoccupation with time and change, and with the Western preoccupation of the emergence of life from the lifeless, even from the dead. Personifying deity themes are not only in the Western pagan and monotheistic religions but in the pantheons of South Asia and in the lingering wonder about the Mandate of Heaven in East Asia. Among the important issues regarding this question is that of influence and the porousness of boundaries, and of structural parallels that might not involve causal influence.

5. A comparative study of form and value across traditions can elucidate the hypothesis that all things have value of a sort, or many sorts, as recognized variously. It would be particularly pertinent to raise the question of how the scientific representation and explanation of various elements of reality in mathematical language, or at least with an ideal of mathematical expression, relates to the widespread experience of value. In the West, this has been shaped as the fact/value distinction, with various strategies for dealing with it, many of which claim that value is a subjective projection. In the Confucian and Daoist traditions, the framing assumptions about the ubiquity of value in experience have made it difficult to relate the traditional cosmologies in which value plays such a large role to scientific work, resulting in a general failure to rethink East Asian traditions in scientific terms and the equal failure to represent science in the cultural comfort zones of East Asia. Although many East Asian people are scientifically adept and culturally adept, these are not easily integrated. Recent debates in India about the Hindutva movement, which claims that many modern scientific ideas were already advanced in the ancient Vedas, much to the scorn and ridicule of scientifically educated South Asians, point to the inability to relate the deep cultural metaphors about consciousness at the base of reality to science. Science thus is too much represented as crassly technological while the Hindu religious traditions (there are many) are too

much represented as preposterous to the modern mind and out of date. Although the question of the bearing of scientific language in mathematical form on cultural expressions of value in experience is one of the most abstract intellectual topics that might be addressed, it has enormous practical importance. To the usual mix of scientists, philosophers, and relevant scholars of religion this research project should add political and cultural critics, including artists, as well as journalists.

6. Although religious and cultural traditions differ interestingly in the contents of their representations of moral and social values, they all, each in its own way, provide grounds for understanding that people lie under obligation. When religious traditions lose their plausibility and force, social groups tend to lose their sense of the importance of obligation. They become relativistic in the sense that nothing of moral weight really counts. This is different from the legitimate relativism that says that different things are valuable in different contexts. A socially as well as intellectually important research project would be to investigate in a comparative way the different paths by which cultural traditions ground obligation. In addition to philosophers and religious and cultural experts, it would be important to include social psychologists and cognitive scientists who study the natural evolution of moral sensibilities. A good guess would be that this research project would include that the grounds for lying under obligation are biological, cultural, and philosophical, all at once, such that the human condition of lying under obligation cannot be represented without all three.

7. Personal wholeness is a widely if not universally shared goal in cultural and religious traditions. Often this is what is meant by spirituality. But in what does wholeness consist? This depends on the kinds of components of human life that are construed as important to be well grounded and integrated in personal life. From the ontological themes of consciousness come the spiritual traditions of meditation and personal discipline, such as in the martial arts. From the ontological themes of emergence come the spiritual traditions of harmonization with nature, society, and other individuals. From the ontological themes of personhood come the spiritual traditions of perfecting body and action, individually and conjointly. These mix together across the large religious and cultural traditions. Under the impact of modernity, the components of historical location, social identity, and relations to family and local community have become items of concern as domains to which individuals should be comported. Dislocation makes

all these problematic. The research into wholeness should involve biological, medical, and psychological experts who approach wholeness in terms of brokenness with responses in the form of therapy. It should also involve those modeling wholeness on growth and discipline, such as theological advocates of theosis in the Orthodox Christian traditions, trainers, coaches, and monastic masters from Daoist, Buddhist, and Christian communities. Finally, it should include those whose framework for wholeness comes from symbols of personal, social, and cosmic narratives.

8. The ultimate reality of otherness, stemming from the location of people in various existential fields, poses two particularly potent research questions today. The first and most obvious is the study of proper and improper relations to others given the biological, personal, and cultural biases toward protecting "our own." The question breaks down into three kinds of "others": persons (or peoples), social institutions, and nature in the sense of the environment. Great importance has been given, rightly, to ingroup/outgroup distinctions and where they arise. Evolutionary theory explores the hypothesis that transmission of genes is an individual matter, and the alternative hypothesis that genetic evolution is a function of groups rather than, or in addition to, that of individuals. Recent evolutionary science in anthropology and cognitive science has grappled with the costs of the default assumption that people are motivated by their own perceived interest, one of which is the difficulty of explaining altruism. The great religions more or less agree that compassion, love, or altruism should be accorded all people regardless of their ingroup or outgroup status. How does this affect the relevant sciences (which usually study within only theistic assumptions about religion)? Treating social institutions as "others" that must be engaged in an existential field is a relatively understudied topic. Some, such as Jonathan Haidt, recognize this as a phenomenon of ingroup identification, but the difficult question comes with regard to prizing and tending institutions of outgroups, for example, nondemocratic societies. The third topic area is engaging the natural environment in many modalities as an "other" that needs respect and care. Sadly, few if any of the great cultural traditions have developed intricate ways of articulating environmental issues, even those associated with nature in the public mind such as the Daoist traditions. Partly this is because the new knowledge derived from science and the alarms arising from environmental disasters postdate the formative periods of those traditions. But all those cultural traditions have also been preoccupied with the human place in the cosmos to the ignoration of the

larger context in which human life is but a causal factor. The collaborative scientific and humanistic study of the engagement of "otherness" is an ultimately important topic in all three of its cases: the otherness of individuals, institutions, and nature.

9. The second topic concerning the cosmological ultimate condition of engaging others in existential fields is the extent to which our ways of conceiving "others" objectifies them so as to distort and, often, demean them. This is a typical concern of postmodern thinkers who stress the ways in which large-scale theories in science or narratives in cultures marginalize and distort those who are viewed as "others." For instance, evolutionary science in the nineteenth century objectified Africans as diminished human beings (Agassiz); medical science in the twentieth century objectified homosexuals as diseased and subjected them to cruel "cures" such as electroshock therapy, lobotomies, and hysterectomies. European colonial powers objectified the "native" cultures they ruled as "primitive" or underdeveloped and destroyed or radically reconstructed them to conform to ideal European standards. Nature, in the era of modern science and technology, has been objectified as valueless in itself and ready for exploitation for the values defining human purposes. Our current intellectual culture is riven by hostilities between outspoken representatives of the scientific community who prize objectivity with its imposition of universal laws and rationality and equally outspoken representatives of humanistic disciplines who construe scientific objectivity as the expression of certain cultural values disguised as a purely realistic representation of what's what. A research project involving collaborative representatives from both sides of this divide could work through the excesses and extremes of both sides through careful consideration of issues in the objectification of human, institutional, and natural "others." In general, current "religion and science" discussions have not sufficiently internalized the lessons to be learned from Foucault, Said, and other postmodern thinkers.

10. The cosmological ultimacy of the fact that each person achieves a complex and usually ambiguous value-identity gives rise to the massive question of life's meaning. All the major religious traditions address the question of the meaning of life in various ways, usually without benefit of what science can teach about the nature of human life, its context within social and historical conditions, and its reach within the cosmos. The

symbols of life's meaning in the various traditions need to be studied comparatively in conjunction with scientific perspectives. Perhaps this research would be enriched by parsing the categories for life's meaning through the other ultimate categories of obligation and value, well-groundedness in the components of life, issues of engaging others in life's existential fields, and human relations to the ontological ultimate reality variously symbolized.

SUMMARY AND CONCLUSION

This chapter sketched a philosophical scheme that identifies five ultimate realities. One is the ontological ultimacy of the contingency of the universe on whatever makes it be. The other four are the cosmological ultimate realities of form, components formed, existential location, and value-identity, which constitute the boundary conditions of human life as being under obligation, seeking well-grounded wholeness, engaging others, and finding meaning in one's value-identity. These cosmological ultimates come from the traits of being determinate, the most abstract notion of what it is to be a thing and thus common to all cultural, philosophical, religious, and scientific ways of representing the cosmos and human life. All religious and cultural traditions have approaches to all five ultimate realities.

The chapter concludes by briefly laying out ten research projects to address issues of ultimacy so understood that would involve collaborative work by scientists of different specialties with thinkers from other disciplines, particularly philosophy and the study of religion. These projects are:

1. Why is there something rather than nothing?

2. Can the theistic approach to ontological contingency be balanced by symbolic approaches deriving from the ontological themes of consciousness and emergence?

3. Within what interpretive frames is science to be understood from the perspectives of the consciousness and emergence ontological themes as well as that of personal theism?

4. What does it mean for the sciences that the consciousness, emergence, and personal theism symbolic themes mix within and across traditions?

5. How, in comparative perspective, does value relate to form, and what does this mean for the scientific representation of form in mathematical language? Can the mathematical sciences express value?

6. What does it mean in scientific and comparative religious perspectives that people lie under obligation?

7. In what does personal wholeness consist, in comparative religious, biological, medical, and other scientific perspectives?

8. Given the common assumption of selfishness in the sciences of human evolution, how can people be understood to engage other people, institutions, and nature in respect to their real and deserving characters?

9. How does scientific objectification affect engagement with other peoples, institutions, and nature?

10. How is the meaning of life to be understood in comparative scientific and religious perspectives?

Each of these research projects is very large and requires multidisciplinary collaborative study. For practical purposes, each might be broken into subprojects, or into sequential stages of research. But the array of questions as a whole articulates an agenda for the study of ultimacy that respects the many contributions of the various sciences and the different cultural perspectives of the world religions.

NOTES

1. For purposes of this chapter, "ultimate realities" means the boundary conditions for the existence of the world. As *ultimate*, they are the last in a series of conditions without which some important aspect of existence would be missing or impossible. The symbols of such ultimate realities are much like what Peter Berger characterized as "sacred canopies." See his *The Sacred Canopy: Elements of a Sociological Theory of Religion* (Garden City: Doubleday, 1967). For a detailed theory of symbols treating ultimate realities, see Robert Cummings Neville, *The Truth of Broken Symbols* (Albany: State University of New York Press, 1996). The theory of ultimate realities

sketched in this chapter is an hypothesis developed at greater length in Neville, *Ultimates: Philosophical Theology Volume One* (Albany: State University of New York Press, 2013). Although this hypothesis can be defended at length in philosophical fashion, it is put forward in here as a heuristic device to organize a discussion of ultimate realities.

2. Stephen W. Hawking, *A Brief History of Time: From the Big Bang to Black Holes* (London: Transworld, 1988), 174. Hawking followed this paragraph with the next two, which conclude the book:

> Up to now, most scientists have been too occupied with the development of new theories that describe *what* the universe is to ask the question *why*. On the other hand, the people whose business it is to ask *why*, the philosophers, have not been able to keep up with the advance of scientific theories. In the eighteenth century, philosophers considered the whole of human knowledge, including science, to be their field and discussed questions such as: Did the universe have a beginning? However, in the nineteenth and twentieth centuries, science became too technical and mathematical for the philosophers, or anyone else except a few specialists. Philosophers reduced the scope of their inquiries so much that Wittgenstein, the most famous philosopher of this century, said, "The sole remaining task for philosophy is the analysis of language." What a comedown from the great tradition of philosophy from Aristotle to Kant!
>
> However, if we do discover a complete theory, it should in time be understandable in broad principle by everyone, not just a few scientists. Then we shall all, philosophers, scientists, and just ordinary people, be able to take part in the discussion of the question of why it is that we and the universe exist. If we find the answer to that, it would be the ultimate triumph of human reason—for then we would know the mind of God. (174–175)

3. See, for instance, Christopher Key Chapple's *Yoga and the Luminous: Patanjali's Spiritual Path to Freedom* (Albany: State University of New York Press, 2008).

4. A splendid example of the morphological shift from the consciousness of intentional agents such as personal gods to pure unintentional consciousness associated with Nirguna Brahman is in the work of the great late-tenth-early-eleventh-century nondual Kashmir Shaivite philosopher

Abhinavagupta. See Paul Eduardo Muller-Ortega's *The Triadic Heart of Siva: Kaula Tantrism of Abhinavagupta in the Non-Dual Shaivism of Kashmir* (Albany: State University of New York Press, 1989) for a study of the cultivation of devotional consciousness.

5. The *Daodejing*, chapter 1, following the Wangbi edition, translated by Wing-tsit Chan in his *Source Book in Chinese Philosophy* (Princeton: Princeton University Press, 1963), 139. Subsequent to his translation, findings of probably earlier manuscripts indicate a different ordering of the chapters.

6. Wangbi's *Commentary on the Lao Tzu*, translated by Ariane Rump in collaboration with Wing-tsit Chan (Honolulu: University of Hawaii Press, 1979), 1. These texts are discussed in Neville, *Ritual and Deference: Extending Chinese Philosophy in a Comparative Context* (Albany: State University of New York Press, 2008), chapter 4.

7. Zhou Dunyi, "An Explanation of the Diagram of the Great Ultimate," translated by Wing-tsit Chan in his *Source Book of Chinese Philosophy*, 463.

8. For a discussion of these and related issues, see Wesley J. Wildman's *Science and Religious Anthropology: A Spiritually Evocative Naturalist Interpretation of Human Life* (Farnham: Ashgate, 2009), especially chapters 3–5.

9. See Whitehead's *Science and the Modern World* (New York: Macmillan, 1925).

10. See Jonathan Haidt's "The Emotional Dog and Its Rational Tail: A Social Intuitionist Approach," *Psychological Review* 108 (2000), 814–834.

Part V

PLAYERS

PRELIMINARY REMARKS

The thinkers discussed in the four chapters of this part have played important roles in the intellectual rituals of philosophy of religion and philosophical theology in which we are commonly interested. Chapter 17 is a memorial address for John E. Smith, who was my undergraduate and graduate teacher and mentor; it was delivered to the Society for the Advancement of American Philosophy in 2010, which accounts for its personal references. Richard Rorty was also a graduate student of Smith's, a little ahead of me, and participated in the New York Metaphysical Club for a number of years; we have interacted since the 1960s, and chapter 18 began as an essay for his volume in the Library of Living Philosophers. William Desmond and I had no common training, but we found in each other a common commitment to systematic philosophy, especially about theological topics, as shown in chapter 19. Chapter 20 began as a talk at Nancy Frankenberry's retirement forum, rounding out but not completing a friendship that began when she was just starting out. Nearly all the themes discussed in this volume come up for discussions tied to the specific intellectual personalities of these players.

Chapter 17

JOHN E. SMITH
Doing Something with American Philosophy

The philosophy of John Smith is not a dispassionate subject for me. He was my teacher from my sophomore year in college through the PhD, which he mentored. I worked in his office nearly every day during that time. He became my intellectual father and framed the way I took up philosophy. He performed my wedding and twenty-five years later taught my two daughters. We worked together philosophically and in the politics of the academy from my first day as his undergraduate typist, when I was utterly naive about both topics until the day he died when I had no innocence left. His daughter Diana informed me of his death by responding to an email I had sent him that afternoon. I preached his funeral, threw frozen dirt on his coffin in the Grove Street Cemetery, spoke at his memorial service, and now am here. I think of myself as one of his intellectual heirs and know that so many others also received philosophic life from him. So perhaps I speak for more than myself here in mourning the loss of an important intimate forebear. My aim in these remarks is to call to mind some of his heritage.

EUROPEAN AND AMERICAN PHILOSOPHY

The first thing to stress about that heritage is that Smith found his earliest philosophic grounding in European philosophy, especially German idealism, and only later in American philosophy. Doubtless his great teachers at Union Seminary, such as Paul Tillich, Reinhold Niebuhr, and Richard Kroner, were responsible for much of this. When he studied American philosophy at Columbia, it was Josiah Royce, the American who most closely identified with German idealism, who became the subject of his dissertation and first book. His early teaching assignments at Yale were heavily weighted toward modern European philosophy. I took four courses with him in the late 1950s and early 1960s on Kant's *First Critique*, and three on Hegel's *Lesser Logic*. His pedagogical method was a classical "explication of the text," moving paragraph by paragraph. Although in none of those courses did we officially get past the "Table of Categories" in the *Critique* or "Being" in the *Logic*, his commentary carried us in detail through the whole of those books, the related works of the authors, their historical contexts, and their contemporary relevance.

Smith's first book, *Royce's Social Infinite*, was his revised dissertation, which has held the high ground in determining Royce scholarship for sixty years and will continue to do so until Randall Auxier's large book on Royce someday is published.[1] But Smith's second book, *Reason and God* (1961), was mainly about the problems arising from the European context, with only two chapters focusing on American philosophers.[2] The solid focus on European philosophy, especially German idealism, had two important consequences for Smith. It helped him see and express just how different and original American philosophy was. And it moved him to be primarily a philosopher of religion, and to read much of American philosophy through the interests of religion.

A NEW THEORY OF EXPERIENCE

So the second point of Smith's heritage, surely the one most familiar to this society, was his elaboration of the new notion of experience in his many interpretations of American philosophers, beginning with Edwards and Emerson but treated most fulsomely with respect to the classical pragmatists, among whom he counted Royce.[3] His most common contrast was between the sense of experience in the British empiricists and that of pragmatism. William James, I think, was Smith's least favorite of the great pragmatists, but he gave James primary credit for radical empiricism that saw relations and change as constitutive of direct experience, not as subsequent observations on something immediately given.[4] In discussing Peirce and Dewey, Smith regularly cited their notions of interpretive interaction in the laboratory and in social affairs, insisting that experience is inclusive of both its objects and its interpretation, not a medium between the world and the interpreter.

An equally important contrast for him was that between the Kantian and idealist problematic of representative knowing and the pragmatic sense of experience as engagement. His magisterial *Purpose and Thought*, an interpretation of the enduring significance of the pragmatists, is a thoroughgoing development of the idealists' themes of purpose and intentionality to interpret the pragmatists. He shows how those idealist themes are radically reshaped within the American tradition to become a robust naturalism, not idealism at all. Even though Peirce once said that matter is frozen mind, though James was fascinated by psychic phenomena, and though Royce called himself an idealist, Smith showed that when the real differences are laid out, they all were naturalists just as much as Dewey. In fact, pragmatism invented a new sense of experience that includes the idealists' concerns for intentionality and the Cartesians' concerns for mental life within a large and robust naturalism that is as friendly to science as to soul, something the continental tradition has tripped over time and again. This was one of Smith's most important lessons.

Smith's own theory of experience emerged from his interpretation of the contrasts of pragmatism with both British empiricism and German idealism. Two points in his theory stand out for me. One is his basic claim that experience is direct but mediated. The British empiricists understood experience as direct but immediate, and therefore their theory was easily swept aside as the "myth of the given." When Wilfrid Sellars came to Yale in the late 1950s all excited about refuting the "myth of the given," Smith's students could not see what the excitement was all about, because we knew that experience as direct and immediate had been refuted by Peirce in his papers of the 1860s and that pragmatism had never been tempted by that myth.[5] Sellars, of course, took his interlocutors to be analytic philosophers for whom Hume was still the last word and so was concerned to set them right about immediacy in direct experience. Smith's students generally have had a hard time taking analytic philosophy seriously precisely because of its frequent underlying assumption of immediacy in the givenness of experience. One of the recurrent themes in Smith's philosophy has been the concept of interpretation as the construction of experience through the purposeful mediation of signs. This was a preoccupation in his construal of the classical pragmatists and in his own systematic works such as *Experience and God* and *The Analogy of Experience*.[6]

The mediation of experience was no problem for the German idealists, of course. Their problem, said Smith, was an inability to show that experience is direct. From Kant onward, the idealists were so concerned with the constructed character of experience and the spontaneous powers of the self that real things can hardly be said to be given or encountered at all. The struggles with representationalist theories of knowing arise from constructed signs construed as a barrier between knowers and the known, a barrier that makes a connection but that nevertheless keeps the real things known outside of the internal constitution of the knowing self. The interactionist theme in the pragmatic theory of experience is a powerful corrective to the failure of the idealist tradition to have a robust theory of the givenness of experience. Smith called this American sense of experience "direct but mediated." He rejoiced in Peirce's doctrine of Secondness precisely because it gives testimony to direct otherness in contact. The problem with the rhetoric of the "myth of the given" is that it obscures the fact that the problem is with the immediacy claimed for givenness, not the givenness itself.

The second point that stands out for me in Smith's theory of experience as direct but mediated is that we can learn from experience. Experience is "shot through" with purpose and valuation, as he liked to say, and we learn when our expectations find something unexpected, especially when we have to invent something new to find or secure what we have valued intentionally, a theme on which he liked to cite Dewey. If the given in experience were immediate, we would not learn from it until after the fact, if then. On the other hand, our intentionality structures and purposes would blind us to learning anything new unless something could be given to interrupt them and cause us to take a new look, to see perhaps some deeper dimension of things. Secondness is a crucial component to the process of experiential interaction.

PHILOSOPHY OF RELIGION

The third point of Smith's heritage on which I want to reflect is philosophically based on the theory of experience as direct and mediated, namely, his approach to philosophy of religion. Before discussing this, however, I want to make an existential point. John Smith was one of the most sophisticated philosophers of our era, deeply erudite, thoroughly imbued with Enlightenment criticism, and closely involved with cross-cultural studies, especially in the second half of his career. Yet he was a Presbyterian minister and a believing Christian (the second does not always follow from the first). How did he put his philosophical sophistication together with his religion? When I went to Yale as a pious seventeen-year-old Methodist from Missouri, I encountered so many things that made my Christian faith seem naive, stupid, narrow-minded, credulous, and embarrassing that I did not see how one could be educated and religious too. My personal freshman-year crisis was emblematic of the religious crisis of midcentury America. Smith gave me Tillich's *The Courage to Be* to read, but more importantly he let me know himself as a religious philosopher.

Part of his lesson was to subject the standard critiques of religion to criticism. One of his favorite characterizations of some of his own arguments was that he was "breaking a lance" for some cause that we all know is lost. For instance, we know the proofs for God's existence all fail, but he showed how their standard refutations all fail too. Chapter 6 of *Reason and God* asks, "Is Existence a Valid Philosophical Concept?" and answers, Yes, in a sense. Kant's claim that existence is not a predicate is crucial for his refutation of the ontological argument, and Smith rebuts that claim by redefining existence. Actually, he said, the proofs are not about God's existence because God is not an object that can exist and, as Tillich said, is beyond the distinction between existence and nonexistence. Once the terms are redefined, the proofs look better and better for what they are.

The major part of Smith's contribution as a philosopher of religion was indeed to redefine many of the major religious terms in ways that let them slide around the standard critiques and take on new meanings and robust vitality. In this he was carrying out the theological project of his teacher Tillich, whose ideas, such as the God beyond God and the polarities of experience, he took up and redefined as his own. But Smith differed from Tillich and advanced beyond him in this very important point. Tillich's theory of experience was heavily indebted to German idealism. It retained as fundamental a distinction between subject and object, and between self and world. When Tillich talked about the Ground of Being, it was the Ground that mediated between subject and object, self and world.[7] Smith employed instead the pragmatic theory of experience in which God can be experienced directly albeit with mediation. Tillich's essay "The Two Types of Philosophy of Religion" was important for Smith, who interpreted Tillich's preference for the Platonic-Augustinian ontological type as adherence to an immediacy of religious experience.[8] Tillich took the soul's journey into itself to find the divinity that was already there to be an uncovering of an immediate presence of the divine light in the human light. Smith argued that this still is not experience until it is interpreted, and the interpretation is mediation. Moreover, even the supposed immediacy of the divine ground in the soul is shaped by mediating cultural signs, he argued. Smith's own position was to balance the Platonic-Augustinian ontological type with the Aristotelian-Thomistic cosmological type that Tillich depreciated.

This balance cannot be achieved without going beyond both, however, for Smith. The way to go beyond both is with his elaboration of the pragmatic theory of experience, now turned toward the experience of God or dimensions of ultimacy. Here I want to make a parenthetical remark about how the interest in philosophy of religion colored Smith's approach to American philosophy. He read all the pragmatists, as well as Edwards, Emerson, and Whitehead, through concerns for religion and ultimacy as well as through concerns for science and community.[9] Beginning with *Reason and God* and continuing through his last book, *Quasi-Religions: Humanism, Marxism, and Nationalism*, he argued for the importance of the metaphysical dimensions of those philosophers because it is metaphysics that mediates questions of ultimacy.[10] This religious theme should not be surprising. Peirce, after all, was a devout Episcopalian, or at least as devout as most Episcopalians get, and he began the first chapter of his 1907 Logic Book with the following prayer: "O Creator out of blank nothing of this universe whose immense reality, sublimity, and beauty so little thrills me as it should, inspire me with the earnest desire to make this chapter useful to my brethren."[11] William James wrote the most famous and influential study of religious experience of our era, *The Varieties of Religious Experience*. John Dewey's *A Common Faith* was a Terry Lecture series at Yale just like Tillich's *The Courage to Be*. So religion and philosophical theology were important strains in pragmatism. This was less so of George Herbert Mead, whom Smith generally mentioned only as an afterthought.

The dominant academic interpretation of pragmatism during Smith's formative years, however, was that of the Columbia school where he took his PhD, which was resolutely secular, perhaps scientific, and often hostile to religion. Justus Buchler, Smith's contemporary and my colleague at Stony Brook, was heir to that secular bias toward pragmatism.[12] So Smith's interpretation of pragmatism through the lens of philosophy of religion was a substantial rejection of his teachers' approach. When I was a college senior and took the GRE exams, they included an exam in specialty fields and I took the one in philosophy. The back of the exam booklet said that it had been prepared by the Columbia University Philosophy Department and, sure enough, about twenty percent of the questions were about Dewey and related topics. But I knew the difference between the Columbia and Yale interpretations, and to my great shame and guilt I gave the Columbia, not the Yale, answers. Mortified by my dishonesty as an interpreter of pragmatism, I confessed to Smith, who absolved me *after* we learned that I aced the exam with an 860, the highest possible grade at the time. The intellectual background of my malfeasance is that Smith had developed a serious new dimension of interpretation of American philosophy through his religious interests. He included Whitehead among the American philosophers as a pragmatist, for instance, in his *The Spirit of American Philosophy*.

Whitehead had inspired the whole movement of process theology, and Smith considered Hartshorne to be his ally in advancing classical American pragmatic thought. Smith viewed his colleague Paul Weiss as a Whiteheadian and Peircean religious thinker, among other interests. Smith showed how tone-deaf to the religious, and ultimately to the metaphysical, dimensions the Columbia school had been in advancing American philosophy.

To return to Smith's brief for religious experience, his pragmatic theory of signs led him to interpret the ultimate dimensions of both secular and institutional religious experience through signs of ultimacy, as elaborated in *Experience and God* and *The Analogy of Experience: An Approach to Understanding Religious Truth*. Where Tillich had backed up on God in the soul, as it were, Smith found direct, mediated, experiential engagements with God up front throughout life. Where Tillich found God as a Ground beyond all distinctions, Smith found God as what he called a "center of intention." Smith wrote, "I start with man and what I call his 'circular predicament' and then proceed to an understanding of God as the transcendent center of intention, passing on to Christ as the concrete manifestation of that center, ending with the community of love (the Beloved Community) as the locus of transforming power in history which holds out the promise of escape from man's predicament."[13]

In these remarks, I have only glanced at the theme of community in Smith's interpretation of pragmatism because it is so complicated. For Smith, as well as Edwards, Emerson, Peirce, James, especially Royce, and somewhat distantly Dewey and Whitehead, the community is culturally if not also institutionally Christian. Smith wrote as a "Christian in philosophy" and was clear about the legitimacy of that identity.[14] The fact that some of the important Columbia interpreters of pragmatism were Jewish perhaps accounts for their lack of enthusiasm for the religious dimension of that part of American philosophy, although Smith himself stressed the importance of the Jewish contribution to American philosophy in Morris Raphael Cohen, Buchler, and Weiss, among others; Richard Bernstein is the most important of Smith's students as an interpreter of American philosophy.

Smith understood the great religious traditions, including Confucianism, Daoism, Islam, Buddhism, and Judaism, as well as the Christianity to which he adhered, as developing great systems of signs by which the ultimate dimensions of life can be engaged; this was also his approach to the quasi-religions. I do not know whether he would say, as I would, that the sign system of God as a center of intention is just one among many for engaging ultimacy and whether alternatives that do not ascribe intentions to the ultimate are also effective for the experience of ultimacy. I suspect that would be a stretch for him. I know he did not like my argument in *God the Creator* that God cannot have intentions and was a bit embarrassed, or provoked, that I dedicated the book to him.

AMBIGUITIES OF PHILOSOPHICAL AMBITION

The fourth and final point I want to make about Smith's heritage for us is somewhat bittersweet. The day I met him he told me that "to hang out your shingle as a philosopher (or philosophy major) is implicitly to say that you will become a peer of Kant and Hegel and do better than they did." What a romantically intimidating inspiration for an undergraduate! He taught the American philosophers, as well as Kant and Hegel, as predecessors to ourselves in the ongoing advancement of philosophy. Our task is not to repeat, not even ultimately to interpret, but to interpret so as to take up and do something new and better than our predecessors. He was ambivalent about the Society for the Advancement of American Philosophy because, despite its title, it seemed to him to ossify American philosophy by keeping the light on the past, however great, rather than to advance to new ground by transforming the resources of the past. I take comfort from the fact that he saw my own philosophy as advancing to new ground, even when he thought it was sometimes in the wrong direction.

The bittersweet part is that Smith's own work was caught on this point. I have construed his philosophy in these remarks as interpreting both European and American philosophy so as to bring about new theories of experience and religion. But he never wrote the big monograph that developed his position from the inside, in its own terms, and as something moving beyond our predecessors. When asked about this, he pointed out that for most of his career he was so involved in academic life, especially the politics of the philosophic community, that he did not have the time or space to write an *Experience and Nature* or a *Process and Reality*.

But I think the issue is deeper than the lack of occasion. Smith was an essayist, which means that he wrote in the vocabulary of the community with which he was engaged. Interpreting other philosophers was natural for him because he could mediate their vocabularies. His essays are transcendently clear and utterly free of jargon. But jargon is what you need for a big systematic monograph, because a new vision needs a new language (like Peirce's or Whitehead's), or old language used and abused in new ways (like Dewey's). Authors of those big monographs generally don't fit into communities well. Dewey was largely misunderstood and Whitehead ignored in their academic contexts. Smith, by contrast, astonishingly carried out Royce's notion of loyalty to the philosophical community, loyalty to loyalty. As Royce knew, this can include criticism, rebellion, and political infighting, all of which Smith practiced and from which most of us here have benefited. His lifelong fight against narrow professional projects and for pluralism in philosophy was a manifestation of his tenacious loyalty to the community. But that loyalty cost him the possibility of disengaging enough to risk the foolishness of a new, monographic vision with its own vocabulary worked out through the "labor of the notion." He was resigned to, but sad about, the irony of the accomplishments of his own work in light of the directions he gave me and others about "hanging out your shingle as a philosopher."

Reflecting on my grief at the passing of my philosophical father, I have come to understand the source of my own sustained embrace of the foolishness of creating a new and improved philosophical vision advancing American philosophy.[15] It is a kind of filial piety working in me since I was eighteen, helping John Smith to be himself when his own fierce loyalty frustrated that, taking upon myself the reverse loyalty of disloyalty and quasi-disengagement, abandoning the fight for the center, and accepting marginalization and relative philosophic homelessness. Although these efforts might turn out to be no more than folly, I am confident that John would want more and better philosophers than I to do something new with American philosophy. In that advancement on our part, John Smith our teacher comes into his own.

NOTES

1. John E. Smith, *Royce's Social Infinite: The Community of Interpretation* (New York: Liberal Arts Press, 1950). Auxier's book, *Time, Will, and Purpose: Living Ideas from the Philosophy of Josiah Royce* (Chicago: Open Court, 2013), has been published and updates Smith's scholarship.

2. John E. Smith, *Reason and God: Encounters of Philosophy with Religion* (New Haven: Yale University Press, 1961). The volume has five chapters about "the past" and eight about "the present situation" regarding philosophy and religion. Chapters on Peirce and Dewey are included in the "past" along with Kant, Rousseau, and Nietzsche.

3. See John E. Smith, *Purpose and Thought: The Meaning of Pragmatism* (New Haven: Yale University Press, 1978), chapter 3, "The New Conception of Experience."

4. See John E. Smith, *The Spirit of American Philosophy: Peirce, James, Royce, Dewey, Whitehead* (New York: Oxford University Press, 1963; new edition, Albany: State University of New York Press, 1983), chapter 2. See also his *Themes in American Philosophy: Purpose, Experience, and Community* (New York: Harper and Row, 1970), chapter 2.

5. Charles S. Peirce, "Questions Concerning Certain Faculties Claimed for Man" and "Some Consequences of Four Incapacities" in many collections, including *The Essential Peirce: Selected Philosophical Writings*, volume 1, edited by Nathan Houser and Christian Kloesel (Bloomington: Indiana University Press, 1992), chapters 2 and 3.

6. John E. Smith, *Experience and God* (New York: Oxford University Press, 1968), and *The Analogy of Experience: An Approach to Understanding Religious Truth* (New York: Harper and Row, 1973).

7. See the plot of Paul Tillich, *Systematic Theology: Volume One* (Chicago: University of Chicago Press, 1952), part 2.

8. Paul Tillich, *Theology of Culture*, edited by Robert C. Kimball (New York: Oxford University Press, 1959), chapter 2, "The Two Types of Philosophy of Religion." Smith discusses Tillich's essay at length in "The Present Status of Natural Theology," chapter 8 of *Reason and God*.

9. See Smith's *America's Philosophical Vision* (Chicago: University of Chicago Press, 1992). Smith for many years was the general editor of the Yale edition of *The Works of Jonathan Edwards*.

10. *Quasi-Religions: Humanism, Marxism, and Nationalism* (New York: St. Martin's Press, 1994). See also chapters 7 and 9 of *Reason and God*.

11. Unpublished in English, I believe. It is manuscript 277 in the Peirce archives at Harvard and was pointed out to me by Hermann Deuser, who translated it into German in his *Charles Sanders Peirce: Religionsphilosophische Schriften, Übersetzt unter Mitarbeit von Helmut Maassen, eingeleitet, kommentiert und herausgegeben von Hermann Deuser* (Hamburg: Felix Meiner Verlag, 1995).

12. See Justus Buchler, *Charles Peirce's Empiricism* (New York: Octagon Books/Farrar, Straus and Giroux, 1980).

13. *The Analogy of Experience*, 43.

14. See *Reason and God*, chapter 7.

15. As a motive for me, it was not the example of Paul Weiss, although that helped.

Chapter 18

RICHARD RORTY
Pragmatism, Metaphysics, Comparison, and Realism

The late Richard Rorty was one of the most influential philosophers of the second half of the twentieth century.¹ If I may be permitted a personal note, we have known each other since we were at Yale in the 1950s, he as a graduate student and instructor, I as an undergraduate who went on to take a doctorate there in philosophy. We had many of the same teachers, for instance, John E. Smith (the main proponent there of pragmatism); Paul Weiss (who was on both of our dissertation committees); Wilfrid Sellars (the leading analytic philosopher at Yale at the time); as well as the great idealist, Brand Blanshard; the amazingly creative Platonist, Robert S. Brumbaugh; the Aristotelian teacher of teachers, Rulon Wells; the pioneering comparativist, F. S. C. Northrop; the architect of America's only truly successful great pluralistic philosophy department, Charles Hendel; and others in that golden age of philosophy at Yale. Richard Bernstein has been a friend to both of us since those days. Strangely, however, although our professional paths have crossed many times since then in conferences, philosophy clubs, and publications, we have gone in almost opposite directions as philosophers. This is even stranger because we both took from Yale a fundamentally pragmatic orientation to philosophy, so we disagree about what is important in pragmatism.² Even yet stranger has been our professional and personal relationship with the late David L. Hall, a soulmate of mine in appreciating the aesthetic dimensions of American philosophy who hailed Rorty as the "prophet and poet of the new pragmatism."³

This essay is an exploration of four main connected themes with regard to which I believe Richard Rorty had every reason to get right, but got wrong; I'm deeply sorry that he did not live to set me right in turn. The first theme concerns the importance of pragmatism. He believed pragmatism, especially that of James and Dewey, sets us free from metaphysics and the view that philosophy is "the mirror of nature," and he attempted to excise from pragmatism all its metaphysics. I believe that pragmatism shows a new way to do metaphysics that gets around its foundationalist roots, its Kantian critics, and any commitment to reference as only mirroring. The second theme concerns metaphysics itself and how to do it without the bad consequences Rorty and others alleged. The third theme is cross-cultural philosophical comparison, as between Western, East Asian, and South Asian philosophies. The last meeting at which Rorty and I were together was at the East-West Philosophers' Conference in Honolulu where he argued that comparative philosophy is both impossible and undesirable and I argued the opposite. The final theme is philosophical realism in a large sense that pertains to what philosophy might hope to accomplish. Whereas Rorty is famous for the claim that philosophy is conversation whose only control is the drift of the conversation itself, a reprise of the rhetorical sophistic claim of antiquity, I shall argue that philosophies can be corrected by reality, however indirect, dialectical, and conversational that corrective process is. Therefore, I defend the pragmatic thesis that philosophy is inquiry, in continuity with inquiry in other fields such as science even though its critical tests are different.

PRAGMATISM

What Rorty mainly appreciated in pragmatism was its rejection of a host of distinctions that gather around the "representationalist approach to knowledge" characteristic of much of the modern period. These distinctions include those between cognitive receptivity versus spontaneity, necessary versus contingent truths, subjectivity versus objectivity, and the mind versus reality that it should mirror to know truly.[4] I agree that pragmatism rejected the representationalist view, in the broad sense about which Rorty wrote, as well as the distinctions associated with it. Rorty correctly cited John Dewey's many critiques of the philosophic tradition in behalf of the project of overcoming the representationalist approach. Pragmatism for Rorty was a creative and imaginative historicism.

Nevertheless, Rorty suspected the pragmatists, at least Peirce and Dewey, of being incomplete historicists. While Rorty wanted to rescue Dewey from this by excising his metaphysics, he dismissed Peirce entirely.[5]

> For all his genius, however, Peirce never made up his mind what he wanted a general theory of signs *for*, nor what it might look like,

nor what its relation to either logic or epistemology was supposed to be. His contribution to pragmatism was merely to have given it a name, and to have stimulated James. Peirce himself remained the most Kantian of thinkers—the most convinced that philosophy gave us an all-embracing ahistorical context in which every other species of discourse could be assigned its proper place and rank. It was just this Kantian assumption that there was such a context, and that epistemology or semantics could discover it, against which James and Dewey reacted.[6]

Rorty's critique of Peirce here misses a crucial distinction that was defended in many ways by Peirce. On the one hand, Peirce knew that all philosophy is situated in its historical context and is limited by the perspectives of its situation. He had many discussions of the historical limitations of ancient philosophy, medieval philosophy, early modern philosophy, and of the philosophical arguments in his own nineteenth century. This historicism was a reflection of the basic point of Peirce, namely, that all thought is hypothetical and fallible, perhaps justified so far as we can tell but limited in its truth claims to what can be known or tested in its historical context.

On the other hand, the *topic* of a philosophical discussion might be "foundational" matters of the "foundations" of the cosmos, issues concerning the fundamental and basic structures within which cosmological causation and epistemological efforts work. Hypotheses about these foundational structures do not have to say that the structures are eternal; both Peirce and Whitehead thought they characterize only our own "cosmic epoch," to use Whitehead's phrase. But these very broadly historical but narrowly stable structures allow us to say metaphysically what change, causation, thing, in/out, value, and other obvious characteristics of our world might consist in.[7] *Foundationalism* claims that certain things are basic and a priori certain, required for justifying anything else. Pragmatic hypothetical study of *foundations* is an historically contextualized account of what those stable foundational structures might be. Whether those foundational structures change within time is itself an empirical question. Like many other philosophers, mistaken on this point, Rorty believed that the historicist contextualism of philosophical hypotheses entails that they cannot be about structures that are not immediately historicized. Yet obviously there can be historically contextual hypotheses about structures that are not historical or are about extremely broad epochal structures. They can be about structures that explain how time itself can flow![8]

So Peirce is by no means a Kantian in the sense Rorty suggests. Peirce called himself a "critical commonsensist," by which he meant "critical" in the sense of Kant's philosophy of examining the grounds for knowledge and "commonsensist" in the sense of the Scottish school by that name that said that there is no a priori foundation for knowledge (as Kant had claimed) but only the deliverances of the historically pruned common sense of humankind.[9] Evolutionary theory gave Peirce a strong reinforcement in the view that opinions that withstand generations of criticism and achieve goals left frustrated by alternative opinions are likelier to be true.

Moreover, Peirce had a philosophic idea that makes Rorty's main point about knowledge plainer than neo-pragmatism ever expressed it. Peirce distinguished three kinds of reference.[10] One is the customary semiotic sort where one sign refers to other signs within the semiotic system or "conversation." Another is iconic reference, which does indeed assert that the world is "like" what the sign says, the mirroring function. Yet another is indexical reference, which Peirce says connects our thinking causally with the world, as a pointing finger causes us to turn our gaze and thus causally encounter something special to intentional attention. Little in Rorty's account of the flow of thought conveys any sense of causal connection of the world with our cognitive faculties. On the contrary, Rorty seemed to be consumed with the wholly noncausal representational theory and why it does not work philosophically. He paid little attention to senses in which representations can be organic causal connections between an organism and its environment, as Dewey might put it. The result was that Rorty's rhetoric suggested only that a philosophical conversation could only be about more conversation, earlier or later, never about the world that often is the conversations' topic.

I would urge an even more basic point, namely, a distinction between the extension of interpretation and its intention.[11] The extension of interpretation is the multitude of ways by which signs relate to one another in terms of meaning and reference within a semiotic system. In this sense, language is about more language, never about what the language seems to be talking about. Peirce's claim that signs are about other signs might be construed in this limited way. The intention of interpretation, however, is the ways by which an entire semiotic system is employed to signify a real object or environment to an interpreter. Intentional interpretation is the direct engagement of the world by interpreters through the direction and mediation of their sign systems. For Peirce and Dewey, if not always for James, *experience* meant the engagement with the local world as that experience is shaped and enabled by the signs the interpreter has for discriminating what's there and worth knowing. This causal, quasi-biological, model of knowing, so basic to the pragmatists, is almost wholly absent from Rorty's accounts. Rather, he took his discussion from a dialectic of philosophical theories, mainly within the analytic tradition, not from analogies of coping with nature.

So Rorty missed some of the serious conceptual innovations of pragmatism, beginning in Peirce, which allowed it to give good arguments in rejection of the representational theory of cognition, even while it acknowledged the use of signs as representations for directing causal interactions with the environment. Peirce's great genius was to provide these arguments against the position of Kant, which Rorty simply had to dismiss as implausible in the currency of the philosophers he liked, for instance, Wittgenstein, Dewey, parts (the nonmetaphysical ones) of Heidegger, Sellars, and others.[12] Rorty's objection to Peirce was that these considerations about semiotics and reference seemed to him to be ahistorical metaphysics, which was verboten. For Peirce, however, these considerations were historical and hypothetical, although at least locally well-grounded, theories about how interpretation works, theories that are alternatives to sophistic versions of Rorty's own theory of conversation, and superior in that they convey the realistic reference to the real world that might correct them far better than Rorty's hope that some future conversationalist will point out flaws.

Rorty's discussion of Dewey's metaphysics was a two-pronged attack.[13] The first prong was to associate Dewey's explicit use of "metaphysics" with an ahistorical foundationalism that Dewey directly rejected. He cited Dewey's own late-in-life lament that his metaphysics could not be dissociated from foundationalist absolutism, seeming to prove that "metaphysics" really does mean "foundationalist metaphysics" rather than hypotheses about foundations. But this point only reflected Rorty's reading of dominant trends in the philosophic conversation. Its plausibility requires a complete ignoration of the discussions within process metaphysics, for instance.

The second prong was the affirmation of the inference that the historical contextualism of philosophical hypotheses entails that the hypotheses themselves must claim that their topics are narrowly historical and contextual. As argued earlier, this is a fallacious inference. Today's hypotheses might well be about transcendent overarching cosmological structures (as in physics) while acknowledging that tomorrow's hypotheses might claim somewhat different things about those cosmological structures. Dewey made many metaphysical claims about the precariousness of the human situation and the function of inquiry to stabilize human responses to that situation, maximizing the human abilities to achieve and critically modify their ends-in-view. Of course, Dewey knew that this was a twentieth-century way of looking at philosophy, but he claimed that it was right over against the history of philosophy, and right until proven deficient. That Rorty wanted to expunge this "metaphysics" from Dewey suggests that he missed the point about hypotheses about foundational issues.

Therefore, I would urge that the importance of pragmatism rests less with its rejection of big-deal, logocentric, modernist pretensions to foundationalist philosophy than with its concrete alternatives for doing philosophy. Even the French, who like to think only one thought at a time, are able to move beyond modernist foundationalism. The pragmatists, especially Peirce and Dewey, were able to offer full-fledged alternatives to modernist foundationalism, not *post*modernism but a new form of late modernism free of foundationalism, mirroring, and all that. Rorty's pragmatism-without-metaphysics is what is called "neo-pragmatism." Against this, it is important to assert the wholeness of pragmatism, perhaps as "paleo-pragmatism."

METAPHYSICS

Now it is important to take a close look at metaphysics, especially as that is part of pragmatism. Pragmatic metaphysics does not attempt to establish an a priori foundation for other kinds of knowledge, as in the modern tradition from Descartes to Husserl. Rather, it attempts to develop hypotheses about the most basic structures of the world as interpretable by human beings. Dewey characterized this as the "generic traits of existence." Whitehead had a more elaborate view of metaphysics or philosophical cosmology as hypothetical. The metaphysical entry point for Whitehead was the question of how the elaborate relations expressed mathematically in modern physics could possible apply to the worldview he called "scientific materialism" presupposed by modern scientific "common sense."[14] He answered that mathematical relations could not apply to that worldview. Therefore, because mathematics steadily was revealing new truths and connections, the worldview of modern scientific common sense had to be changed. His "process metaphysics" was an original invention concerning how to conceive the world of nature so that science might be true. Someone like Rorty might object that the various sciences make their advances in small and uncoordinated pockets of inquiry without need of metaphysical coordination. Whitehead would answer that this is possible only by the scientists blinding themselves to the contradictions between what they assert scientifically and what they assume as the background conditions. Whitehead rightly defined philosophy as the effort of civilization to reconcile discordances such as this.[15]

Many contemporary philosophers, perhaps including Rorty, would say it is simply impossible to do metaphysics in this broad sense of developing hypotheses that reconcile such divergent aspects of experience as our commonsense assumptions with the advances in science (and the arts, imaginative literature, politics, and the rest). The decisive trumping argument against this position is that Whitehead in fact did it. Esse proves posse. The only arguments against Whitehead are that his metaphysics is inadequate, incomplete, wrong here or there. That he cannot do what he did is a silly claim.

Nevertheless, pragmatic metaphysics needs to distinguish itself from lookalikes that fall prey to Rorty's critical arguments. Does not metaphysics attempt to present a conceptual mirror to nature? Even Peirce said that reality is the "object" of the opinion to be held by the community of inquirers in the infinite long run, after all the mistakes have been purged.[16] Doesn't this suggest that reality is like what the opinion says it is?

The key to this issue is Peirce's distinction made earlier between iconic and indexical reference. If a metaphysical hypothesis is intended to refer only iconically, it is meant to function as a mirror. But why would anyone want reference in this instance to be only iconic? If reality is puzzling in itself, why duplicate the puzzle by adding a second version of it in the mind, and then adding the problems of the mind versus body on top of that? On the contrary, the point of trying to map reality at all is to satisfy some human interest or purpose. This is the primordial point of pragmatism: we interpret the world so as to be able to identify what serves our purposes or, as Dewey called them, our ends-in-view. To engage the world is to interpret it with signs that stand for their objects *in certain respects*, as Peirce said. The respects in which we interpret the world are those that are relevant to our interests and purposes. At a crude level, these concern staying alive, eating without getting eaten, finding shelter, and so forth. Evolutionary theory fills in many of these pragmatic details. Facilitating evolutionary survival for the passing on of genes, human beings developed semiotic systems that allow them to ask far-ranging questions. The linguistic structures that allow us to get the family to the water hole safely and back again also allow us to ask about God, freedom, and immortality (Kant's big questions). Peirce said that the best questions are those about what should be the objects of our purposes. The linguistic structures also allow, and indeed demand for the sake of thoroughness, metaphysical speculation.

So metaphysics is the attempt to develop ways of looking at the world that, on the one hand, allow us to discriminate the most important features for fulfilling our ultimate purposes and, on the other hand, to determine through critical reflection what our ultimate purposes ought to be. In good pragmatic fashion, there is no easy distinction between reality and its values on the one hand and human interest on the other. Rather, human beings evolved to discriminate humanly important from trivial matters in the world. Clams make different and equally, for them, correct discriminations that we neglect and miss entirely. Furthermore, the evolution of human beings has allowed us to ask deeper and deeper questions about what should be our purpose. Mere survival has limited purposive value, though crucial in its sphere. Passing on the genes is something our ancestors thought of not at all, and that we think of, ironically, under the hood of the ethics of population explosions. Nevertheless, human beings for at least ten thousand years have been able to ask theological questions about the boundary questions of worldliness and human hope.

If it ever was, metaphysics is not now practiced by a squatting solitary reflection on the lip of the cave overlooking the valley with the setting sun in the distance and the rising moon over the right shoulder. Now metaphysics needs to coordinate evidence for what is important in human life that comes from all the sectors of civilized experience. Whitehead lists, as those sectors, science, aesthetics, ethics, and religion.[17] That list might be expanded or contracted according to argument. Shortly I shall add to it the comparative understanding of different world cultures. Metaphysics needs to coordinate whatever is important for human life, as well as to reverse the process and ask what is important for human life.

All of this makes the pragmatic argument, so dear to Rorty, that human interests and purposes determine how we take the world, both in our piecemeal excursions and our metaphysical inquiries.[18] A proper pragmatic way of putting this is that we do not want a mere map mirroring reality. That would be as confusing as reality itself. Rather, we want a map that leads us to our goals, and to the recursive improvement of our goals. Metaphysics is not just iconic then, but also indexical. It should lead us to engage reality in many causal senses, better and more discriminately. It should help us discriminate the real distinctions that are relevant to our ends-in-view as well as show us what is important enough to engage our ends-in-view.

Whereas Rorty was surely on board regarding the direction of inquiry by human interests, he balked at the pragmatic point that reality itself might tell us that certain ways are sure to fail and that some ways of looking at nature and society are simply false with regard to the discriminations important for human life. He seemed to think that the concrete pursuit of human purposes was so disengaged from life itself that only conversation, not the bumps of reality itself, could correct that pursuit. Or, to put it more subtly, he thought that, because any bump in reality has to be registered in philosophic language before it could refute a position, and that philosophy does not register nonphilosophic bumps, philosophy does not learn from reality, only from other philosophies. Hence, the world is well lost.

Of course, there is something false in this argument about Rorty. Despite his being a consummate dialectician and critic of other philosophers' arguments, his main point was that philosophical opinion shifts because of nonrational factors, a dying of interest in certain topics, or the overwhelming power of a new perspective. The very edginess of his view of philosophy as conversation, which offends so many philosophers, is that the brute reality of changing interests, as opposed to good philosophical argumentation, shifts the conversation. Yet Rorty's polemic against reality, or the world, as a corrective to philosophy disabled him from acknowledging the truly edifying element in his point about what moves philosophic conversation.

Peirce, and many others since him, including Whitehead, noted that we interpret reality only in certain respects, and that these respects are a function of human interests and purposes. So metaphysics does not mirror alone, except in ways in which maps are helpful for getting around the territory. It lifts discriminations that are humanly relevant, and it seeks out discriminations that are relevant to determining what ought to be humanly relevant. More important than the map is the indexical connection with reality so that the causal interactions between it and us are felicitous. Rorty would applaud the reference to felicity. But he would have little means for determining how it is justified by what is really felicitous. Metaphysics is a comprehensive guide to felicity, better or worse depending on how well it discriminates the conditions for felicity.

COMPARISON

The conditions for felicity are, of course, culture bound. These conditions can be imagined hierarchically from top to bottom or vice versa. From the top are ideals of human happiness and high civilization, moving downward through practices and institutions that might achieve those ideals under various particular circumstances, to elementary-level survival needs. From the bottom are attempts to satisfy survival needs that ritually organize human individuality and society, to achieve somewhat stable institutions that make possible the realization of the ideals of friendship, rich family life, community organization, which in turn allow for attention to be paid to what might be ultimately important.

The Western philosophic world has isolated itself from attention to alternative systems of the elementary-to-ultimate cultural considerations by means of its commitment to an internal dialectic. It's hard enough to deal with those critics who are part of one's own conversation. Learning enough of a radically different worldview to make that part of one's own conversation has seemed an unnecessary pain for many Western philosophers. Ironically, this was true for Rorty, who construed his own turns on the dialectic of Western philosophy to be sufficient in themselves. He did not examine whether South Asian or East Asian philosophies might have presented alternatives to the representationalist versus edificationist dialectic he saw in his grand narrative of Western philosophy. As a Deweyan, we might have expected him to look to other cultures for ways of surmounting the troubling distinctions of Western philosophy that continued to trouble him. But he did not.

In contrast, I would like to defend the fallibilist principle that one's philosophical public ought to include all those who might contribute to the discussion, including those whose cultures are so different that they would dispute the initial ways of setting up philosophic issues. This means that graduate education in philosophy (like undergraduate education) should include sufficient introduction to the world's philosophic traditions that representatives of any should be welcome in any philosophical discussion. Enormous consequences for philosophical education follow from this, although they will not be pursued in this place. Here is the point at hand: a properly fallibilist pragmatic philosophy will seek to make itself vulnerable to correction and therefore needs to seek out critical perspectives from which it might learn—hence the double need to embrace as many philosophic traditions within one's public as possible and to frame one's philosophy so as to enter the publics of other traditions. As American (nonanalytic) philosophical education once assumed that a general knowledge of the history of Western philosophy was a baseline for getting started, now a fallibilist pragmatist needs to assume familiarity with the cross-cultural comparative issues as a baseline. This is an observation about how philosophy goes about its business. There are also more urgently practical reasons for philosophers to be cross-culturally educated, namely, that we deal with those other cultures, with their philosophical values and habits of mind, in everyday business, travel, and affairs of war and peace. How can we afford to be philosophically ignorant of the philosophies of those in other cultures? My concern here, however, is with philosophy itself.

Now the logic of comparison is by no means innocent. Many comparative methods have recommended themselves, including cross-cultural debate and dialogue, the "neutral" reading of texts from different traditions, and so forth. All the methods attempt to flesh out in practical ways a certain logical structure to comparison. There are at least three elements of that logical structure: (1) the ascertainment of the respect in which comparison is being made, (2) the fair elaboration of what each of the positions compared says about the respect of comparison, and (3) the analytical drawing of comparative conclusions regarding commensurability and incommensurability, similarities and differences, overlap, contradiction, consistency, and so forth.[19]

Comparisons are often slipshod when they neglect precision about the respects in which different positions are being compared. Commonly, mere similarity of language (usually with one or both sides in translation) suggests a comparison when in fact the similar terms are not taken by the respective traditions or positions to interpret their objects in the same respect. A "respect of comparison" is a comparative category, and the elaboration of comparative categories is an extremely difficult and complex matter. Part of the correct objection of "anti-colonialist" philosophers to comparison is that it usually starts out assuming that Western categories mark out the obvious and proper respects in which philosophies across cultures can be compared. So the process of comparison involves the continuous criticism of comparative categories to make them less biased and fairer. This cannot be done prior to the examination of the different philosophies themselves. Rather, it is an ongoing process whose corrections come from frustrated attempts to use biased categories. No ending point exists that guarantees wholly neutral comparative categories or respects of comparison, but the critical process can steady down until some newly encountered factor raises the question of a previously unnoticed bias.

The elaboration of what each of the compared positions says in the respect of comparison is extremely complicated. It involves moving from the native ways of speaking about the comparative category to expression in terms of the category. Thus, it develops a new language, transforming the very vague neutrality of the comparative category into a much more concrete language expressing the comparative category as specified or filled in by the compared positions. The different native expressions of the positions need to be translated into a new common language of the comparative category so that it will be possible to see how they agree, disagree, and so on. Such a process is rife with opportunities for distortion and bias. Here it is good to remember Peirce's claim that the formal terms of one's theory dictate what classes of experience might count as evidence for or against the theory, but that before the assessment of the evidence it is necessary to look at the theoretical terms from the standpoint of the phenomena and reject those theoretical terms if they distort the phenomena.[20] Critical consideration of problems of "specification" of the respects of comparison with the positions compared are what drive the fallible revisioning of the respects themselves.

It is not enough to find common terms to compare culturally different philosophies. The comparisons themselves need to be stated. The fairness of the statements is subject to debate and the different perspectives from which the comparisons are stated need to be understood and rationalized together. Perhaps the conclusion would be that the positions compared are simply incommensurable, despite their expression in a common language. In all of this, (1) the statement of the comparison, (2) the specifications of the comparative category in terms of the things compared, and (3) the development of the comparative categories or respects of comparison, the interests and values of competing comparers, need to be identified and taken into account. Comparative categories are developed because someone thinks it is *important* to compare in those respects. Philosophic positions are specified with these expressions rather than those because someone thinks these are the *important* statements. Pragmatism is highly sensitive to the interaction of interest and sense of importance with interpretive direction.

My point here, over against Rorty's dismissal of comparative philosophy, is that a culture of comparative competence is important for pragmatic philosophy today as it operates on a global stage. Without this, Western philosophy cripples itself with arbitrary[21] invulnerability to correction. Against this, Rorty would be extremely non-sanguine about philosophy actually learning something from a process of correction.

REALISM

My final theme is a defense of realism in philosophy against what David Hall called Rorty's "default nominalism," with which he claimed to agree. By realism here I do not mean a doctrine of independent universals, although that is something I would defend. Rather I mean that many of philosophy's topics are real things about which we can be wrong. Reality is anything we can be wrong about. Moreover, by engaging philosophy's real topics, we can find correction sometimes and learn something new. We can learn when we have been mistaken, and we can learn new ways of interpreting that allow for broader and deeper critical engagement.

I agree with Rorty that philosophy has the form of conversation; this is part of our pragmatic heritage, that philosophy is inquiry within a community of inquirers. Rorty's default nominalism, however, is the supposition (to which he was driven by the historical dialectic he recounted in *Philosophy and the Mirror of Nature*) that the content of the conversation is the words of the conversation itself. Nominalism. Argument is words that get us to replace certain words by others, even in the event that interest merely shifts from one set of problems to another, from one language to another. We make the rhetorical shift because we think the move is edifying.

I disagree with Rorty, however, about the content of the conversation. I believe that the conversation is about our actual engagement with realities about which we might be wrong. We get at these realities only through interpretations shaped by our philosophic and other signs (to use Peirce's metaphors). To understand how philosophic signs engage is so complicated that we understand what we are doing in part through engaging other philosophic traditions that seem to do it differently. We engage the physical world in connection with our engagement with the sciences, the social world through our engagement with politics, ethics, and the social sciences, the ultimate dimensions of reality with our engagement with religion, the aesthetic dimensions with our engagement with the arts, and so on. In all these philosophic moves, our philosophical claims are hypotheses that are vulnerable to correction and are worthy to the extent that they have been subjected to the relevant corrections. No one knows what future corrections will need to be made.

Richard Rorty was interpreted by a generation of philosophers as saying that philosophy can make no progress in getting closer to the truth and that it wanders about in conversational mode blown by the winds of shifting interest. This is a somewhat unfair characterization, because he surely believed that we can learn that we were mistaken: *Philosophy and the Mirror of Nature* argued that much of the modern tradition was a vast mistake, based on a mistaken view that there is a world out there to which philosophy should conform. His very rhetoric, attacking a "world well lost," funded that interpretation of him as an advocate of classical sophistry.

My own view, by contrast, is that philosophy can indeed make progress toward the truth, not by any simple emulation of experimental sciences as Peirce sometimes suggested, but by engaging reality in direct experience and through critical modes of engaging many other engagements of reality, including other philosophies, the sciences, the arts, religion, and ethics. More particularly, what philosophy can do is to function in its metaphysical mode to elaborate hypotheses about the fundamental structures of reality that can show how all these other forms of engagement can be coordinated. Metaphysical hypotheses, of course, are historically contingent and fallible. They have an aesthetic character that comes from their breadth and intensity of vision and a utilitarian character that comes from their function to coordinate different conversations. As every pragmatist knows, the idiosyncratic sensibilities, values, and interests of a philosopher inevitably shape philosophic work and are not completely disciplined by a larger community. Indeed, the function of every genuinely original philosopher is to correct a community's sensibilities, values, and interests. In some sense, a philosophy is better thought of as a work of art that allows new things to be envisioned, heard, or danced, than as a scientific theory that conceives itself to map its subject matter. Envisioning, hearing, and dancing are not mere subjective activities. They are responses to reality by which reality is engaged and its importances registered in human experience.

Although Rorty was mistaken to downplay the importance of reality for disciplining our engagements, and hence inappropriately abandoned the quest for truth, he was right, I believe, to insist that philosophy's functions are to edify. Edification makes us better able to discriminate and respond appropriately to what is important in reality. He will rightly be remembered more as a moralist, or perhaps as a critical theologian in the tradition of his maternal grandfather, Walter Rauschenbusch, than as a critical epistemologist, however much he thought the opposite of himself.

NOTES

1. This essay was commissioned only days before his death in early June 2007.

2. See Richard Rorty, *The Consequences of Pragmatism* (Minneapolis: University of Minnesota Press, 1982); he discusses pragmatism throughout nearly all of his works, including the most influential book, *Philosophy and the Mirror of Nature* (Princeton: Princeton University Press, 1979). For my

divergent view of pragmatism, see *The Highroad around Modernism* (Albany: State University of New York Press, 1992), especially the introduction that directly addresses Rorty's interpretation. For a more general context for the debate, see *Pragmatism, Neo-Pragmatism, and Religion: Conversations with Richard Rorty*, edited by Charley D. Hardwick and Donald A. Crosby (New York: Peter Lang, 1997), which contains essays by Rorty and myself, among many others; his is a defense of William James, and mine is a defense of paleo-pragmatism against Rorty's neo-pragmatism.

3. See David L. Hall's elegant book, *Richard Rorty: Prophet and Poet of the New Pragmatism* (Albany: State University of New York Press, 1994). See also his "The Culture of Metaphysics: On Saving Neville's Project (from Neville)," *American Journal of Theology and Philosophy* 18/3 (September 1997), 195–214, and my reply in the same issue, 281–294. See also *Metaphilosophy and Chinese Thought: Interpreting David Hall*, edited by Ewing Chin and Henry Rosemont, Jr. (New York: Global Scholarly Publications, 2005) for essays on Hall by both Rorty and me.

4. See, for instance, Rorty's essay "The World Well Lost" in *The Consequences of Pragmatism*. The world is any sense of "reality" that philosophy should be about.

5. See his essay "Dewey's Metaphysics" in *The Consequences of Pragmatism*.

6. *Consequences of Pragmatism*, 161. On the question of Peirce's semiotics in the context of his system, see Douglas R. Anderson, *Strands of System: The Philosophy of Charles S. Peirce* (West Lafayette: Purdue University Press, 1995); Vincent M. Colapietro, *Peirce's Approach to the Self: A Semiotic Perspective on Human Subjectivity* (Albany: State University of New York Press, 1989); Robert S. Corrington, *An Introduction to C. S. Peirce: Philosopher, Semiotician, and Ecstatic Naturalist* (Lanham: Rowman & Littlefield, 1993).

7. See, for instance, the first chapter of Whitehead's *Process and Reality*, corrected edition, edited by David Ray Griffin and Donald W. Sherburne (New York: The Free Press, 1978).

8. See, for instance, the heavy duty metaphysical hypothesis in my *Eternity and Time's Flow* (Albany: State University of New York Press, 1993).

9. See Peirce's essay "Issues of Pragmaticism," best edited in *The Essential Peirce: Selected Philosophical Writings*, volume 2 (1893–1913), edited by Nathan Hauser (Bloomington: Indiana University Press, 1998), chapter 25.

10. Peirce discussed reference in many places. Perhaps the most convenient is in Hauser's *The Essential Peirce*, volume 2, chapters 2–3. See my discussion in *The Truth of Broken Symbols* (Albany: State University of New York Press, 1996), introduction.

11. See my *The Truth of Broken Symbols*, throughout.

12. See my discussion of this, with appropriate texts, in *The Highroad around Modernism*, 27–29.

13. See his essay "Dewey's Metaphysics" in *Consequences of Pragmatism*.

14. This is the plot of Whitehead's *Science and the Modern World* (New York: Macmillan, 1925).

15. See the preface to *Science and the Modern World*.

16. See Peirce's essay "How to Make Our Ideas Clear," for instance, in Hauser and Kloesel, editors, *The Essential Peirce: Selected Philosophical Writings*, volume 1 (1867–1893), chapter 8. "The opinion which is fated to be ultimately agreed to by all who investigate, is what we mean by the truth, and the object represented in this opinion is the real" (139).

17. *Science and the Modern World*, ix. For a detailed discussion of Whitehead's point, see David L. Hall's *The Civilization of Experience: A Whiteheadian Theory of Culture* (New York: Fordham University Press, 1972), chapters 1, 7–9.

18. See John E. Smith's fine interpretation of pragmatism, *Purpose and Thought: The Meaning of Pragmatism* (New Haven: Yale University Press, 1978).

19. I have analyzed the logic of comparison in *Normative Cultures* (Albany: State University of New York Press, 1995). This theory of comparison was used and further elaborated in the three volumes of the Comparative Religious Ideas Project: *The Human Condition*, *Ultimate Realities*, and *Religious Truth*, all edited by Robert Cummings Neville (Albany: State University of New York Press, 2001); see especially the analytical essays by Wesley J. Wildman and myself.

20. See Peirce's essay "A Neglected Argument for the Reality of God," for instance, in Hauser, volume 2, chapter 29.

21. Hall, *Richard Rorty*, chapter 5.

Chapter 19

WILLIAM DESMOND'S PHILOSOPHICAL THEOLOGY

William Desmond is one of those rare philosophers who has a philosophy, indeed a philosophical system. In this he is like Plato, Aristotle, Plotinus, Thomas Aquinas, Duns Scotus, Descartes, Leibniz, Spinoza, Hegel, and Whitehead; I too aspire to be in this small circle. Desmond brings his philosophy to the study of theological topics, expanding and elaborating his philosophy, to be sure, but not waiting for the theological topics to generate a philosophical idea. The history of Western theology, in Christianity, paganism, Judaism, and Islam, is shaped far more by the great systematic philosophers who engaged its issues than the other way around. Philosophical theology in the most productive sense is not theology approached with philosophic tools but philosophy that deals, among other things, with theology. William Desmond's philosophical theology is very important in our time just for this reason.

So many theologians today, philosophical and otherwise, are preoccupied with religious identity, concerned with whether to be faithful to a religious community.[1] When it comes to inquiry into the truth about theological issues such as the nature of God, that preoccupation is a serious detraction. William Desmond is a deeply religious man and writes with an existential sense of the urgency and depth of theological topics. But he is able to take a giant step over the problems of religious identity and get straight to the serious topics.

METAXOLOGY

Let me begin with a comparative remark about the central rhetorical and conceptual trope of Desmond's system, the "between," the "middle," the "metaxology." The term "between" immediately forces the question, between what? To be sure, Desmond's extensive system provides many answers to that question. A recurring pattern in his system is getting between univocity, equivocity, and dialectic.[2] The point here is that the terms one operates between are something like substances in relation, or reference points, or orientation points. Generally put, for Desmond the truth does not lie wholly, or even at all, in any of the reference points, only in between.

This is especially true of his treatment of the history of Western philosophy. One of the major argument strategies of *God and the Between* (like most of his other books) is the sequential discussion of philosophers on the topic at hand, showing how each can be pushed to limits on the other side of which truth lies, although it is not squarely on the other side either, but somehow between. What Desmond calls "dialectical" thought attempts to synthesize what lies on both sides of the limit, and he credits dialectic with much insight. But better than a totalizing synthesis is the recognition that the truth lies around the limits, and in something less than the total synthesis. Desmond's superb grasp of the history of Western philosophy makes his discussions insightful in a properly poetic way, even when he wants to get between all the philosophers he discusses.

Another major argument strategy he employs is a kind of dialectical phenomenology of the world as experienced. This is a bit reminiscent of Hegel's *Phenomenology of Spirit*, which is not surprising given Desmond's long preoccupation with Hegel.[3] Yet what I call "dialectical phenomenology" is not really Hegel's totalizing dialectic but something far closer to the philosophical method of Paul Weiss.[4] It is an inspection of some aspect of reality as experienced, in such a way that the experience pushes beyond its own limits. The truth of the experience is beyond the limits of that experience, but not squarely in some other experience. Nor is it in the sum of the experiences. It lies, for Desmond, rather around the limits of the experiences and is grasped in the dialectic of passing through the limits.

All these remarks are about rhetorical and conceptual strategies in Desmond's philosophy, especially his philosophical theology. He is an apophatic philosopher about nearly all philosophical topics, not just about God. On the one hand, he is a classical metaphysician. On the other hand, his philosophical apophaticism lifts him above the postmodern critiques of metaphysics because his cannot be (1) nailed down to a univocal logocentric view, nor (2) reduced to nihility by constant postmodern erasures (what he calls equivocity) nor (3) to overly ambitious dialectical synthesis. By staying in the middle with constant apophatic movement he is the poet of new insight that is positive but that must simply be "seen" through following his movements around the substantial reference points between which truth lies.

HARMONY

Permit me to contrast this rhetorical and conceptual strategy with another that looks much like his but is different, focusing on the trope of "harmony." Let me give first a metaphysical exposition of this and then an epistemological one, both of which parallel Desmond. By harmony I mean something whose components just fit together.[5] That they just fit together means that they are not held together by some overarching "third term." They just fit, and we see that they fit with a kind of aesthetic judgment.[6]

Patterns of Harmony. The components of a harmony have a pattern of their fit together, and that pattern has to be formally consistent in some sense. But the components do not fit together because of the pattern: the pattern exists because they fit together. Agreeing with Desmond's philosophy of the between, the philosophy of harmony says there is no intrinsic core of the harmony that holds it together in the middle, only the fit.

Components of Harmony. I mean the notion of harmony to be metaphysically absolutely general. To be determinate at all is to be a harmony. Therefore, the components of a harmony are themselves harmonies, with components that are harmonies, and so on down. Hence, every harmony has infinite depths in its components, and this is one of several senses in which this philosophy agrees with Desmond about the too-muchness of being, which he sometimes calls its "over-determination." Most of the time our pragmatic interest in a harmony does not need to trace out its components very deeply. But reflection on its metaphysical character can give rise to Desmondian "astonishment" at its infinite complexity. Moreover, because the components of a harmony are infinite, so is the complexity of its pattern.

Existential Location of Harmonies. A harmony gets its components together in its pattern in an existential location. Noting the metaphysical generality of this, existential location might be of the space-time sort, of the imaginative sort, the formal mathematical sort, or whatever sorts there turn out to be (they are all sorts of harmonies). To understand existential location, we need to recognize that a harmony needs component features of two kinds. One, which I call conditional features, is those features by virtue of which the harmony is related to other harmonies so as to be determinate with respect to them. Every harmony is determinate in the absolutely general sense that it is what it is and *not some other things*. Determinateness requires conditional features so that the harmony can be related enough to other things so as to be different from them. The other kind of component feature, which I call essential, is whatever component contributes to the integration of the conditional features so that the harmony has its own being. Without essential features, the harmony would reduce, not to its conditional features but to the other harmonies that would condition it if there were an "it" to condition. Every harmony necessarily has both essential and conditional features; neither is more important than the other. And they just fit together in some pattern.

Now a harmony might contain some other harmonies wholly as its components, such that the contained harmonies' essential features are included in containing harmony. A harmony might also contain the conditional features of certain other harmonies but not their essential features. In this sense, the other harmonies are external to the harmony that receives conditional features from them. This is the definition of "externality" and, hence, of existential location. A harmony is "located" with respect to the harmonies that are external to it but condition it (or that it conditions). The shape of the existential field is constituted by the patterns of the harmonies that are determinate with respect to one another and external to one another in this sense.

Examples of Patterns. Given the absolute generality of the notion of harmony, it is important to remind ourselves of the variety of patterns that a harmony might have. It might be a synchronic pattern, like a mathematical proof, the organic structure of a body, or a fleeting situation. It might be diachronic like a melody, an argument, the tumble of a landslide, the career of a life. Reality is filled with a rush of processes that take shape in fleeting patterns that instantly dissipate as things move on; such fleeting patterns have components whose careers are almost entirely external to the pattern, and the pattern is hardly more than a spot defining a location in a broader existential field.

The interesting harmonies are those that either tend to keep their patterns through various changes in the environment or that are themselves discursive patterns that take time to play out. In the former case, some of the components (both conditional and essential) hold to the same pattern or change patterns slowly, while others of the components (only conditional ones) change so as to make a changing environment. In the latter case, there are essential features of the harmony from the past and future that help give own-being to any present moment in the discursive development. Suppose two strangers sit next to one another on a train and have a fascinating conversation that changes the lives of both, although they never see one another after that ride. The harmony that is the conversation has a discursive pattern that includes the being of the people as they talk as well as the course of their discourse. It includes their bodies that have stable existential location in the train that itself has conditional features from the surrounding terrain as its speeds along. With each breath, the people take in air that has its own harmonic history, chemically change it, and exhale it again. Each person brings a whole personal history that had been wholly external to the conversation until the conversation happened and then entered the conversation only in those components that made a difference to the encounter. In the sense that their pasts are past, they are external to what they themselves bring to the conversation. The same holds for their respective, separate, futures. The conversational exchange involves the language and other semiotic aspects that they share and that enables their conversation; the semiotic systems are internal to the conversation in certain respects, and external in others. Each person changes in certain important ways in the conversation, responding to the new other and becoming new in response. With all the inherited conditions, there still is much freedom in a conversation like that; whereas the persons are steadily determinate in certain respects, they are freely indeterminate in other respects relevant to the interaction, and they create new realities between them and within each of them. The closer they become, the more intimate in speaking of and revealing important things, the more they become intimately other to one another. That cumulative otherness is an important part of the shape of the existential location of each. The existential field of their conversation is the whole of the patterns of harmonies entering one another from without and returning outside again, from their physical movement down the tracks to their biological occupation of their place in the train to the creation of new human interaction and intrapersonal realities in each. Whereas the components of a harmony, considered as internal to it, give infinite existential depth or intensiveness, the components of the existential field in which a harmony has location give infinite existential extensiveness. This also agrees with Desmond's too-muchness.

Value of Harmonies. In addition to pattern, components, and existential location, a harmony has the value of getting these components together with this pattern in this existential location. The value would be different if the pattern were different, although the components and location were the same. The value would be different in there were different components together with the same pattern in the same place. And it would be different if the same components were together with the same pattern in some other place. To be is to be determinate, which is to be a harmony, which is to have the value of harmonizing certain components with a certain pattern in a certain existential location. As Desmond argued in *Ethics and the Between*, to be is to have value. To apprehend a being is to have an aesthetic appreciation, however dulled and denied, of its value insofar as the being's pattern, components, and existential location are correctly apprehended.[7]

The Counterintuitive Meaning of Harmony. That a thing has a value does not mean that the value is necessarily a good thing from another perspective. The word "harmony" often has the connotation of "nice," and this does apply in contexts in which our purposes are to pull things together. But given the metaphysical generality of the term, anything determinate is a harmony and it might have a value that conditions other things disastrously. A perfect storm is a harmony; so is an imperfect one. Human immunodeficiency virus (HIV) is a harmony; so is an oppressive dictatorship, or rape and mayhem: anything determinate is a harmony, with the particular value of getting its components together in its place with its pattern. That value might be devastatingly deleterious in the larger picture. The harmonies that we prize in human life, civilization, and aesthetic appreciation of reality are vulnerable to being destroyed by the harmonies in microbes, barbarians, and the things that ruin attention. Desmond's work is eloquent with its phenomenological analysis of this morally ironic state of affairs: everything, every harmony, is an achievement of value, and this makes the course of life a bloody jungle in which the microbes win until the sun goes supernova. He is right that it takes a metaphysical vision to see the pervasive goodness of being behind the terrors of causation and dissipation.

THE INFINITY OF RESPECTS OF INTERPRETATION

Turn for a moment from this dry metaphysics to an epistemological set of remarks that will seem even dryer to Desmond's typical audience because they come from American pragmatism. To know or cognitively engage a determinate thing, a harmony, is to interpret it in some respect. Any harmony in principle can be interpreted in an infinite number of respects: in all the respects of its infinitely complex pattern, its infinitely grounded components, its infinitely extensive existential location, its infinitely intensive internal value, and its infinitely extensive values for other harmonies. The very stance of interpretation therefore bears the contrast of a finite respect against a background of an infinity of respects in which interpretation is possible. Although we are not conscious of this most of the time, a little reflection will tell us that interpretive engagement bears this penumbra of infinitude of reality to be interpreted by means of the single respect at hand. What a humbling and astonishing way to engage reality!

In practice, we interpret things in the respects to which our cultures, semiotic systems, and purposes direct us. So we have an extremely limited set of interpretive signs that can be identified in the respects in which we interpret things. But much of experience is learning pragmatically that the respects in which we interpret things do not pick up on all that is important, that is, valuable, about them. The process of interpretation therefore is constantly casting about for better signs and more relevant respects in which to interpret things. From a crude pragmatic perspective, we interpret things in the respects that are important for us to stay alive. But once we have complicated enough semiotic systems to do that, we have the powers, and inherit the history, to question our world much more broadly. As we do this, we become aware of the limitedness, and usually inadequacy, of our habitual respects of interpretation. We are forced to become poets to ask new questions of things. Or, to use another metaphor, interpretation in its subtler phases is always apophatic. This is because of the character of harmonies, infinite in interpretability, and because of the character of interpretation, finite in its respects of interpretation and aware of what is missed in the shadow of interpretations.

METHODS COMPARED

This metaphysics of harmony and epistemology of interpretive engagement resonates with astonishing exactitude the story Desmond's metaxology tells of our world. Why do I prefer it to Desmond's approach, which is so much more poetic and comes up with such similar results? Desmond's philosophical dialectic is an inside story, one that needs to be entered and followed and that defines the subject matter. My approach moves through an inside story but also tells an external story. The metaphysical theory of harmonies is an hypothesis, to be measured against competitors. So is the epistemology of interpretive engagement. The status of my theory as hypothesis situates it both as an internal story, in the poetics of constructing the hypothesis, and an external story that makes the hypothesis vulnerable to correction from the outside. If I might say so, this puts me more in the "between" than Desmond. Whereas his philosophic method, like Paul Weiss's, is pure thinking, mine is thinking as well as testing.

Consider this consequence of the point. Desmond's story is almost exclusively devoted to attaining the wise middle of the Western tradition. He modestly claims to have only an "educated person's" knowledge of the other world philosophical and religious traditions. In fact, he is a super-educated person. But he does not engage the Confucians and Daoists, the Hindus and Buddhists, or even the Muslims and Jews, the way he does the philosophers and theologians of the European Greek and Christian West. They rarely enter any of his critical analyses of strengths and limitations. Of course, we all are limited to what we know. Desmond is the very model of knowing in depth—I always feel superficial talking with him. But lurking in some non-Western philosophical master might be a mode of thought that overthrows the univocity/equivocity/dialectic/metaxology structure of his argument. Unless he treats his whole approach as an hypothesis and makes it vulnerable to correction by the other great traditions of philosophy, his analysis remains strangely private to the Western tradition.

Desmond's readings of classical figures in Western philosophy and theology are extraordinary. His philosophical grid of four approaches (listed earlier) leads to astonishing new perspectives for understanding them, and his poetic genius enables a new language for philosophy. But what if his reading is seriously mistaken? That I agree with it does not make it true! His reading is one reading, an hypothesis that needs to be articulated as such and tested against alternative readings. Richard Rorty has made us aware of the great philosophical value of "strong misreadings."[8] Do not misunderstand me. Hegel's reading of the history of philosophy is a great philosophy in itself, even if it is mainly wrong about each of the philosophers. Each of them, of course, is infinitely interpretable and is lied about when forced into a single story. So the best form for a reading of great philosophers is that of an hypothesis whose tools and suppositions are brought to the fore for analysis and criticism. Every comprehensive reading of the history of philosophy (even if it includes the non-Western philosophers), should be apophatic in the sense of making each reading vulnerable to correction.

DETERMINATENESS AND THE ONTOLOGICAL GROUND OF MUTUAL RELEVANCE: GOD

Now let us turn to the philosophical theology of God. Consider the preceding account of determinateness and remember its generality: univocal determinateness, equivocal determinateness, dialectical determinateness, metaxological determinateness; the determinateness of physical objects in the modes of past, present, and future, of enduring objects, of evanescent objects, of pure subjectivity, of abstract entities of any sort, of fictions, falsehoods, counterfactuals, contradictions, of things so indeterminate as to be only infinitesimally determinate—anything that has any character that makes it something rather than something else or nothing. Metaphysical theories differ in their accounts of the kinds of things there are, but this account of determinateness cuts beneath all of them: any of them might be true and it would still illustrate the theory of determinateness per se.

This theory is that to be determinate is to be a harmony among other harmonies with conditional features relating to those other harmonies and essential features integrating them all into the own-being of the harmony. For any harmony to have the being appropriate to its kind (or to its singularity), it needs to be a contrast in which its essential and conditional features fit together. If a harmony is to condition another harmony, it needs to have its being in which its essential and conditional features fit. Similarly, if a harmony is to be conditioned by another harmony, receiving conditional features from it, it needs to have its being in which its essential and conditional features fit. Therefore, the very ground of a plurality of harmonies together, which is necessary for any of them to be determinate, or for anything at all to be determinate, is that the harmonies be together in their whole respective "beings," each a contrast of its conditional and essential features. This can be called the "ontological ground of mutual relevance": "ontological" because it grounds the being of the harmonies as each a contrast of essential and conditional features, "of mutual relevance" because the harmonies must be relevant to one another in conditioning ways so as to be determinate with respect to one another, albeit without reducing to one another.

BEING AND BEINGS

What can this ontological ground of mutual relevance be? This is an alternative to Heidegger's famous question about being in contrast to beings. The ontological ground of mutual relevance is what allows determinate things to have their determinate being vis-à-vis one another and in distinction from there being nothing at all.

Of course, as the determinate harmonies condition one another, they constitute all sorts of togetherness through their conditional features as traced earlier, in existential fields, mutual participation, entering and leaving one another, and so forth. But this "cosmological" ground of mutual relevance cannot account for the togetherness of the being of the mutually conditioning harmonies, precisely because the essential features of the other are not included in the conditional features constituting the conditioned harmony. If the essential features of the other were to be contained in the conditional features a harmony receives from the other, the other would cease to be other and would be merely a wholly contained component of the original harmony. Real plurality, real otherness, so necessary for a thing to be determinately what it is and not another thing, requires that the essential features of different things be external to their cosmological conditionings. Remember, if the essential features of the other are not in a real contrast with the other's conditional features, the other has no real being; hence, it would not even be able to function as a conditioning harmony—plurality would be impossible.

If the ontological ground of mutual relevance is not the interactive cosmological field of mutual relevance, then what is it? Suppose it is a common feature to all beings, "being." Is being in this sense determinate? If so, then it must be something rather than something else and thus be a harmony among the other harmonies, and it cannot be the ontological ground that makes its determinate character mutually relevant to anything that is different from itself. Is being as *ens commune* then indeterminate, as Hegel suggested? If so, as purely indeterminate, by itself it cannot ground the mutual relevance of determinate things. On Hegel's view, being can be the ground of determinate things only when caught up in the larger dialectic of the Absolute, along with nothing and becoming and indeed determinate things; as Desmond has so often pointed out, the Hegelian dialectic cannot stop, or even be its own determinate self, short of the whole.

Perhaps then "being" as the ontological ground of mutual relevance is not *ens commune* but rather the whole, *ens perfectissimum*. Is this whole a determinate totality that includes all the determinations as parts? If so, then it is just one more determinate thing that needs yet a deeper ontological ground of mutual relevance to make it determinate with respect to those other things; in this case, it could not be the ontological ground of mutual relevance. If the whole is completely indeterminate—not just mainly indeterminate or determinate but always changing, like Hegel's "good infinite"—then it is just the de facto togetherness of whatever plural things happen to be. Some things are determinate with respect to one another, and others are not. The cosmos has pockets of tight order in vast oceans of relative indeterminacy. There is no totality or "wholeness" to things, only the de facto array of determinate things. And that cannot be the ontological ground of mutual relevance, although the de facto array of determinate things exhibits that ground.

ONTOLOGICAL CREATION

What else could the ontological ground of mutual relevance be than an ontological creative act that produces the determinate things as its creative terminus? All the determinate things of the world are created, all the world's objects, traits, characteristics, patterns, component groundings, existential locations, values, and everything else are created, because they are determinate with respect to one another. The world has temporal and spatial, and n-dimensional extensiveness, and all this is created. Therefore, the ontological creative act has no extensiveness. It is not located in time, nor does it last through time: the ontological creative act is eternal and immense (unmeasurable, not huge). The ontological creative act that grounds the mutual relevance of determinate things is not a creator at the beginning of time, because that would give creation a date and dates are all created. Nor is it a continual creative act through time, because time is itself created in the temporal things.

Nevertheless, the ontological creative act is singular in that it is one act that creates all the determinations with their mutual conditionings. Through those conditionings, the determinations interact through space and time and exhibit many forms of determining of indeterminacies within the cosmic flow. Not only is there no time when these things are created, their mutual temporal and spatial interactions, all of them, are ontologically created together. Otherwise, they could not stand apart from one another to be in different times and places, nor could their earlier phases be different from their later phases. The singularity of the eternal and immense act of ontological creation is a good ground for calling it God. (Nontheistic traditions have other rhetorical devices for naming it.)

GOD

The ontological creative act is not determinate at all apart from creating. And then it has the determinate character of being the creator of this world. In classical medieval terms, this is to say that the divine will precedes the divine nature (Scotus over Thomas). What is the divine nature that is created in the creating of the world? We must look to the world to find out. Does it have unity? That depends on whether the world has unity, and of what kind: the divine nature as the end product of the ontological creative act has whatever kind of unity that the world has, although it has the absolute singularity of creating the world with whatever unity de facto is there.

The complete indeterminacy of God apart from creating stands in contrast to some main themes of Western philosophical theology. It is common to say, as the Neo-Platonists and Thomists do, that God transcends all distinctions and is internally simple. To be simple is to be indeterminate. But those traditions also say that the determinate things created (or emanated) have a divine character that is delimited but somehow derives from a fullness of being in the transcendent indeterminate God. I see shadows of this in Desmond's philosophical theology. Yet in these traditions there is no real creating of novelty, only the introduction of negations that delimit the infinite fullness of being into finite beings. And insofar as it makes sense at all to say that there is character in God apart from creating, for example, perfect goodness, wisdom, unity, or beauty, that character is either determinate in some mysterious fullness sense or utterly indeterminate. If it is determinate in any sense, then the mutual relevance of God apart from creating and the created determinations needs a deeper ontological ground. If it is utterly indeterminate, then creation is the real making of novelty, not the mere self-diremption of some infinite stuff such as pure Act of To Be.

From the perspective of the theory of divine creation as the ontological ground of mutual relevance, the created world, including its creator, is absolutely astonishing. It is not what we would expect from a good God, or an intelligent God, or a powerful God, or a beautiful God, or a unified God. All those antecedent properties of God, magnified to infinity, are cheats if they are supposed to mean anything determinate. Rather, God creates the determinate world in all its de facto character, which is absolutely accidental and astonishing if looked at against an impossible background of deeper potential explanation. The ontological act creates intelligibility itself, and this is quite intelligible within the logic of creating novel things, the logic of making.

THE DIVINE NATURE

Popular theistic religion sometimes asks about the character of the Creator as it would ask about the character of a person. The ontological creative act that grounds the mutual relevance of all determinate things cannot be a person, of course, since persons are determinate and hence created. But we can ask whether the created cosmos as a whole is the sort of thing a person would create, such that God's created nature is indeed personal. To this question I think we must remain agnostic because we have such a small sample of the created cosmos from which to judge. Contrary to popular readings of the Bible, God does not create a cosmos in which the just are rewarded and the wicked punished, at least so far as we can tell.

Nevertheless, there are some transcendental traits of creation that characterize God. To the extent the preceding account of harmonies is correct, the world is a process of making and unmaking harmonies, as the Spirit blows where it will. The harmonies have patterns and so there is a transcendental Logos. The harmonies have infinite depth, so God is a too-muchness, to use Desmond's term. The harmonies have place so there is a pluralism in the divine creative act. And the harmonies all have value: so God in creating anything is creating something good, even if that good is a disaster for some other good. Moreover, given the character of time, all things in the mode of past time are together in the singular creative act with all things in the modes of present and future time. Any given "dated event" is together in all its future possibilities with its present actualization and with its roles in the actual past. The spontaneous present is always moving on, changing the shape of the future and adding new actuality, meaning, and value to the past. Whereas within time we experience ourselves only as present with memories and anticipations, in the singular creative act, all the dynamism of the present is ontologically together with the dynamism of the constantly changing future and the dynamism of the constantly accreting past. The dynamism of the divine life is not limited to having to take place in some present. God is not "present" but is the togetherness of all things in all their temporal embodiments as past, present, and future.

COMPARISONS

I beg forgiveness for the staccato abstractness of these points about God. They feel like telegraphic summaries of arguments I've given in much greater detail elsewhere, which they are.[9] In these concluding remarks, however, I want to return to some comparative points about William Desmond's philosophical theology. Earlier I characterized his approach as a kind of phenomenological dialectic, a pure thinking that weaves its way across the limits of philosopher and the limits of individual "takes" on philosophic topics. My own approach does that in part, and with much less poetry than Desmond's, but also externalizes the treks of pure thinking by making them hypotheses to be adjudicated as such, which I claimed to be more of a "between" than the course of pure thinking.

Now the argument I have given about harmonies, determinateness, the ontological ground of mutual relevance required for determinateness, ontological creation, and God is a kind of complex hypothesis, or set of hypotheses. The dialectic by which I presented the argument is my clumsy version of philosophical poetry. I have not weighed the hypothesis against alternatives here, save in this respect: The analysis of determinateness is so abstract and basic as to get underneath all the hypotheses I know of concerning kinds of determinateness. So in a certain sense all the alternatives are possible instantiations of my hypothesis, not alternatives. But that might simply be my limited vision.

IN DESMOND'S MIRROR

My final question is how my hypothesis looks if it is right about reality when analyzed in Desmond's way. I believe there is extraordinary congruence between our visions. Here are some ways.

A persistent, and perhaps the most basic theme, of Desmond's work in the trilogy of *Being and the Between*, *Ethics and the Between*, and *God and the Between* is astonishment, wonder, getting-knocked-off-your-horse surprise. He traces that theme through countless trails. The theology of the total origination of determinateness in the creative act explains at a metaphysical level why we should be so astonished. There is nothing in the creator apart from creation to suggest a reason for the world we have.

A related theme in his work, to which I have alluded several times, is the overdetermination of being, its too-muchness. Desmond's genius is to call attention to this in philosophical or ordinary situations in which we (univocally, equivocally, or dialectically) block out the surplus with our finite representations. The metaphysical account of the infinite density of harmonies shows why we should expect the too-muchness.

Desmond's theme of idiocy, the sheer that-it-isness, of things is mirrored in the radical contingency, but in-your-face reality, of things, of being in general, and of God. The account of God as ontological creator *ex nihilo*, absolutely indeterminate apart from creation, absolutely free from any constraints in creating, and absolutely de facto in the terminus of the creative act in determinate things, provides a ground for that idiocy. Desmond shows how we think that in philosophical experience. My hypothesis shows why we should expect that when we think philosophically.

Desmond's second "hyperbole," the aesthetics of happening, highlights the aesthetic dimension in all experience, particularly philosophical experience that is alert to pervasive issues. This is to say, on my account, that the grasp of harmonies as contrasts of features that just fit together is an aesthetic one and thus pervasive in all experience, even if not thematized. Moreover, the theory of harmonies shows how all harmonies have value, such that to grasp them as harmonies is, among other things, to appreciate them in their particular values. As an hyperbole reverses, as Desmond argues, the creator is the ground of the intrinsic value in the things created, the harmonies.[10] Perhaps Desmond would want to say that this is because of some primordial beauty and goodness in the creator. But I want to say that this is because of the sheer, arbitrary act of creating determinate things such that they necessarily have value. The astonishing thing is not God's goodness but God's goodness-making.

Desmond's third hyperbole is the erotics of selving, a topic that I have not addressed here. To see how human beings need to make better, more complicated harmonies of their lives, which are always emerging in new harmonies as old ones dissolve, is not difficult. The reversal of this hyperbole is the apprehension of our selving before God, on the one hand being who God makes us, including our created freedom within limits, and on the other hand being who we are (eternally) within the singular life of God. As Desmond frequently puts it, selving is a bottom-up approach to God.

Desmond's agapeics of community, the fourth hyperbole, is a top-down approach in which God comes to us as the creator of the community of being of which we have a part and to which we have various forms of responsibility. Although I have not developed the normative aspects of the community of being here, it is not difficult to see that the mutual relevance involved in determinateness as such puts creatures with some control over what harmonies they make and lose into many relations of benefit and obligation. To be with others is to be ontologically grateful, and there is no other way to be.

My argument in this chapter has been that the exquisitely nuanced philosophical theology William Desmond has developed can be complemented helpfully by a pragmatic metaphysical philosophical theology of the sort I have sketched. Many aspects of complementarity exist, perhaps the most important of which is the reinforcement of vision, especially those aspects of vision that are prayers. Crazy as it may seem, I do pray with my hypotheses. The aspect of complementarity stressed in this chapter, however, is the advantage of externalizing a philosophical theology as an hypothesis, while also inhabiting it as a spiritual and philosophical way.

NOTES

1. This is particularly true in conservative forms of Roman Catholicism and Protestantism, and in Orthodox Christian communities in the diaspora. The issue is whether to be more concerned with firming up one's religious identity or pursuing inquiry into the truth of theological matters, the result of which should determine one's identity. See my discussion in *Realism in Religion* (Albany: State University of New York Press, 2009), chapter 1.

2. This pattern occurs in *Being and the Between* (Albany: State University of New York Press, 1995), *Ethics and the Between* (Albany: State University of New York Press, 2001), and *God and the Between* (Oxford: Blackwell, 2008).

3. See his *Beyond Hegel and Dialectic: Speculation, Cult, and Comedy* (Albany: State University of New York Press, 1992) and *Art and the Absolute: A Study of Hegel's Aesthetics* (Albany: State University of New York Press, 1986). All of his books take Hegel extremely seriously. For an interesting discussion of his various views on Hegel, see *Clio: A Journal of Literature, History, and the Philosophy of History: Philosophy Studies* 20/4 (Summer 1991).

4. The late Paul Weiss was a friend and admirer of William Desmond and one of my important teachers. An example of Weiss's "dialectical

phenomenology" is his *Being and Other Realities* (Chicago and LaSalle: Open Court, 1995).

5. This is analyzed by Whitehead as a "contrast." See his *Process and Reality*, corrected edition, edited by David Ray Griffin and Donald W. Sherburne (New York: The Free Press, 1978), 24, 228.

6. For a detailed analysis of this, see *Realism in Religion*, chapter 8.

7. I have analyzed this in much detail in *The Cosmology of Freedom* (New Haven: Yale University Press, 1974; reprint edition Albany: State University of New York Press, 1995), part 1, and my three-volume *Axiology of Thinking*: *Reconstruction of Thinking* (Albany: State University of New York Press, 1981), *Recovery of the Measure* (Albany: State University of New York Press, 1989), and *Normative Cultures* (Albany: State University of New York Press, 1995). *Reconstruction of Thinking* argues that form (pattern) is a function of value rather than the other way around.

8. See the defense of this in David L. Hall's *Richard Rorty: Prophet and Poet of the New Pragmatism* (Albany: State University of New York Press, 1994).

9. See, for instance, *God the Creator: On the Transcendence and Presence of God* (Chicago: University of Chicago Press, 1968; reprint with a new introduction, Albany: State University of New York Press, 1992) and *Eternity and Time's Flow* (Albany: State University of New York Press, 1993).

10. See *God and the Between*, 164ff.

Chapter 20

NANCY FRANKENBERRY
Philosopher of Religion,
Radical Empiricist,
Herald of Contingency

INTRODUCTION

In the 1978 volume of *Process Studies*, Nancy Frankenberry published an article called "The Empirical Dimension of Religious Experience" that I thought was so good that I wrote her a short fan letter about it.[1] She responded by saying that she was flattered by my praise because I was a model for her younger generation. For the first time in my life I felt old. And I wasn't yet forty. But here I am, still fully employed, presenting a *long* fan letter at her retirement. Nice irony!

I want to begin laying out some of the themes and accomplishments of her distinguished career as a model philosopher of religion by discussing her early book *Religion and Radical Empiricism* (1987).[2] The context in which she wrote then was the stream of analytical philosophy of religion that had descended from Hume. She could have, but did not, write in the context of continental philosophy of religion descended from Hegel. Her overall point, which has remained at the center of her work down to today, is that philosophy of religion depends on a philosophy of experience, and that the British empiricist philosophy of experience is wrong. (She has since substituted "language" for "experience" in ways to be discussed shortly.)[3] The American pragmatic and Whiteheadian traditions of experience are the better way to go. The plot of her book is as follows. First, she locates philosophy of religion as concentrating on the issues of justifying religious or theological beliefs. This was Hume's trajectory. Many philosophers and scholars of religion have downplayed the centrality of belief, but Frankenberry has made it central throughout her career. The two main modes of theological justification have been metaphysics and appeals to experience, both of which she rejects in the forms they take in the Humean analytical orientation but defends in a careful milking of Whitehead's metaphysics and pragmatic appeals to experience.

The second chapter of her book details, with many criticisms, the trajectory of empiricism from Hume to Ayer and the logical positivists to analytical linguistic empiricism, where beliefs are turned into sentences, and finally to the neo-pragmatists, mainly Quine, Davidson, and Rorty. The neo-pragmatists almost get it right, Frankenberry says, Rorty building on Davidson who builds on Quine. Her dialectical development of their views is exquisite. I'm not sure whether her title for this chapter, "Shaking the Foundations of Empiricism," is an intentional play on the title of Tillich's book of sermons, *The Shaking of the Foundations*.[4] Frankenberry is generally critical and often dismissive of Tillich. The main theme common to Quine, Davidson, and Rorty is what Frankenberry calls "holism" or "semantic holism." I'll come back to this.

The third chapter argues that the people who really did set the philosophy of experience on the right track in reference to religion were the classical pragmatists, especially James and Dewey. Their work is what she calls "radical empiricism," which she adopts as the title for her own philosophy with the phrase from William James's *Essays in Radical Empiricism*.[5]

The fourth chapter explores the attempt of the Chicago School to develop a religiously robust *theism* on radically empirical bases, treating Henry Nelson Wieman, Bernard Meland, and Bernard Loomer. These figures are of little or no interest to analytic philosophers early or late. But the reason Frankenberry finds them interesting is that they do get the point that radical empiricism can penetrate even into religious thinkers who take theism seriously.

The fifth chapter of *Religion and Radical Empiricism* is a shocker. It argues first that Alfred North Whitehead's philosophy can provide a metaphysical justification for radical empiricism. Or rather, it describes in metaphysical terms what the world is such that radical empiricism is the very process of experience. To defend Whitehead this way requires excising his conception of God, and perhaps reinterpreting his theory of eternal objects, while bolstering his theory of causal efficacy. (I am an enthusiastic supporter of all this surgery.) The shock is that her empirical defense of Whitehead's metaphysics is a long, critical argument to the effect that Whitehead's theory makes perfect sense of the 2,500-year tradition of Buddhism in its various schools. In fact, for the Buddhists

Whitehead's metaphysics would be common sense, not the weird speculations that turn off analytic philosophers.

Frankenberry has continued the themes and historical sources introduced in *Religion and Radical Empiricism* throughout her career. To be sure, she has treated other themes as well. For instance, her entry on "Feminist Philosophy of Religion" in the *Stanford Encyclopedia of Philosophy* is a tour de force discussion of the whole field of recent religious studies, theology, and philosophy of religion, focused around the contributions of feminist thinking. As an important woman in the field, she willy-nilly has made feminist contributions, and without the common ideological strutting.

Perhaps the most astonishing thing about *Religion and Radical Empiricism* is that it demonstrates a singular virtue that has characterized Frankenberry's entire career. Our is a time of philosophical Balkanization. Analytic philosophers talk only to those who play their game, continental philosophers devote themselves to inventing private discourses, and creative philosophers in the American tradition have retreated to the mountains of North Carolina and Colorado.[6] Frankenberry is almost unique among us in being able to get on the inside of just about any philosophical approach, gain the respect of those in that gang, and then make an argument that moves across all, developing a singular position. The Humeans; the logical positivists; the linguistic analytic philosophers; the classical pragmatists; the Chicago School; Quine, Davidson, and Rorty; Whitehead; and the Buddhists! That breadth of vision and creative synthesis was the reason I published *Religion and Radical Empiricism* in my SUNY series in Religious Studies way back then. Shortly, I shall discuss one of Frankenberry's latest writings, a paper entitled "Contingency All the Way Down: Whitehead among the Pragmatists," which was not yet published when I read it and wrote this.[7] This paper is a remarkable maturation of the broad vision and creative synthesis begun in *Religion and Radical Empiricism*.

FRANKENBERRY, WHITEHEAD, AND DAVIDSON

Anyone who knows much of anything about Frankenberry's work will have been surprised to find that, in *Religion and Radical Empiricism*, the neo-pragmatists Quine, Davidson, and Rorty are just steps on the way to the radical empiricism of the classical pragmatists, especially James and Dewey. She has been known for many years as a staunch defender of Davidson and Rorty, especially the former.[8]

I confess that over these years I have never been able to appreciate Frankenberry's high regard for the historical importance of Davidson, try as I might to be in sympathy. I read his "On the Very Idea of a Conceptual Scheme" shortly after its publication and generally agreed with it but thought it was pretty unremarkable.[9] I never much appreciated any significant distinction between conceptual schemes and their content, and so, not having fallen down that hole, was not turned on by a ladder by which to climb out. Only if one has bought into much of Kant's project, in which knowledge consists in justifying content for a subjectively constituted conceptual scheme, or perhaps the other way around, would the scheme-content distinction be significant.

The pragmatists and Whitehead did not buy into that. What might look a little similar is their view that our engagements of the world are shaped by signs that exist in various semiotic networks. The signs in their networks guide our interactions with things and in turn are modified by the feedback from those interactions. There are many kinds of signs in semiotic networks, and many contexts for interpretive engagement, and many values and purposes orienting those engagements. In all cases, the interpretive engagements are what Whitehead called "simplifications," because the signs and semiotic networks involved interpret what they engage only in certain respects, to use Peirce's formula for interpretation.[10] Whitehead was particularly concerned toward the end of his life that science be understood to simplify reality only in the respects that are subject to mathematical expression, and that this leaves out a lot of concrete reality.[11] As a critic of abstractions, philosophy, for Whitehead (and the same can be said for the classical pragmatists) needs to develop certain signs in semiotic networks that have the form of theories that lift up for attention the sorts of things that might get left out on more reductive theories. His magnificent original categorial scheme in *Process and Reality* was designed to call attention to how the relations among things expressed in mathematical physics could apply to the things of the world (they could not if the world were made of substances), how causation could have real force (it could not if it were mere regularity), and how things could have the values we experience in them across the "breadth of civilized experience," which is inconceivable if the world were only facts. Whitehead's metaphysical scheme is only an hypothesis aimed to let us grasp the world less reductively, being applicable to everything in a consistent way and adequate to acknowledge everything we have reason from other parts of experience to want to think together with yet other parts of experience.¹² He was happy with the thought that his hypothesis might be improved upon, and he even suggested that it might only apply to the nature of the physical cosmos in our limited cosmic epoch. Frankenberry beautifully presents this Whitehead from her earliest writings to the latest.

I would say that in our own time we need to improve upon Whitehead by developing a metaphysical scheme that is responsive to two things missing in his vision. His appeal to the breadth of civilized experience needs to be problematized by the large array of critiques of Western colonialism or imperialism concerning what counts as important experience. And in judging how to be sensitive to the habits of simplifying thinking, we need now to operate within a public that includes those from intellectual traditions beyond the West. I suspect Whitehead in Heaven and Frankenberry in Hanover would agree with these needs for modification.

The moral here is that Whitehead's (or Peirce's or James's or Dewey's) theories or categorial schemes are not schemes with *content* but rather are schemes that *illustrate* what needs attention in the world we engage. They have moral force, calling us not to neglect one thing just because it is hard to think it along with something else. They function as parts of processes, not as finished pictures or descriptions. Frankenberry is wonderfully adept at characterizing "contingency" as the ongoing processive nature of things, which, in the case of human beings, sometimes involves metaphysical interpretive engagement of the most generally imaginable world so as to keep us alert to the dynamic relation between the concrete and abstract or simple.¹³ There are, to be sure, many kinds of signs in semiotic networks other than those shaped like schemes, theories, and the like. But all involve semiotically shaping the dynamics of engagements.

In trying to develop sympathy for Davidson, my sense is that what irked him was some Kantian or Neo-Kantian philosophy that the objective world is in fact some kind of filled-in framework, or a framework of categories organizing the content of experience that differs from some other framework that organizes it differently, say, in a different culture. Davidson's argument is a good critique of that "knowledge as a content-filled scheme" view, which is beside the point if you already have a pragmatic or Whiteheadian orientation.

Why then, does Frankenberry take it so seriously? Compared with the rich visions of Peirce, James, and Dewey with all their implications for how to live and think, isn't Davidson's pragmatism thin gruel? What makes it noteworthy?

THE LINGUISTIC TURN

The answer, I think, is that it is very important if you have taken the "linguistic turn," to use Rorty's phrase.[14] In its most elementary sense, the linguistic turn is when you stop talking about the world in engaging it and limit yourself to talking about how to talk about the world, or not to talk about it. Or to put the point more academically, the linguistic turn transforms philosophy from speaking about the world to speaking about language about the world and the various normative uses of language. This is an extension of the Kantian transcendental turn that says philosophy (or at least epistemology, metaphysics, and philosophical cosmology) cannot speak about the world, only about the transcendental conditions for knowing the world, with the "content" of knowledge of the natural world coming exclusively from science. The linguistic turn had been taken by analytic philosophy long before Rorty and Davidson, focusing on formal and informal language use. Perhaps in some sense the linguistic turn defines analytic philosophy.

What makes the linguistic turn so attractive to analytic philosophers is that it supports their sense that there is an immediate quality to linguistic thinking about which we ought to be able to get clear. Analytic philosophers groove on clarity and often believe that the right kind of thinking is argument of the sort that can be followed in a potentially intuitive way. Continental Husserlian phenomenologists, having taken the *transcendental* turn, believe that we have an immediate intuitive grasp of *experience*, but that it takes fallible and inferential thinking to describe the experience. The analytic *linguistic* turn eliminates the leap from consciousness to its fallible, often metaphorical, description and instead revels in the immediacy of clarity of language and reason giving. Some of us, though not Frankenberry, are old enough to remember analytic philosophers telling us that we should not even think about things for which immediate and comprehensive clarity is not possible, for example, metaphysics. Rorty knew well that clarity is a mirage. For clarity he substituted rhetorical persuasiveness: what counts is what persuades.[15] Part of Rorty's genius was to articulate how imaginative literature can be persuasive in a far more powerful way than a clear argument in the vocabularies of various analytic philosophers. One of the meanings of "holism" in Frankenberry's philosophy of religion is that there might be a patch of persuasiveness that does not need anything external to refer to, nor special claims made about truth, only the living reality of being on the inside of the conversation. Among the many kinds of conversation she likes are religious ones that can have their own integrity without being analyzed from above or below. Rorty's student, Robert Brandom, has extended his point to develop a neo-pragmatics of persuasive inference conditions and has proposed an Hegelian-style ideal of holistic cascades of persuasive inference, with a logic about how to do so.[16] Frankenberry does not carry holism that far.

I have never ever even been tempted to take the linguistic turn and find myself alienated from its assumptions that seem to pervade analytic philosophy. Let me say again how amazed I am that Frankenberry escapes this alienation. Rather, I am still living off of the old-fashioned, classical, non-linguistically turned pragmatists and have to call myself a paleo-pragmatist to be distinct from the neo-pragmatists. Remember what Rorty said about the classical pragmatists. Peirce should be thanked for inventing the name but should otherwise be plainly rejected as a metaphysical realist. James was great for his critique of overwrought absolutist thinking and should be scolded for his neutral monism of the blooming, buzzing experience stuff when he should have had a neutral monism of language entering the human conversation. Dewey, Rorty thought, should be approved in all his critique of the history of philosophy but rejected in his metaphysics aiming to describe the "generic traits of existence."[17] Richard Bernstein, Rorty's close friend, writes glowingly of Rorty and the other neo-pragmatists but objects strenuously to their abandoning the category of experience in favor of persuasive rhetoric. Most specifically, Bernstein objects to Rorty's failure to hold on to Peirce's category of secondness.[18] Secondness was Peirce's proof positive that there is a world out there to which we refer but for which we have not got the referring semiotic habits right. According to Peirce, secondness is the corrective force of externality, but the most secondness you can get in Rorty's holism is a conversation-stopper.[19]

Let me back up a bit and illustrate again what I mean by the sense of experience in my interpretive-engagement pragmatism. An infant develops leg muscles as signs interpreting gravity so that it can stand up. A driver has habitual signs that interpret the speed and pitch of the car and that pick up on the visual conditions of the road and traffic without ever being conscious of those interpretations until some other driver does a foolish thing or the brakes fail. A monk lives in a cell on Mt. Athos, building his whole life into a sign of what he would tell you is God, with minimal verbalization. The semiotic network of muscles and nerves helps the baby engage standing up against gravity, the driving habits are a quasi-holistic semiotic network that engages the road for the trip, and the congeries of diet, loneliness, keeping "hours," and performing liturgies with words that don't count much constitute a very complicated semiotic network for engaging God in a whole religious life. These interpretations might in fact be false: the baby may fall, the driver crash, and the monk be wrong about the existence of God. But all are pragmatic interpretive interactions with the environment, all are vulnerable to secondness, and all require further interpretive experience to check up on their truth when that comes into question. As Peirce said, we do not ask the question of truth about our various interpretive engagements of life unless something comes up to lead us to doubt them. And if we have reason to doubt, we have a direction for inquiry into what is true or false in the matter.

Let me now make a formal philosophical distinction to express why I advise against the linguistic turn. In making an interpretation of something, the sign stands for its object in a certain respect, and the interpreter, in context and with some purposes or values, interprets the sign to stand for the object in that respect. I call this an "intentional" interpretation, "intending" to interpret the object. The sign in the interpretation is actually a sign plus its semiotic system or network. The sign and its network function together in mediating the engagement of the interpreter with its object. It is possible also to interpret how a given sign relates to other signs within its network. Every interpretation itself is a sign that operates within and often changes the semiotic network. I call the interpretive work within the network the "extensional" interpretation, connoting the semiotic network itself as the extension of the interpretation. The crucial point to notice is that with most conscious and unconscious or preconscious experiences, every intentional interpretation can be restated as an extensional interpretation, and so the whole series of interpretations of real things in the environment can be re-represented as extensional interpretations of interpretations of interpretations. Thinking is about thinking about thinking. Taking the linguistic turn, all experiential interpretation is like talking about talking about talking. This intra-extensional interpretive process is friendly to continental semiotics' dyadic signifier-signified analysis. It is also friendly to the holism of the linguistic turn and the ready abandonment of the necessity of reference and truth to which Frankenberry is often drawn. But what it sacrifices is any robust intentional interpretation of environments with real things, things that can block or correct interpretive engagements with secondness. It also gives up our usual robust sense that we are engaging a real world with objects that are what they are regardless of what anyone thinks about them (that last is Peirce's line).

Now my position here already has been refuted elegantly by Nancy Frankenberry in an essay imaginatively entitled "On the Very Idea of Symbolic

Meaning."[20] That title is *not* a clever riff on a title by Tillich! But her elegant arguments all depend on the linguistic turn in which we are always talking about what we are saying, not about what we are talking about as real objects. If we do not take that turn, then the capturing of the argument for extensional analysis alone is arbitrary in not acknowledging intentional interpretation with real reference and where the interpretations might need to be assessed as to their truth or falsity. Whitehead and the pragmatists, especially Peirce, had metaphysical hypotheses that make good sense of real objects, real reference, and dicey truth claims, and I share that part of philosophy with them.

Frankenberry, along with many others, defines religion as belief in superhuman beings.[21] I agree that belief has some importance in religion but understand belief in a Peircean way as a habit that shapes our interactions with things. It might be possible to represent our belief-habits in a linguistic way. But the coherence of those belief-habits is a function of the vastly complicated coherence of the environment engaged, the coherence of habits in an individual's and perhaps a community's life, and the coherence of the values and purposes motivating the engagements that involve the belief-habits. Or the incoherencies in all these. The coherence of linguistic belief-statements of those habits might have barely any relevance to the coherence of the belief-habits of lived religion. The medieval search for a system of linguistically expressible doctrines has very little bearing on the search for a coherent religious life shaped by belief-habits.

What picture of the world emerges from my path away from the linguistic turn? An emphasis on holism seems excessive, even when it is reduced to an ideal of bringing unanimity to a philosophical conversation, and especially when it comes to mean a Brandomist whole of inferential connections. Rather, we engage the world with a great many, often uncoordinated, semiotic networks, each developed with some pragmatic efficiency in some domain of life. The world seems, to my best estimation, to contain only pockets of humanly meaningful order, swimming in chaotic maelstroms of little or no order of a humanly measurably scale. We need grand metaphysical systems to bridge these multitudinous and barely commensurable domains of life, each with its set of semiotic networks for interpretation. Metaphysics is not to connect these in a systematic framework that rationalizes its content: metaphysics rather is to keep our attention on the rich diversity of things, perhaps bringing them into some kind of abstract meaningful relation with one another. Experience itself lurches from one pocket of order to the next, with many surprises and breaks in inferential or conversational continuity. The real world is constantly sending us secondness signals that some domain of life is simply not to be addressed with the semiotic network appropriate to some other holistically mastered domain. The loss of reference, truth, and the robust sense of engaging external things is not a "world well lost," as Rorty named it.[22] It is the loss of world.

FRANKENBERRY'S VISION

If Frankenberry has been as enamored of Rorty's and Davidson's philosophy as she claims, then you would expect her own religious vision to be some pallid holism. But listen to what she writes in a recent essay that begins saying, "To my mind, Richard Rorty and Donald Davidson are the most original and significant pragmatists of the second half of the twentieth century, as Whitehead was the most important thinker of the first half of the century."[23] In a section called "A Whiteheadian-Pragmatist Vision," which she espouses for herself, she writes:

> For both Whitehead and contemporary pragmatists, contingency and chance mark the universe as unfinished. All inquiries are therefore open to revision, and every life is itself a matter of invention and experiment. To live with dedicated awareness and sensitivity to this radical contingency is, I claim, a religious or at least quasi-religious way of life, a spiritual discipline, something worthy of surviving the de-theologizing of process thought. It leads to a very different quality of existence than is available to those individuals within religious traditions in which notions of an immutable divine will and predestination prevail, or in which a karmic system of merit and demerit inexorably plays out. The style of spirituality entailed in the acceptance of radical contingency is a far cry from doctrines of any kind or from the grandiosity and sublimity sometimes sought by religious minds. A nontheistic spirituality, closer to an aesthetic mysticism than to morals, may better suit our times than the "panentheism" ascribed to Whitehead or the atheism espoused by contemporary pragmatists. The spirituality I associate with a Whiteheadian-pragmatist vision is more akin to what Keats meant by "negative capability": a capacity for "being in uncertainties, mysteries, doubts, without any irritable reaching after fact and reason." This is an exacting spiritual practice, not reserved for poets alone, but available for all those willing

to embrace uncertainty, to live with mystery, and to make peace with ambiguity. It is precisely the style of spirituality that Rorty has in mind when he commends pragmatism as a guard against our desire to find something to worship.[24]

Now I applaud this vision and am so pleased that Frankenberry and I are fellow travelers, or vision sharers, or contingency-prehensive partners. In this important paper, she argues against the separation of pragmatism and analytic philosophy and cites their common attachment to rigor and logic. She does not point out that analytic philosophers have never had a good word to say about us pragmatists who also follow out its metaphysical and speculative dimension, such as Sandra Rosenthal, Frederick Ferré, Joseph Grange, and George Allan (whom she cites approvingly on Whitehead). We metaphysical pragmatists are highly resistant to the linguistic turn and its loss of real reference and the question of truth. But the most powerful part of Frankenberry's paper is its careful exposition of Whitehead, jettisoning its explicit theology and showing how he gives a meticulous account of the possibility of a world of radical contingency. Everything in the world, she points out for Whitehead, is a becoming of something that was not wholly determined in advance and, moreover, we can experience this if we do not impose fictitious certainties, especially about our metaphysical hypotheses.

I think Whitehead himself does not go far enough in the matter of contingency. His account deals with contingency within the temporal world of process and does not question the contingency of why there is such a world at all. His Category of the Ultimate describes the workings of finite contingent things, creativity as such, and interactions with God. Scratch his account of God and he still leaves this category as "just the way things are." His hypothesis about this, of course, is contingent, but the hypothesis says that the reason why things are as they are is that this is the necessary condition for temporal process. It would have been far better for him to have said that these ultimate conditions and the very process of the temporal world are contingent on an ontological act that creates them contingently, just as every other contingent thing is created. The ontological act has no nature apart from creating and is contingently gratuitous, arbitrary, and from our side undeserved and utterly surprising.[25] Moreover, this act can be experienced with the right training. One meaning of Whitehead's "ontological principle" is that any complex thing or process is to be understood in terms of the various contingent decisions that go into making it up.[26] He should have applied that to the contingent cosmos as such and to the Category of the Ultimate. Such an ontological creative act does nothing to answer uncertainties or provide noncontingent handholds. But it does offer a contingent depth dimension to contingency everywhere. Without acknowledging something like the contingent ontological creative act, Frankenberry's contingency goes all the way back and all the way forward, but *not* all the way down.

But if she does acknowledge something like this ontological creative act, then she finds herself in unwonted proximity to Tillich. My ontological creative act is one version of Tillich's Ground of Being theologies. One of the meanings of Tillich's title, *The Shaking of the Foundations*, is precisely to do away with a priori foundational structures and to make way for the sort of radical contingency Frankenberry wants. His argument is from the presuppositions of contingency, which he defines as the tension between individuation and participation, dynamics and form, and freedom and destiny, and he surely was no linguistic philosopher, being so distrustful of language.[27] Frankenberry's argument is mainly epistemological. But she also should track the path from the pragmatists to Tillich, veering from analytic philosophy as she tracks the other path to analytic pragmatists such as Rorty and Davidson.

Now I want to return to the topic of symbolic meaning, the very idea of which Frankenberry rejects. Recall the statement of her vision that I quoted earlier. This is a spirituality, not a philosophical conclusion, although the practice is justified as realistic because of her philosophical conclusions about contingency. To symbolize this way of life, she quotes Keats's capacity for "being in uncertainties, mysteries, doubts, without any irritable reaching after fact and reason." She says this "exacting spiritual practice" is "available for all those willing to embrace uncertainty, to live with mystery, and to make peace with ambiguity." Tillich is with her all the way on this. She is not talking about particular uncertainties, mysteries, or ambiguities. Rather she takes those terms as deep and broad symbols characterizing the nature of reality to which we should be true. "Embracing," "living with," and "making peace with" are powerful symbols for shaping a life fit for a contingent cosmos. Of course, none of these symbols are to be taken literally. If they were, they would not be functionally fit to orient a spiritual lifestyle, only particular responses to things.

Notice also that Frankenberry advocates symbolizing the context of human life with these contingency symbols because she believes the cosmos really is contingent like this. Her spirituality embraces symbols that are epistemologically realistic and metaphysically refer to the real world. Only because she takes the world to be really contingent does she say that these symbols are true guides for spiritual life. If the world were not really contingent, as symbolized in various ways, but were instead filled with Thomistic principles and essences, or Calvin's predestination, then her spiritual advocacy would be mere fiction writing. Like the classical pragmatists, the meaning of spiritual symbols lies in the difference they call for in living, and that difference had better be based on the way things are going down, not on finding a clever epistemology that obviates the need for checking up on the truth for our philosophy.

Then would it not be a great help, philosophically, if she were to develop a theory of symbols, not symbols as signs in an extensional semiotic network of inferences but rather symbols shaping decisive, concrete, engagements with the pervasive character of contingency? The networks of these symbols need not be reconciled or fitted into a holistic pattern in inference. Rather they are to be understood as shaping decisive engagements with the ultimate conditions of contingency, engagements filled with secondness, shock, and existential transformation. All those symbols would have to be "broken" as Tillich said. But they would be important for interrupting idealistic pressures for continuity within holistic contexts so as to be more flexible in responding to real contingencies.

Of course, Frankenberry has plenty of valid targets in her campaign for a spirituality of contingency. Throughout Christian history there have been people who want to insist on simple, eternalist, noncontingent answers to the stresses of life. She has even gone so far as to define religion as necessarily involving belief in superhuman intentional agents. This has currency in Christian popular religion. But this is false for the Christian traditions of Neo-Platonism and Thomism, as well as the tradition from Schleiermacher to Tillich. For South Asian religions, intentionality is what must be expunged from the root metaphors of consciousness. Confucian religiosity carefully deletes divine intelligences from the nonintentionality of ontological conditions. I myself have argued for a long time for a view that says that what is created sets up conditions for obligation and moral identity, with the ontological creative act being exempt from this. Thus, morals are continent on the situation, which is contingent on contingent factors from the past, which are contingent on existing with later presents and futures.[28]

The question I want to pose for Frankenberry is where we can get popularly and publically accessible symbols for dealing with an ultimately contingent world, if we want a properly late-modern pragmatist-Whiteheadian spirituality. I suggest that we need appropriately naturalized symbols in five areas. First, we need symbols to address the contingency of the whole show. These have been plentiful in a great many religions and now need to be brought up to date with new scientific descriptions of the cosmos. Second, we need to have symbols that address the ultimate of question of choice. Is there something ultimately important about how we relate to the choices that seem to have different values? Third, are there symbols that indicate what is it to be a person or soul in relation to what is ultimately important, embracing existential contradictions? What about failure, guilt, and restoration? Fourth, we need symbols that address others that have an existence of their own, with their own self-organization that might be quite beyond our comprehension (I don't mean only radically different, cultural groups but also mountains, trees, plains, and conditions of existence outside the whole human environment). Fifth, we need symbols to reset the default on questions of the meaning of life. Tillich said we have a crisis about human meaningfulness generally. I suspect we now face the problem of the frustration of an attempt to achieve global justice anywhere, especially under the grinding conditions of capitalism that seem so important to bear through to attain the wealth necessary to consider liberal equations of equality and responsibility.

Whence will Frankenberry derive symbols for facing these issues head on? Can they derive from the narrow academic base of analytic philosophy? Or the broader base of professional pragmatists, paleo- and neo-? Whitehead in his metaphorical moments as in *Adventures of Ideas*? Or do we need a thoroughgoing examination of the myriad of religious symbols that are present or that can be culled in our culture? Or all of these, my own position?

My final question for Frankenberry and many of our colleagues in the naturalism camp is whether we can summon symbols that allow us to engage the depths we all acknowledge in one way of another. To what extent do we engage the radical contingency of the cosmos? Many people have touted divine freedom, but we need a metaphysics to explain what that might be. There is no greater contingency than that of the existence of the cosmos itself! How do we understand ultimately lying under obligation when there are so many perspectives to determine what is good? How can we relate to religious issues of suffering and wholeness, including the tough-minded spirituality Frankenberry urges, without ways to give existential symbolism to this issue? How do we find symbols for engaging others that acknowledge not only ingroup/outgroup distinctions but also differences in social institutions and the natural world? Both histories of religions and current environmental science need to be incorporated into this conversation. How do we find symbols for articulating and communicating about the issues of the meaning of life, especially in a cosmos contingent backward and forward, and all the way down? We philosophers might build a robust spirituality out of the metaphysics of contingency in all these areas, but most people engage better in symbols that resonate richly across many symbol systems. I urge Frankenberry to embrace eagerly The Very Idea of Symbolic Meaning and analyze critically the various affirmations of contingencies or flight from contingency in the many religious symbol systems of the world.

A final tease: Frankenberry commends "the style of spirituality that Rorty has in mind when he commends pragmatism as a guard against our desire to find something to worship." That makes sense if finding "something to worship" means hankering after some noncontingent deity that gives noncontingent meaning to our lives, guarantees of community, noncontingent still points within the soul, a divinely authoritative ethic, which worship has sometimes meant. But that is not the only meaning of worship. Does not Frankenberry's call for a spirituality of contingency imply as well finding a way to worship that contingency with gratitude, love, and commitment to attend to suchness?

NOTES

1. "The Empirical Dimension of Religious Experience," *Process Studies* 8/4 (Winter 1978), 259–276.

2. *Religion and Radical Empiricism* (Albany: State University of New York Press, 1987). I congratulate myself that this book was published in the SUNY series in Religious Studies that I edited at the time.

3. See her defense of "the linguistic turn" in, for instance, "The Study of Religion after Davidson and Rorty," *American Journal of Theology and Philosophy* 35/3 (September 2014), 195–210, and "The Fate of Radical Empiricism and the Future of Pragmatic Naturalism," in *Pragmatism, Naturalism, and Religion*, edited by Matthew C. Bagger (New York: Columbia University Press, 2015).

4. Paul Tillich, *The Shaking of the Foundations* (New York: Charles Scribner's Sons, 1948).

5. James's *Essays in Radical Empiricism* was first published in 1912 (New York: Longmans, Green and Co.) and then republished along with

James's 1909 *A Pluralistic Universe* in a volume edited by Ralph Barton Perry with the names of both books (New York: Longmans, Green and Co., 1942).

6. I am referring to the boisterous and growing Institute for American Religious and Philosophical Thought, previously known as the Highlands Institute for American Religious and Philosophical Thought.

7. Frankenberry, "Contingency All the Way Down: Whitehead among the Pragmatists," in *Thinking with Whitehead and American Pragmatism: Experience and Reality*, edited by Brian G. Henning, William T. Meyers, and Joseph D. John (Lanham: Lexington Books/Rowman & Littlefield, 2014), 97–116.

8. For recent work praising Davidson and Rorty, see the essays cited in note 3 for her discussions of the linguistic turn, as well as "Contingency All the Way Down: Whitehead among the Pragmatists." Quine once visited a theological gathering at Boston University and, when asked what kind of pragmatist he was, said hotly that he was no kind of pragmatist at all and that he wished people would stop associating him with a movement he disliked. So Frankenberry's forced baptism of Quine by the sword, or the pen, was no better appreciated by him than Charlemagne's similar attempts to make Christians by a forced performative ritual.

9. Donald Davidson, "On the Very Idea of a Conceptual Scheme," in his *Inquiries into Truth and Interpretation* (Oxford: Clarendon Press, 1984).

10. See the discussion of Peirce on this topic in my *On the Scope and Truth of Theology* (Albany: State University of New York Press, 2006), especially chapters 2 and 5.

11. See Whitehead's essays "Mathematics and the Good" and "Immortality," in *The Philosophy of Alfred North Whitehead*, The Library of Living Philosophers, edited by Paul Arthur Schilpp (New York: Tudor, 1941), 666–700.

12. This is how Whitehead described it in the famous first chapter of *Process and Reality: An Essay in Cosmology*, corrected edition, edited by David Ray Griffin and Donald W. Sherburne (New York: The Free Press, 1978).

13. See her "Contingency All the Way Down."

14. See Richard Rorty, editor, *The Linguistic Turn: Recent Essays in Philosophical Method* (Chicago: University of Chicago Press, 1967). This anthology includes most of the important essays leading to and expressing the linguistic turn, plus a superb introduction by Rorty that sets the terms for the linguistic turn. For the basic essays on the linguistic turn in the study of religion, see Nancy K. Frankenberry and Hans H. Penner, editors,

Language, Truth, and Religious Belief: Studies in Twentieth-Century Theory and Method in Religion (Atlanta: Scholars Press, 1999).

15. This is the powerful positive moral drawn in his *Philosophy and the Mirror of Nature* (Princeton: Princeton University Press, 1978).

16. Robert B. Brandom, *Making It Explicit: Reasoning, Representing, and Discursive Commitment* (Cambridge: Harvard University Press, 1994).

17. See Rorty's *Consequences of Pragmatism* (Minneapolis: University of Minnesota Press, 1982).

18. See Richard J. Bernstein, *The Pragmatic Turn* (Malden, MA, and Cambridge, UK: Polity Press, 2010), especially chapter 6, "Experience after the Linguistic Turn," and chapter 9, "Richard Rorty's Deep Humanism."

19. See my defense of the kind of pragmatism Rorty did *not* like, especially metaphysical realism, in chapter 18 that is a version of chapter 5 in *The Philosophy of Richard Rorty*, The Library of Living Philosophers, edited by Randall E. Auxier and Lewis Edwin Hahn (Chicago and LaSalle: Open Court, 2010), 139–155. Rorty was ill when this essay was commissioned for The Library of Living Philosophers and died before having a chance to respond, though he did to many of the other essays in this significant volume. I am sorry that an essay on Rorty by Nancy Frankenberry was not included.

20. Nancy K. Frankenberry, "On the Very Idea of Symbolic Meaning," in *Interpreting Neville*, edited by J. Harley Chapman and Nancy K. Frankenberry (Albany: State University of New York Press, 1999), 93–110.

21. On Frankenberry and her colleagues on this point, see the preface to her edited volume, *Radical Interpretation in Religion* (Cambridge: Cambridge University Press, 2002), xiii–xiv. Parts of it are worth quoting here:

> As a collection, these studies focus primarily on religion as a form of linguistic behavior. . . . Despite the variety of viewpoints and subject matter, all of the authors share at least three things. First, the move away from older models of representation and symbolic expression to holistic ways of thinking about the interrelations of language, meaning, belief, desires, and action. If beliefs have inferential relations to other beliefs, an interpreter can ascribe a single belief to a person only against the background of a very large number of other beliefs. . . . Second, they stand in a critical tradition that explains religion in entirely naturalistic terms, rather than on superhuman or faith-based premises. . . .

Far from treating religion as a *sui generis* phenomenon, they assume that whatever explains how language and minds work generally explains how religious language and religious minds work. Third, all recognize that, to be descriptively adequate, a definition of religion must include "superhuman agent" or one of its variants as characteristic of what makes ritual action or belief specifically "religious" for believers and interpreters alike.

22. Frankenberry includes herself in this collection, with her essay "Religion as a 'Mobile Army of Metaphors.'"
23. See Rorty's "The World Well Lost," chapter 1 of *Consequences of Pragmatism*.
24. "Contingency All the Way Down: Whitehead among the Pragmatists," 97.
25. Ibid.
26. This is the theory I have been defending since *God the Creator* (Chicago: University of Chicago Press, 1968) and most recently in *Ultimates: Philosophical Theology Volume One* (Albany: State University of New York Press, 2013).
27. This criticism of Whitehead is elaborated in my *Creativity and God: A Challenge to Process Theology* (New York: Seabury Press, 1980; new edition, Albany: State University of New York Press, 1995).
28. See Tillich's *Systematic Theology*, volume 1, part 2 (Chicago: University of Chicago Press, 1952).
29. See my *Existence: Philosophical Theology Volume Two* (Albany: State University of New York Press, 2014), part 1.

INDEX

Actual occasion (Whitehead's technical term), 221–22, 227–28, 245–47
Advaita Vedanta, 59
Aesthetic, 1, 10, 13–14, 228, 260, 266–67, 270, 303, 310, 315–16, 321, 324, 333, 346
Affections, religious, 134
African tribal religion, 4
Ahn, Christopher, xv
Al-Ghazali, 75
Allah, 57
Allan, George, 214, 347
Alpert, Richard, 115
Ames, Roger T., 154
Anderson, Douglas, 91–92, 317
Anselm, 75
Apophaticism, 55, 81–83, 89, 182, 188–90, 205, 211, 233, 239, 255, 262–65, 269, 320, 325, 327
Aquinas, Thomas, 7, 58, 65, 82–83, 149–50, 168, 222, 241, 263, 271, 319
Architecture, 3, 10
Aristotle (Aristotelianism), 1, 7–9, 11–12, 15, 64, 82, 125, 174, 194, 223, 289, 297, 303, 319
Arjuna, 43, 57
Art, xv. 3, 10, 42, 81, 144, 157, 172, 182, 185, 188, 205, 285, 309, 315–16

Asad, Talal, 270
Atkinson, Brooks, 144
Augustine of Hippo, 6, 74–75, 109, 241, 297
Auxier, Randall, xv, 294, 301, 353
Axial Age, 4, 40, 48, 79, 86, 105, 110, 178–85, 189–90, 205, 276, 280
Ayer, A. J., 338
Bagger, Matthew C., 351
Barth, Karl, 147, 178, 227, 269
Beauty, xv, 10, 30, 33, 44, 121, 135, 196, 202, 263, 298, 330, 333
Berdyaev, Nicolas, 226, 262
Berger, Peter, 41, 53, 85, 92, 154, 168, 233, 258, 270, 288
Berkeley, George, 215
Bernard of Clairvaux, 75
Bernstein, Richard, 299, 303, 343, 353
Biology (Biological, Biologists), 8–9, 15–16, 20, 36, 88, 121, 168, 169, 186, 201–02, 256, 284–85, 288, 307, 323
Blanshard, Brand, 303
Boehme, Jakob, 226, 262
Bonaventura, 75
Bowden, John, 271
Boydston, Jo Ann, 114
Bracken, Joseph, S. J., xiii-xv, 211, 213, 236, 243–54

Bradley, F. J., 249
Brahman, 3, 39, 57, 59, 61, 150, 164, 178, 182, 204, 274–75, 289
Brandom, Robert, 343, 345, 353
British empiricism, 138, 294–95
Buber, Martin, 250
Buchler, Justus, 223, 298–99, 302
Buddha (Buddha-mind, Buddhism, Buddhist), 4–5, 21, 26, 38, 43, 47, 48, 56, 59, 86, 93, 102, 105, 107, 115, 147–50, 156–57, 164–65, 168, 173, 178, 180, 189, 204, 225, 236, 248, 274, 276, 283, 285, 299, 326, 338–39
Bultmann, Rudolf, 191
Cahoone, Lawrence, 240
Calvin (Calvinist, Calvinists), 121, 135, 229, 232, 349
Capps, Walter H., 160
Cathars, 7
Chapman, J. Harley, xv
Chapple, Christopher Key, 289
Cherbury Herbert, 7–98,
Chin, Ewing, 317
Christianity (Christian, Christians), 4, 6–7, 20, 47–48, 57, 75, 81, 90, 93, 105, 111–12, 118, 122–24, 126, 145, 147, 156–57, 163–65, 172–73, 177, 180–82, 189–90, 192, 226–27, 233–36, 240, 245, 251, 262, 285, 296, 299, 319, 326, 334, 349, 352
Cicero, 6, 21
Cohen, Morris, 299
Colapietro, Vincent M., xiii, 91, 317
Collins, Randall, 154, 161
Colonialism, xi, 4–6, 20–21, 143, 188, 265, 286, 313, 341
Comparison, xii, 6, 21, 48, 51–52, 55, 58, 61, 145, 147, 149–61, 170, 173, 187–92, 243, 269, 277, 282–89, 303–04, 310–14, 318

Components, conditional and essential, 8–14, 19–37, 39–40, 51, 56–57, 61–69, 73, 86, 174–76, 194–96, 198, 224, 227, 237, 240, 247–253, 258–60, 268–69, 278–81, 284, 287, 321–29
Confucianism (Confucius, Confucians), xii, 4, 38, 47–48, 56, 60, 102, 105, 149–50, 168, 173, 178, 182, 189, 205, 218, 236, 265, 275, 283, 299, 326, 349
Contingency, 28–35, 40, 204, 218–20, 225, 261, 268, 273, 287, 304, 316, 333, 337, 341, 346–51
Corrington, Robert S., 53, 72, 197, 209, 214, 317
Crosby, Donald A., 192, 317
Cross, Richard, 271
Culture, xi, 1, 3–7, 10, 14–17, 20–22, 31–35, 38–49, 51, 57, 66, 68–70, 76–77, 79–81, 85–92, 99–105, 111, 113, 121, 129, 134, 138, 154–55, 158, 161, 169–70, 176, 178–89, 192, 201–05, 215, 225, 235, 257–58, 267, 273–79, 283–88, 296–97, 299, 304, 310–14, 325, 341, 350
Cusa, Nicholas, 7
Dance, 3, 10, 103, 157, 171, 203, 236, 316
Dao (Daoism), 3, 21, 38, 43, 47–48, 56, 60, 67, 86, 105–06, 147, 150, 164, 168, 173, 178, 182, 189, 205, 222, 226, 262–64, 275, 284–85, 299, 326
Davidson, Donald, 338–42, 346, 348, 352
Dawkins, Richard, 88, 93, 209
Deacon, Terrence, 139
Dean, William, 199, 203
Definition, xi–xii, 3–19, 24, 34, 39, 44–45, 62, 71, 89, 95, 156,

195, 219, 255, 322; *see* Religion, definition of.
Dennett, Daniel, 88, 93
Derrida, Jacque, 78
Descartes, Rene, 80, 90, 140, 142, 215, 240, 308, 319
Desmond, William, xiii, xv, 291, 319–334
Determinateness, 8, 13, 25, 27, 37–41, 51, 61–62, 71, 86, 175, 194, 205, 219, 220–26, 245, 249, 251–52, 262, 268, 277, 322, 327, 332–34
Deuser, Hermann, xiii, 92, 192, 302
Dewey, John, 50, 79, 91, 97, 113–14, 136, 142–44, 167, 169, 200, 214–15, 256, 294–01, 303–09, 312, 338–43
Dialectic, 38, 51, 61, 83, 138–39, 142, 150, 156, 198–203, 207, 223, 243, 264, 282, 304, 307, 311–12, 315, 320, 325–28, 332–34, 338
Diamond, Jared, 270
Dias, Maria G., 191
Diller, Jeanine, xiii, 71
Dilworth, David, 154, 161
Diversity, 25, 49, 59, 136, 219, 275, 283, 345
Dorrien, Gary, 190–91
Durkheim, Emile, 16–17, 20, 32, 36, 187, 200
Eckel, Malcolm David, 92, 161
Eckhart, Meister, 226, 262
Ecology (Ecological, Ecologists), 12–14, 16, 32, 39. 105, 213, 280
Edwards, Jonathan, 69, 72, 134–36, 168, 294, 298–99
Eliade, Mircea, 20, 36, 114, 173
Ellegate, Nancy, v, xv-xvi
Emerson, Ralph Waldo, 133–35, 139, 294, 298–99

Emptiness, 148–150
Engagement, 1–2, 4, 9–14, 19–21, 23–24, 27–35, 37, 41–45, 49–52, 55–58, 66–70, 73, 77–89, 93, 95–114, 119–30, 138, 141, 143–44, 165–74, 184, 186, 189, 202–05, 215, 255–57, 261, 263, 269, 280–81, 286, 288, 294, 299, 301, 306, 315–16, 325–26, 340–45, 349
Equivocity, 320, 326
Eternity, 60, 64, 197, 218–22, 232, 234–39, 247–54, 275, 305, 329, 333, 338, 349
Existential field, 8–9, 12, 27–28, 40, 174, 195–97, 259, 278, 280–87, 322–23, 328; location, 8, 12, 27–29, 35, 37–40, 51, 62, 65–69, 86, 174–76, 195, 198, 223–24, 237, 240, 259–60, 268–70, 278–80, 287, 321–25, 329
Experience, human, xii-xiii, 4, 11, 22–23, 44, 51–52, 56–59, 66–71, 73, 80, 84–89, 95–105, 108–14, 119–30, 134–35, 137–44, , 147, 167, 169, 183, 186–88, 190, 199, 202–05, 215, 224–26, 239, 250, 258, 264, 266, 276, 283–84, 294–301, 306, 309–10, 314, 316, 320, 325, 331, 333, 337–45, 327
Ferre, Frederick, 214
Feuerbach, Ludwig, 88, 93
Fichte, 137
Finite/infinite contrast, 65–70, 82–83, 172–73, 176, 259–60, 268–69
Firstness (and Secondness and Thirdness), 78, 82, 197, 114–15
Frankenberry, Nancy, xiii, xv, 193, 199–203, 208, 291, 337–54
Frei, Hans, 158
Freud, Sigmund, 20, 24, 30, 36, 88, 93, 103

358 ❦ INDEX

Frisina, Warren G., 114
Gadamer, Hans-Georg, 186
Gallistel, C. R., 72
German idealism, 53, 136, 163, 293–97
Gibson, W. R. Boyce, 113
God (gods, goddesses), xiii, 3,, 5–7, 11, 21–22, 26, 31, 33, 38, 56–59, 65, 68, 77, 81–84, 90, 102, 105–06, 110–12, 118–24, 127, 129, 135, 143, 147, 149–50, 154, 156, 164, 168, 171–73, 178, 182, 185, 196, 204, 206–07, 211, 218–35, 237, 239–41, 244–48, 251–54, 261–67, 271, 275–77, 282, 289, 297–300, 310, 319, 320, 327, 330–33, 338, 344, 347
Godlove, Terry F., xi, xvi
Goldstein, Jonathan, 71
Graham, Jesse, 191
Grange, Joseph, 214
GRE exams, 298
Great Ultimate, 38, 60, 275–76, 203
Green, Garrett, 269
Griffin, David Ray, xiii-xv, 72, 211, 213–40, 254, 270, 317, 335, 352
Hahn, Lewis Edwin, xv, 242
Haidt, Jonathan, 179–81, 191, 278, 285, 290
Hall, David L. 154, 335
Hardwick, Charley D., 192
Harmony, 1–3, 5, 7–17, 19, 24–35, 60–66, 72, 86, 105–07, 135, 174–75, 194–95, 223–25, 231, 237, 240–41, 247, 249–52, 259, 264, 268, 270, 281, 284, 321–28, 331, 334
Hartshorne, Charles, 90, 92, 114, 161, 198, 213–14, 218–19, 222–23, 227–28, 234–37, 241, 245–48, 299
Hawking, Stephen, 273, 281, 289

Hegel, G. W. F., 82, 90, 95, 114, 137–38, 294, 300, 319–20, 326–29, 334, 337, 343
Heidegger, Martin, 25, 138, 141, 165, 214, 218, 307, 328
Heimbrach, Hans-Guenter, xvi
Hellenism, 112
Heltzel, Peter G., 241
Hendel, Charles, 303
Henning, Brian G., 352
Heuristic, xii, 1–2, 19–24, 35, 255, 289
Hindu (Hinduism, Hindus), 4–5, 21, 38, 47–48, 56–59, 86, 105, 118, 150, 156, 178, 189, 204, 263, 274, 276, 283, 326
Holism, 338, 342–46
Hopkins, Gerard Manley, S.J., 202, 226
Humanities, xiii, 17, 202, 208–281
Hume, David, 137, 140, 165, 215, 295, 337, 339
Huntington, Samuel P., 22, 36
Husserl, Edmund, 113–14, 138, 140, 165, 308, 342
IARPT, 199–200
Ibn al-Arabi, 75
Ibn Rushd, 75
Iconic reference, 38, 51, 53, 56, 59, 67–71, 79–82, 91, 98, 104, 117–25, 131, 171–72, 184–85, 193, 198–99, 203–08, 236, 239, 306, 309–10
Indexical reference, 38, 51, 53, 56, 67–71, 80–83, 91, 104, 117–25, 171–72, 185, 193, 198–99, 202–07, 236, 239, 306, 309–11
Ingroup (and outgroup), 3–4, 41, 110, 118, 178–83, 285, 351
Inquiry, 1, 4, 13–17, 19, 23–24, 32–34, 37, 82, 108, 126, 130, 144, 148, 152, 156–57, 161, 166, 177,

183, 186, 188, 190, 192, 193, 200, 208, 215–16, 219, 258, 304
Institute for American Religious and Philosophical Thought, xiv, 352
Interpretation, 10, 20, 41–43, 51, 67, 71, 77–91, 96, 98, 101–15, 117–29, 135
Islam, 4, 22, 48, 57, 75, 105, 154, 156–57, 165, 173, 262, 265, 299, 319; *see also* Muslim
Jainism, 47, 59, 178
James, William, 23, 30–31, 36, 44–45, 53, 113, 135, 143, 215, 294–95, 298–99, 303, 305–06m 317, 338–43, 351–52
Jaspers, Karl, 178–79, 91
Jefferson, Thomas, 7
Jesus, 57, 68, 76, 102, 105, 111–12, 118, 123–24, 148, 171, 180, 244
Jews, 4, 7, 47, 75, 90, 93, 118, 124, 147, 178, 189–90, 265, 299, 326; *see also* Judaism
Joas, Hans, xiii
John, Joseph D. 352
Johnson, Roger A., 7, 18
Judaism, 6, 48, 58, 90, 105, 112, 124, 156, 173, 262, 299, 319; *see also* Jews
Jung, Matthias, xiii
Kabbalism, 75, 83, 276
Kali, 118, 171
Kant, Immanuel (Kantian, Kantians), 16, 30, 90, 113–14, 122, 136–39, 142, 144, 163, 169, 182, 187–89, 192, 200, 214–15, 232, 239, 256, 269, 289,, 294–97, 300–01, 304–09, 340–42
Karma, 5, 275–76, 280–81
Kasher, Asa, xiii, 71
Kaufman, Gordon, 191, 203
Keats, John, 346
Keller, Catherine, 251, 254

Kierkegaard, Soren, 30, 43, 120
Kimball, Robert, 241, 302
Knepper, Timothy D., xi, xvi
Koller, Silvia Helena, 191
Krauss, Lawrence M., 196, 209
Kripal, Jeffrey, J., xi, xvi
Kroner, Richard, 293
Lactantius, 6
Leary, Timothy, 115
Legge, James, 7
Levinas, Emmanuel, 225, 250
Levy-Strauss, Claude, 16
Lewis, Thomas A. xi, xvi
Lindbeck, George, 158
Linguistic turn, 342–45, 347, 351–52, 75
Literature, 3, 309, 342
Liturgy, 6, 30, 34, 45, 90, 121, 157, 227, 343
Loomer, Bernard, 338
Luckmann, Thomas, 270
Lull, Ramon, 7
Maassen, Helmut, 92
Maimonides, 75
Marx (Marxism, Marxists), 16, 23, 88, 93, 138
Masuzawa, Tomoko, 36
Mathews, Shailer, 186
McKeon, Richard, 154
McNamara, Patrick, 192
Meaning, 3, 5–6, 16, 28–29, 33, 35, 45–52, 56, 70, 79–86, 101, 106–11, 115, 121–22, 128, 138, 141, 153, 163–65, 185, 203–07, 215, 222, 230, 253, 260–67, 274, 278–81, 286–88, 297, 306, 324, 331, 345, 348–51, 353
Meland, Bernard, 338
Metaphysics, 30, 51–52, 68, 70, 92, 115, 118. 142, 143, 167, 176, 182, 185–92, 195, 199, 207, 215–16, 235–36, 240, 261, 268,

Metaphysics (*continued*)
298, 303–10, 317, 320, 324–25, 338–45, 351
Metaxology, 319–20, 325–27
Methodism, 232–33, 244, 296
Meyers, William T., 352
Miller, A. V., 113
Modernism, 214–15, 216–17, 308
Mohammed, 4, 102,
Moses, 4, 57, 76, 102, 121
Muller, Max, 7, 148
Muller-Ortega, Paul Eduardo, 290
Music, 3, 10, 30, 135, 157, 182–86, 202–08, 224
Muslims, 4, 7, 47, 147, 189–90, 265, 326
Mysticism, 11, 28, 30, 79, 83, 87, 96–97, 102–94, 127, 182
Narrative, 40, 57–58, 80, 102, 113, 117–18, 121–22, 202, 227, 266–67, 285–86, 312
Native American, 139
Nature (as in "world," not "nature of"), 30, 56, 59, 69, 72, 78, 86, 98, 134, 169, 198–99, 202–03, 225, 280, 284–88, 303, 307–10
Neville, Beth, iv, xv
Niebuhr, Reinhold, 191
Nietzsche, Friedrich, 138, 234, 301
Nishitani, Keiji, 165
Nominalism, 83, 134, 314–15
Northrop, F. S. C., 154, 161
Obligation, 28, 39–40, 50, 56, 58, 62, 69, 86, 156, 173–74, 180, 205, 232, 239, 259–62, 268, 278–84, 287–88, 334, 349–50
Ontological context of mutual relevance, 26, 63–65, 175, 195–97, 250–51
Ontological creative act, 26–35, 37–40, 51–52, 55–56, 60–72, 176, 194–99, 204–07, 219, 222, 225, 245, 251–54, 262, 268, 329–31, 348–49
Ontological Principle (Whitehead's technical term), 218, 347
Origen, 75
Otto, Rudolf, 108, 114
Paganism, 105, 176, 283, 319
Pahnke, Walter, 115
Paleo-pragmatism, 308, 317
Parsons, Talcott, 16
Paul, St., 4, 68, 112, 121, 128
Peden, Creighton, deck of, 199
Peirce, Charles S., 53, 67, 72–74, 76–84, 90–92, 97, 101, 107, 110, 113–15, 117–19, 126, 134–35, 139–44, 139, 161–71, 198, 200, 215, 236, 294–302, 304–11, 314–18, 340–45, 350
Penner, Hans H. 352
Phenomenology (Phenomenologist, Phenomenology of Religion), xii, 20–21, 78, 95–97, 112–14, 78, 141, 151–52, 155–56, 161, 165–68, 173, 213, 218, 320, 324, 332, 335, 342
Phillips, D.Z., 164
Philosophical Theology, xiii, 70, 164, 194, 199, 208, 211, 226, 236, 243–44, 291, 298, 319–20, 327, 330, 332, 334
Philosophy (or Philosophers), xi, xv, 17, 21, 23–26, 29, 34, 37–39, 42–43, 47, 51–52, 58, 60, 64–66, 70, 76, 78, 83–85, 88–90, 100, 108, 113–14, 124–25, 133–39, 141, 143–45, 154–58, 160–61, 163–69, 172–76, 178, 180, 185, 189–90, 194–99, 202, 205, 208, 211, 214–17, 219–23, 226, 236–38, 243–46, 250, 253, 255–56, 258, 268, 273–77, 281–2, 284, 287, 289, 291, 293–301, 303–09,

311–17, 319–22, 325–27, 330, 332–34, 337–39, 341–51 10
Philosophy of religion, 144, 163–64, 236–37, 291, 296–98, 337, 339, 342
Phlogiston, 137
Plotinus, 219–22, 319
Possibilities, 28, 33, 39, 50, 62, 69, 86–87, 172–76, 237–38, 252–54, 258, 261, 270, 278, 331
Postmodernism, xi, 5–8, 17, 19, 23, 49, 82, 136, 138, 141, 143, 165, 186, 189, 191, 202, 213–17, 240, 286, 308, 320
Pragmatism (or Pragmatist, Pragmatic), xii, 9, 19, 29, 37–40, 43, 47, 50–53, 66, 68, 70, 73, 76, 81, 97–98, 113, 134, 136–44, 152, 165, 167–69, 172, 180–89, 192, 200–04, 208, 215–17, 227, 256–57, 263–64, 268, 270, 281, 294–99, 303–18, 321, 325, 334, 337–53
Principle (*li*), 149
Proudfoot, Wayne, 93
Psalm 23, 205–06
Psychology (*and* Psychology of Religion), xii, 1, 10, 13–16, 22, 24, 29–34, 42, 153, 158, 167, 179–80, 185, 201, 255–56, 278, 284–85
Pugliese, Marc a., xiv
Purva Mimamsa, 6
Quine, Willard, 338–39, 352
Ramsey, Paul, 72
Raposa, Michael, 92
Rauschenbusch, Walter, xiii, 316
Realism, philosophical, 19, 108, 119, 186, 189, 216, 303–04, 314, 353
Reductionism, 14, 16, 87–89, 96, 163–67, 182, 256
Reference, 13, 22, 38–40, 51, 53, 61, 67, 79–84, 91, 96–104, 108–09, 112–14, 117–27, 164–72, 184–85, 193, 196, 198, 202–03, 236–37, 244, 255, 304, 306–09, 317, 344–46
Religion, xi-xii, 1–8, 10–11, 13–18, 20–25, 27–34, 36, 37–53, 55, 58, 64, 68, 70, 76–87, 89, 91–92, 102, 104–06, 108, 110–11, 113, 118–19, 122, 128–30, 145, 148–49, 156–58, 160, 163–76, 177–78, 180–83, 185–90, 200–02, 205, 207–08, 215, 226, 231–32, 236, 239, 251, 255–59, 265–68, 276–87, 294, 296–301, 310, 315–16, 331, 338, 345, 349–51, 353–54; definition of, 1, 9–10, 23–24, 31, 34–35, 37, 52, 73, 166–67, 255; defining, xi-xii, 1–24, 31, 34–35, 37, 73, 145, 165–68, 255–58, 270, 354; *see also* Philosophy of religion.
Religious belief, 165, 236, 345
Religious experience, xii-xiii, 2, 73, 75, 84–93, 95–115, 119–31, 144–45, 165, 168, 182–83, 186–90, 225–26, 297–99
Religious Studies, xii, 17, 166–67, 187, 255–56, 339
Ricci, Matteo, 5
Richardson, Robert D., 113
Ricoeur, Paul, 186
Righteousness, 28–29, 35, 40, 48, 86, 180, 206, 278
Rorty, Richard, xiii, xv, 192, 291, 303–18, 326, 338–39, 342–43, 346–48, 351–54
Rosemont, Henry, Jr., 317
Rosenthal, Sandra, 347
Ross, James F., 164
Royce, Josiah, 293–95, 299, 301
Rump, Ariane, 290

Samkhya, 59
Sanderson, J. Burdon, 113
Sartre, Jean Paul, 138
Saussure, Ferdinand, 78
Schaab, Gloria L., SSJ, xiv
Schilbrack, Kevin, xi, xvi, 18, 35, 55
Schleiermacher, Friedrich, 78, 137, 177, 191, 225, 349
Schlette, Magnus, xiii
Science (natural and social), xiii, 8, 15–16, 20–23, 29, 34, 47, 67, 75, 78–79, 93, 133, 137–44, 154–55, 157–58, 163–69, 177, 182, 184–89, 193, 196, 199–203, 207–08, 214–16, 219, 233, 243, 255–56, 264–67, 273, 277–78, 281–89, 295, 298, 304, 308–10, 315–16, 340, 342, 351
Scotus, Duns, 188, 263, 265, 271, 319, 330
Sellars, Wilfrid, 295, 303, 307
Semiotics, 1, 10, 13–14, 30–38, 42, 51–53, 66, 71–73, 78–01, 95–115, 119–27, 131, 169–71, 182–84, 186–87, 200, 230, 236, 257–58, 306–09, 317, 323, 325, 340–49
Shangdi, 5, 226
Sherburne, Donald,, 72, 228, 254, 270, 317, 335, 352
Shiva, 57, 236, 275
Smid, Robert W., 160
Smith, Barbara Herrnstein, 269
Smith, Diana, 293
Smith, Huston, 115
Smith, John E., xiii, xv, 91, 270, 291, 293–303, 318
Society (Whitehead's technical term), 234–35, 245–46
Sociology, 16–17, 32, 34, 42, 53, 85, 147, 153, 157–59, 201, 255, 258
Speirs, E. B., 113

Spinoza, Baruch, 78, 197, 215–16, 221, 319
Stalnaker, Aaron, 149,160
Stump, Eleonore, 164
Substance (Aristotelian), 1, 8–11, 83, 174, 277, 320, 341
Suchocki, Marjorie, 213, 227, 235–06
Supernatural beings or agents (Supernaturalism), 3–4, 20–22, 24, 57, 145, 168, 177, 182, 193, 199, 203, 207, 276–77
Symbols, 30–34, 38, 41–43, 47–49, 55, 58, 68–79, 84–87, 90–91, 99, 105–07, 111, 114, 118–20, 122, 126, 147–48, 159, 165, 167, 171–73, 177, 184, 193, 203–08, 225–27, 233, 236–39, 242, 257–68, 274–80, 285, 287–88, 348–51

Thatamanil, John J., 161
The One and the Many, 25, 35, 176, 218, 220, 222, 227, 235–236, 244–247
Theissen, Gerd, 271
Theology, 6, 17, 23, 41–43, 48–52, 79, 81–90, 93, 96, 104, 114, 135, 145, 147–60, 163–64, 177–78, 181–92, 194, 199, 201, 208, 211, 213–14, 217–20, 222, 225–30, 233, 236, 239–40, 243–45, 255, 262–64, 299, 319–20, 326, 333, 339, 347; *see also* Philosophical theology
Tillich, Paul, 6, 33, 53, 84, 92, 101, 110, 115, 149–50, 161, 165, 167, 171, 177, 182, 191, 197, 232, 241, 293, 296–99, 302, 338, 345, 348–51
Togetherness, temporal, ontological or cosmological, 25, 32, 63–64, 195–97, 224, 237–38, 248, 253, 328–29, 332

Troeltsch, Ernst, 191
Tyler, E. B., 20, 36, 114
Ultimacy (Ultimate realities, ultimate concern), xiii, xv, 3–6, 9–17, 19, 21–35, 37–53, 55–61, 65–71, 73, 76, 80, 83–88, 92–93, 95–96, 98–111, 115, 118–30, 138, 144, 148–51, 156, 158, 164, 166–86, 189, 193–99, 203–08, 211, 218–19, 226, 233, 236, 241–42, 244, 255–69, 273–89, 298–300, 310, 312, 347–350
Ultimate of Non-being, 38, 60, 275
Unity, 25, 32–33, 53, 102–05, 118, 122, 196, 219, 222, 225, 228–29, 237, 244, 248, 252, 279, 330
Univocity, 320, 326
Value, 8, 10, 12–14, 27–30, 33–35, 37, 44, 50–51, 56, 58, 62, 65–69, 72, 86–88, 117, 125, 135, 142–44, 148, 155, 172–74, 195, 198, 202–04, 224, 228–37, 241, 252–53, 258–61, 268, 270, 278–88, 296, 306, 310–16, 324–33, 335, 340, 344–45, 350
Van der Leeuw, Gerardus, 20, 36, 114
Vishnu, 57, 275
Wangbi, 275, 290
Ward, Keith, 160
Watson, Walter, 154, 161

Weber, Max, 191
Weiss, Paul, 26, 36, 90, 92, 114, 161, 223, 244, 299, 302, 303, 320, 326, 334
Wells, Rulon, 303
Whitehead, Alfred North, 31, 90, 143, 172, 213–41, 243–54, 258–59, 270, 277, 282, 290, 298–302, 306–11, 317–18, 319, 335, 337–42, 345–47, 349–52, 354
Wholeness, 10, 17, 28, 31, 35, 39–45, 49, 56, 69, 86, 105, 172–74, 202, 205, 226, 259, 268, 279–81, 284–88, 308, 329, 349
Wieman, Henry Nelson, 186, 214
Wildman, Wesley J., xi, xvi, 36, 161, 191, 193, 196, 203, 206–08, 220, 241, 290, 318
Wittgenstein, Ludwig, 79, 81, 92, 164, 214, 289, 307
Wolter, Allan, O.F.M., 271
Worldview, xiii, 42, 45–52, 79, 104, 110, 119, 182–83, 190, 211, 215, 255, 258–69, 308, 312
Worship, 5–7, 10–14, 16, 29–33, 43, 48, 106, 121, 171, 182, 233, 235, 247, 351
Yahweh, 57, 227
Yong, Amos, 241
Zhou Dunyi, 60, 71, 275, 290
Zoroastrianism, 178

www.ingramcontent.com/pod-product-compliance
Lightning Source LLC
Chambersburg PA
CBHW020218240426

43672CB00006B/343